Rabindranath Tagore's Theatre

This book analyses Rabindranath Tagore's contribution to Bengali drama and theatre. Throughout this book, Abhijit Sen locates and studies Rabindranath's experiments with drama/theatre in the context of the theatre available in nineteenth-century Bengal, and explores the innovative strategies he adopted to promote his 'brand' of theatre. This approach finds validation in the fact that Rabindranath combined in himself the roles of author-actor-producer, who always felt that, without performance, his dramatic compositions fell short of the desired completeness. Various facets of his plays as theatre and his own role as a theatre-practitioner are the prime focus of this book. This book will be of great interest to students and scholars in Theatre and Performance Studies and most notably, those focusing on Indian Theatre and Postcolonial Theatre.

Abhijit Sen is a former Professor of English, Department of English, Visva-Bharati, Santiniketan. His chief areas of interest include Renaissance Studies, Theatre Studies and Rabindranath Tagore.

Rabindranath Tagore's Theatre
From Page to Stage

Abhijit Sen

LONDON AND NEW YORK

First published 2022
by Routledge
2 Park Square, Milton Park, Abingdon, Oxon OX14 4RN

and by Routledge
605 Third Avenue, New York, NY 10158

Routledge is an imprint of the Taylor & Francis Group, an informa business

© 2022 Abhijit Sen

The right of Abhijit Sen to be identified as author of this work has been asserted in accordance with sections 77 and 78 of the Copyright, Designs and Patents Act 1988.

All rights reserved. No part of this book may be reprinted or reproduced or utilised in any form or by any electronic, mechanical, or other means, now known or hereafter invented, including photocopying and recording, or in any information storage or retrieval system, without permission in writing from the publishers.

Trademark notice: Product or corporate names may be trademarks or registered trademarks, and are used only for identification and explanation without intent to infringe.

British Library Cataloguing-in-Publication Data
A catalogue record for this book is available from the British Library

Library of Congress Cataloging-in-Publication Data
Names: Sen, Abhijit, author.
Title: Rabindranath Tagore: from page to stage / Abhijit Sen.
Description: Abingdon, Oxon; New York: Routledge, 2021. | Includes bibliographical references and index. |
Identifiers: LCCN 2021009183 (print) | LCCN 2021009184 (ebook) | ISBN 9780367626785 (hardback) | ISBN 9781003110279 (ebook)
Subjects: LCSH: Tagore, Rabindranath, 1861-1941--Criticism and interpretation.
Classification: LCC PK1726 .S395 2021 (print) | LCC PK1726 (ebook) | DDC 891.4/414--dc23
LC record available at https://lccn.loc.gov/2021009183
LC ebook record available at https://lccn.loc.gov/2021009184

ISBN: 978-0-367-62678-5 (hbk)
ISBN: 978-0-367-62680-8 (pbk)
ISBN: 978-1-003-11027-9 (ebk)

DOI: 10.4324/9781003110279

Typeset in Times New Roman
by Taylor & Francis Books

To the memory of my father and my mother

Contents

List of illustrations ix
About author xi
Acknowledgements xii

Introduction 1

SECTION 1
The historical context 11

1 The Bengal Renaissance theatre and Rabindranath 13

SECTION 2
Rabindranath as dramaturge and theorist 37

2 Theatre and Nation 39
3 Theatre at the *asram*-school 63
4 Theories of theatre 76

SECTION 3
Rabindranath as theatre-practitioner 93

5 Preparing the playtext 95
6 Selecting the cast 116
7 Rehearsing the play 129
8 Setting the stage 149
9 Acting the role 162

10	Theatricalizing cultures	186
11	Translating the playtext	195
12	Conclusion	217

Appendix I: Plates (of photographs/paintings of Rabindranath's performances) 225
Appendix II: Rabindranath Tagore: A brief chronology of select events and works, 1881–1941 245
Bibiliography 313
Index 320

Illustrations

Figures

Plate 1	*Valmiki Pratibha*: Rabindranath Tagore as Valmiki (an early performance, c.1881)	225
Plate 2	*Valmiki Pratibha*: Rabindranath as Valmiki, with the robbers (later performance)	226
Plate 3	*Valmiki Pratibha*: Rabindranath as Valmiki; Indira Devi Chaudharani as Luxmi	226
Plate 4	*Visarjan*: Rabindranath as Raghupati, bent over the dead body of Joysingha (Arunendu Tagore) in the last scene (early performances, from 1890 to 1900)	227
Plate 5	*Visarjan*: Rabindranath as Joysingha; the stage décor by Gagendranath Tagore (later performance in Calcutta in 1923)	228
Plate 6	*Phalguni*: Rabindranath with the cast of the prologue, added for the later performance in Calcutta (1916)	229
Plate 7	*Phalguni*: Rabindranath as Kavisekhar in the prologue; painting by Abanindranath Tagore (production in Calcutta, 1916)	230
Plate 8	*Phalguni*: Rabindranath as the blind *baul* in the main play; painting by Abanindranath Tagore (production in Calcutta, 1916)	231
Plate 9	*Dakghar*: Rabindranath as Thakurda (Gaffer), Ashamukul Das as Amal and others; the stage décor was by Nandalal Bose and others, supervised by Abanindranath Tagore (production in Calcutta, 1917)	232
Plate 10	*Dakghar*: Rabindranath as Thakurda (Gaffer), Ashamukul Das as Amal and others in the final scene of the play	232
Plate 11	Programme brochures for several productions (*Natir Puja, Sesh Varshan, Navin* and *Shapmochan*)	233
Plate 12	Programme brochure for *Natir Puja*, first performance in Calcutta (1927)	234

x *List of illustrations*

Plate 13	Programme brochure for *Natir Puja*, first night of later performances in Calcutta (1931)	235
Plate 14	*Natir Puja*, a scene from the film made by New Theatres studio (1932); Lalita Sen replaced Gouri Bose as Srimati in the film	236
Plate 15	*Natir Puja*, a scene from the film; Upali (Rabindranath) pays his homage to the dead Srimati; the film replicates the stage performance	237
Plate 16	*Natir Puja*: Upali and Srimati, at the beginning of the play; painting by Gaganendranath Tagore	238
Plate 17	*Natir Puja*: painting by Abanindranath Tagore	239
Plate 18	*Natir Puja*: the dance of the Nati (dancing girl), made famous by Gouri Bose (who was cast as the first Nati) showing how she discards her ornaments as she dances; painting by Nandalal Bose, who was also in charge of costumes	240
Plate 19	*Tasher Desh*: a poster for the play by Nandalal Bose, who also designed stage-setting and costumes	241
Plate 20	*Tasher Desh*: Rabindranath with the cast of the play	242
Plate 21	*Chitrangada* (dance drama): performance at New Empire (1936); Rabindranath is seated on stage, left of the dancers; the singers and musicians are seated at the rear of the stage	242
Plate 22	The Poet and the Dance: woodcut by Ramendranath Chakravarty, suggesting the proximity of Rabindranath to the dancers as he sat (possibly onstage) reciting lines	243
Plate 23	Event celebrating the Poet's last birthday (1941), performed on the porch of Udayan, his residence in Santiniketan; he sits on a chair facing the dancers	244

About author

Abhijit Sen is a former Professor of English, Department of English, Visva-Bharati, Santiniketan. His chief areas of interest include Renaissance Studies; Theatre Studies; Rabindranath Tagore.

He has made presentations at seminars/conferences – regional, national and international, and has also published widely in areas related to his fields of interest. Apart from being the Guest Editor of *Sangeet Natak*, vol. XLVI, nos. 1–4, 2011: Special issue on 'Rabindranath's East-West Encounters: Performance and Visual Arts' (New Delhi: Sangeet Natak Akademi, 2013), he has also edited Shakespeare's *Macbeth*, with introduction and annotations (New Delhi: Pearson Longman, 2009). Among some of the translations he has carried out is the English translation of Rabindranath Tagore's *Tasher Desh*, translated as *The Kingdom of Cards*, in *Essential Tagore*, eds. Fakrul Alam & Radha Chakravarty (Cambridge, Mass.: Harvard UP, 2011): 450–487.

Abhijit Sen has also been actively engaged with the theatre, working with students and colleagues at Visva-Bharati, Santiniketan, as well as producing plays with theatre troupes in Kolkata. At Santiniketan, he has worked on Shakespearean productions like *The Merchant of Venice, The Merry Wives of Windsor, Romeo and Juliet, The Wars of the Roses,* and *A Midsummer Night's Dream*. Among the plays of Rabindranath Tagore that he has produced are *Visarjan, Raja* and *Tasher Desh* (as prose play).

Acknowledgements

This study draws upon my long-standing passion for the theatre, on the one hand, and my love and admiration for the works of Rabindranath Tagore, on the other. After I joined Visva-Bharati more than three decades ago, I felt all the more the extraordinary presence of Rabindranath in the very ambience of Santiniketan wherever I turned. My work with the theatre continued alongside through collaborations with students, colleagues and peers in Santiniketan as well as with friends and theatre enthusiasts in Calcutta. My admiration for Rabindranath provoked me to work with some of his plays in the theatre. When I had seen Bohurupee's productions of *Raktakarabi* and *Raja*, directed by Sombhu Mitra, I realised how powerfully Rabindranath can reach out with his plays to the audiences. My first-hand experiences with some of his plays in the theatre strengthened my conviction further. I have reasons to believe that our productions of *Visarjan, Raja* and *Tasher Desh* (as a prose play), in particular, made some impression upon (at least) certain viewers who were present during the performances of these plays. I realised how singularly unfortunate the Bengali theatre has been in veering away from Rabindranath in its theatrical practices, failing to comprehend what makes him so contemporary and so relevant to the times we live in. It was this realisation that encouraged me to focus on Rabindranath's career as a theatre-practitioner and attempt a serious study of his plays – less as literature, more as theatrical texts. Even as my study and my experiences in the theatre went hand in hand, I was thrilled every time I experienced how the words on the page burst into a life of their own on the stage, invoking a theatrical idiom that was rich, poetic, even musical. I was convinced that Rabindranath was fully aware of the strength of that theatrical idiom, through which he was trying to create a different kind of theatre. It is time we give him his rightful credit and recognise the power of the theatre that we have inherited from him.

All this increasingly motivated me to undertake an academic exploration into Rabindranath's own work in the theatre to which I could bring my own perceptions of stage performance. I was extremely fortunate to have Rabindra Bhavana, with its invaluable library and archival holdings, situated in Santiniketan, which was also now my place of work. It was indeed a privilege to find a position not only in Visva-Bharati but also in a department that had a rich tradition of Tagore scholarship. I was able to exchange ideas both with former professors and senior colleagues like Shyamal Kumar Sarkar, Bikash Chakravarty, Santa Bhattacharyya and with later generations of colleagues who continued the rich legacy through their own scholarly contributions. I was also encouraged by colleagues and reputed scholars of other departments/centres of Visva-Bharati, including Sankha Ghosh, Swapan Majumdar or Prasantakumar Pal who, as directors/professors at Rabindra Bhavana, spearheaded the academic pursuits there, particularly related to Tagore Studies. Even beyond Visva-Bharati, I had the good fortune of being in touch with stalwarts in the field like my teachers Sukanta Chaudhuri and Supriya Chaudhuri, or friends and peers like Swapan Chakravorty or Ananda Lal, Krishna Sen or Tapati Gupta, former/emeritus professors of Jadavpur University and Calcutta University. Their scholarly contributions as well as their valuable advice have always been a source of inspiration for me. I have learnt much from my interactions with them and I take this opportunity to express my sincere gratitude to all of them.

I am also grateful to the administration of Visva-Bharati for granting me a year's sabbatical leave that allowed me to collect material and engage in research work for this volume. The staff at Rabindra Bhavana, Visva-Bharati, had always been ready to extend their kind assistance and cooperation, which made the work so much easier and more pleasurable.

I am grateful to all my colleagues of the Department of English, Visva-Bharati, for their ceaseless encouragement and unstinting support throughout this period. I must record my particular gratitude for Ananya Datta Gupta's kind assistance; despite her busy schedule, she readily agreed to read through some of the draft chapters and offered insightful observations that have helped me to revise and reshape some of the matter.

I convey my indebtedness to Sudakshina Ghosh, who has been an enthusiastic participant not only in my theatrical endeavours but also in my academic ventures. Through the entire duration of writing and revising the chapters of the book, she has been a source of continuous support, providing important information and material related to the work, and proposing constructive suggestions and perceptive comments.

My special thanks are due to Samiran Nandy, Mainak Biswas and Joydip Das, who helped me to access photographs and plates from online and offline sources in the public domain as well as with other necessary reprographic technicalities. I expressly thank the members of "Birutjatio" for coming forward to help with the indexing.

My sincere thanks also to the team of the publishing house, Routledge (of Taylor and Francis Group), for kindly helping with the different stages of publication of the volume, at a time that was made considerably difficult for all by the global pandemic.

Finally, I am grateful to all those who have both inspired and nudged me to complete this book and make it available for a wider readership.

Introduction

I

Though Rabindranath Tagore, with his experiments and innovations in the field of theatre, created a new model for the modern Indian theatre, his contribution has not quite received the wide acclaim it deserves – whether in the academia or in the theatrical arena. His plays have been studied primarily as creative literature, and mostly appreciated for their literary/philosophical value.[1] At times, Rabindranath has been credited as a playwright with innovative dramas to offer on the page, and attention has been drawn to the new style of dramaturgy that he was trying to evolve.[2] Yet – except for a handful of discerning critical analyses[3] – there has been little acknowledgement, and less of serious academic discussion, of the theatrical potentiality of his plays.

Unfortunately, in the theatre, too, the stage worthiness of Rabindranath's plays has been generally viewed with condescension, if not downright disparagement; these have hardly been considered fit for serious production. Despite the enthusiastic – though commercially disastrous – early endeavours of theatre professionals like Sisirkumar Bhaduri or Ahindra Chowdhury or the subsequent more notable stage success of the plays staged by Bohurupee, a pioneer of the Group Theatre movement in Bengal, the situation has not changed appreciably in Rabindranath's favour. A flurry of events, engaging plays and/or dance dramas were precipitated by the birth centenary (1961) or the more recent sesquicentennial celebrations (2011), but it is yet to be seen whether these would remain as mere sporadic events occasioned by the celebrations or would have more long-ranging effects on serious negotiations with Rabindranath in the theatre.

As for Rabindranath himself, he could hardly remain contented with the mere writing of a play; he was restless till he had it staged, and that too on multiple occasions, with adequate revisions/modifications/innovations made for each event. What is hardly remembered today is how effortlessly he was able to fuse together the roles of author, actor, director, producer and even designer, and refashion himself as a versatile man of the theatre.[4] Initially he seems to have emerged as an actor,[5] but soon took up the reins of production. He started with the performances within the household that kept him engaged in his early formative years. After he

DOI: 10.4324/9781003110279-1

shifted to Santiniketan and was able to experiment with his productions at the *asram*-school, he developed further as a producer/director. At a later phase, his productions staged in Calcutta or other metropolitan venues exuded a distinct note of confidence, so much so that they could even involve the sale of tickets, mostly to raise funds for the university. In fact, he often returned to the theatre at the Jorasanko residence to stage his later productions for the Calcutta audiences. Not only were early productions like *Valmiki Pratibha* (1881, again 1890) or *Kal Mrigaya* (1882) performed at Jorasanko, but he also made use of the Vichitra stage at Jorasanko for *Phalguni* (1916, the charity show for the Bankura famine),[6] *Dakghar* (given there several times between late 1917 and early 1918), *Sesh Varshan* (in 1925), *Natir Puja* (in 1927), *Rituranga* (in 1927), *Sundar* (in 1929), to cite a few instances. Performances at the *asram*-school continued through the rest of his career after he relocated himself to Santiniketan. Santiniketan served as the testing ground for his recent dramatic compositions; the plays written during this phase usually premiered there – so, *Sarodotsav* in 1908, *Raja* in 1911, *Achalayatan* in 1914, *Phalguni* in 1915, *Natir Puja* in 1926, *Nataraj-Riturangasala* in 1927 and so on. But plays performed earlier elsewhere were also revived at the *asram*-school (generally with his support, if not direct participation) – like *Raja o Rani* in 1912 (in which Sudhiranjan Das played Queen Sumitra) or *Visarjan* in 1909, 1919 and again in1935. Late in his life, after the school evolved into the university (Visva-Bharati), not only did he mount several productions in Calcutta but also toured different parts of India and abroad with his troupe of performers, enacting dramas and dance dramas. After his shift to Santiniketan, among the dramatic compositions[7] he produced in Calcutta (in many of which he acted/participated himself) were *Dakghar* in 1917 at Vichitra,[8] *Varsha-mangal* in 1922 at Madan Theatre and Alfred Theatre, *Visarjan* in 1923 at Empire Theatre, *Arupratan* in 1924 at Alfred Theatre, *Rituranga* at Vichitra in 1927, *Tapati* in 1929 at New Empire Theatre, *Shapmochan* in 1933 at Empire Theatre, *Chandalika* and *Tasher Desh* in 1933 at Madan Theatre, *Raja* in 1935 at New Empire Theatre, *Chitrangada* (dance drama) at New Empire in 1936 and *Shyama* at Sree Theatre in 1939. Again, at the invitation of Sarojini Naidu, *Shapmochan* and *Tasher Desh* were performed at the Excelsior Theatre, Bombay, in November 1933, and *Chitrangada* was presented in Bombay, Ahmedabad and Nagpur. *Chitrangada* also toured successfully Khulna, Kumilla, Chittagong, Sylhet and Mymensingh of East Bengal (now Bangladesh) in March 1938, while *Shapmochan* had an enthusiastic reception in Sri Lanka (then Ceylon) in May 1934. These performances were chiefly given in an effort to replenish the university exchequer with the sale proceeds.[9]

As an author, who also combined in himself the roles of actor, director and producer, Rabindranath was always on the lookout for an opportunity to perform and produce his own plays, both recently written ones and also reworked versions of earlier compositions. His penchant for novelty and freshness nudged him to explore new grounds and move in new directions, in the writing as well as the staging of his plays. Even when reviving earlier plays, he so inscribed the script and/or the performance with revisions/modifications, even improvisations/innovations, that they became new texts. He was ever learning from the practical experience of the theatre, which, in turn, helped to shape his dramaturgical structure, on the one hand, and bring a remarkably 'modern' approach to the business of play production, on the other.

This process of fashioning a new theatre, for Rabindranath, became related to the requirements of an emergent nation that he could envision through his own notions of nation-building. His contribution to the Bengali theatre has to be understood in the context of the theatre to which he arrived in the late nineteenth century, and for which he tried to create an alternative model that would be more in tune with local aspirations. He was, in effect, imagining a 'new' theatre for a new nation. Veering away from contemporary practices, in the writing and staging of plays, Rabindranath conceptualized a new theatre that he tried to locate in the socio-politico-cultural context of his age. There is a pressing need, therefore, not only to historicize the arrival of Rabindranath in the arena of the Bengali theatre of that period, but also to evaluate his significant contribution in conceptualizing a new model for the modern Bengali theatre, which, in turn, was intertwined with his vision of a new cultural space for the emergent nation.

Only when we appreciate how Rabindranath's role as a dramatist is complemented by his role as an actor-director would we be able to view how these roles engraft themselves onto that of a performance-theorist who conceptualizes a modern Indian/Bengali theatre. Not much of this has been given the critical attention it deserves. As pointed out, there have been some insightful explorations written in Bengali – whether by scholars like Sankha Ghosh and Bishnu Basu, or theatre-personalities like Sombhu Mitra and Kumar Roy. In English, however, there is a dearth of adequate critical analysis in this area. Not enough seems to have been done after Edward Thompson's *Rabindranath Tagore: Poet and Dramatist* (1948). A recent contribution in this area has been Mala Rengathanan and Arnab Bhattacharya (ed.), *The Politics and Reception of Rabindranath Tagore's Drama: The Bard on the Stage* (2014); though a significant addition, the thrust of that volume is considerably different from that of the present study, which attempts to explore Rabindranath's own role as author-actor-director-producer and stress the major changes he achieved in writing and staging plays for Bengali theatre. For this, it has depended heavily upon what has already been researched, investigated and/or published in this area. Building on that, the study has tried to reassess the uniqueness of Rabindranath as a dramaturge who evolved smoothly through many phases of playwriting, who shifted effortlessly from writing to staging of plays, who was able to forge a happy blend between author and practitioner, and all the while, who was dreaming of a new model of theatre relevant not only for his times but for future times as well. That is what makes him so much our contemporary even today.

II

It needs to be made clear at the very outset that the present study, in trying to focus on Rabindranath's theatre, will presuppose a distinction between *drama* (as a written/printed text on page) and *theatre* (as performance, and therefore a text created on the stage). The point of concern, here, will primarily be on the shift from the page to the stage, and, by corollary, on Rabindranath more as a theatre-personality than as a dramatist. Yet, for one who combined in himself the roles of author, actor and director it would be impossible to keep drama and theatre segregated from each other. As such, appraisals of his plays – whether of their narrative format, or thematic concerns, or dramaturgical structure – would have to enter at relevant junctures. His theatrical output was automatically influenced by, and, in turn, was further influencing, his dramaturgical strategies in shaping his plays. If in writing the plays potential staging was kept in mind, the experience of staging those plays would be carried over into the writing of later plays. Theatrical exigencies would be the invariable prerequisite for both the composition and the mounting of the plays; even his theorizing about theatre would be largely conditioned by actual praxis.

There are, however, some major hurdles to be confronted in this projected area of study. The first of these is related to lack of adequate documentation of theatrical activities. This a major problem when dealing with a cultural artefact like theatre which, with its ephemeral character, inevitably exists in the here and the now. The moment a performance is over it becomes history. With the development of visual aids in more recent times, it has perhaps become relatively easier to preserve evidence of performances. Even then, the wholeness of the performance cannot really be kept intact; the immediacy of a theatrical experience – whether actorly or productional or spectating in kind – can hardly be relived to the same degree as available in its originary moment. The magic of that moment, which a living theatre thrives upon, defies any form of documentation or preservation. Though this problem is common to theatres of all cultures, in the Indian context, it is further compounded by the lack of adequate means of – as well as awareness for – proper documentation of theatre. Moreover, theatre, being a living art, constantly evolves and outgrows its older modes. The styles of acting and/or production of one period become obsolete within a couple of decades. As Amritalal Bose, a leading theatre-personality and a senior contemporary of Rabindranath once remarked: "The style of acting changes every twenty years, if not sooner."[10] We cannot expect visual documentation of Rabindranath's productions to have been preserved for posterity, and the one such attempt made (a performance of *Natir Puja* captured on celluloid by New Theatres in 1932) does not do justice to the original event. More often than not, we may be left feeling more dissatisfied than contented – one reason being the loss of the immediacy of the theatrical experience; another, the 'outdated' manner of acting and production.[11]

Under such circumstances, for our evaluation of Rabindranath as a man of the theatre, we have to access eyewitness accounts, available in the memoirs and reminiscences of his contemporaries. Here yet another hurdle threatens to thwart our attempts. For, when the subject of study is Rabindranath, a formidable preponderance of adulation, verging on adoration, often tends to swamp critical/objective perception, both among his contemporaries and his following generations. With the towering presence of Rabindranath amidst them, most among his generation were usually left so awestruck that much of their assessments – even of his career in the theatre – betrayed signs of hero-worship tending towards bardolatry. For instance, Sita Devi has left us eye-witness accounts of different plays that he staged and performed in. Recalling Rabindranath's acting in the 1911 production of *Raja* in Santiniketan, she writes: "And the Poet dancing as Thakurda amidst them [the young boys] was a moving sight. He could dance remarkably well. Those who have seen him only in his mature years have missed much [of this]."[12] But one could suspect that her assessment may not have been free from her personal admiration for Rabindranath's greatness:

> Whenever I saw his acting I always felt whatever be the role it was impossible for us to forget that it was Rabindranath. Though he was an excellent actor of the first grade, it was hardly possible for him to remain incognito. *Just as the sun cannot be made to take on the guise of a star, it was impossible to disguise him as any other self.* [13]

So, when recapitulating the sixty-two-year-old Rabindranath in the role of the young Joysingha (in the 1923 production of *Visarjan*), Sita Devi notes that he "could be easily mistaken for a youth, so bold was his gait, so resonant his voice",[14] we are not sure how far this may be considered an objective evaluation of the Poet's histrionic abilities. However, upon cross-checking, her comments seem to agree with those given in contemporary press reviews like: "He looked so young when he first appeared.... some of his poses were the acme of histrionic art"[15] or "As Joy Singh, his [Rabindranath's] every utterance and gesture drew applause from the vast and admiring audience."[16] We are then on surer ground and can accept Sita Devi's remarks as reliable eyewitness record.

The reviews carried in the newspapers of the period are another important source of information, usually written by specialist drama critics. So, the Poet's acting in *Sarodotsav* [17] was said to be "of another order. It was something uplifting and ennobling, bringing out subtle inner meaning of the play, making it plain to the least intelligent among the audience and imparting to the whole performance a wonderful dignity and charm."[18] The 1916 *Phalguni* [19] was described as "a feast of colour and sound and joy. ... [in which all the actors] acted as the birds sing – because of the happiness they feel; and as the flowers grow, because the spring is in their veins"[20] in which Rabindranath's "magnetic personality in the double role of the poet gay and the ministerial grave made the oratorio a complete success which it so eminently deserved"[21], and with his impersonation of the blind *baul*, "(t)he dramatic motif crystallizes at the appearance of the blind singer."[22] Some reviews, at times, astutely drew parallels between a particular production and a contemporary context. So, when Rabindranath produced *Tapati* in 1929, *Nachghar* carried a long report in its 1929 Autumn issue where it observed: "The incongruities in the contemporary political scenario that disturb Rabindranath have been articulated in this symbolic drama, *Tapati*."[23]

Particularly insightful are comments made about Rabindranath's theatre by noted litterateurs and/or theatre-personalities of the day. Satyendranath Dutta was moved by the 1916 *Phalguni* production and wrote a long appreciative review. Hemendrakumar Roy not only admired Rabindranath's acting on the stage but was all praise for his vocal acting and elocutionary style: "If voice be the chief implement of theatre, then one would unhesitatingly class Rabindranath's voice as matchless.... The varied intonations in his voice would be fitting for any first grade actor"[24] or again, "Rabindranath possessed a gifted voice, which could articulate any manner of emotion – a talent often lacking in the best of actors.... I have never heard anyone – in the theatre or literary circle of Bengal – to recite like Rabindranath."[25] Sajanikanta Das was pleasantly surprised to see how the induction of dance as a theatre idiom (for a dance drama like *Shyama*) enhanced the quality of the production and quickly dispelled all his initial qualms:

> *the language of the body is in no way less than the language of poetry.* I had misgivings about the propriety of the students of Visva-Bharati enacting this tale of physical love by. In reality I found *the touch of genius* could make everything possible. The expressiveness of the soft bodily postures dissolved away the sense of the physical to recreate a world of cerebral perception.[26]

Amritalal Bose, a theatre stalwart of the period, commended Rabindranath both as actor and director. Having seen the production of *Goray Galad* staged in 1900 for the Sangit Samaj, under the direction of Rabindranath, Amritalal is reported to have composed a humorous rhyme, which praised the abilities of the director in charge of this production: "*Sobe sakhe abhineta, ke jane eder neta/ Pratibha je sikshadata bujhi parichay*" ["All are amateur actors, one wonders who their leader is/ That this trainer is decidedly gifted is most perceptible"].[27] And after witnessing the *Visarjan* of 1923,[28] he applauded the performance in no uncertain terms:

> the performance of "Visarjan" was, begging the captious critic's pardon, an unqualified success.... (Rabindranath) has achieved greatness and greatness courts him too.... In endowing Rabi Babu with a great mind, Providence seems to have prepared a special mould to cast the golden casket in which that mind was to find its home.[29]

III

It is sources like these, then, that one would have to fall back upon in the course of this study. Help will also be sought from notable critical contributions already made in this field, both by theatre-scholars and theatre-practitioners. The contributions of scholars like Bishnu Basu or Sekhar Samaddar have directed our attention to the career of Rabindranath in the theatre, while the writings of theatre stalwarts like Sombhu Mitra, who having worked with some of the plays on the stage, have alerted us to their immense theatrical potential. Apart from other scholarly works, particular mention may be made of Rudraprasad Chakrabarty's *Rangamancha O Rabindranath: Samakalin Pratikriya* (Calcutta: Ananda Publishers, 1995). A helpful compilation of reviews/reports of Rabindranath's stage career that appeared in newspapers, journals and personal memoirs, this serves as a valuable source of much relevant information. The two major biographical works – Prabhatkumar Mukhopadhyay, *Rabindra Jibani*, 4 vols. (Calcutta: Visva-Bharati Granthalay, 1936–52) and Prasantakumar Pal, *Rabi Jibani*, 9 vols. (Calcutta: Ananda Publishers, 1982–2003) – have also proved to be rich repositories of valuable data. It may be mentioned here that though in 2001 the name of Calcutta was officially adopted as "Kolkata", because the accepted name of the city during Rabindranath's lifetime and for decades after had remained "Calcutta", this name (Calcutta) has been retained throughout this study for purposes of uniformity. This has been done also to refer to works published subsequent to 2001, unless the title of a work specifically mentions "Kolkata" (e.g., Ananda Lal, "Tagore in Kolkata Theatre: 1986–2010", in *Towards Tagore*, ed. Sanjukta Dasgupta, Ramkumar Mukhopadhyay and Swati Ganguly, Calcutta: Visva-Bharati, 2014: 515–46).

Precisely because so many of the Tagore household were involved with the theatre, in this study Rabindranath has been referred to by his name (omitting the surname); for the other members, too, this has been mostly followed (so, Abanindranath, Gaganendranath, Rathindranath, and so on). Also, where Rabindranath has used translations/equivalences for original Bengali names/terms, these have been indicated (usually in parentheses) as with *The Autumn Festival, Sacrifice, Karna and Kunti, Red Oleanders*, etc. Where these have not been readily available, translations/equivalences have been provided here for purposes of this book.

The book will comprise three sections. The first section, in surveying the historical context, will attempt a general overview of the Bengal Renaissance theatre and the involvement of the Tagore family in this area. This is expected to set the stage for a discussion of Rabindranath's emergence on the scene, the kind of theatre he was exposed to in his formative years, and the kind of theatre he envisioned as a departure from that model. The second section, focusing on Rabindranath as a dramaturge and theorist, will consist of three chapters: "Theatre and nation", which will underscore his vision of a new model for the theatre vis-a-vis his involvement in the nation-building programme and his awareness of the sociocultural requirements of an emergent nation; "Theatre at the *asram*-school", which, in continuation of the previous chapter, will concentrate on how his new notions of theatre were put into practice after his relocation to Santiniketan; and "Theories of theatre", in which his conceptualization of this new theatre would be analysed. The third and final section will devote itself to investigating Rabindranath's role as a theatre-practitioner through a study of his engagement with theatre-related issues like "Preparing the playtext", "Selecting the cast", "Rehearsing the play", "Setting the stage", "Acting the role", "Theatricalizing cultures" and also "Translating the playtext"; the purpose of these chapters is to draw attention to the metamorphosis of a dramatic text into a performance text, and the consequent reconstitution of the text as it shifts from page to stage. The chapter on "Translating the playtext" has been included to alert us to the fact that not only do the playtexts (in Rabindranath's self-translated versions) become significantly transcreated, but often the dramaturgical and/or theatrical codes are also radically reinscribed.

Through this analysis, the book hopes to add to our understanding of Rabindranath as a leading innovative theatre-practitioner who not only had expertise in the different segments of performance (acting, singing, designing, choreographing, directing, producing) but also a distinctive vision for a modern Indian theatre – different yet inclusive. The visionary playwright and the pragmatic theatre-practitioner blended in Rabindranath to gift us with a unique theatre-personality – a gift we have unfortunately tended to overlook.

This book had to necessarily depend upon several works written in Bengali – for both primary and secondary sources. When excerpts have been cited from these sources, if an already available (and dependable) translation of the Bengali original was accessible it has been made use of; in all such cases the source of the translation has been mentioned and acknowledged. Unless specified thus, the (remaining) translated passages are my translations done for the purposes of this book. A select bibliography, comprising primary and secondary reading, has been provided at the end to indicate the works consulted and/or cited. Also, a brief chronology of select events and works (between 1881 and 1941), with particular focus on dramatic/theatrical achievements, has been included as an appendix.

Notes

1 To cite a few instances: Jatindramohan Bagchi, *Rabindranath o Jug sahitya* (Calcutta: Brindaban Dhar & Sons Ltd, 1947); Upendranath Bhattacharya, *Rabindranatya Parikrama* (Calcutta: Orient Book Company, 1960); Asutosh Bhattacharya, *Rabindra Natyadhara* (Calcutta: Sanskriti Prakashan, 1966); Abu Sayeed Ayub, *Pantha Janer Sakha* (Calcutta: Dey's Publishing, 1973); Soumendranath Basu, *Rabindranatake Tragedy* (Calcutta: Tagore Research Institute, 2009).
2 Pramathanath Bishi, *Rabindra Natya-prabaha*, 2 vols. (Calcutta: Orient Book Company, 1958); Asrukumar Sikdar, *Rabindranatye Rupantar o Aikya* (Calcutta: Patralekha, 1998); Edward Thompson, *Rabindranath Tagore: Poet and Dramatist* (Delhi: Oxford University Press, 1948); Bishweshwar Chakraverty, *Tagore the Dramatist: A Critical Study*, vols. 1–4 (Delhi: B.R. Publishing, 2000).
3 Mention may be made of Sankha Ghosh, *Kaler Matra o Rabindra Natak* (Calcutta: Dey's Publishing, 1971); Sombhu Mitra, *Natak Raktakarabi* (Calcutta: M.C. Sarkar & Sons, 1992); Bishnu Basu, *Rabindranather Theatre* (Calcutta: Pratibhas, 1987); Dilip Kumar Roy, *Rabindra samakale Rabindranataker Abhinoy* (Calcutta: Sramik Press, 1999); Kumar Roy, *Rabindranatak: Rup ebong Ruper Bhasya* (Calcutta: Pratibhas, 2010); Sekhar Samaddar, "Rabindranather Natyabhavna", in *Punascha Rabindranath*, ed. Sabyasachi Bhattacharya and Bratin Dey (New Delhi: National Book Trust, India, 2012) 215–83. Certain Bengali journals have brought out special numbers devoted specifically to Rabindranath's dramas, like *Uddalak*, 2nd year, nos. 2 & 3, April–September, 2002, or *Balaka*, 19th year, no. 29, November 2010. As evident

Introduction 9

here, these are critical discussions in Bengali. Not much seems to have been done in English to evaluate critically Rabindranath's contribution as a theatre-practitioner.

4 Memoirs by many of his contemporaries recall his active engagement as a theatre-personality, though not much attention seems to have been paid to these in critical studies. Apart from his own reminiscences in *Jibansmriti* and *Chelebela* (both of which have been translated into English), mention may be made of *Jyotirindranather Jibansmriti* as reported by Basantakumar Chattopadhyay (Calcutta: Prajnabharati, 1919); Abanindranath Tagore (transcription by Rani Chanda), *Gharoa* (Calcutta: Visva-Bharati Granthan Vibhaga, 1941; rpt. 1983); Asitkumar Haldar, *Rabitirhe* (Calcutta: Anjana Prakashani, 1958); Sahana Devi, *Smritir Kheya* 5th edn. (Calcutta: Prima Publications, 2011; originally 1978); Sita Devi, *Punya Smriti* (Calcutta: Probasi, 1942); Indira Devi Chaudhurani, *Rabindra Smriti* (Calcutta: Visva-Bharati Granthan Vibhaga, 2010; originally 1960); Sudhiranjan Das, *Amader Santiniketan* (Calcutta: Visva-Bharati Granthalay, 1959); Pramathanath Bishi, *Rabindranath O Santiniketan* (Calcutta: Visva-Bharati, 1959; rpt. 1975); Santidev Ghosh, *Rabindrasangeet* (Calcutta: Visva-Bharati Granthalay, rev. edn. 1958; originally 1942); Hemendrakumar Roy, *Soukhin Natyakalaye Rabindranath* (Calcutta: Indian Associated Publishing Co. Pvt. Ltd., 1959); Charuchandra Bandyopadhyay, *Rabi-Rashmi: Purba bhag*, vol. 1 (Calcutta: University of Calcutta, 1938) and *Rabi-Rashmi: Paschim bhag*, vol. 2 (Calcutta: A. Mukherjee & Co., 1939); etc. Details of his life events, including his explorations in the world of theatre, are to be found in the two foremost biographical works, Prabhatkumar Mukhopadhyay, *Rabindra Jibani*, 4 vols. (Calcutta: Visva-Bharati Granthalay, 1933–56; rev. 1960–64) and Prasantakumar Pal, *Rabijibani*. 9 vols. (Calcutta: Ananda Publishers, 1982–2003). Particularly useful for this study has been Rudraprasad Chakrabarty, *Rangamancha O Rabindranath: Samakalin Pratikriya* (Calcutta: Ananda Publishers, 1995) with its well-documented and informative source of reports of the reception of the Poet's career in the theatre.

5 In the early days of *Valmiki Pratibha* (1881) or *Raja o Rani* (1889), the details of production seem to have been supervised by his elder brothers, Jyotirindranath or Satyendranath.

6 This, according to his biographer, was the first appearance of the students of Santiniketan before a Calcutta audience. See Prabhatkumar Mukhopadhyay, *Rabindra Jibani*, vol. 2 (Calcutta: Visva-Bharati Granthalay, 1936) 534–5.

7 These compositions cover the wide range that spans his dramatic oeuvre: verse plays like *Visarjan*; prose plays like *Achalayatan, Dakghar, Raja, Arupratan*; musical plays like *Varsha-mangal* or *Rituranga*; and dance dramas like *Shapmochan, Chandalika, Chitrangada* or *Shyama*.

8 This play has a unique stage history. The first production of the play was not of the Bengali original but of the English *Post Office* by the Irish Abbey Theatre, first in Dublin (17 May) and then in London (10 July) in 1913. The first performance of the Bengali *Dakghar* was not organised by Rabindranath but given under the aegis of the Brahmo Samaj at Mary Carpenter Hall on 3 May 1917. Rabindranath first produced the play on 10 October 1917 at Vichitra; for this, he recruited Ashamukul Das for the role of Amal, as he had played the role for the May production at Mary Carpenter Hall. The Bengali *Dakghar* was subsequently performed many times at Vichitra, including the one on 31 December 1917 before the Congress delegates including Gandhi, Besant, Malaviya and others. Incidentally, among all his plays staged overseas, *The Post Office* remains perhaps the most frequently performed, given in different languages.

9 After the success of *Natir Puja* (1926), Rathindranath proposed that the production be taken to Calcutta (in 1927) to raise funds for Visva-Bharati. For the Bombay tour of *Shapmochan* in 1933, the advertisement in *The Times of India* (22 November 1933) mentioned: "Proceeds will go to Visva-Bharati the International Institution at Santiniketan." Immediately after the Calcutta performances of *Chitrangada* (March 1936),

10   Introduction

the Poet moved to Patna with his contingent, as reported in *Anandabazar Patrika*: "Rabindranath has arrived in Patna with boys and girls of Santiniketan to raise funds for Visva-Bharati." The very next year (1937), when *Chitrangada* was taken to Bombay, *The Times of India* announced the event on consecutive days (20, 23, 24, 25 Feb) as: "THE EXCELSIOR/In aid of/Viswa-Bharati/For three days only..." and on 27 February as: "Last Performance today!/THE EXCELSIOR/In aid of/Vishva-Bharati..." (as cited in Rudraprasad Chakrabarty, *Rangamancha O Rabindranath: Samakalin Pratikriya*, 207, 250–1, 288, 294–5).

10 Amritalal, in fact, made this remark in his evaluation of Rabindranath's 1923 production of *Visarjan*, of which he wrote a long review with the title, "Visarjan – an appreciation', in *Indian Daily News*, 4 September 1923; this has been cited in *Rangamancha O Rabindranath: Samakalin Pratikriya*, 64–5.

11 Closer to our times, audio recordings have been made of Bohurupee's monumental productions like *Raktakarabi* or *Raja Oidipous*, yet younger generations tend to find the style of acting archaic and stylised.

12 Sita Devi, *Punya Smriti*, 19.

13 Sita Devi, *Punya Smriti*, 19; emphases added.

14 Sita Devi, *Punya Smriti*, 242.

15 *Indian Daily News*, 27 August 1923; cited in *Rangamancha O Rabindranath: Samakalin Pratikriya*, 62.

16 *The Statesman*, 26 August 1923; cited in *Rangamancha O Rabindranath: Samakalin Pratikriya*, 62.

17 This was a production in Calcutta given on September 1922 to raise funds for Visva-Bharati.

18 *Indian Daily News*, 18 September 1922; cited in *Rangamancha O Rabindranath: Samakalin Pratikriya*, 91.

19 This was a Calcutta performance in aid of the Bankura famine.

20 *The Statesman*, 1 February 1916; cited in *Rangamancha O Rabindranath: Samakalin Pratikriya*, 125–6.

21 Amritabazar Patrika; cited in *Rangamancha O Rabindranath: Samakalin Pratikriya*, 125.

22 *The Bengalee*, 30 January 1916; cited in *Rangamancha O Rabindranath: Samakalin Pratikriya*, 127.

23 Quoted in *Rangamancha O Rabindranath: Samakalin Pratikriya*, 235.

24 Hemendrakumar Roy, *Soukhin Natyakalaye Rabindranath* (Calcutta: Indian Associated Publishing Co. Pvt. Ltd., 1959) 112.

25 Hemendrakumar Roy, *Soukhin Natyakalay Rabindranath*, 124–5.

26 *Anandabazar Patrika*, 8 February 1939; cited in *Rangamancha O Rabindranath: Samakalin Pratikriya*, 301; emphases added.

27 Cited in Khagendranath Chattopadhyay, *Rabindra Katha* (Calcutta: Jayasri Pustakalay, 1941) 221.

28 Amritalal is reported to have seen the performance of *Visarjan* on 25 August 1923.

29 "Visarjan – an appreciation" in *Indian Daily News*, 4 September 1923; as cited in *Rangamancha O Rabindranath: Samakalin Pratikriya*, 64–5.

Section 1
The historical context

1 The Bengal Renaissance theatre and Rabindranath

I

The Bengali theatre, emerging in the nineteenth century largely as a by-product of the Bengal Renaissance, remained first, a colonial importation, and second, an urban phenomenon. The theatres of the British, constructed in Calcutta from the mid-eighteenth century primarily for the entertainment of the local British residents, provided the model for the Indian/Bengali theatres. In the words of Sudipto Chatterjee: "The Bengal Renaissance was the outgrowth of the grafting of a foreign culture onto a more-than-willing native culture ... It is in the wake of this endeavour to assume/regain a respectful self-identity, that in the 1840s, several theatres were spawned in the native quarters of Calcutta."[1]

The English theatres in Calcutta, built by the British theatre enthusiasts, were emulating the contemporary European realistic theatre, with its proscenium stage heavily adorned with Victorian 'pictorial realism'. The Russian Herasim Lebedeff is credited with having staged the first Bengali plays (Bengali translations of *The Disguise* and *Love is the Best Doctor*); his Bengally Theatre, built at No. 25 "Dom-Tollah" (Ezra Street), would have been very much a replica of the available European model. He writes in his memoir:

> I set about building a commodious Theatre on a plan of my own, in Dom-Tollah, (Dome-Lane) in the centre of Calcutta; and in the mean while I employed my Linguist to procure native actors of both sexes, ...[2]

The staging took place on 27 November 1795, and was repeated on 21 March 1796. Interestingly, Lebedeff claims to have used male as well as female players also for his production. However, it is difficult to say how far he could cater to the average Bengali playgoers, as the rather exorbitant admission rates may have been near-prohibitive for them.[3] Also, the stilted Bengali translation may not have found favour with the Bengali populace, used to more colloquial language used in indigenous forms of entertainment like *jatra, akhrai, half-akhrai, tarja*.[4] Moreover, despite its historical importance, Lebedeff's attempt, ultimately, was one initiated by a foreigner (he was a Russian) and remained an abortive one, as

DOI: 10.4324/9781003110279-2

he had to put an end to his ventures when his theatre was closed after a fire and he ran into financial insolvency.

When the Bengali *nouveaux riches*, in turn, decided to have their own theatres, they, too, followed the European model. Prasannakumar Tagore, the first Bengali *bhadralok* to erect a theatre in imitation of the Western model, flamboyantly called it the 'Hindoo Theatre', yet went on to stage plays in English – the first night saw productions of scenes from Shakespeare's *Julius Caesar* and an English version of Bhavabhuti's *Uttar-Ramcharit* (translated by an Englishman, Wilson).[5] Scholars mention that among the actors who later appeared in this theatre – usually playing Shakespearean roles in English-language productions – were Ramtanu Lahiri (in 1833) and Madhusudan Dutt (in 1834, then aged ten), playing the Duke of Gloucester in *Henry IV*.[6]

Against this Anglicist or Reformist trend, with its overt dependence on the Western cultural models, emerged an Orientalist/Revivalist backlash. Sanskrit plays (in Bengali translations) were revived and quasi-Sanskrit plays were also composed and staged. So, while there were productions of Sanskrit masters (in translation) like Kalidas and Vasa, there were also quasi-Sanskrit plays like Kaliprasanna Singha's *Sabitri-Satyaban Natak* (published 1858) or Monomohan Basu's *Ramabhishek Natak* (performed 1868), for which there were no Sanskrit antecedents but which followed the classical sources using the Bengali language.[7] When Kalidas's *Sakuntala* was given at Ashutosh Dev's (Satu babu) theatre on 30 January 1857, *Hindoo Patriot*, on 15 February 1857, noted that "(t)he announcement [on the invitation card] had the further attraction that the play announced was *a genuine Bengalee one* ..."[8]. Not only was Kalidas appropriated for the Bengali theatre, but he was also stridently promoted as the champion of the Indian/Bengali legacy against Shakespeare, the supreme cultural icon of the Western colonizer. So, when the Bengali poet Hemchandra Bandyopadhyay, in his eulogy of Shakespeare, had gushed: "*Bharater Kalidas, jagater tumi*" ["Kalidas is of India, you are of the world"], no less than Vidyasagar retorted with: "*Hembabur e katha bolibar adhikar nai. Se to Sanskrito jane na*" ["Hembabu has no right to say this. He has no Sanskrit learning"].[9]

When, in the post-Lebedeff era, Bengali theatre stirred back to life on 6 October 1835 with the staging of *Vidyasundar*, at Nabinchandra Basu's house at Shyambazar, it took recourse to the Indian love story of Vidya and Sundar, but also borrowed from Western theatrical codes. The *Hindoo Pioneer* reviewer noted, with approval, the intermixing of the "English style" and the "native language" in the performance. Interestingly, this performance also deployed women in the female roles, and the actress Radhamoni was particularly applauded for her impersonation of the character of Vidya, the heroine.[10] For that matter, when Taracharan Sikdar wrote his *Bhadrarjun* (1852), he used a tale from Indian mythology but worked into it a Western dramaturgical style; in his introduction, having declared how he eschewed the details given in Sanskrit dramaturgical prescriptions, he wrote: "Done according to the principles of European drama, I offer this play."[11] The very next year, Harachandra Ghosh published his translation of Shakespeare's *The Merchant of Venice* as *Bhanumati Chittabilas* (1853) and announced in the English preface[12] of the play how he

> undertook to write it [the play] in the shape of a Bengali *Natuck* or Drama, taking only the plots and underplots of the Merchant of Venice, *with considerable additions and alterations to suit the native taste*, but at the same time losing no opportunity *to convey to my countrymen, who have no means of getting themselves acquainted with Shakespeare, save through the medium of their own language, the beauty of the author's sentiments...* the work being of a novel character, professing, as it does, to be a *Bengali Natuck though written much after the manner of an English play.* [13]

Though *Bhadrarjun* or *Bhanumati Chittabilas* were early indications, it was finally through the efforts of Michael Madhusudan Dutt that a happy conciliation was achieved between the Reformist and Revivalist positions in the Bengali theatre. Aware of Western traditions, he was able to use these for his dramaturgical structure, while for the dramatic narrative resorting to Indian epics/myths/legends. In fact, Madhusudan's role as a playwright of the period encapsulates the dilemmas involved vis-à-vis the realization that the British presence in India had a two-fold Janus-like influence, "one destructive, the other regenerating."[14] On the one hand, Madhusudan had an undisguised disgust for the mindless borrowings from Sanskrit drama, which impelled his conscious efforts to import Western models for Bengali dramaturgy, and which he justified thus:

> I am aware, my dear fellow, that there will, in all likelihood, be something of a foreign air about my drama: but if the language be not ungrammatical, if the thoughts be just and glowing, the plot interesting, the characters well maintained, what care you if there be a foreign air about the thing?[15]

On the other hand, he was acutely aware of his sociocultural position as an Indian and hence the need to relocate his Western borrowings within that context. This may have been the reason why he did not dabble in Shakespearean translation/adaptation – though that was one of the foremost preoccupations in the contemporary theatre. In a letter to his friend Rajnarain Basu he wrote:

> Some of my friends – and I fancy, you are among them – as soon as you see a drama of mine begin to apply the canons of criticism that have been given forth by the masterpieces of William Shakespeare. They perhaps forget that I write under different circumstances. Our social and moral developments are of a different character.[16]

In his earliest play, *Sarmishtha* (1859), while importing the model of tragic drama from European sources, Madhusudan used it to retell a well-known story that had its roots in the Indian tradition[17]; in doing so, he not only provided the model for his other plays but also for the kind of "transculturation" later adopted in the Bengali theatre. We need to contextualize Madhusudan's efforts within that dialectical relationship, which informed the cross-cultural exchanges between the European/English culture (of the colonizing master) and the new urban educated Bengali elite (the colonized subject) in nineteenth-century Bengal: "English literature was not merely a literature of the masters but it was literature, a source of non-denominational spirituality, a harbinger of a secular outlet."[18] But the fact remains that though Madhusudan's *Sarmishtha* or Ramnarayan Tarkaratna's *Ratnabali* or the many Indianized Shakespearean adaptations (*Hamlet* as *Hariraj*, *Macbeth* as *Rudrapal*, *Othello* as *Bhimsingha*) all emerged as Bengali playtexts, their performances were conditioned by the Western staging principles. The theatre semiology on the Bengali stage, therefore, remained – and has remained – a Western importation.

The other important characteristic of this Bengali theatre was its urban nature: it evolved primarily in the city, for the entertainment of the Calcutta residents, under the patronage of the rich *bhadralok* (elite) classes. In its early phases, it was kept confined to the premises of these social elites, though usually at their 'garden-houses' and not quite their official residential quarters. The invited guests who went to the theatres also came from the upper echelons of the society; these performances were meant primarily for select audiences and not for the common people.[19] In fact, even for these invited *bhadralok* classes, a hierarchical system of seating arrangements was, perhaps, practised. There is at least one reference to the ushers showing seats to the spectators in keeping with their social ranking (the dress they wore being the marker); the incident left quite a few feathers ruffled and, in turn, elicited hasty explanations that the organizers were not aware of this development.[20] The performances of the theatrical troupes of that period were chiefly bolstered by the generosity of the city-based wealthy patrons. Even when later amateur theatrical companies tried to carve out identities for themselves – Jorasanko Theatre (1865), Sovabazar Private Theatrical Society (1865), Bowbazar Amateur Theatre (1868) and Bagbazar Amateur Theatre (1868; in 1872 renamed as Shyambazar Theatre Society) – their performances still depended on private patronage.

This urban theatre, emerging as an offshoot of the contemporary *bhadralok* culture, eventually pushed to the margins the earlier forms of popular/folk performance, which included not only the *jatra* (of which Gopal Udey was a major impresario) but also the non-dramatic forms of entertainment like *kathakata, kabigan, panchali,* or *kirtan*. With the arrival of the colonizer's model of theatre, these indigenous forms were increasingly treated with disdain as being fit only for the riff-raff. The English-educated Bengali elite were not only hostile towards these popular modes of entertainment but even advocated for the promotion of the Western model for emulation. Rajendralal Mitra, for instance, wrote:

> It is difficult to indicate within the codes of decency to what extent *kheur* and *kabi* were odious. One deeply regrets to assess the mental state of those who feel entertained by them ...

> It may easily be said that vulgar forms like *kabi* and *kheur* cannot survive for long in any decent society; they would cease to exist with time .... In the past four years, at several venues in Calcutta proper plays are being performed. The rich, the elite, the scholar all assemble to witness them and derive the pure pleasure of theatre. It is our sincere hope and earnest request to all well-wishers of this land to ensure that this pleasurable form of entertainment is promoted throughout the country, including the villages, so that the impure arts like *jatra, kabi, kheur*, etc. are removed, and thereby immorality eradicated and respectable behaviour inculcated in Bengal.[21]

The indigenous performance forms were severely criticized for what was seen as their attempts to vulgarize the Hindu pantheon to generate cheap entertainment for the lower sections of the society: "Thanks to the present type of jatras, Krishna and Radha look like *goalas* [milkmen]; in the past, the qualities of a good poet made them appear as divinities" (*Bangadarshan*, Kartik 1280: 1873).[22] And when a performance of *Sakuntala* (spelt as 'SAKONTOLLAH' in the original source) was given as *geetabhinaya* [song-enactment], it was hailed as "the first Opera in Bengalee" written in a "simple and elegant style" with "appropriate and exquisite" songs; it was fervently hoped that "the Opera will supersede the degenerate JATTRA" (*The Hindoo Patriot*, 22 May 1865).[23]

Yet, it may be argued that the indigenous modes of performance were 'non-dramatic' only in the context of Western notions of theatre, in particular the illusionistic theatre. In India/Bengal, the local drama/theatre constituted a composite body of performing narratives, adopting various styles of ritual/performance/presentation/celebration; apart from *jatra*, there were also forms like *palagaan, panchali* or *kirtan* which used a mode of "geeti-natya" [song-enactment]. Scholars are of the opinion that works like Joydeva's *Geetagovinda* or Bipradas Pipilai's *Manasa-vijaya* (1495) or Chandidas's *Sri Krishna Kirtan* (1500) are diverse manifestations of this "geeti-natya".[24] According to Sukumar Sen,

> Around this time, indigenous tales like those of *Manasa* or *Dharma* or *Chandi*, or mythical stories from the *Ramayana* or *Krishnaleela* would be presented through short/long songs or *panchali*, accompanied by music and dance during village festivals or worship of deities in the temples.[25]

Chandidas inducted Krishna, Radha and Jashoda among the characters, who presented their dialogues in songs (with the particular *raga* and *tala* mentioned), so much so that the work may be considered a specimen of musical drama.[26] In fact, it is unlikely that Chandidas's entire work was presented on a single day and may have required consecutive days for performance; its several sections, strung up together, would seem to resemble the cycle plays of medieval Europe, while also being inflected with the available conventions of local folk-drama or *jatra*.[27] Again, *kathakata* required the orator/narrator (*kathak*) to impersonate various roles and also adopt the narrator's voice, effortlessly shifting from one *persona* to another.[28]

The arrival of Chaitanya not only ushered in an age of religious and social reforms in medieval Bengal, but also encouraged the use of such performance/narrative modes to disseminate his teachings. Chaitanya and his compatriot Nityananda are known to have arranged for performances which used verse-dialogues not only between onstage characters but also between actors and spectators. The dialogues also indicate that Sribas played the role of Narada, Brahmananda of Barai, and Haridas that of Kotwal. It is believed that Chaitanya did not follow the classical conventions stipulated by Bharata's *Natya-shastra*, but took recourse to available folk traditions, possibly *jatra*. Apart from *Sri Krishna Kirtan*, he is said to have taken part in performances of *Rukmini-haran* and *Brajalila* (playing the female role of a Gopini in the latter).[29] Chaitanya's movement also triggered off further performances of ritual-narratives celebrating the Vaishnavite cult.[30] These medieval models of Bengali performance, including forms like *jatra, palagaan, kirtan* or *panchali*, were quickly marginalized with the arrival of the Western model of theatre during the Bengal Renaissance.

If Michael, with his *Sarmishtha* and other tragedies, set the parameters for cultural importation from Western sources, Dinabandhu Mitra's *Nildarpan* foregrounded yet another major trend in the Bengal Renaissance theatre. Recounting the horrors of oppression by European indigo-planters, *Nildarpan* was important historically not only because it was the play with which the National Theatre chose to launch itself (on 7 December 1872) but also because, with its anti-colonial stand, it became one of the most frequently acted plays in the nineteenth century.[31] That drama was not merely a form of entertainment but also an effective medium of instruction, perhaps even propaganda, was quickly realized by the nineteenth-century Bengali society – playwrights, practitioners and spectators alike. In fact, the theatre was seen as a channel through which educational and social reforms could be promoted: "The theatre plays the role of both a social reformist and an educator of society. We hope the National Theatre will succeed in carrying out this responsibility effectively."[32] This was the reason why social reformers of the Bengal Renaissance, like Vidyasagar or Keshabchandra Sen, chose to associate themselves with the theatre: both were personally involved with Metropolitan Theatre's production of *Bidhava Vibaha* (1859), which spoke in favour of widow remarriages. After the establishment of the National Theatre, the *Education Gazette* (on 13 December 1872) not only advised the Bengali people to "encourage and promote rapport with the National Theatre … so that the obscene and vulgar forms of amusement are replaced by unadulterated and innocent entertainment" but also reminded the actors of their responsibility to "uphold the morals and conventions of the nation in the theatre".[33] Commenting on the National Theatre's double bill of *Jamai Barik* and *Bharatmata* (a single scene), a newspaper reporter observed:

> Those who were present at the National Theatre on that day have come away so moved and so instructed that would never be obliterated. The theatre is a social reformer as well as an instructor. Our hopes are kindled that the National Theatre will succeed in bearing out the dual responsibilities.[34]

What was particularly significant about *Nildarpan* was the manner in which the social consciousness in the play was predicated on an anti-colonial ideology. It was a powerful play, and its performance often provoked violent reactions among the spectators – colonizers and colonized alike. Immediately before the second scheduled performance of the play (21 December 1872) by the National Theatre, the editorial in *The Englishman* (20 December 1872) fumed:

> A Native paper tells us that the play NIL DARPAN is shortly to be acted at the National Theatre in Jorasanko. Considering that the Revd. Long was sentenced to one month's imprisonment for translating the play, which was pronounced by the High Court a libel on Europeans, it seems strange that Government should allow its representation in Calcutta, unless it has gone through the hands of some competent censor, and the libellous parts excised.[35]

The secretary of the theatre company (in a letter published on 23 December) was quick to explain to the readers of the daily that the libellous portions had indeed been excised, that the purpose of the performance was not to satirize the English but to depict the village life of rural Bengal, and that the players held the English in considerable esteem. The celebrated actress, Binodini, gives a detailed description of how a performance in Lucknow (in May 1875) was violently interrupted by the English spectators present:

> One night, when we were performing *Nildarpan* in the Chhatramandi area of Lucknow, almost all the sahibs of the city had come to see the play. When Rogue Sahib attempts to rape Kshetromoni, Torap enters breaking down the door and assaults Rogue, while Nabinmadhav escapes with Kshetromoni. The play was going extremely well; moreover, Babu Motilal Soor and Abinash Kar Mahasay were enacting the roles of Torap and Mr Rogue most adroitly. Seeing this, the Europeans became extremely agitated. A commotion ensued, and one Sahib clambered onto the stage and was about to strike Torap. This incident left us in tears, the actors in fear, and the Manager Dharmadas Soor in shivers. The performance was called off, the costumes and furniture were packed, and we fled from the site. Only after leaving Lucknow early next morning, did we all breathe easy.[36]

Earlier, on 29 March 1873, when the play had been staged for a charity show in aid of the Mayo Hospital, there had been a parallel response, but now from the colonized. The same actors had taken on the respective roles of Torap and Rogue. On this occasion, too, the spectators (mainly consisting of locals) were so moved that they almost forgot they were witnessing a performance and gave vent to their upsurging anger. A certain Deendayal Basu, who was a clerical assistant to an eminent English barrister, is said to have been "so overcome [with passion] that he leaped onto the stage and joined Torap in beating Rogue, till he fainted himself".[37] A widely circulated anecdote mentions that when Vidyasagar saw the performance of *Nildarpan* staged by the National Theatre, he was so incensed with the role of the devilish Wood (performed by Ardhendusekhar Mustafi) that he hurled his slippers at the actor; the actor is said to have picked up Vidyasagar's slippers as the greatest reward for his performance. This, however, is probably a mere anecdote without much historical evidence.

Anecdotes like these, however, point to the strident anti-colonial ideology with which the performances of *Nildarpan* were palpably inscribed. This anti-colonial/nationalist ideology was being generated through other theatrical events too. As noted earlier, during its first phase, the National Theatre presented a single scene entitled *Bharatmata*, after its performance of *Jamai Barik* (on 15 February 1873). In its second phase, the National Theatre (on 10 May 1873), appearing for the last time at the premises of the Sovabazar palace (with a dramatization of Bankimchandra's novel *Kapalkundala*), concluded the event with what was advertised (in *Amrita Bazar Patrika*, 8 May 1873) as 'BHARAT SANGIT'.[38] When the Great National Theatre went to Lucknow (mentioned by Binodini), *Bharat-sangit* was a part of its repertoire.[39] Even in the field of Shakespeare translations/adaptations, the scales seemed to be overtly tilted in favour of the appropriated Shakespeare rather than the 'original' version. So, while Girishchandra Ghosh's more faithful (and more poetic) rendition of Shakespeare's *Macbeth* (1893) failed miserably at the box office despite his indisputable histrionic and dramaturgical talents, Amarendranath Dutt gained commercial success with the Indianized *Hamlet* as *Hariraj* (1899).[40] The nationalist concern, therefore, was making itself more and more visible in the workings of the nineteenth-century theatre, so that, by the turn of the century, it would take the centre stage in Bengali theatre.

The nineteenth-century Bengali stage was inundated, in particular, with three forms of drama – the historical, the mythological and the social. The historical plays were stoking the nationalist ardour sweeping through the age then. The mythological plays were revisiting myths and legends of ancient India, in accordance with the Revivalist trends of the Bengal Renaissance. Moreover, the combined impact of Hindu Revivalism, Theosophist movement, neo-Vaishanivism (of Vijaykrishna Goswami) and the ministry of Ramakrishna and his school propelled a surge of *bhakti* (devotion), so much so that some of the plays qualified as religious drama. There were also plays that underscored social awareness negotiating with social issues, both seriously and satirically. Therefore, the plays written and staged from what has been termed as the "Age of Girishchandra" (1870–1912) to the "Age of Sisirkumar" (1920–59) – with Amarendranath Dutt bridging the two – were primarily historical, mythological/religious and social drama. This is borne out by the dramatic output of some of the major playwrights of this period, like Girishchanda Ghosh, Kshirodprasad Vidyabinode, Dwijendralal Roy and Sachindranath Sengupta. Though Rabindranath was a contemporary of these dramatists, he was not contributing to this trend but rather moving in a different direction.

Among the historical plays that ran successfully during this period were Girishchandra Ghosh's *Rana Pratap* (1904), *Sirajuddaulah* (1905), *Mir Kasim*

(1906), *Chhatrapati Shivaji* (1907); Kshirodprasad Vidyabinode's *Pratapaditya* (1903), *Padmini* (1906), *Palashir Prayaschitta* (1906), *Nandakumar* (1908), *Alamgir* (1921); Dwijendralal Roy's *Rana Pratapsingha* (1905), *Mebarpatan* (1908), *Noorjahan* (1908), *Shahjahan* (1909), *Chandragupta* (1912); Sachindranath Sengupta's *Gairik Pataka* (1930), *Sirajuddaulah* (1938), *Rastrabiplab* (1944), *Dhatri Panna* (1948). Even a lesser dramatist like Jogeshchandra Chowdhury was deployed by Sisirkumar Bhaduri to write *Digvijayi* (1928), a play on Nadir Shah, which Sisirkumar carried through with his deftness as a producer. These historical plays were not always of great literary merit, but they contributed to the anti-colonial/*swadeshi* discourse of the times. Not only did they invoke the pre-colonial past of ancient/medieval India, but also bolstered an image of Indian maleness as a prerequisite to confront the atrocities of the colonial masters. The historical framing sought to provide a sense of remoteness; yet it was more often than not obvious that they were commentaries upon the unwelcome presence of the colonizer. Smarting under these blows, the colonizer, on his part, resorted to the Act of Dramatic Performances Control (1876) to prohibit plays that were considered seditious or libellous. Under this Act, not only plays like Girishchandra's *Sirajuddaulah, Mir Kasim, Chhatrapati Shivaji* or Kshirodprasad Vidyabinode's *Pratapaditya, Palashir Prayaschitta* but even dramatized versions of Bankimchandra's novels (*Chandrasekhar* or *Anandamath*) were banned from the stage.

The impact of contemporary religious movements saw the emergence of mythical and religious drama. The epics (*Ramayana* and *Mahabharata*) and the scriptures (the *Puranas*) were rummaged for source material for several plays. Girishchandra believed that the national character of India was fundamentally spiritual. Only through highlighting the spiritual core the national cause could be promoted: "No poem or drama can benefit the nation (*jati*) without pursuing the spirit of the nation. Religion constitutes the national core of India…. Religion resides in the heart of India. To address that heart, the play has to be premised on religion."[41] This was the role assigned to the contemporary mythological/religious drama So, while Girishchandra used the epics for *Sitar Banabas* (1880), *Abhimanyuvadh* (1881), *Pandaver Ajnatavas* (1882) or *Jana* (1894), he scoured the *Puranas* for *Daksha Yajna* (1889) or *Kamale Kamini* (1891). At the same time, he created religious plays around the lives and ministries of saints and holy figures – *Chaitanya-leela* (1884),[42] *Bilwamangal Thakur* (1886), *Buddhadev-charit* (1887), *Sankaracharya* (1910). Kshirodprasad Vidyabinode's contribution to mythological drama came with *Babhrubahan* (1899),[43] *Raghubir* (1903), *Bhisma* (1913), *Naranarayan* (1926). Dwijendralal Roy used the epics to create his *Sita* (1904) and *Bhisma* (1913). Plays of this category had been popular even prior to the emergence of the National Theatre – Manomohan Basu's *Ramabhishek* (1867), or Ramnarayan Tarkaratna's *Rukmini-haran* (1871) provide instances. In the times of Girishchandra and Sisirkumar even dramatists other than the ones named above continued to cater to this category – so, Apareshchandra Mukhopadhyay's *Karnarjun* (1923) or Jogeshchandra Chowdhury's *Sita* (1924) and *Vishnupriya* (1931) achieved notable commercial success.

The sociocultural concerns of the age were also being articulated in the writings of many of these dramatists. Girishchandra, as a theatre-practitioner, was left disgusted with the murkier aspects of the contemporary society that he had seen at close quarters. He considered the realistic depiction of that society akin to "stirring the gutter".[44] Yet, his astute analyses in plays like *Prafulla* (1889) or *Balidan* (1904) betray both his anguish at social injustice and his compassion for its victims. He also mocked the social evils through his farces and burlesques like *Bellik Bajar* (1887), *Saptamite Visarjan* (1893), *Baradiner Bakshish* (1894), *Sabhyatar Panda* (1894), *Panch Kone* (1896), *Jaysa-ka-taysa* (1907). Dwijendralal Roy's plays *Paraparey* (1912) and *Banganari* (1916) offered serious social commentaries, while he also excelled in farcical plays like *Kalki Avatar* (1895), *Viraha* (1897), *Trahya-sparsha* (1900), *Prayaschitta* (1902), *Punarjanma* (1911) or *Ananda Biday* (1912). The last mentioned was a scathing criticism of Rabindranath, of which more details are provided below. Another contemporary playwright well known for his satires, burlesques and farces was Amritalal Bose; among his major achievements were *Chorer upor Batpari* (1876), *Chattuje o Banrujje* (1884), *Sabash Atash* (1900), *Sabash Bangali* (1908), *Byapika Biday* (1926). Jyotirindranath, Rabindranath's elder brother, contributed to this category with his *Kinchit Jolojog* (1872), *Emon karma aar korbo na* (1877)[45] or *Hathath Nabab* (1884). Sometimes, however, these burlesques and farces, in the name of chastising social evils, degenerated into foul language and low taste. "One wonders how the (theatre) authorities decided to present before the viewers such farces that revelled in such foul language. Shame!"[46] If such farces and burlesques were meant to satirize social evils, an alternative route – an escape from the social problems – was provided through a kind of wish fulfilment in musicals and romances. Girishchandra invoked the *Arabian Nights* in his *Abu Hossain* (1896), but a larger share came from Kshirodprasad Vidyabinode with his *Bhuter begar* (1908), *Daulat-e-duniya* (1908) or *Alibaba* (1897).

Among the nineteenth-century farces, *Mohanter ei ki kaj* (1873) and *Gajadananda O Yuvaraj* (1876) deserve special mention. The former was a scathing attack on religious hypocrisy and fraudulent spiritual heads. It recounted the public scandal that had erupted around the illicit relationship between the Mohanta (head priest) of the Tarakeswar temple and Elokeshi, the sixteen-year-old wife of a government employee, leading to the beheading of the woman by her husband. A trial followed, where the European judge overturned the verdict of the Indian jury, which was construed as interference by the British administration into local matters. When first performed by Hindu National Theatre in Chuchurah in 1873, the farce created a noticeable stir. Later, by staging the same play in 1874 in Calcutta, Bengal Theatre was able to exploit the public scandal and the ensuing courtroom drama, and, in turn, reap huge profits for itself.[47]

Gajadananda O Yuvaraj was of greater historical significance in that it not only foregrounded the anti-colonial question, but also precipitated the momentous Act for Dramatic Performances Control (1876), which allowed the administration to censor all subsequent dramatic writings and productions. *Gajadananda O Yuvaraj* was presented by the Great National Theatre on 19

February 1876, lampooning the hospitality extended to the Prince of Wales (the future Edward VII) by the noted advocate Jagadananda Mukhopadhyay during the prince's Calcutta visit in January 1876. The prince was welcomed into the Bhowanipur residence of Jagadananda to the sounds of ululation and blowing of conch shells by the ladies of the house. This was considered ample material for a farcical representation; hence, *Gajadananda O Yuvaraj*. After the second performance on 23 February, the police administration took serious note of the embarrassment caused to a 'loyal' subject and ordered the prohibition of the play. But the theatre company changed the name to *Hanumancharitra* and staged the farce once again on 26 February, along with another play, *Karnatak-kumar*. Both plays were now banned from the stage, instigating the company to poke fun at the police in yet another farce *The Police of Pig and Sheep* (staged 1 March). The same day, the *Indian Mirror* noted:

> A GAZETTE OF INDIA EXTRAORDINARY was issued last evening containing an Ordinance to empower the Government of Bengal to prohibit certain dramatic performances, which are scandalous, defamatory, seditious, obscene or otherwise prejudicial to the public interest ...
>
> We need hardly say that the Ordinance is issued consequent on performance of that scandalous farce, entitled "Gajanund" on the stage of a disreputable Native Theatre in Calcutta. All honor to Lord Northbrook for the prompt action taken by him to uphold the cause of public morality and decency. The Ordinance shall remain in force till May next by which time a law be passed by the Viceregal Council on the subject.[48]

Discouraged by the steps taken, the Great National Theatre withdrew the play from circulation. In spite of this, when the innocuous *Sati ki Kalankini* was being performed on 4 March, the police stepped into the playhouse and arrested the director of the company, Upendranath Das, its manager Amritalal Bose and eight actors including Amritalal Mukhopadhyay (Belbabu) and Motilal Soor. The charge against them was that the play *Surendra-Binodini*, staged on 1 March (along with the farce *The Police of Pig and Sheep*), was obscene. The trial began on 6 March, and on 8 March the magistrate handed sentences of one month's imprisonment to Upendranath Das and AmritalalBose; the rest were acquitted. The sentence was challenged at the High Court, which, in its verdict on 20 March, cleared the play from the charge of obscenity and released the two accused. This trial had caused quite a stir, not only in the world of the theatre, but in the whole of Bengal. Yet, despite the protests and challenges, in March 1876 the Dramatic Performances Control Bill was passed into an Act.

II

It is this historical context that helps to define the responses of the Tagore family – and of Rabindranath, in particular – to the nineteenth-century Bengali theatre. The Tagore family had a long history of rapport with the contemporary

24   *The historical context*

theatre. Dwarakanath Tagore, Rabindranath's grandfather, had been among the early patrons of the Calcutta theatres; he was a member of the Amateur Dramatic Society, and even made a handsome contribution towards the building of the Sans Souci Theatre after the burning down of the Chowringhee Theatre.[49] When other rich patrons of the theatre had started to promote Bengali theatrical performances at their private premises[50] – Pearymohan Basu at Jorasanko (1854), Kaliprasanna Singha also at Jorasanko (1856), Ashutosh Dev (Satubabu) at Simla (1857), Ramjoy Basak at Charakdanga Road (1857), the Rajas of Paikpara at Belgachia (1858) – the Tagores were not to be left behind. So, Jatindramohan Tagore set up a playhouse at Pathuriaghata (1865), while Girindranath, the second brother of Rabindranath's father Devendranath, wrote *Nabababoobilas*, satirizing the contemporary *baboo* culture. Girindranath's sons, Ganendranath and Gunendranath, were avid theatre enthusiasts. The former initiated a competition for plays about the social evil of multiple marriages and arranged for the premiere of the resultant best play, Ramnarayan Tarkaratna's *Nabanatak* at the Tagore residence (7 January 1867). The latter, Gunendranath, joined Jyotirindranath (Rabindranath's elder brother) and Saradaprasad Gangopadhyay (a relative by marriage) to form the Jorasanko Theatre and went on to stage Michael Madhusudan Dutt's *Krishnakumari* and *Ekei ki bole sabhyata* [*Is this Civilization?*].[51] The Jorasanko Theatre, in following the European model, was a proscenium stage, complete with painted scenes. Jyotirindranath's memoir mentions how reputed artists were commissioned to paint the scenes, and "there was no dearth of effort to represent the scenes as realistically as possible. For the forest scene, different plants were used and actual fireflies were stuck on with glue to add to the beauty of the scene."[52] It may be worthwhile to mention here that the popular indigenous *jatra* was also invited for performance at the Tagore residence. Jyotirindranath reports in his reminiscences:

> The best *jatrawallahs* (jatra actors) of the day, Nemai Das and Nitai Das performed their *jatra* in this house. Their costumes included *zaree chapkan* (glossy tight pyjamas), *zaree* cummerbands (shimmering belts) and crown-like glistening toupees, with feathers stuck on. The zaree, of course, was fake. The *jatrawallahs* usually imitate the fashion of the contemporary dressing habits.[53]

Rabindranath himself also mentions the performance of *jatra* in their household in his childhood reminiscences.[54]

Rabindranath and his elder brothers, too, were in close contact with the public stage of their generation. Rabindranath's early induction to theatre seems to have been under the tutelage of his elder brothers, particularly Satyendranath and Jyotirindranath. Jyotirindranath himself was a skilled actor, and often played female roles as well. His impersonation of Natee (the Actress) in *Nabanatak*, in particular, was much admired: "*Beginning with the graceful bow of the Natee*, the representation of every succeeding character, elicited loud shouts of applause from all sides, and rendered the whole scene an object of peculiar amusement to the audience."[55] It was in Jyotirindranath's farce *Emon karma ar korbo na* that Rabindranath played the lead role of Aleekbabu (in 1877);[56] in fact he was so good in the role that the play was subsequently renamed as *Aleekbabu*. He also performed in two other household plays – Jyotirindranath's *Manmoyee* (published in 1880) and *Vivaha-utsav* (published in 1892, in which several members of the family collaborated).[57]

The early performances of *Valmiki Pratibha* may have been given under Jyotirindranath's supervision. When the play was to be performed before Lady Lansdowne, Satyendranath, who had invited her, objected to the dacoits appearing bare-chested before the European guests; so they were dressed in long kurtas and pyjamas, somewhat like the Kabuliwallahs (traders coming from Kabul, Afghanistan).[58] Satyendranath was also in charge of the *Raja o Rani* production, reportedly performed at his Birjitala residence (in 1889).[59] Significantly, Satyendranath's wife, Jnanadanandini played Queen Sumitra to Rabindranath's (nine years her junior) King Vikramdev; Satyendranath played Devdutta, with Narayani being played by Rabindranath's wife, Mrinalini.[60] Snide remarks were passed in contemporary press reports about brothers-in-law and sisters-in-law pairing as husbands and wives for their onstage roles; but the Tagore family continued unabated with the performance.[61]

Not only male members, therefore, but even the women of the Tagore family were given roles in several productions; among them were not only daughters of the family, like Abhijna, Pratibha, Indira and Priyamvada, but also daughters-in-law, like Jnadanandini, Kadambari and Mrinalini. This was a significant contribution by the Tagore family, given the prevailing hostility towards female actors being deployed for performance in those days. Rabindranath – and the Tagore family in general – were confronted with this contemporary antagonistic attitude, not only during the time of *Valmiki Pratibha* or *Raja o Rani*, but even in later periods.

Among his mentors, Rabindranath was perhaps most inspired by his brother Jyotirindranath, who not only interpolated his plays with songs but also used his considerable knowledge of Western music for his own melodic improvisations and innovations. Jyotirindranath had also written several plays for the public stage – *Purubikram-natak* (1875), *Sarojini*[62] (1875), *Asrumati* (1879), as well as farces like *Hathat Nabab* (1884) and *Emon Karma Aar Korbo Na* (1877).[63] As mentioned, Rabindranath is known to have played the role of Aleekbabu with such élan that the farce subsequently became popular as *Aleekbabu*.

Jyotirindranath was not only one of the prime initiators of the Tagore household theatre but also had several of his plays (histories, tragedies and farces) performed on the public stage – *Purubikram-natak* (1874), *Sarojini*[64] (1875), *Asrumati* (1879), *Kinchit Jalojag* (1873), *Emon Karma Aar Korbo Na* (1877) and *Hathat Nabab* (1884).[65] As mentioned earlier, Jyotirindranath experimented extensively with Western melodies, and, in turn, encouraged Rabindranath to try his hand at similar experimentations in his early operatic pieces like *Valmiki Pratibha* (1881), *Kal Mrigaya* (1882) and *Mayar Khela* (1888). The Poet himself reminiscences how Jyotirindranath would be "engrossed in the creation of new tunes" on the piano while he and Akshay Chowdhury (a family friend) would be kept busy "fitting words to the tune"; some of this was carried over into the making of *Valmiki Pratibha*.[66]

III

There was a fair degree of transaction between Rabindranath himself and the contemporary professional theatre. It is reported that Rabindranath performed in a family production along with Ardhendusekhar Mustafi, a renowned professional actor of the period.[67] Another contemporary actor (and playwright), Amritalal Bose saw and admired Rabindranath's productions on several occasions. He described the production of *Visarjan* (1923) at the Empire Theatre as "an unqualified success".[68] Rabindranath's novel, *Bouthakuranir Haat* was dramatized as *Raja Basanta Roy* and staged by the Great National Theatre as early as in 1886.[69] His *Raja o Rani* was appropriated by the professional theatre, almost immediately after their in-house production (1889), and was continued on the public stage till at least 1914.[70] In fact, between 1886 and 1940, there were about thirty-eight productions in the commercial theatre based on his plays or dramatized versions of his fictional works.[71] Rabindranath applauded the histrionic talents of younger generations of professional actors, like Sisirkumar Bhaduri and Ahindra Chowdhury, and even permitted them to perform his plays on the public stage, sometimes tailoring the texts for that purpose. For instance, an advertisement for Sisirkumar's production of *Visarjan* (in 1926) mentioned: "For the performance by Natyamandir, this play has been revised and expanded with the kind permission and meticulous supervision of Kabindra Rabindranath"; it also referred to Dinendranath's training for accurate renditions of the songs.[72] However, despite such elaborate arrangements, among the plays produced by either Sisirkumar Bhaduri or Ahindra Chowwdhury, comedies like *Chirakumar Sabha*[73] or *Sesh Raksha*[74] enjoyed a relative success, while serious plays like *Tapati*[75] or *Grihapravesh*[76] and dramatized versions of novels like *Gora*[77] or *Jogajog*[78] failed at the box office.

It also needs to be put on record here that there were certain signs of apathy towards Rabindranath's plays in the contemporary professional theatre. There were manifold attacks on Rabindranath and his works, which ultimately had an adverse effect on the reception of his plays in the commercial theatre. First, he was faulted for not being contemporary enough; his plays were seen as obscure and irrelevant to the needs of the age. Second, he was considered as hailing from a class – and a family – that was affluent and elite, and, hence, removed from the common people. The Brahmo Samaj (to which his family belonged), despite its significant contributions to the contemporary nationalist discourse, was often seen as an esoteric, walled-in community, following a faith that differed from mainstream Hinduism, and, in general, remained distant from the populace. Third, Rabindranath and his followers were seen as promoting a culture that was effete, unmanly and decadent, and invited scornful censure from, among others, Kaliprasanna Kavyavisharad and Dwijendralal Roy. The former, after the publication of *Kori o Komol* (1886), passed snide remarks that the cooped-in poet should stay cloistered in his pigeonhole. And the latter launched scathing attacks on Rabindranath on several counts – ranging from eroticism in the verse drama *Chitrangada* (1892) to abstruseness in the poems of *Sonar Tari* (1894) – till, casting aside all codes of civility, he lampooned Rabindranath in his satire *Ananda Biday* (1912). In fact, this vein of hostility towards Rabindranath and his plays was carried well into the second half of the twentieth century. As late as in 1973, we find Hirendranath Bandyopadhyay making uncharitable remarks about Rabindranath's drama in the journal *Bingsha Satak*:

> The theatre audiences had no expectations from the plays of Rabindranath because they lacked the spirit of life and indulged in artificiality. That Rabindranath could not find his place in Bengali theatre was not only because of the opposition of the contemporary dramatists, but more because his drama fell short of that vital life of which Shakespeare is the master... The dramatists of Bengal rejected Rabindranath for reasons more than their mere orthodox mentality. They sought for a certain masculinity in life, in literature, in poetry, in drama. They wanted to emulate that male virility in their plays and their theatre. The poets and dramatists of that age missed this maleness in the personality of Rabindranath. His poetic idiom, too, lacked masculine flourish; all that was there was a mellifluous tinkling of glass. They found an unmanly effeminacy in Rabindranath's person as well as in his art, and this they ridiculed in their writings. Moreover, they were also vehemently opposed to Rabindranath's philosophy of life.[79]

In the nineteenth-century public theatre, the general response to Rabindranath's plays ranged from indifference to downright animosity. As discussed earlier in this chapter, the historical, mythological/religious and social plays were the three major forms of drama dominating the Bengali stage then. Rabindranath, however, eschewed these prevalent forms of drama in his playwriting and moved in a different direction. This nonconformist approach might have incurred the dislike of the other theatre-personalities of the period. The nature of this animosity was encapsulated, for instance, in the negative responses of Girishchandra Ghosh. Though revered for his playwriting and his histrionic talent as the 'Shakespeare' and the 'Garrick' of the nineteenth-century Bengali theatre, Girishchandra did not seem to care much for Rabindranath or his plays. When Girishchandra joined the Emerald Theatre in October 1887, *Raja Basanta Roy* (Kedar Chowdhury's dramatization of Rabindranath's novel *Bouthakuranir Haath*) was being staged. Girishchandra immediately stopped this production and moved on to other plays. Only after Girishchandra left Emerald Theatre on 3 February 1889, the play was revived (from 7 April 1889), with *Raja o Rani* also being added to the repertoire from 1895.[80] In fact, as long as Girishchandra remained associated with any playhouse, Rabindranath's plays would be shelved away from that stage – whether at Bengal, or Emerald or Minerva Theatres. When Classic Theatre was being run by Amarendranath Dutt, he decided to stage Rabindranath's novel *Chokher Bali* and asked Girishchandra, the resident dramatist, to draft the stage version. Girishchandra is reported to have fumed at the proposal and declared that he would not allow that "morally decadent text" be staged at any theatre with which he was associated. The adamant Amarendranath went ahead with his plans, dramatizing *Chokher Bali* himself; as a result, Girishchandra stormed out of Classic Theatre.[81]

Adverse responses were voiced even by Amritalal Bose,[82] who later, however, changed his opinion after witnessing Rabindranath's plays on the stage. But the one who was particularly vociferous in denigrating Rabindranath was Dwijendralal Roy. The tussle between these two literary giants had spilled out into the open; though Rabindranath seems to have been more restrained in his rebuttal of Dwijendralal's censure, the latter spewed venom publicly. This, in turn, created a sharp rift between their respective followers. The strife reached a climax with Dwijendralal's demeaning sketch of Rabindranath in his satire *Ananda Biday*, staged at the Star Theatre on 16 November 1912. It reeked with such pungency that it was summarily rejected by the audience, who demanded that the performance be stopped. To add fuel to the fire, the bellicose Dwijendralal, from his seat in the box, entered into a heated exchange with the spectators. This so infuriated the assembled spectators that they had to be pacified and the playwright had to be whisked away to a safer shelter. Such hostile audience reception sealed the fate of the play and *Ananda Biday* was banished from the stage.[83]

As mentioned earlier in the chapter, the vital role of theatre in arousing a socio-politico-cultural awareness in its spectators was repeatedly emphasized, more so after the founding of the National Theatre (1872): "The 'National Theatre' is a lofty name, which carries potentials higher than mere entertainment. Have the bearers of this name forgotten their promise?"[84] This assumed a deeper significance when, in the context of the anti-colonial/*swadeshi* stirrings, the nineteenth-century theatre was expected to play an instructive role in honing the nationalist aspirations of the people. The more alert among the playwrights and practitioners were aware of this onerous task, but they were often constrained by the popular demands of production/reception. No less than Girishchandra is reported to have lamented, "Nowadays I do not write plays but only turn in some high-strung scenes. The theatre authorities retain whatever they wish to, the rest they discard."[85] Apareshchandra Mukhopadhyay, another playwright of the period, pointed to the decline of ideals in the contemporary theatre: "When ideals begin to collapse, it is not difficult to guess the outcome. Greed for this aberrant thrill and decadent clapping has caused many a dramatist to wallow in melodrama; good drama of literary worth is becoming increasingly rare."[86] The immediate aim was merely to excite the audience to mindless applause, without any attempt to instruct or alert them.

Unfortunately, instead of pursuing any lofty goal, the playwrights, actors and managers of the theatre were often embroiled in bickering with one another, with fierce competition between rival theatre companies. So, when Dwijendralal Roy, apart from demanding a hefty sum for his mythological play *Bhisma*, also stipulated extra conditions, the proprietors of Minerva Theatre rejected his play but commissioned Kshirodeprasad to write another *Bhisma*, which, completed in a fortnight, was staged at Minerva, much to the chagrin of Dwijendralal.[87] Again, when Sisirkumar Bhaduri had set his heart upon staging Dwijendrala's *Sita* but was unable to procure the rights to the play, he encouraged Jogeshchandra Chowdhury to pen a play on *Sita* (1924), which scaled great heights of theatrical success through Sisirkumar's histrionic talent.[88] This rivalry between Sisirkumar Bhaduri and Art Theatre (with Ahindra Chowdhury in the lead roles) was made evident even during the staging of Rabindranath's *Chirakumar Sabha*.[89]

Rabindranath was steering clear of these pitfalls of the commercial theatre. In 1927, in an article in the journal *Nachghar*, edited by Hemendrakumar Roy, he voiced his definite reservations against the public theatre: "The manner in which the public theatre is conducting itself hardly holds any promise. One with refined tastes and aesthetic acumen can hardly bear to remain there for long."[90] In this same piece he refers to the 'little theatres' of the West which were venues for experimental/avant-garde productions. He was yearning for a performative space away from the humdrum of the public stage where he could experiment with the kind of theatre that he was imagining; Santiniketan provided him precisely with this 'alternative' space. Through his experiments at Santiniketan, Rabindranath was not only trying to break free from the tradition of Girishchandra and the commercial stage but also to promote a different cultural imaginary that would enable the contemporary audience to move beyond the cocoon of cultural mediocrity. He articulates his notions of a perceptive/sensitive spectator ("*sahriday darshak*") in his essay "Rangamancha" (1902); this has been analysed further in the subsequent chapter on "Theories of theatre". Not only is he hopeful that the perceptive spectator would be able to receive the performance sensitively, but he is also not willing to play to the unimaginative viewer for easy popularity. Not only in "Rangamancha" of 1902, but also in that article he penned for *Nachghar* in 1927, he had shown his preference for the perceptive viewer: "Let the public theatre cater to the populace, the alternative theatre would have nothing to do with that."[91] There have been occasions when, disappointed with the interruptions of the audience, he has taken measures to 'educate' the viewers to mould them into adequately responsive individuals.[92] With such measures Rabindranath was, first of all, taking a stand against the practices and expectations of the nineteenth-century public stage; second, setting before his viewers an alternative cultural imaginary that could create a different audience expectation; and third, trying to give a shape to the kind of theatre that he was imagining.

It would probably be in order to make a couple of observations here regarding the charges levelled against Rabindranath, particularly by those associated with the commercial theatre. First, in recalling the genesis of the Bengali public theatre in Calcutta one would remember that it was both an urban occurrence and primarily entertainment for the *bhadralok* (elite) classes. This theatre has been identified as "bourgeois", catering to the materialist culture of the contemporary *nouveaux riches*.[93] With a social hierarchy already promoted by the urban elites in this theatre, it does not seem justified to hold Rabindranath alone guilty of elitism or class superiority. Second, it is also undeniable that the Tagore household, as frontrunners of the Bengal Renaissance, had already carved a niche for themselves in the sociocultural matrix of the times. The distinctiveness of Rabindranath was an inheritance of the cultural ambience of his household which left an indelible impression in his formative years. Recalling his "Home Environment" he writes: "One great advantage which I enjoyed in my younger days was the literary and artistic atmosphere which pervaded our house."[94] This atmosphere at home – elite and affluent perhaps, but certainly exuding a cultural discernment – helped him to think differently. This difference, not comprehensible to many, prompted some to brand him and his circle as effete, ineffectual, even unmanly. But because Rabindranath was rethinking the gender roles in a radical manner, his idea of agency did not comprise mere physical prowess but an inner moral strength. The virile masculinity, readily associated with the nationalist cause in the historical plays, was replaced by an inner resilience available equally in his kings and princes like Govindamanikya (*Visarjan*) and Abhijit (*Muktadhara*), minstrels like the blind *baul* (*Phalguni*) and Dhananjoy Bairagi (*Muktadhara* and *Prayaschitta*), and indeed in female characters like Sumitra (*Raja o Rani/Tapati*), Srimati (*Natir Puja*) or Nandini (*Raktakarabi*). To dismiss this as unmanly or ineffectual is an unfair and incomplete reading of Rabindranath's position. The bias in this reading becomes all the more blatant when we recall the Tagore family's, and Rabindranath's own, passionate engagements with nation-building.[95] How Rabindranath, working within this environment, negotiated with the nationalist discourse, engrafting his ideas of the theatre with his notions of the nation, will be our concern in the following chapter on "Theatre and Nation".

The other major charge often levelled against Rabindranath – both in the nineteenth century and later – was that his plays failed to address the contemporary social problems. In this regard, it may suffice to refer here to a famous exchange of correspondences between Rabindranath and Saratchandra Chattopadhyay on this issue of contemporariness. Saratchandra had dramatized his novel *Denapaona* as *Sorosi*, which first appeared in *Bharati* in 1926 and was staged by Sisirkumar Bhaduri in 1927. When Saratchandra sent a copy of his play to Rabindranath for his opinion, the latter praised his effort but sounded a note of warning: "Through *Sorosi* you have tried to please the contemporary times, and have been rewarded for it, but, in doing so, you have dented your own talent. You have constructed *Sorosi* to reflect the aspirations of the immediate times." To Saratchandra's query as to how – and why – could/should the demands of the contemporary times be avoided, Rabindranath replied: "You have written that the contemporary is an inevitable presence. It is inevitable, and great, precisely where it is able to gain entry into the time not immediately present."[96] Even as he prioritizes the timeless over the merely contemporary, he seems to point in the direction of what he has tried to achieve in his own plays; they are not chained to any particular "time present", but project a larger matrix in which "time past" and "time future" are also included. A play like

Raktakarabi, for instance, captures both the contemporary present and the time beyond. For instance, the issues of power or of social hierarchy that the play engages with may be sited in a given social set-up within a given time frame, or, again, may be seen as available in a different spatio-temporal locale where the same/similar problems between oppressor and oppressed persist. If one stops to think, one would find most of his plays are informed with this plurality of spatio-temporal situatedness – in the quasi-historical narratives of *Raja o Rani* and *Visarjan*; in the seasonal celebrations of *Sarodotasav* and *Phalguni*; in the symbolic overlayings of *Raja* and *Dakghar*; in the sociopolitical questionings of *Tasher Desh* and *Kaler Jatra*; or even in the dance-based recycling of myths and legends in *Chitrangada, Chandalika* or *Shyama*.

To label these plays as effete, ineffectual, even irrelevant, failing to address contemporary concerns, is a grossly unjust and incomplete appraisal of Rabindranath's dreams. His ideas were so much more progressive that his contemporaries, who were unable to grasp them, lagged behind. Their inability to understand the range of the cultural imaginary that he was envisioning was unfortunate; it was even more unfortunate that they translated their inability into vituperative attacks against him and the ideas he was envisaging. His dreams of an emergent nation/*swadeshi samaj* were deeply entrenched with contemporary concerns involving social, political and cultural issues. In certain respects, it may even be argued, his concerns were less nationalist, more patriotic, and, therefore, perhaps, less political, more sociocultural. That is why he engaged so passionately not only with problems of education, communal amity, social inequalities or rural reconstruction, but also with the kind of cultural space that the new nation was to create for itself, with its own literature, music, dance and even theatre. Rabindranath's role as an ideologue in the nationalist discourse has to be viewed in the context of these cultural concerns. This is what he was bringing to the theatre of his age, and trying to refashion it vis-à-vis the new sociocultural imaginary.

With Santiniketan serving as his principal 'testing laboratory', Rabindranath was increasingly negotiating with the possibilities of an alternative/experimental theatre, which would mark a departure from both the imported Western model and the urban commercial Bengali theatre. In eschewing both, he was striving towards that alternative model which would be in tune with the cultural aspirations of an emergent nation/*samaj*. Because for Rabindranath the 'nation' was never limited by narrow visions of the nationalist agenda, his vision of the emergent nation was always collapsed together with his dreams of a new *samaj* or community. His theatre, too, would try to break free from the shackles of Western staging principles and yet would remain aloof from the constricting labels promoted in the name of the nationalist discourse. This 'different' road that he chose to tread – and in what way – will be our major concern in the following chapters.

Notes

1 Sudipto Chatterjee, "Mise-En-(Colonial)-Scene: The Theatre of the Bengal Renaissance", in *Imperialism and Theatre*, ed. J. Ellen Gainor (London: Routledge, 1995) 19–37; here quoted from 20.
2 Herasim Lebedeff, "Introduction", *A Grammar of the Pure any Mixed East Indian Dialects* (1801) vi–vii; as cited in Brajendranath Bandyopadhyay, *Bangiya Natyasalar Itihas, 1795–1876*, 7th edn. (Calcutta: Bangia Sahitya Parishad, 1998; originally 1933) 14.
3 Admission rates were for boxes and pit 8 sikka rupees and for gallery seats 4 sikka rupees (advertised in *The Calcutta Gazette*, 26 November 1795); cited in Brajendranath Bandyopadhyay, *Bangiya Natyasalar Itihas*, 16.
4 Opinions of different scholars have been cited in Subir Roy Chowdhury and Swapan Majumdar, *Bilati Jatra theke Swadeshi Theatre* (Calcutta: Dey's, 1999; originally 1972), 17–8.
5 This translator was possibly H.H. Wilson, the noted English professor of Hindu College. For details, see Brajendranath Bandyopadhyay, *Bangiya Natyasalar Itihas*, 21–2.
6 See Nazmul Ahsan, *Shakespeare Translations in Nineteenth Century Bengali Theatre* (Dhaka: Bangla Academy, 1995) 16–7.
7 See Brajendranath Bandyopadhyay, *Bangiya Natyasalar Itihas*, 46, 67.
8 Quoted in Brajendranath Bandyopadhyay, *Bangiya Natyasalar Itihas*, 37; emphases added.
9 Quoted in Bepinbehari Gupta, *Puratan Prasanga*, ed. Asitkumar Bandyopadhyay (Calcutta: Pustak Bipani, 1989; originally 1966) 26. Also cited in Subir Roy Chowdhury and Swapan Majumdar, *Bilati Jatra theke Swadeshi Theatre*, 59.
10 See Brajendranath Bandyopadhyay, *Bangiya Natyasalar Itihas*, 23–4.
11 Cited in Pinakesh Sarkar (ed.), *Harano Diner Natak* (Calcutta: Sahitya Samsad, 1999) 22.
12 There were two prefaces – one in English, the other in Bengali.
13 Pinakesh Sarkar (ed.), *Harano Diner Natak*, 77; emphases added.
14 As diagnosed by Karl Marx in "The Future Results of the British Rule in India", in Karl Marx and Frederick Engels, *On Colonialism* (Moscow: Foreign Languages Publishing House, 1853; rpt. Moscow: Progress Publishers, 1959) 84.
15 Undated letter to Gourdas Basak; cited in Subir Roy Chowdhury and Swapan Majumdar, *Bilati Jatra theke Swadeshi Theatre*, 30.
16 Cited in Nazmul Ahsan, *Shakespeare Translations in Nineteenth Century Bengali Theatre*, 84–5.
17 An earlier attempt in this direction seems to have been made in *Kirtibilas Natak* (c.1852) by G.C. Gupta, in the preface of which is proclaimed: "Many may be under the misconception that the performance which generates intense pity may naturally not be desired by humans. Yet, after some consideration it becomes evident that pity stirs up a kind of pleasure in our hearts. That is why the great English poet Shakespeare has written that our hearts may be inflamed by pity but our minds have an unending craving for such pity." A few lines later he also happens to mention Aristotle and the Greek custom of rewarding the best tragedian/tragic actor. Cited in Pinakesh Sarkar (ed.), *Harano Diner Natak*, 57.
18 Jasodhara Bagchi, "Shakespeare in Loin Cloths: English Literature and the Early Nationalistic Consciousness in Bengal", in *Rethinking English: Essays in Literature Language History*, ed. Svati Joshi (Delhi: Oxford University Press, 1994) 146–59; here quoted from 149–50.
19 Almost 400 respectable persons, among them several European gentlemen and ladies, assembled at Pearymohan Basu's house for a performance of *Julius Caesar*, in spite of inclement weather. The *Sangbad Pravakar* (5.5.1854) urged the

organizers to make such performances available to the common people, at nominal prices for tickets (see Brajendranath Bandyopadhyay, *Bangiya Natyasalar Itihas*, 32).
20 Mahendranath Mukhopadhyay's reminiscences of a performance he attended at Ashutosh Dev's house, as mentioned in Bepinbehari Gupta, *Puratan Prasanga*, 80; cited in Subir Roy Chowdhury and Swapan Majumdar, *Bilati Jatra theke Swadeshi Theatre*, 20–1.
21 *Bibidhartha-samgraha* (Magh 1780 Saka, Jan–Feb 1858) 234–5; as cited in Brajendranath Bandyopadhyay, *Bangiya Natyasalar Itihas*, 17–8.
22 As cited in Sumanta Banerjee, *The Parlour and the Street: Elite and Popular Culture in Nineteenth Century Calcutta* (Calcutta: Seagull Books, 1989) 162.
23 As cited in Brajendranath Bandyopadhyay, *Bangiya Natyasalar Itihas*, 81.
24 See Sukumar Sen, *Bangala Sahityer Itihas*, 4th edn. vol. 1, Part I (Calcutta: Eastern Publisher, 1963; originally 1940) 42; also, Gourisankar Bhattacharya, *Bangla Loknatya Samiksha* (Calcutta: Rabindra Bharati University, 1974) 128–30, 138, 151.
25 Sukumar Sen, *Bangala Sahityer Itihas*, vol. 1, Part I, 82.
26 See Gourisankar Bhattacharya, *Bangla Loknatya Samiksha*, 145–51.
27 Gourisankar Bhattacharya, *Bangla Loknatya Samiksha*, 145, 151–2.
28 This is somewhat similar to what Brecht would later posit as his theory of 'Alienation-effect', where a constant 'alienation' between actor and character is required.
29 For details, see Gourisankar Bhattacharya, *Bangla Loknatya Samiksha*, 152–60.
30 Gourisankar Bhattacharya, *Bangla Loknatya Samiksha*, 160–3; also, see Salim Aldin, *Madhyjuger Bangla Natya* (Dhaka: Bangla Akademi, 1996) 48; 161–2.
31 Between December 1872 and December 1876, *Nildarpan* was acted no less than fourteen times (by several companies).
32 *Amrita Bazar Patrika*, 20 February 1873; as cited in Brajendranath Bandyopadhyay, *Bangiya Natyasalar Itihas, 1795–1876*, 7th edn. (Calcutta: Bangia Sahitya Parishad, 1998; originally 1933) 125–6.
33 Cited in Brajendranath Bandyopadhyay, *Bangiya Natyasalar Itihas*, 103.
34 *Amrita Bazar Patrika*, 20 February 1873; cited in Brajendranath Bandyopadhyay, *Bangiya Natyasalar Itihas*, 125–6.
35 Quoted in Brajendranath Bandyopadhyay, *Bangiya Natyasalar Itihas*, 105.
36 Binodini Dasi, *Amar Katha*, ed. Soumitra Chattopadhyay, Nirmalya Acharya, et. al., revised and expanded (Calcutta: Subarnarekha, 1987; originally 1912) 23.
37 As cited in Subir Roy Chowdhury and Swapan Majumdar, *Bilati Jatra theke Swadeshi Theatre*, 42.
38 Cited in Brajendranath Bandyopadhyay, *Bangiya Natyasalar Itihas*, 143.
39 Reported by the newspaper *Sadharani* (31 May 1875), as mentioned in *Bangiya Natyasalar Itihas*, 188.
40 Yet, an eyewitness account is sharply critical of the production: "We saw *Hariraj* at the Classic Theatre with Amarendra Datta and Kusumkumari. ... The standard of acting was poor. It was pure ranting." (Kanti Mukherjee, in an interview cited in Subir Roy Chowdhury and Swapan Majumdar, *Bilati Jatra theke Swadeshi Theatre*, 62)
41 Girishchandra Ghosh, "Pouranik Natak", in *Girish Rachanabali*, ed. Rabindranath Roy and Debipada Bhattacharya, vol. 1 (Calcutta: Sahitya Samsad, 1944) 731–5; here quoted from 732.
42 In this play Binodini played the role of Nemai; Sri Ramakrishna witnessed this performance and blessed her.
43 Conferred the title of "Vidyabinode" for this play
44 Girishchandra's observation to his contemporary Amritalal Basu ("I had hoped to write a few good plays in my final years; yet in this old age I have to be stirring the gutter. To write plays on such realistic issues and to stir the gutter are the same")

has been reported in Rabindranath Bandyopadhyay, "Kaljoyee natakkar Girishchandra Ghosh", in *Korok Sahitya Patrika: Bangla Natak o Natyamancha*, ed. Tapas Bhowmik, Autumn issue (2013): 76–88; here cited from 79.
45 This farce was rewritten as *Aleekbabu* in 1900.
46 Reported in the periodical *Anusandhan, Ashar* 1296 BS (June 1889); as cited in Ramenkumar Sar, "Sadharon rangamanche Rabindranath byartho", in *Balaka*, ed. Dhananjoy Ghosal, year 19, no. 19 (November 2010): 181–8; here quoted from 187.
47 See Brajendranath Bandyopadhyay, *Bangiya Natyasalar Itihas*, 140, 151–2.
48 As cited in Brajendranath Bandyopadhyay, *Bangiya Natyasalar Itihas*, 193.
49 Ajitkumar Ghosh, *Thakurbarir Abhinay* (Calcutta: Rabindra Bharati Society, 1988) 4.
50 Usually, these rich patrons ('babus' and 'rajas') located the theatres in their 'garden-houses', kept aside for purposes of entertainment, and not at proper residential quarters.
51 Mentioned in Abantikumar Sanyal, *Kabir Abhinay* (Calcutta: Rabindra Bharati University, 1996) 8.
52 See Basantakumar Chattopadhyay, *Jyotirindranather Jibansmriti*, ed. Prasantakumar Pal (Calcutta: Subarnarekha, 2002; originally1919) 37–8.
53 Basantakumar Chattopadhyay, *Jyotirindranather Jibansmriti*, 38.
54 See *Chelebela*, in *Rabindra Rachanabali* [Complete Works of Rabindranath. Birth Centenary edition] 15 vols. (Calcutta: West Bengal Government, 1961) vol. 10, 138–40. This work will subsequently be referred to as *RR*.
55 *The National Paper*, 9 January 1867; as cited in Ajitkumar Ghosh, *Thakurbarir Abhinay*, 10–11; emphases added.
56 *Jyotirindranather Natya Sangraha*, compiled by Sushil Roy (Calcutta: Visva-Bharati Granthan Vibhaga, 1969) 657.
57 Controversies regarding the dates of these plays (and their performances) have been mentioned in Rudraprasad Chakrabarty, *Rangamancha O Rabindranath: Samakalin Pratikriya* (Calcutta: Ananda Publishers, 1995) 22, 25.
58 See Ajitkumar Ghosh, *Thakurbarir Abhinay*, 18–9.
59 There is some difficulty in ascertaining the exact date of this staging, but it was probably staged in the autumn of 1889; for details, see Rudraprasad Chakrabarty, *Rangamancha O Rabindranath: Samakalin Pratikriya*, 46.
60 This is the only instance when Mrinalini is known to have performed in a play, persuaded by Satyendranath. For details, see Prabhatkumar Mukhopadhyay, *Rabindra Jibani*, vol. 1 (Calcutta: Visva-Bharati Granthalay, 1933; rev. 1960) 349; Abanindranath Tagore, *Gharoa* (Calcutta: Visva-Bharati Granthan Vibhaga, 1941; rpt. 1983) 104–6. This is corroborated by Rathindranath: "My mother was persuaded to take the part of Narayani, in *Raja-o-Rani*, the first and only time she appeared on the stage": see "Looking Back", in *Rabindranath Tagore: A Tribute*, ed. Pulinbihari Sen and Kshitis Roy (New Delhi: Sangeet Natak Akademi, 2006; originally 1961) 45–52; here quoted from 46.
61 See Indira Devi Chaudhurani, *Rabindra Smriti* (Calcutta: Visva-Bharati Granthan Vibhaga, 2010; originally 1960) 36.
62 This play was also performed in the *jatra* form.
63 See Bishnu Basu, *Rabindranather Theatre* (Calcutta: Pratibhas, 1987) 19–20.
64 This play was also performed as *jatra*.
65 See Bishnu Basu, *Rabindranather Theatre* (Calcutta: Pratibhas, 1987) 19–20.
66 See *My Reminiscences* (London: Macmillan, 1917; rpt. 1933) 128–9, 193.
67 See Khagendranath Chattopadhyay, *Rabindra Katha* (Calcutta: Parul Prakasani, 2015; originally 1941) 205.
68 *Indian Daily News*, 25 August 1923; cited in Rudraprasad Chakrabarty, *Rangamancha O Rabindranath: Samakalin Pratikriya*, 64.
69 The dramatization of the novel was done by Kedar Chowdhury; see Rudraprasad Chakrabarty, *Rangamancha O Rabindranath: Samakalin Pratikriya*, 100.

70 See Prasantakumar Pal, *Rabi Jibani*, vol. 7 (Calcutta: Ananda, 1997) 78–80.
71 See details in Subroto Ghosh, *Rabinataker Natyakatha* (Calcutta: Signet Press, 2017) 58–9. A detailed discussion of Rabindranath's plays staged in the public theatre is also provided in Harindranath Dutta, *Rabindranath o Sadharan Rangalay* (Calcutta: Tagore Research Institute, 1983) 7–9, 12–5, 19–28.
72 *Nachghar*, 3rd year, no. 5, 10 *Ashar* 1333 BS (1926); as cited in Sekhar Samaddar, *Visarjan: Rupe, rupantare* (Calcutta: Papyrus, 1992) 94, n. 17.
73 The staging of this play generated some controversy between Sisirkumar Bhaduri and Ahindra Chowdhury both of whom were interested in the play. Ultimately, Ahindra Chowdhury's Art Theatre Limited was able to procure the rights of production and the first performance was staged on 18 July 1925; Rabindranath saw the second performance on 25 July. For details, see Prabhatkumar Mukhopadhyay, *Rabindra Jibani*, vol. 3, 239, and Prasantakumar Pal, *Rabi Jibani*, vol. 9, 194–5, 237–8. See also n. 89 below.
74 Staged by Sisirkumar Bhaduri at Natyamandir in 1927, opening on 14 September 1927. Rabindranath, at the request of Sisirkumar, revised his *Goray Galad* as *Seshraksha*, though Sisirkumar seems to have preferred the original title. The performance was advertised almost as an invitation to a twin marriage celebration. These details are mentioned by Rudraprasad Chakrabarty, citing the authority of Sourindramohan Mukhopadhyay (*Kabiguru Rabindranath o Nataraj Sisirkumar*, 17–20) in Rudraprasad Chakrabarty, *Rangamancha O Rabindranath: Samakalin Pratikriya*, 79.
75 Staged by Sisirkumar Bhaduri at Natyamandir on 25 December 1929; see Subir Roy Chowdhury and Swapan Majumdar, *Bilati Jatra theke Swadeshi Theatre*, 90; also Rudraprasad Chakrabarty, *Rangamancha O Rabindranath: Samakalin Pratikriya*, 242–4.
76 Art Theatre premieres *Grihapravesh* at Star Theatre, with Ahindra Chowdhury, Sushilasundari and Niharbala in the lead roles. Dinendranath and Gaganendranath were in charge of music and stage design, respectively. The Poet went to see the third performance on 19 December. Rabindranath was, on the whole, pleased with the performance but thought some revisions were needed. He made the changes in the original, reduced the number of songs and even introduced a couple of new characters (including that of a young girl). He was supposed to go and see the revised text in performance on 9 January 1926, but no records are available to confirm whether he actually went on that day. See Prasantakumar Pal, *Rabi Jibani*, vol. 9, 264.
77 Staged by Ahindra Chowdhury for Natyaniketan on 19 December 1936; see Subir Roy Chowdhury and Swapan Majumdar, *Bilati Jatra theke Swadeshi Theatre*, 91.
78 Staged by Sisirkumar Bhaduri for Nabanatyamandir in December 1936; see Subir Roy Chowdhury and Swapan Majumdar, *Bilati Jatra theke Swadeshi Theatre*, 91.
79 Hirendranath Bandyopadhyay, "Bigoto Kaler Katha", in *Bingsha Satak* (2nd year, no. 1, January 1973); as cited in Harindranath Dutta, *Rabindranath o Sadharan Rangalay*, 5–6.
80 As reported in Subroto Ghosh, *Rabinataker Natyakatha*, 61–2.
81 For details, see Harindranath Dutta, *Rabindranath o Sadharan Rangalay* (Calcutta: Tagore Research Institute, 1983) 10–1.
82 Amritalal Bose took an unkind swipe at a poem by Rabindranath in a public lecture at Albert Hall, which had the audience rolling in laughter; see Harindranath Dutta, *Rabindranath o Sadharan Rangalay*, 6.
83 See details in Harindranath Dutta, *Rabindranath o Sadharan Rangalay*, 51–3.
84 Amritalal Bose, "Puratan Panjika", in *Masik Basumati*, Baisakh 1331 BS (April 1924); as cited in Brajendranath Bandyopadhyay, *Bangiya Natyasalar Itihas, 1795–1876*, 119.
85 As reported by Girishchandra's contemporary Apareshchandra Mukhopadhyay, who also regretted that Bengali plays often failed to show any literary merit and mostly declined to tedious melodrama merely to arouse the spectators to clap insensibly; cited in Ramenkumar Sar, "Sadharon rangamanche Rabindranath byartho", in

36 *The historical context*

       Balaka, ed. Dhananjoy Ghosal, year 19, no. 19 (November 2010): 181–8; here quoted from 185.
86 Apareshchandra Mukhopadhyay, *Rangalayer Trish Batsar* (1933); as cited in Ramenkumar Sar, "Sadharon rangamanche Rabindranath byartho", in *Balaka*, ed. Dhananjoy Ghosal, year 19, no. 19 (November 2010): 181–8; here quoted from 185.
87 Details in Harindranath Dutta, *Rabindranath o Sadharan Rangalay*, 47–8.
88 For details, see, for instance, Pinakesh Bhaduri, "Natyacharya Sisirkumar and Natyasurya Ahindra Chowdhury", in *Korok Sahitya Patrika: Bangla Natak o Natyamancha*, ed. Tapas Bhowmik, Autumn issue (2013): 304–26; here referred to 307–8.
89 There was some problem over *Chirakumar Sabha*. Sisirkumar Bhaduri claimed that Rabindranath had initially revised and given the play to him for staging. But as Sisirkumar was then busy with *Sita* (and also had not found actors with good singing voices) he had held it in reserve. The Art Theatre Limited, with Ahindra Chowdhury in the lead, convinced Rabindranath that Sisirkumar was not interested in doing the play in the immediate present, and the rights of production be given to them for two years in exchange of royalty. They probably acquired the rights around April, and, as per contract, staged the first performance within six months, on 18 July 1925. Rabindranath saw the second performance on 25 July. The play was well received in the commercial theatre. See details in Prabhatkumar Mukhopadhyay, *Rabindra Jibani*, vol. 3 (Calcutta: Visva-Bharati Granthalay, 1952; rev. 1961) 239, and Prasantakumar Pal, *Rabi Jibani*, vol. 9 (Calcutta: Ananda, 2003) 194–5, 237–8.
90 *Nachghar*, 3 June 1927; as cited in "Natyamancha samparke Rabindra-chintan" ["Rabindranath's thoughts on the Stage"], *Gandharva, Rabindranatya sankha* [Number on Rabindranath's Theatre], 1368 BS (1961): 72–3; here quoted from 72.
91 *Nachghar*, 3 June 1927; as cited in *Gandharva, Rabindranatya sankha* [Number on Rabindranath's Theatre], 1368 BS (1961): 72–3; here quoted from 73.
92 There have been occasions when the programme-brochures carried instructions for the audiences not to clap till the end of the performance. His experiences of restless spectators at New Empire during a staging of *Vasanta* in 1932, or at Waltair for a *Shapmochan* performance in 1934, prompted him to take this measure. For details, see Harindranath Dutt, *Rabindranath o Sadharan Rangalay* (Calcutta: Tagore Research Institute, 1983) 38; Parimal Goswami, *Smriti-chitran* (Calcutta: Prajna Prakashani, 1958) 227–8; Rudraprasad Chakrabarty, *Rangamancha O Rabindranath: Samakalin Pratikriya,* (Calcutta: Ananda, 1995) 261–2.
93 See, for instance, Utpal Dutt, *Ashar chalaney bhuli* (Calcutta: Paschimbanga Natya Academy, 1993) 58–9.
94 *My Reminiscences*, 116.
95 One may point to their participation in events like the Hindu Mela, Sakhi Samiti, Rakhi Bandhan (during the anti-Partition movement). In fact, the building of a theatre within their residential premises and encouraging performances, in which male and female family members took part, was a way to promote the moral and cultural imaginary of the people beyond the accepted norms of the period.
96 As cited in Ramenkumar Sar, "Sadharon rangamanche Rabindranath byartho", in *Balaka*, ed. Dhananjoy Ghosal, year 19, no. 19 (November 2010): 181–8; here quoted from 183.

Section 2
Rabindranath as dramaturge and theorist

2 Theatre and Nation

I

Between *Visarjan* of 1890 and *Sarodatsav* of 1908, there was what may well be considered as a lull of almost eighteen years in Rabindranath's serious theatrical activity. Admittedly, there were some sporadic attempts at dramatic composition made during this interim period. There were two significant verse-plays, *Chitrangada* (1892) and *Malini* (1896),[1] and a few comedies, farces and sketches like *Goray Galad* (1892),[2] *Bini Poysar Bhoj* (1893),[3] *Swargiya Prahasan* (1894), *Baikunther Khata* (1897), *Lakshmir Pariksha*[4] (1899), *Bashikaran* (1901) and others.[5] The verse-play *Chitrangada*, despite being a major achievement – both in its depiction of an empowered female protagonist and its use of the erotic to an extent hardly again attempted by him in drama – was never produced by Rabindranath. It was performed under his supervision only after he transformed it into the dance drama *Chitrangada* (as late as in 1936) – where much of the erotic was subsumed in the melody of the songs if not totally abandoned, and the protagonist also lost some of her original verve. *Malini* also was a significant work – on the one hand, it brought compassionate love in conflict with blind fanaticism, and raised the problems of politicking in the name of religion (issues he had dealt with in *Visarjan*); on the other, it introduced into a dramatic work his fondness for the Buddhist faith. Yet, it somehow did not seem to have inspired Rabindranath enough to arrange for its production, in sharp contrast to his usual habit of arranging for performance almost immediately after completing a play. He did not have anything to do with its first performance, when the students staged *Malini* at Santiniketan to welcome Rathindranath and his new bride on 8 February 1910. There was a second performance of the play in April 1910 (possibly on 23 April), when Rabindranath appears to have supervised the production but not played any role.[6] By 1910, of course, *Sarodotsav* (1908) had happened, marking his return to writing and staging of drama (albeit of a different brand). Among the farces, it is reported that he acted in *Baikunther Khata* for the Khamkheyali Sabha (1897)[7] and directed the *Goray Galad* production of Sangeet Samaj in 1900, when his meticulousness as director was much applauded.[8]

However, it is the return to serious playwriting with *Sarodatsav* in 1908 that signifies a major shift, not merely dramaturgical but even ideological, for it

DOI: 10.4324/9781003110279-3

may be seen as directly issuing out of his concerns with nation-building. Here, perhaps, we need to move away from the theatre arena for a while and focus on Rabindranath's ideological engagement with the Nation, if only to realize that the theatre with which he emerged after 1908 is largely a consequence of this engagement.

On 1 January 1877, the title of 'Empress of India' was conferred upon Queen Victoria. To commemorate the occasion, Sourindramohan Tagore (1840–1941) composed a song in her honour, hailing her as "rajrajeshwari" [empress].[9] Within a month, the not-yet-sixteen Rabindranath sounded a markedly different – even defiant – note in a poem, "Dillir Darbar" ["The Royal Court of Delhi"], which he read at the Hindu Mela:

> *British bijay kariya ghosona*
> *Ar je gay gak, amra gabo na,*
> *Amra gabo na harasa gaan*
> *Eso go amra je kajan achi*
> *Amra dharibo arek tan.*
> [Whoever else may sing the glory of the British,
> We shall not do so,
> We shall not sing any merry song,
> Come, let us few who remain,
> Sing a different tune.][10]

Again, in response to Eleanor Rathbone's insensitive comments made in an open letter (28 May 1941), on 4 June 1941 (just a couple of months before his death) Rabindranath had this to say:

> It is not so much because the British are foreigners that they are unwelcome to us ... as because while pretending to be trustees of our welfare they have betrayed the great trust and have sacrificed the happiness of millions in India to bloat the pockets of a few capitalists at home. I should have thought that the decent Britisher would at least keep silent at these wrongs and be grateful to us for our inaction, but that he should add insult to injury and pour salt over our wounds, passes all bounds of decency.[11]

Between the teenager of 1877 and the octogenarian of 1941 came various phases of Rabindranath's ideological negotiations with the notion of the Nation, which need to be historicized in relation to events, both at home and abroad, to which he was a witness and which etched their deep impressions upon him. There was his early emphasis on the indigenous society (*swadeshi samaj*) – which, according to some recent Western theorists of nationalism, would point towards an 'organicist' view of Nation as an ancestrally inherited sociocultural community; or, according to others, it might correspond to the idea of the *Gemeinschaft* (emotional community). Against this, loomed large the Eurocentric notion of the Nation-State, which, some hold, is a product of 'modernization', with the political community as its constituent, or, for others, would be equivalent to *Gesellschaft* (rational/political community or state).[12]

The more Rabindranath experienced the power of the authoritarian state organ, the deeper grew his aversion for such impersonal and structured authorities. This is voiced through his protests against brutal measures by repressive regimes – whether the British-perpetrated genocide in Amritsar or the Japanese intervention in China. The more these regimes were efficient and organized, the more were they to be distrusted, and the Poet's perception of the European kind of nationalism bristled with this distrust. But Rabindranath's engagement with the Nation also trod several paths in between: from his early support of the *swadeshi* movement, to his shying away from the movement as it turned increasingly violent; from his early admiration of Gandhi's social reforms to his later rather severe criticism of Gandhi's cult of the *charkha* [13]; from his early eulogies of Japan to his subsequent disgust at Japanese atrocities. It would not be out of place here to recall that his response to the British was also multilayered: his sense of regard for the "boro Ingrej" (the "great English", whom he associated with all that was good in the English culture) was played off against his condemnation of the "choto Ingrej" (the "small English", whom he identified with the colonizing masters who had taken possession of this country and unleashed an oppressive system of control).[14] But the trust he reposed in the justness of the "great English" was rudely battered after incidents like the British Parliament's apathetic response to the Jallianwala Bagh massacre (perpetrated by the "small English").[15] And, in his final moments, he was articulating his anxious misgivings of the crisis in civilization precipitated by the rabid nationalism that had begun in the West and had spread its tentacles worldwide. All these are evidences of Rabindranath's dialectical and complex relationship with the concept of Nation, in general, and of nationalism in India, in particular.

Between 1890 and 1908 Rabindranath had begun to articulate more consistently his views of the Nation in his essays. These essays, mostly written between 1893 and 1908, were compiled into volumes with tell-tale names, like *Raja Praja* [*The King and the Subjects*], *Bharatbarsha* [*India*], *Swadesh* [*Country*], *Samaj* [*Society*], *Atmasakti* [*Self-empowerment*], all published between 1905 and 1908. Scholars have further located three phases within this period[16]: the first, when Rabindranath derides hankering for British sympathy ("Ingraj o Bharatbashi" ["The English and the Indian"], 1893), condemns British excesses ("Kantharodh" ["Stifling"], 1898) and upholds the significance of the syncretic Indian civilization, the worth of which the British colonizer has failed to understand ("Bharatbarsher Itihas", 1902); second, when realizing the futility of mere protests – even violent ones – he suggests a more constructive agenda ("Swadeshi samaj", 1904); and third, when he makes plain his disenchantment with the contemporary leadership and criticizes the political programmes of agitation and violence, which fail to address socio-economic needs like education, communal harmony and village welfare ("Byadhi o Pratikar" ["Disease and Cure"], 1907 or "Path o Patheya" ["The Way and the Means"], 1908). His negotiation with the nationalist discourse continued beyond – as in his insistence for a new historiography in "Bharatbasher Itihaaser Dhara" ["The Course of Indian History"] (1912),[17] or in the reiteration of his convictions in "Rabindranather rashtranitik mot" ["The Nationalist Views of Rabindranath"] (1929), or in the insightful essays of *Palli Prakriti* where he stresses the need for rural reconstruction to rejuvenate India.

Alongside, one would need to remember that during this period (1890–1908) Rabindranath was taken up with several projects related to nation-building. In 1901, he founded the *asram*-school (hermitage-school) at Santiniketan, in a definite departure from the pedagogical system established and institutionalized by the British. Through approximation – not replication – of the model of the *tapovan* of ancient India, he was trying to reinvigorate the Indian system of education by moving away from the British template and providing a viable alternative, appropriate to the Indian context. Again, in 1905, he became involved with the mass movement against the British policy of partitioning Bengal. It is reported that, while chairing a meeting in Calcutta on 27 September 1905, it was the Poet who proposed that the day of Partition (16 October) be observed as a day of union (between Hindus and Muslims) through *rakhi bandhan*.[18] On that particular day, he himself stepped out into the streets singing songs and tying the *rakhi* (a yellow-coloured thread) on others' wrists to signify unity between the Hindu and Muslim communities. Though later he withdrew from direct involvement in the movement and retired to Giridih, he spent his time there composing more than twenty memorable patriotic songs, within a month's time. Again, when in 1906, the National Council of Education was established (to give shape to an institution of higher learning as an alternative to the British-structured Calcutta University), Rabindranath was among the founder members.

Central to Rabindranath's engagement with the discourse of nationalism in India is his postulation that: "in our country the society/community (*samaj*) is above all things."[19] It is this idea of a close-knit organic cultural community, with its ancestral legacies, that was subsequently more fully articulated in that seminal essay, "Swadeshi samaj" (1904):

> The core of a nation is where the collective welfare of the people is located. To inflict any damage to this core is to cause injurious harm to the entire nation. In England, if the governing power ('*rajsakti*') is dented, the entire nation feels the wound. That is why politics is such a serious affair in Europe. In our country, if the society ('*samaj*') is maimed, the entire country suffers from a crisis.[20]

It is the syncretic character of the *samaj* that gives it a centrality in Indian life, and this, for Rabindranath, is the result of a historical process peculiar to India. This is an idea that he reiterates elsewhere too – notably in the "Bharat-tirtha" poem and "Jana Gana Mana" (later set to tune and the first stanza chosen as India's national anthem). For him, "Hindu" did not signify a particular religious body, but a larger social system that accommodated several races, religions, cultures: "Hindu is a racial consequence (*jatigata parinam*) of Indian history."[21] So, the terms "Hindu" and "Mussalman" denote identities of different categories; and, Christian converts like Krishnamohan Bandyopadhyay are "Hindu by race (*jati*) but Christian by religion."[22] Even the English essays dating from his 1916-tour of Japan and America, and later compiled in *Nationalism* (1917), stress this point: "Races ethnologically different have in this country come into close contact. This fact has been and still continues to be the most important one in our history."[23] The homogenization of races that enabled the European nation-states to emerge as unified organs is alien to the Indian experience.

An automatic consequence of this, for Rabindranath, is the distinction between state power involving political governance, and society/*samaj*, functioning as an organic socio cultural unit: "In our country, *sarkar-bahadur* (the government) is not part of the society, it remains outside the society."[24] In a sequel, added later to "Swadeshi samaj", he went on to re-emphasize this feature of the Indian community:

> What is power for Europe is not power for us. ... The powerhouse of Europe is the State. ... The well-being of our country lies in its community (samaj). ... So, the freedom of the community is the true freedom of India.[25]

The welfare of the *samaj* is the collective responsibility of its constituent members, and therein lies the power of the Indian society. The collaborative nature of the citizens' duties necessitates each member of the society doing his/her bit to ensure all-round social development. If one recalls the original context for the "Swadeshi samaj" address,[26] one would remember how Rabindranath reminds his fellow countrymen that the Indian tradition stressed the need for collective responsibility, which, he held, was the hallmark of the Indian society, as distinct from the European Nation-State, where governance and social welfare were the responsibility of those in control of a centralized political system:

> That which is called State in English, in our regional languages has been termed '*sarkar*' (government). In ancient India, this *sarkar*/government was manifest in the form of *rajshakti* (kingly power, i.e., political governance). But there is a difference between the English State and our *rajshakti*. Whereas, in England, the entire responsibility for the national welfare is entrusted to the State, in India this is done only partially.[27]

The driving force of the Indian *samaj*/society, for Rabindranath, was its *atmasakti* (self-empowerment):

> I shall say this, to depend on others' charity is the sign of the 'pessimist'. I shall never concur that there is no hope for us unless we beg on our knees.[28] I believe in our land (*swadesh*), I salute the spirit of self-empowerment (*atmasakti*).[29]

It was the lack of this *atmasakti* that had made the Indian people increasingly dependent on the political machinery, in contradiction to its traditional reliance on self-help. To drive home this point, Rabindranath uses an allusion that is most appropriate to the immediate situation that occasioned the "Swadeshi samaj" address:

> It is not that the kings would not dig up reservoirs for the common people, but any citizen of means would be expected do the same. So, even if the king paid no heed, the water-vessel of the land would not dry up.[30]

In an essay written much later ("Rabindranather rastranaitik mot", 1929), he reiterates the same idea: "The country belonged to the people; the king was only a part of it, as the crown is a part of the head."[31]

In opposition to this coherent indigenous society, Rabindranath views the European Nation-State as a political entity that often proves heedless of, even antagonistic to, basic human concerns: "In the West, the national machinery of commerce and politics turns out neatly impressed bales of humanity."[32] This pronouncement, from one of the essays of *Nationalism* (1917), betrays his awareness (and distrust) of the Western notions of nation-building.[33] It is evident that the thrust of Rabindranath's polemics in these essays is to construct the Nation primarily in the negative: as a product of the politically belligerent, dehumanizingly industrialized West, with its colonialist Empire-building enterprises. And, when Japan, in imitation of this Western model, shows signs of an equally aggressive nationalist design, Rabindranath is scathing in his criticism, as is available in his correspondences with Yone Noguchi:

> When you speak, therefore, of "the inevitable means, terrible it is though, for establishing a new great world in the Asiatic continent" – signifying, I suppose, the bombing of Chinese women and children and the desecration of ancient temples and Universities as a means of saving China for Asia – you are ascribing to humanity a way of life which is not even inevitable among the animals and would certainly not apply to the East, in spite of her occasional aberrations. You are building your conception of an Asia which would be raised on a tower of skulls.[34]

He had no hesitation in categorically denouncing this brand of Nationalism, especially in India, as a derivative discourse that poses a "great menace".[35] He posits India as "a country of No-Nation"[36] as opposed to the ultra-nationalism of Europe, which was dependent on political-scientific-militaristic-bureaucratic systems of governance, and which by the nineteenth century had launched upon aggressive colonialist expansion and imperialistic ventures.[37] And when the Indian nationalist movement showed signs of floundering, Rabindranth criticized it for its want of a "constructive ideal" and a lack of understanding of the need of "constructive work *coming from within herself*".[38] These were the reasons why, to borrow Ashis Nandy's words, "nationalism itself became gradually illegitimate" for him, leading to his distancing himself from the project of Indian nationalism.[39]

Though evolving through several phases, Rabindranath's perception of Nation ultimately remained informed with his prioritization of the "organicist" *nation as community* (*swadeshi samaj*) over the "modernist" *nation as state*. His theory of India as "a country of No-Nation" is a reassertion of the primacy of the village community in the Indian *swadeshi samaj*. Rabindranath, like Gandhi, exalted the village as the nucleus of Indian society. But, unlike Gandhi, he was not in favour of an inflexible rusticity: "When I desire that our villages may spring to life, I do not wish that rusticity to be revived which, with its own beliefs and practices, remains cut off from the outside world – not only is it different from the progressive spirit of the times but even opposed to it."[40] Differing from Gandhi, therefore, he did not hold the notion of the state *per se* at fault, but was against *that* form of nationalism that was fiercely competitive, rapaciously expansionist, deliriously power-hungry;[41] in fact, "for Tagore, the state and the community were not competing categories; they were, in the best of times, complementary."[42] At a point, when his differences with Gandhi had reached a crescendo, he wrote:

> … it hurts me deeply when the cry of rejection rings loud against the West in my country with the clamour that the Western education can only injure us. It cannot be true. What has caused the mischief is the fact that for a long time we have been out of touch with our own culture and therefore the Western culture has not found its proper prospective in our life, often found a wrong prospective giving our mental eye a squint.[43]

Elaborating on this issue further, he had written in 1928:

> The knowledge which had made the demons powerful also gave power to the gods. *There can be no separate classes for Knowledge.* Nowadays we get to hear in our country that there is evil in the knowledge of the West, so we have no need for it. I do not say so. I do not hold that because power is destructive, powerlessness should be our goal. To withstand the destruction of power, one needs to *know* that power; to ignore it is to invite more havoc.[44]

For Rabindranath, self-empowerment (*atmasakti*) came through Knowledge; denial of Knowledge meant denial of *atmasakti*, and hence denial of Truth.

Moving away from the Gandhian position as well as from other more rabid forms of Indian nationalism, Rabindranath started to envisage a form of universalism/ internationalism. It was this ideology of internationalism that prevented him from supporting narrow sectarian notions of nationalism, for which he was widely vilified at home and abroad. In a rejoinder to Gandhi's brand of political activism, Rabindranath referred to the altered global situation, particularly after the First World War:

> The awakening of India is a part of the awakening of the world ... From now onward, any nation which takes an isolated view of its own country will run counter to the spirit of the New Age, and know no peace. From now onward, the anxiety that each country has for its own safety must embrace the welfare of the world.[45]

It was this spirit of universalism for which his university, Visva-Bharati, would serve as a cradle. The motto of Visva-Bharati ("where the world makes its home in a single nest") indicates precisely this. In fact, late in his career, Rabindranath was thinking in terms of the citizenship of the world, not merely of India. Recent scholarship has attempted to forge links between this attribute in him and the tenets of cosmopolitanism, and to see how he attempted a symbiosis between the civilizations of the East and West.[46]

What eventually comes across is a more inclusive concept of Nationalism, which, while harping on the centrality of the village community, does not exclude other possible potentials, provided they were geared towards the welfare of the people. One might even suggest here that Rabindranath ultimately seems to have made a distinction between *deshprem* (patriotism) and *jatiyatabad* (nationalism); the former is anchored in emotion, while the latter provides the ideological basis of the nation-state. He did support the cause for India's political independence, but he felt that true independence could only come when the standards of life would be raised through education, economic freedom and cultural emancipation. This explains, on the one hand, his rejection of outright boycott of foreign goods, and, on the other, his consent to introduce tractors and machinery for agricultural development at Sriniketan. In fact, Rabindranath continuously tried to engage local resources to shape up the community at Santiniketan-Sriniketan as an embodiment of his "imagined community"; his was one among "many similar experiments throughout the twentieth century at creating in a microcosmic locality the forms of the large political community, whether of the nation or of socialism or something else."[47] As late as in 1939, in a message to the inmates of his *asram*-school, he recalled his early "Swadeshi Samaj" days and remarked:

> I had tried to imply then that one need not bother about the entire nation. One alone cannot take responsibility for the whole of India. One should take charge of a village or two. One will have to win their hearts, to gain strength enough to work with them. It is no easy task, and will require a lot of sacrifice. If one can liberate even a couple of villages from ignorance and incapacity, one would be able to recreate an ideal of India in miniature.[48]

The Santiniketan-Sriniketan community, then, would have served as a capsule of his vision of the Indian community, his *swadeshi samaj*.[49]

II

If between 1900 and 1910 Rabindranath had started to imagine a new nation, he had also started to imagine a new theatre. As pointed out at the start of this chapter, after the early experimentations with the Western models there was a virtual withdrawal from serious playwriting for a period of about eighteen years (1890 to 1908). In this eighteen-year gap between *Visarjan* (1890) and *Sarodotsav* [*The Autumn Festival*] (1908), when there was not much of serious dramatic/theatrical activity,[50] he was formulating new theories of theatre, even as he was negotiating with new theories of nation-building. Unfortunately, Rabindranath has left us only a handful of writings in which he articulates his theories of theatre. It was in 1902 that his seminal tract on theatre, "Rangamancha" ["The Theatre"], was published.[51] The date is important, coming between the setting up of the *asram*-school at Santiniketan in 1901 and the Bengal Partition movement in 1905, and alongside the writing of several early essays on nation-building, with "Swadeshi samaj" appearing in 1904. In "Rangamancha" he derided the conventions of Western naturalistic theatre and, in particular, the painted scenery. Against that, he upheld the form of *jatra*, with which he (and his family) had close contact within the Tagore household precincts in his boyhood days. He promoted this indigenous theatre as a sample of the more nuanced staging principles of the Indian performance traditions:

> Assisted by performance, the poetry, which is the real thing, flows over the thrilled hearts of the spectators like a fountain. The gardener-woman roams her barren garden all day in search of flowers – you do not need to cart whole trees on to the stage to demonstrate that: the entire garden should spontaneously spring to life in the gardener herself. Or else what is so special about her, and what is the purpose of having spectators sit there like wooden dummies?[52]

Rabindranath's espousal of the cause of *jatra* is particularly significant because this signals his departure from the colonial and urban character of the nineteenth-century Bengali theatre. He was conceptualizing a "parallel theatre" that would be largely rid of the colonial trappings and the urban inflections. It would also be a theatre where the imagination of the audience would not be circumscribed by the "crude European barbarisms" of the Western realistic stage: "is the spectator who has come to see you perform destitute of any resources of his own?"[53] He would reiterate his disregard for Western naturalism and champion the cause of indigenous resources (folk and classical) in subsequent writings, too – notably in the "Prologue" ("*Suchana*") added to *Phalguni* (in 1916; the original play was composed and performed in 1915),[54] and the preface to *Tapati* (1929). More of this has been elaborated in a subsequent chapter (Chapter 4) where his theorizing about theatre has been discussed.

III

With Rabindranath shifting base to Santiniketan, much of this conceptualization of a "parallel theatre" could be realized in practice through the productions in the open-air ambience of the *asram*-school. This ambience not only determined the production and reception of his plays, but also helped to crystallize his theories about theatre. While he was imagining an alternative way of life for the community/nation, he was also imagining an alternative style of production for the theatre. This was notably evident in the open-air productions of seasonal plays like *Sarodotsav* and *Phalguni* [*The Cycle of Spring*], which engaged not only with a different style of acting but also with a different style of stage design, costuming and make-up. For the 1911 *Sarodatsav* production at Santiniketan (in which Rabindranath played the Sannyasi), he preferred to keep the stage bare, only decorated with "lotus flowers, *kash* [55], leaves and foliage", and a blue backcloth representing the sky.[56] In *Phalguni* (1915)[57], the dramaturgical configuration went yet a step further in collapsing together topographic and psychic spaces: "Beginnings: the Street" (Scene1), "Search: the *Ghat*" (Scene 2), "Doubt: the Field" (Scene 3), "Revelation: the Cave-mouth" (Scene 4). If in the context of the nation, the geographical territory gave way to an imagined space, where a group of people, sharing a historical memory, consented to live together, here, in the context of the dramaturgical/theatrical structure, the topography of the stage-space dissolved away to make room for the psychic space, which represented the actual arena of the dramatic 'action'. *Phalguni* was first performed at Santiniketan on 25 April 1915; and in 1916 the charity show for the Bankura famine was given at Jorasanko. In performance, the language of the theatre tried to approximate the fluidity of the text on page. So, as Indira Devi has recounted: "In place of the earlier incongruous Western imitation, a blue backdrop had been used; it is still used now. Against it, there was a single branch of a tree, with a single red flower at its tip, under a single ray of the pale moonshine."[58] And the poet Satyendranath Dutta was all praise for the innovative stage decor: "A tinge of green on the blue backdrop – as though the sky and the forest had fused together into a oneness."[59] In writing and staging of this new crop of plays, therefore, Rabindranath proved that he had arrived with an alternative theatre, which could serve as a cultural equivalence to his notions about a nascent nation.

The relocation to Santiniketan held two-fold benefits for Rabindranath. Apart from providing him with a space and ambience conducive to his innovations in theatre semiology, this relocation also allowed him to experiment with the Santiniketan community itself and mould it as a model for his ideal *swadeshi samaj*. Rabindranath was trying to interpenetrate the local community with his vision of the *swadeshi samaj* and propel it towards *atmasakti* or self-empowerment. One of the obvious ways to achieve this was to encourage all members to participate in community life. For this, the residential character of the *asram*-school was particularly conducive. As has been argued, "The distinctive feature of the local experiment is always that it retains the immediacy of the face-to-face community, and uses its vast resources of deep and dense interpersonal memories to invoke trust and innovate subtle solutions."[60]

With a holistic approach to education,[61] Rabindranath was consciously trying to engage the potentials of the students and teachers in different ways; the visual and the performing arts, therefore, were intrinsic to the pedagogical methodology adopted at Visva-Bharati:

> In the educational programme emphasis is given to Music and Art, for it is clearly recognised that the great use of Education is not merely to collect facts, but to know man and to make oneself known to man. Every student is expected to learn, at least to some extent, not only the language of intellect, but also the language of art – to obtain a mastery of lines and colours, sounds and movements.[62]

Edward Thompson, in a telling remark about Rabindranath's *asram*-school, observed:

> It should be noted first, that the poet planned much more than a school. He sought a home for the spirit of India, distracted and torn in the conflicting storms of the age. The unity of India has been a dream present with some of her greater sons. Here he felt it might begin to be realized with a completeness hitherto unattained.[63]

The theatrical performances became a means (among others) to achieve this end. Alert to the possibility that theatrical performances could afford him with just such an opportunity to build up an interactive *swadeshi samaj* in Santiniketan-Sriniketan, Rabindranath kept a sharp lookout for human resources locally available. He had to make his theatrical experiments pleasurable experiences, without being either too exacting or too compromising. Local talents had to be honed to cater to aesthetic demands of the experiment, factoring in the logistics of production and reception. So, in the early years of the school, when the student community comprised primarily male students, he made boys impersonate roles of women, which was in tune with what he had stated in "Rangamancha": "It is time we rid ourselves of such crude European barbarisms as demanding that a garden must be presented by an exact painting or *female roles acted by bona fide females*."[64] It appears, then, that in the early years of the *asram*-school, with a group of talented young boys at hand (and, by corollary, a dearth of girls), he was putting his theory about female impersonation into practice. The theoretical formula and the theatrical exigency, therefore, went hand in hand.

Not only the students, but even the teachers at the *asram*-school of Santiniketan were involved in theatrical performances – whether as onstage performers or as backstage designers/assistants. For instance, if the daughters, Gouri and Jamuna, were cast respectively as Srimati in *Natir Puja* and as Chitrangada in the dance drama *Chitrangada*, the father, Nandalal Bose, a teacher and an eminent artist, was engaged in stage and costume design for several productions of

50 *Rabindranath as dramaturge and theorist*

Santiniketan. Teachers and students contributed collectively to the collaborative enterprise of each performance – not only in matters of performance, but also in stage decoration, make-up and costuming – and all this usually under the close supervision of the author himself.[65] The theatrical experiments at the *asram*-school were used by Rabindranath with a definite purpose. On the one hand, his new crop of plays promoted a new theatre semiology, a new style of production, and hence underscored his ideological impetus to create an alternative *swadeshi* model for the Indian theatre. On the other hand, his ability to engage the greater part of the Santiniketan-Sriniketan community in such sociocultural activities, like theatre performances, indicated that the macro-vision of the *swadeshi samaj* was being actually situated within the micro-location of the *asram*-school. Imagining nation and imagining theatre now almost went hand in hand for Rabindranath.

IV

Apart from the seasonal dramas, there was the rich repertoire of prose plays like *Raja* (1910, performed 1911), *Dakghar* (1911, performed 1917),[66] *Muktadhara* (1922; the attempt to stage this play in the same year was eventually abandoned),[67] *Raktakarabi* (1924; not staged by Rabindranath), *Tapati* (1929; also performed in 1929),[68] *Kaler Jatra* (1932; not staged by him),[69] or *Tasher Desh* (1933; revised 1939); and the dance dramas of his last phase – *Shapmochan* (1931), *Chitrangada* (1936), *Chandalika* (1938) and *Shyama* (1939).

Though Rabindranath was not able to produce either *Muktadhara* or *Raktakarabi* or *Kaler Jatra*, he read aloud some of these plays before gatherings on several occasions and had expressed his desire to produce them. The story of *Tapati* is considerably different; it was performed in 1929, with Rabindranath himself in the lead role of King Vikramdev. Refashioned from the early blank verse tragedy, *Raja o Rani* (1889), it first took the shape of *Bhairaber Bali* (February 1929) and finally emerged as *Tapati* (August 1929), and as early as in September 1929 it was staged at Jorasanko. Some of the more alert among the spectators found contemporary significations in the play: "The incongruities in the contemporary political scenario that disturb Rabindranath have been articulated in this symbolic drama, *Tapati*."[70] *Tasher Desh* was produced under the Poet's supervision, and despite an initial setback at the premiere show in Bombay (1933),[71] it was performed subsequently with much fanfare after the text was revised. Most of these plays, loaded with Rabindranath's ideological assumptions about Nation, often depict an opposition between two communities – an organized political community of the rulers that is both repressive and acquisitive; and a community of the common people, seemingly loose but closely bound by emotional ties and collective memories. For instance, in *Muktadhara*, the king's decision to dam the river – implemented by his engineer with the help of a monstrous machine, and supported by the elites – is injurious to the needs of the ordinary people.

That Rabindranath's concerns with nation-building inform most of these prose plays could best be viewed through a somewhat close analysis of two samples from his mature phase – *Raktakarabi* and *Tasher Desh*. The stage setting of *Raktakarabi*, dominated by the symbolic net, reflects a stiflingly mechanistic space, where the political ("modernist") community of rulers, spearheaded by the Governors/Sardars and Headmen/Morols, unleash a repressive regime, with the King/Raja at its centre. The commoners, like Bishu, Chandra or Phagulal, share memories of rituals and celebrations of their rural ("organicist") community but are engulfed in the dark labyrinths of the gold mine. Nandini hails from that 'other' locale, replete with emotional bondings, and promises to liberate the rest. The conflict between the two kinds of communities here may be seen to correspond to Rabindranath's ideas of the *samaj* (an "organicist" community) pitted against that of the nation-state organ (a "modernist" political set-up). If one were to consider a comment by one of the characters in the play (Bishu):

> After the first day comes the second, after the second the third. There's no such thing as getting finished here. We're always digging – one yard, two yards, three yards. We go on raising gold nuggets – after one nugget another, then more and more and more. In Yaksha Town figures follow one another in rows and never arrive at any conclusion. That's why we are not men to them, but only numbers[72]

alongside what Rabindranath himself wrote in the essay, "Nationalism in the West":

> In the West, the national machinery of commerce and politics turns out neatly impressed bales of humanity …[73]

the affinities would become more than obvious. The two statements placed side by side make it evident that Rabindranath's structuring of *Yakshapuri*/Yaksha Town as the setting of *Raktakarabi/Red Oleanders* (1924/1925) recalls his polemical discourses on European nationalism. The dehumanizing, impersonal, aggressive and organized state power at *Yakshapuri* tries to erase human identities and create automatons, "neatly impressed bales of humanity". At a climactic moment in the play, when Nandini is horrified by the sight of men reduced to mere shadows – described as "the King's leavings"[74] – the Professor explains to her the mechanism of exploitation at work in Yaksha Town:

> That marvellousness [of the King's strength] is the credit side of the account, and this ghastliness [of the shadow-men] is the debit. These small ones are consumed to ash, that the great ones may leap up in flame. This is the principle underlying all rise to greatness.[75]

Though Nandini rejects this principle as "fiendish", this is what provides the base to the acquisitive and exploitative state organ, and enables it to operate with such organized aggressiveness. This, for Rabindranath, would largely correspond to the Western formulation of the Nation-State, with its expansionist agenda.

Raktakatabi is also Rabindranath's retelling of the story of the *Ramayana*. Not only does he locate a modern-day Ravana in the King of Yakshapuri:

> There is a king in my drama. Writing in the present times, I did not have the courage to equip him with more than one head or two hands. Had I the nerve of the ancient poet, I would have done so. The powers of science and technology have added innumerable but invisible hands, feet and heads to the human entity. That the king of my drama extracts and devours by such excessive powers is indicated in the play[76]

but also hints at the schizophrenic split within the nature of this King (Ravana and Vivisana rolled into one)[77] that would result in an inevitable collapse of the power system he has generated. Notably, the region is given the name of *Yakshapuri*.[78] The *Yaksha*, in Indian mythical sources, was a follower of *Kubera*, the god of acquisitive wealth that is hoarded and accumulated, not expended fruitfully. This is in sharp contrast to the role of *Sree* or *Lakshmi*, the goddess of grace and abundance, whose benediction brings prosperity and welfare to all. This very idea of the contrariness between *Kubera* and *Lakshmi* was expressed by Rabindranath in an essay, "Sikshar Milan", written after a tour of America:

> For seven continuous months I had resided in the monstrous palace of wealth in America. I do not say 'monstrous' in a negative sense; perhaps in English one would say 'Titanic wealth' – the wealth of formidable power, immense magnitude. Every day I would sit at the window of the hotel, under the frown of the thirty thirty-five storied buildings. *And I would say to myself, Lakshmi is of a kind, Kubera of another – the difference is vast. The inner essence of Kubera is acquisition, which leads to amassing of wealth. There is no end to this amassing. Two into two is four, four into two is eight, eight into two is sixteen – the calculations leap on like a frog; and the range of the leaps keep growing.* [79]

Letters written around this time also bear out his similar attitude to the avaricious Western materialism.[80] Against this acquisitive might of *Kubera*, Rabindranath upholds the value of *Lakshmi* or *Sree*. *Sree* was a major concept for him – he refers to the loss of "*sree*" (prosperity) in the Indian villages with the influx of the British colonizing system in India which has left the Indian "*swadeshi samaj*" increasingly depleted – materially and spiritually. The Indian people have progressively become more dependent upon the centralized political system of the British administration and have lost their ability for self-help/self-empowerment ("*atmasakti*"). He voices his concern for the "lack of *sree*" (hence, lack of grace and plenitude; "*sree-bhrasta*" in the Bengali original) in the contemporary village community; earlier, because each member of the community (*samaj*) contributed to the agenda of social welfare, *samaj* was blessed with elegance and prosperity (*sree*).[81] It may be noted here that the name "Sriniketan" for the Surul School of Agriculture (established in February 1922) officially came into circulation by the end of 1923.[82] *Raktakarabi/Red Oleanders*, then, champions the cause of the elegance of *Sree* against the oppressive exploitation of *Kubera*, and, in doing so, privileges Rabindranath's concept of *nation as community* over that of *nation as state*. *Raktakarabi*, engaging with so many pressing concerns (social/economic/political/cultural) through its rich multilayered dramaturgical structure, remains one of his most significant achievements in dramatic composition. It is, therefore, all the more unfortunate that Rabindranath did not get the opportunity of producing this unique play – reportedly for the lack of a suitable Nandini.[83]

Tasher Desh was first written in 1935, and then was radically revised by 1939. Though initially written as a prose play, perhaps the advice of well-wishers (Sarojini Naidu among them) after the cold reception of its early performance at the Excelsior Theatre in Bombay in 1935 may have prompted Rabindranath to introduce more songs and dances, to entertain audiences who were not versed with the language. The play was thoroughly revised by 1939, making room for such entertainment. The later stage history of *Tasher Desh* suggests that it has been customarily presented as a dance drama, or at least as a musical, with little or no importance given to the prose dialogues. Yet, on closer scrutiny, *Tasher Desh* appears to belong to the same category as Rabindranath's other prose plays like *Raja*, *Muktadhara* or *Raktakarabi*, where the songs not only add to the dramatic situation but function as extensions of the prose dialogue.

Tasher Desh, which has its genesis in the fairy-tale-like short story "Ekti ashare galpo" ["A Fanciful Tale"], is set in a fantasy land of cards, somewhere beyond the seas. Interestingly, no specific geographical territory is mentioned. "We started from one shore and were shipwrecked in mid-sea; now we have been washed ashore in an alien land", is how the Prince describes the transportation.[84] This strange land has strange inhabitants, as the Merchant, the Prince's companion, after a quick look around, comes back to report: "What I saw was a wooden bower made by a carpenter. I saw people flat in shape, walking in stiff geometrical gait, making clicking noises with their feet as though they had put on wooden ankle bells, no doubt made out of tamarind timber."[85] The card-people swear by their own myths, legends, traditions and customs, which, however ludicrous they may seem to an outsider, assures them of a safe sanctuary. Yet, the Prince is astute enough to note that, because these have been imposed by the rulers (hailing from higher social classes), they serve less as sanctuary more as bondage.

In contrast to this card-land, there is another land in the play – not the one the Prince hails from, for that is equally repressive with its customs and regulations, but the one he dreams of. It comes to him in visionary flashes, and he sings of its beauty:

> In the midst of the vast blue is the emerald isle
> Surrounded by red corals ...
> There if I arrive, I'll surely find
> All those ancient kings' treasure mine.[86]

He names this treasure (*manik*) of his mind "Navina", the "new one"; it comes to him in elusive dreams, decked with flowers from unknown heavens, playing tunes of unknown melodies. Inscribed with these indeterminacies, the land of his dreams, too, has no territorial specificities, lodged as it is in the imaginary of his inner cravings.

So, when the Prince strives to don the mantle of the deliverer of the card-community, does he intend to invest one imaginary space (the card-land) with the ideals of another (the land of his dreams)? Is he, then, reconfiguring the card-land in tune with his own ideas? In other words, is he rejecting the present form of the card-community and replacing it with an imagined community of his own aspirations?

As for the card-people, to attain the ideals of the Prince – who, after all, is an outsider – they have to arouse themselves; theirs, therefore, is a journey towards self-help/self-empowerment/*atmasakti*. Significantly, it is the women who first respond to the Prince's wake-up call. The first among them is Haratani, who is able to defy the rules of the card-land because, prompted by the Prince's external influence, she experiences an inner realization dawning within herself:

> The bee came humming into my chamber.
> Whose message did it carry to my ears? ...
> How can I then remain confined to my room?
> When my heart aches with untold pain?
> How may the days be counted at such slow pace?
> What magic has overpowered me, making me forget my chores?
> And why do I spend my days weaving a net of tunes?[87]

Disgusted with her card-life, she resolves to break free, undeterred by the impediments on the way to freedom:

> The black boulders scowl menacingly before us; we have to smash them to smithereens, even if they break upon our heads. We have to split open the rocky mountains, carving our way through them. Why have we come here? Why do we linger here? O shame! What meaningless days, what lifeless nights have we been spending? What futile moments have entangled us![88]

Her enthusiasm is infectious, and soon others join her, each moving towards her/his own self-realization: her partner, Ruhitan ("Tear away this shroud, shred it to pieces. Be free, be pure, be whole")[89]; her friends, Iskaboni and Chiretoni ("I told her clearly that I would rather be a live woman than a dead card")[90]; the courtiers, Chakka and Panja ("I'm ashamed to look at myself. Fool! Fool! What have I been doing all this while?")[91]; and even the sceptical Dahalani ("Last night I dreamt that I had suddenly become human, and was moving around just like a human being. I felt so ashamed of myself upon waking up. But ... The bird that is chained during the day is set free in dreams!").[92]

In the final scene, the card-people boldly begin their tirade against the age-old laws, and sing praise of the power of the Will:

> Will, Will, the power of the Will,
> That which creates, and dissipates,
> That which knocks at bolted locks,
> That which breaks free from all bonds,
> And yet turns around to bind oneself.[93]

They find an unexpected leader in the Queen herself. She joins the rebels, sings paeans of the Will and prepares to go into exile from this dead kingdom of cards. In this play about breaking down the shackles to create a new living community, the women form an inner core of rebellion and display remarkable fortitude and *atmasakti*. So much so, that the three pillars of this 'State' of cards – the King (the political head), the Priest (the religious head) and the Editor (the cultural head) – submit before the collective might of the community, proving Rabindranath's point that the power ultimately rests with the people, sometimes even with the more marginalized among them. Is this a fairy-tale? Or, a play about decolonization – of the mind, the community, the nation?

At this point, one may make a return to the essay "Swadeshi Samaj", where among other requisites, Rabindranath mentioned the need for a *"samajpati"* (a leader of the society). In fact, along with the notion of the community/*samaj*, he was also negotiating with the concept of a model ruler. One might recall here that the source of the early tragedy *Visarjan* was the novel *Rajarshi* (Royal Sage), where King Govindamanikya emerges as an ideal king, a sage-king. Kings/princes move in and out of several of his plays, from the early *Raja o Rani* (1889) to the late *Tasher Desh* (1932), coming in variegated hues and shades. One could even suggest that through these characters Rabindranath was in search of a model leader, one who could merge in himself the ideals of the king and the sage. That is exactly what happens in *Sarodotsav* when the king disguises himself as the hermit (Sannyasi) to acquire first-hand knowledge about the welfare of the community; the king/sage steps out on the streets with his concern for the well-being of his subjects. On the other hand, the king in the prologue to *Phalguni* is much too taken up with his greying hair to be bothered about the plight of his people; he has to be jolted out of his inertia by the poet. *Raja* not only explores the mystical nature of the King of the Dark Chamber but also presents a critique of good governance: the song *"Amra sabai raja amader ei Rajar rajatwe"* ["We are all kings in this kingdom of our King"] is a telling observation on the ideal democratic situation of this "kingdom", which political rulers from neighbouring lands misread as mere kingless anarchy.

Nandini in *Raktakarabi* alerts the King of Yakshapuri to the exploitative threats of his acquisitive power system. The Prince of *Tasher Desh*, arriving at the Kingdom of Cards, strives to free the cards from the regimentation of their social order, imposed upon them by their social superiors. All of this may well converge into a reading of Rabindranath's vision of an ideal national leader for the new emergent nation.

In "Swadeshi samaj" (1904), he had emphasized the need for a leader or *samajpati*, in whom would repose the trust of the entire community, and who, in turn, would be entrusted with the responsibility of leading the rest in the right direction:

> We need to perceive the nation embodied in a particular individual. We need one in whom the image of the entire society is encapsulated. ... Earlier, when the State and society were together, the king would fulfil this role. Now that the king is external to the society, the society is without its leader. ... Now we need a leader (*samajpati*). He may have his advisory committee (*parshad sabha*), but he will directly be the leader of the society.[94]

On the one hand, he is aware of the daily ravages of colonial forces that exercise their hegemonic control over all spheres of life (ranging from schools to markets); this makes the election/selection of a leader all the more necessary:

> The society has to rise up now against these forces and safeguard itself. The only way to do this is to select a leader, who will represent the interests of all, and whose dictates will not be seen as demeaning but respected as part of our freedom.[95]

On the other hand, he is alert to the possibility of the misuse of power by an undeserving leader, but reposes faith in the supreme powers of the society: "If the society is alert, no person can inflict any permanent damage upon it."[96] He feels that this very need to select the proper leader, capable of the responsibility, only unites the society and gives it a greater cohesiveness.

He had written two essays with the identical title – "Deshnayak". The first was written in 1906, two years after the "Swadeshi samaj" essay; the second, as late as in 1939. In the second, addressing Subhaschandra Bose, he wrote: "I am a Bengali poet; on behalf of Bengal I bestow upon you ["*baran kori*", in the original] the role of the *deshnayak* [leader/hero of the land]."[97] He went on to implicitly invite his countrymen to invest Subhaschandra in the role of a leader: "Let the collective will of the Bengali people accept you as their leader; let their will mould you in the shape appropriate for that onerous responsibility."[98] Around the same time, in the preface to the revised version of *Tasher Desh* (1939), Rabindranath dedicated the play to Subhaschandra, lauding him for his vow to instil new life into the nation. Even as in the fictionalized world of the card-land the card-people collectively chose to follow

Theatre and Nation 57

the leadership of the Prince, here, too, the *samajpati* is to be elected from among the people, by the collective will of the people.

Rabindranath's narration of the nation, then, has made a journey from "Swadeshi samaj" to "Deshnayak", via the intermediary discourse of "Rangamancha" and the 'fictional' narratives of plays like *Raktakarabi* and *Tasher Desh*.

Notes

1 Though *Malini* first appeared in *Kavyagranthabali*, edited by Satyaprasad Gangopadhyay, it was published as an individual playtext only as late as in 1912.
2 This was Rabindranath's first attempt at a full-length comedy; it was later rewritten as *Sesh Raksha* (1928), possibly for performance on the commercial stage by Sisirkumar Bhaduri.
3 A farce for mono-acting; this was performed several times by Akshaykumar Majumdar, a family friend, who, with a penchant for slapstick comedy, was a regular actor in the Tagore in-house productions.
4 A comedy in verse, with an all-female cast.
5 Many of these comic sketches and farces were later compiled in the two collections, *Hasya-kautuk* and *Vyanga-kautuk*, in 1907.
6 See Rudraprasad Chakrabarty, *Rangamancha O Rabindranath: Samakalin Pratikriya* (Calcutta: Ananda Publishers, 1995) 98–9; also Prasantakumar Pal, *Rabi Jibani*, vol. 6 (Calcutta: Ananda Publishers, 1992) 124, 146–7.
7 For details, see Abanindranath Tagore, *Gharoa* (Calcutta: Visva-Bharati Granthan Vibhaga, 1941; rpt. 1983) 120–1.
8 For details, see Rudraprasad Chakrabarty, *Rangamancha O Rabindranath: Samakalin Pratikriya*, 76–8.
9 Sourindramohan Tagore, *Victoria Samrajyan [Empress Victoria]* (Calcutta: I.C. Bose & Co, 1882) 162.
10 Cited in Anuradha Roy, "Bangali buddhijibir chokhe British sashan", in *Unish Sataker Bangalijiban o Sanskriti*, ed. Swapan Basu and Indrajit Chaudhuri (Calcutta: Pustak Bipani, 2003) 254–72; here quoted from 255.
11 *Hindusthan Standard*, 4 June 1941; cited in Niharranjan Ray, *Aitihya o Rabindranath* (Calcutta: Dey's Publishing, 1994) 207.
12 Anthony Smith shows how in the writings of late nineteenth- and early twentieth-century thinkers these two opposite ideas about Nation occur: the "perennialist"/"organicist" view of Nation as organic cultural community; and the "modernist" view of Nation emerging as a product of "modernization", with political community as its constituent. See Anthony D. Smith, *Nationalism and Modernism: A critical survey of recent theories of nation and nationalism* (London & New York: Routledge, 1998) 22–3. See also Ferdinand Tonnies, *Community and Civil Society*, ed. Jose Harris and Margaret Hollis, trans. Jose Harris (Cambridge: Cambridge University Press, 2001) 22–91, where Tonnies plays off the notion of *Gesellschaft* (rational community or state) against that of *Gemeinschaft* (emotional community).
13 Rabindranath, though supportive of the spiritual strength of Non-Cooperation, disagreed with Gandhi's modes of practical politics – his siding with the narrow-minded Khilafat movement to achieve Hindu-Muslim unity; his boycott policies, including boycott of education by students in the schools; or even his proposition that *swaraj* could be gained by spinning the *charkha* for six months. When Gandhi invited him to join in spinning the wheel, the Poet retorted: "Poems I can spin, Gandhiji, songs and plays I can spin, but of your precious cotton what a mess I would make!" Even after several meetings between them, Rabindranath remained

unconvinced about Gandhi's *modus operandi*. In fact, though their meeting of 6 September 1921 (in Calcutta) was held behind closed doors, Elmhirst learnt about it later from the Poet himself and noted down the gist. Krishna Kripalani, in recounting Elmhirst's version, reports: "Tagore said, 'Come and look over the edge of my verandah, Gandhiji. Look down there and see what your non-violent followers are up to. They have stolen cloth from the shops in the Chirpore Road, they've lit that bonfire in my courtyard and are now howling round it like a lot of demented dervishes. Is that non-violence?'" (*Tagore: A Life*. New Delhi: National Book Trust, India, 1986; originally 1961, 169); also cited in Prasantakumar Pal, *Rabi Jibani*, vol. 8 (Calcutta: Ananda, 2000) 143–4.

14 "Choto o boro" ["The Small and the Great", as translated by Surendranath Tagore] was delivered as a public address on 14 and 16 November 1917 at Vichitra and Rammohun Library Hall respectively. The English translation by Surendranath was published in *Modern Review* in December 1917. The essay appears in *Rabindra Rachanabali* [Complete Works] vol. 13 (Calcutta: West Bengal Government Centenary Edition, 1961) 248–64; in subsequent citations *Rabindra Rachanabali* will be denoted as *RR*.

15 Protesting against the massacre at Jallianwala Bagh (13 April 1919), the Poet wrote an open letter to the Viceroy, Lord Chelmsford, and renounced his knighthood (given by the British Empire). He was hopeful that when in 1920 the British Parliament, in both its Houses, discussed the atrocities committed in Punjab, it would redress the wrongs done. But the Poet (present in England from June) was dismayed with the lackadaisical response of the British Parliament and left for Europe, disgusted and disappointed.

16 Sabyasachi Bhattacharya, *Rabindranath Tagore: An Interpretation* (New Delhi: Penguin/Viking, 2011); see 93ff.

17 This was first read at the Overtoun Hall in Calcutta on 16 March 1912. What Rabindranath was arguing in the essay is that, unlike Europe, India does not have so much of a political history as a cultural history, and so there was need for a new historiographical approach. Though Jadunath Sarkar later made an English translation as *My Interpretation of Indian History*, "The Course of Indian History" comes closer to the original title.

18 "The Chairman (Rabindranath) then delivered a short speech at the end of which he suggested that if Partition of Bengal were carried out on the 16th October next the people of entire Bengal Eastern and Western, should celebrate the day as an occasion of their union. That might be observed as an anniversary and Rakhi Bondhan, by exchange of yellow thread between the people of Eastern and Western Bengal on that day, might be observed. A national song terminated the meeting at 9–20 p.m." in *The Bengalee* (28 September 1905); as cited in Prasantakumar Pal, *Rabi Jibani*, vol. 5 (Calcutta: Ananda, 1990) 261.

19 "Bharatbarshiya Samaj", *Atmasakti o Samuha*, *RR*, vol. 12, 678–83; here quoted from 680.

20 "Swadesi Samaj", *Atmasakti o Samuha, RR*, vol. 12, 685.

21 "Atmaparichay" (1912–13), *RR*, vol 12, 175.

22 "Atmaparichay", *RR*, vol 12, 174.

23 "Nationalism in the West" (1917), in *The English Writings of Rabindranath Tagore*, ed. Sisir Kumar Das, vol. 2 (New Delhi: Sahitya Akademi, 2004) 419.

24 "Swadeshi samaj", *RR*, vol. 12, 686.

25 "Swadeshi samaj prabandher parishishta", *RR*, vol. 12, 703.

26 The speech, titled "Swadeshi samaj", occasioned by the need to resolve the problem of severe drought, was first read on 22 July 1904 at Minerva Theatre, Calcutta, and again on 31 July at Curzon Theatre. A sequel followed, "Swadeshi samaj prabandher parishishta", and a "Constitution" was drafted as well. The essay was first pulished in *Bangadarshan* in August 1904.

27 "Swadeshi Samaj", *RR*, vol 12, 684–5.
28 The original uses the image of putting the *kacha* (part of the *dhoti*) around one's neck; the image has been changed here in translation.
29 "Swadeshi Samaj", *RR*, vol 12, 690.
30 "Swadeshi Samaj", *RR*, vol 12, 684–5.
31 "Rabindranather rastranaitik mot", *RR*, vol. 13, 369–75; here quoted from 373.
32 "Nationalism in the West" in *The English Writings of Rabindranath Tagore*, vol. 2, 420.
33 See Anthony D. Smith, *Nationalism and Modernism: A critical survey of recent theories of nation and nationalism* (London & New York: Routledge, 1998) 22–3.
34 Tagore to Noguchi, 1 September 1938; as cited in *The English Writings of Rabindranath Tagore*, vol. 3, 837.
35 "Nationalism in India", in *The English Writings of Rabindranath Tagore*, vol. 2, 458.
36 "Nationalism in the West", in *The English Writings of Rabindranath Tagore*, vol. 2, 434.
37 Rabindranath, in fact, analyses the historical phases that resulted in this form of nationalism as the product of a certain process of 'modernization' in the West.
38 "Nationalism in India", in *The English Writings of Rabindranath Tagore*, vol. 2, 458; emphases added.
39 Ashis Nandy, *The Illegitimacy of Nationalism: Rabindranath Tagore and the Politics of Self* (Delhi: Oxford University Press, 1994) 2.
40 "Uposamhar", *Russiar Chithi* ["Conclusion" to *Letters from Russia*], in *Rabindra Rachabali*, Popular edition, vol. 10 (Calcutta: Visva-Bharati, 1989) 602.
41 See Asok Sen, "Rajnitir pathakrame Rabindranath", *Bangadarshan*, 11 (July–December 2006) 100.
42 Bikash Chakravarty, "Swadeshi Samaj: Rabindranath and the Nation" in *Rabindranath Tagore and the Nation: Essays in Politics, Society and Culture*, ed. Swati Ganguly and Abhijit Sen (Calcutta: Punascha & Visva-Bharati, 2011) 25–35; here cited from 29.
43 Published originally in *The Modern Review* of May 1921 in response to Gandhi's non-cooperation movement; reprinted in *The Mahatma and the Poet: Letters and debates between Gandhi and Tagore, 1915–1941*, ed. Sabyasachi Bhattacharya (New Delhi: National Book Trust, 1997; rpt. 1999), 54–62; here quoted from 62.
44 "Palliprakriti" (6 Feb 1928) in *Rabindra Rachabali* [Complete Works] Popular edition, vol. 14 (Calcutta: Visva-Bharati, 1991) 362–7; here quoted from 367; emphases added.
45 *The Call of Truth* (1921); originally published in Bengali in *Prabasi*, and later in English in *The Modern Review*. Reprinted in *The Mahatma and the Poet: Letters and Debates between Gandhi and Tagore 1915–1941*, ed. Sabyasachi Bhattacharya (New Delhi: National Book Trust, 1997; rpt. 1999) 68–87; here quoted from 84.
46 See, for instance, Martha Nussbaum, "Patriotism and Cosmopolitanism", *The Boston Review*, XIX (5), Oct–Nov 1994, 3–16.
47 Partha Chatterjee, *Lineages of Political Society: Studies in Postcolonial Democracy* (New York: Columbia University Press, 2011) 118.
48 "Sriniketaner Itihas o Adarsha", *Palliprakriti*, in *RR*, vol. 13, 536–40; here quoted from 540.
49 This would, in effect, be in consonance with the theoretical perception of Nation as a "form of cultural elaboration", as argued by Homi Bhabha in *Nation and Narration*, ed. Homi Bhabha (London & New York: Routledge, 1990) 3.
50 As indicated earlier, during this period he had written – along with some comedies and farces – two important verse-plays, *Chitrangada* (1892) and *Malini* (1896), but did not make the effort to produce them.
51 The essay was first published in the *Pous* 1309 B.S. issue (on 30 December 1902) of *Bangadarshan*; the essay was later included in *Bichitra Prabandha* ["Miscellaneous Essays"] published in 1907.
52 The essay has been translated as "The Theatre" by Swapan Chakravorty in *Rabindranath Tagore, Selected Writings on Literature and Language*, ed. Sukanta

Chaudhuri (Oxford, New York & New Delhi: Oxford University Press, 2001) 95–9; here quoted from 97–8.
53 "Rangamancha" ["The Theatre"], trans. Swapan Chakravorty, 97.
54 See Prabhatkumar Mukhopadhyay, *Rabindra Jibani*, vol. 2 (Calcutta: Visva-Bharati Granthalay, 1936) 535–6.
55 A kind of long white grass that grows in autumn.
56 Prabhatkumar Mukhopadhyay, *Rabindra Jibani*, vol. 2, 327.
57 The play was written at Sriniketan when Rabindranath was residing at the '*kuthi bari*' he had bought there.
58 Indira Devi Chaudhurani, *Rabindra Smriti* (Calcutta: Visva-Bharati Granthan Vibhaga, 2010; originally 1960) 38.
59 Satyendranath Dutta's review of the production, titled "Sahare Phalguni", appeared in *Bharati*, ed. Monilal Gangopadhyay and Sourindramohan Mukhapadhyay, 39th year, no. 11, *Phalgun* 1322 (1916), 1098–110; here quoted from 1104.
60 Partha Chatterjee, *Lineages of Political Society*, 118.
61 The "Memorandum of Association" of Visva-Bharati (of which Rabindranath Tagore is named the "Founder-President") notes as Clause III: "To study the Mind of Man in its realization of different aspects of truth from diverse points of view." This was declared on the inside back covers of all four numbers of the first volume of *Visva-Bharati Quarterly* (April, July, October, 1923 and January 1924).
62 *Visva-Bharati Quarterly*, ed. Rabindranath Tagore (14 April 1923) 1; this, in fact, was the very first number of the *Visva-Bharati Quarterly* and it may be presumed this introductory announcement about Visva-Bharati, though published anonymously, in all likelihood would have been written by Rabindranath himself, or, at most, by one under his close supervision. The same announcement was reprinted on the first page of the next number of *Visva-Bharati Quarterly*: July 1923 (ed. Surendranath Tagore).
63 Edward Thompson, *Rabindranath Tagore – Poet and Dramatist* (Delhi: Oxford University Press, 1948) 188.
64 "Rangamancha" ["The Theatre"], trans. Swapan Chakravorty, 99; emphases added.
65 Among the teachers who acted in different plays were Dinendranath Tagore, in charge of music lessons; Jagadananda Roy, the much-revered but much-feared science teacher; Kalimohan Ghose, the *Adhyaksha* (Principal) of Sriniketan, and even the venerable Kshitimohan Sen. The stage decor was often by Abanindranath Tagore or Nandalal Bose, working with groups of students; the costuming and make-up by Nandalal Bose or Pratima Devi, the Poet's daughter-in-law. See details in Biswajit Sinha, *Encyclopaedia of Indian Theatre – 5: Rabindranath Tagore*, Part I (Delhi: Raj Publications, 2003) 17.
66 The English translation of the play (by Devabrata Mukherjea, with a preface by W.B. Yeats) was performed by the Irish Abbey Theatre in Dublin on 17 May and in London on 10 July 1913. Despite arrangements for a performance of the Bengali original at Santiniketan about eight months later, it was called off. The first performance of the Bengali play came as late as in 1917. For details, see Rudraprasad Chakrabarty, *Rangamancha O Rabindranath*, 138–9; Biswajit Sinha, *Encyclopaedia of Indian Theatre – 5: Rabindranath Tagore*, Part I, 294.
67 An arrangement was made in 1922 for the staging of *Muktadhara* during *Vasantotsav* at Santiniketan, but when Gandhi was arrested on 10 March, Rabindranath cancelled the celebrations of *Vasantotsav*, along with the performance of the play. See Prasantakumar Pal, *Rabi Jibani*, vol. 8 (Calcutta: Ananda, 2000) 276.
68 This was the reworked version of the 1889 *Raja o Rani*, which had been written in blank verse.
69 This was a collation of two earlier dramatic pieces, *Rather Rashi* and *Kabi Diksha*, given a final shape in 1932, and dedicated to Saratchandra Chattopadhyay. *Visva-*

Bharati News, October 1932, 31, reports a production of the play at Santiniketan in September 1932, directed by Dinendranath Tagore, in which students and staff participated.
70 *Nachghar* (Autumn issue, 1929); quoted in Rudraprasad Chakrabarty, *Rangamancha O Rabindranath: Samakalin Pratikriya*, 235.
71 On the very first evening (27 November 1933), the spectators (at the Excelsiot Theatre, Bombay), not conversant with the Bengali language, were unable to follow the dialogues of the play, which therefore failed to garner the expected response. Rabindranath worked on the play overnight and introduced more songs (to be accompanied with dances) for the next evening's performance at the same venue. For details, see Prabhatkumar Mukhopadhyay, *Rabindra Jibani*, vol. 3 (Calcutta: Visva-Bharati Granthalay, 1952; rpt. 1961) 489.
72 Rabindranath Tagore, *Red Oleanders* (Delhi: Macmillan India, 1973; 1st edn. 1925) 44.
73 "Nationalism in the West" in *The English Writings of Rabindranath Tagore*, vol. 2, 420.
74 *Red Oleanders*, 95.
75 *Red Oleanders*, 98.
76 *Raktakarabi* (Calcutta: Visva-Bharati, 1926) 107–8; this prose piece appeared first in *Probasi*, Baisakh 1332 B.S. (May 1925) and was later appended to the playtext.
77 *Raktakarabi*, 108. In *Ramayana*, Ravana and Vivisana were brothers, but of diametrically opposite dispositions, so much so that Vivisana later deserted Ravana to join Rama in his battle against Ravana.
78 Many held that the play had initially been titled *Yakshapuri*, but none of the drafts found bear this name: some early manuscripts use the name *Nandini*, to be replaced by *Raktakarabi* from the eighth draft. This puzzling situation may have been caused by the fact that Rabindranath himself referred to the play as *Yakshapuri* in some letters, while he was still in the process of composing it; see, for instance, letter to Ramananda Chattopadhyay, dated 19 Bhadra 1330 BS (1923) in *Chithipatra*, vol. 12 (Calcutta: Visva-Bharati, 1986) 86.
79 "Sikshar Milan" (Aswin 1328, 1921), *Siksha, RR*, vol. 11, 664–98; here quoted from 669; emphases added.
80 See Rabindranath Tagore, *Letters to a Friend*, ed. C.F. Andrews (London: Allen & Unwin, 1928) 105.
81 "Swadeshi Samaj", *RR*, vol. 12, 684.
82 Sriniketan was a project close to the Poet's heart where, as a major extension of the university, his ideas of rural reconstruction would be put into practice under the supervision of Leonard Elmhirst, Rathindranath and Kalimohan Ghosh. See Prasantakumar Pal, *Rabi Jibani*, vol. 9 (Calcutta: Ananda, 2003) 79, 85.
83 The Poet was trying out Reba Roy in the role of Nandini (presumably around 1927), but the production was stalled because she fell ill. Later, after her successful portrayal of Sumitra in *Tapati*, he wanted to cast Amita Tagore in the role; but because she remained diffident, the production could not happen. As reported in Rudraprasad Chakrabarty, *Rangamancha o Rabindranath: Samakalin Pratikriya*, 192–3.
84 The cited passages are from my translation of the play as *The Kingdom of Cards*, in *The Essential Tagore*, ed. Fakrul Alam and Radha Chakravarty (Cambridge. Mass.: Harvard University Press, 2011) 450–87; here cited from 456.
85 *The Kingdom of Cards*, 457.
86 *The Kingdom of Cards*, 454.
87 *The Kingdom of Cards*, 472–3.
88 *The Kingdom of Cards*, 476.
89 *The Kingdom of Cards*, 476.
90 *The Kingdom of Cards*, 471.
91 *The Kingdom of Cards*, 476.

92 *The Kingdom of Cards*, 479–80.
93 *The Kingdom of Cards*, 484.
94 "Swadeshi Samaj", *RR*, vol. 12, 693–4.
95 "Swadeshi Samaj", 693–94.
96 "Swadeshi Samaj", 694.
97 "Deshnayak", *Kalantar, RR*, vol. 13, 387–90; here cited from 387.
98 "Deshnayak", 389.

3 Theatre at the *asram*-school

I

Rabindranath's relocation to Santiniketan, with the founding of the *asram*-school there in 1901, helped to consolidate his vision of – among other things – an alternative mode of theatre, which relied more on indigenous traditions and less on Western borrowings. Rabindranath's theatrical engagements at the *asram*-school had a two-fold purpose: on the one hand, serious explorations into dramaturgical and/or theatrical innovations were undertaken; on the other, these were loaded with ideological underpinnings that informed his ideas of a 'modern' Indian theatre, in a definitive rejection of the colonial mimicry then practised on the Bengali public stage. The essay "Rangamancha" (1902),[1] as noted in the earlier chapter, marked this ideological shift even as he conceptualized his vision of the 'new' Indian theatre, advocating a rejection of Western theatrical models and a return to indigenous cultural traditions, *jatra* in particular. Not only did the open-air ambience of the *asram*-school provide Rabindranath with an appropriate venue where these new theories of theatre could be experimented with in actual practice, but it also allowed a radical departure from his earlier approaches to drama/theatre – whether in writing of the plays or in performing them.

The move to Santiniketan was followed by a series of bereavements in Rabindranath's personal life – the death of his wife, Mrinalini (1902), of a daughter, Renuka (1903), of a favourite colleague, Satishchandra Roy (1904), of his father, Devendranath (1905) and of his youngest and perhaps most-loved child, Samindranath (1907). It was his deep-seated resilience and faith in the unalterable process of life that perhaps enabled him to prevail over the seemingly unending shockwaves of personal grief. Some have wondered whether this may have caused him to turn inwards and write his symbolic plays, which they have chosen to label as "enigmatic"[2] or "mystical"[3] or even "thesis plays"[4]. While we need not make light of the impact of each of these bereavements, yet it does not do justice to the genius of Rabindranath to locate merely in such moments of personal grief the impetus for the decisive turn towards a new dramatic articulation that he took in 1908 with *Sarodotsav*.[5] In fact, it may be recalled here that as early as in 1884, even before these several

DOI: 10.4324/9781003110279-4

bereavements came his way, Rabindranath had already experimented in *Prakritir Pratisodh* with the kind of material that would shape his later "enigmatic"/ "metaphysical"/"thesis" plays. Though relatively weak in its dramaturgical structure, that Rabindranath attached considerable importance to this play is attested by his repeated references to it in later writings. He went on to suggest that this play held the key to his later works: "This *Nature's Revenge* may be looked upon as *an introduction to the whole of my future literary work*; or, rather this has been the subject on which all my writings have dwelt – *the joy of attaining the Infinite within the finite.*"[6] *Prakritir Pratisodh*, in a way, set out the "thesis" that his later mature plays would expound. One may even argue that the moments of personal grief were experienced, surmounted and engrafted onto a larger vision of meaningful human existence as hinted at in *Prakritir Pratisodh*. The mature "thesis plays" give expression to that meaning of human existence through a redefining of human relationship with Divinity (as in *Raja* or *Dakghar*), Nature (as in *Sarodotsav* or *Phalguni*) or fellow humans (as in *Raktakarabi, Muktadhara* or *Tasher Desh*).[7] As has often happened with Rabindranath, the personal is given a broader perspective in being set off against the all-pervasive presence of Life (which affected not only individual human lives but also extended to envelop the larger matrix that defined the national/social/cultural ways of living). Turning away from the storytelling narrative structure of *Raja o Rani* or *Visarjan*, he seems to embark upon a different route in trying to fashion a drama/theatre more relevant to the immediate requirements of the Indian ethos.

That this decisive turn – dramaturgical/theatrical/ideological – had been taken in the writing and staging of plays became evident in compositions like *Sarodotsav* and *Phalguni*. The open-air arena of the *asram*-school afforded a natural platform for the performance of these seasonal plays in particular. The novelty of staging, with innovative stage decor and a spontaneous style of acting, won appreciation both in the *asram* and elsewhere. Even in musical dramas, celebrating the different seasons, the Poet made the most of the new arena now at his disposal. And the concerted efforts of the *asram* residents, who contributed to the theatrical events collectively, enabled Rabindranath to expand the scope of his kind of theatre and give it a definitive identity.

II

The shift to Santiniketan allowed a smooth transition in Rabindranath's theatrical experiments from Western borrowings towards a more Bengali/Indian identity. In fact, his plays in performance came to acquire a uniqueness of their own, marked by his signature style of production, with the *asram* residents his as collaborators. This made possible the rich repertoire of his plays that included not only seasonal plays like *Sarodotsav* (1908) and *Phalguni* (1915) but even the more musical (if less dramatic) celebrations of seasons in *Vasanta* (1923), *Sundar* (1925), *Sesh Varshan* (1925), *Nataraj-Riturangasala* (1927), and *Navin* (1931); prose plays that explored male–female relationships whether through serious probings as in *Grihapravesh* (1925), *Sodhbodh* (1926) or *Bansari* (1933), or in a more light-hearted vein as in comedies like *Chirakumar Sabha* (1926) or *Sesh Raksha* (1928); the mature prose plays[8] like *Raja* (1910, performed 1911), *Achalayatan* (1911, performed 1914), *Dakghar* (1911, performed 1917)[9], *Muktadhara* (1922; an attempt to stage it the same year at *Vasantotsav* was aborted after receiving the news of Gandhi's arrest[10]), *Raktakarabi* (1924; not staged by Rabindranath), *Kaler Jatra* (1932) and *Tasher Desh* (1933; revised 1939); and the dance dramas of the last phase – *Shapmochan* (1931), *Chitrangada* (1936), *Chandalika* (1938) and *Shyama* (1939).

As already suggested above, this wide repertoire and their varied modes of performance could effectively be carried out precisely because Rabindranath had among his *asram* residents enthusiastic collaborators who contributed to each theatrical event. In fact, he had enthused and inspired them to join as collaborators in these ventures. This was the other kind of the experiment that he was carrying out at the residential *asram*-school at Santiniketan, which was related to his concept of the Indian nation as community. In his essays on nation-building, he had incessantly stressed on the centrality of the Indian *samaj*/society ("We have to realize that in our country the community [*samaj*] is above all things": "Bharatbarshiya samaj", 1901) and the strength of which lay in its *atmasakti* or self-empowerment/self-reliance. Around the time Rabindranath founded the *asram*-school (1901), he had also started to imagine an Indian *swadeshi samaj* (a national society/community of India). It was expected, therefore, that in tune with this emphasis on self-reliance and collective working of the entire community, Rabindranath would try to mould the community at Santiniketan as a bedrock for that *swadeshi samaj* of his dreams, and, by corollary, would try to engage as much of the Santiniketan community as possible in different spheres of activities – even in matters of theatrical productions. This would, in course, help to concretize to his vision of an alternative model for a new Indian theatre, breaking free of the shackles of Western naturalistic theatre and harking back to the indigenous traditions of his own culture. If he was imagining a new Indian nation vis-à-vis his dreams of *swadeshi samaj*, he was also imagining a new Indian theatre, firmly anchored in the rich traditions of this great nation.

When Visva-Bharati was established (1921) with a holistic approach to education, Rabindranath was consciously trying to engage the potentials of the students and teachers in diverse ways. The visual and the performing arts, for instance, were made an intrinsic part of the pedagogical methodology adopted at Visva-Bharati:

> In the educational programme emphasis is given to Music and Art, for it is clearly recognised that the great use of Education is not merely to collect facts, but to know man and to make oneself known to man. Every student is expected to learn, at least to some extent, not only the language of intellect, but also the language of art – to obtain a mastery of lines and colours, sounds and movements.[11]

We may recall once more the remarks of Edward Thompson:

> It should be noted first, that *the poet planned much more than a school. He sought a home for the spirit of India*, distracted and torn in the conflicting storms of the age. The unity of India has been a dream present with some of her greater sons. Here he felt it might begin to be realized with a completeness hitherto unattained.[12]

The Santiniketan-Sriniketan experiment constituted the embryo of his vision of the *swadeshi samaj*, not as a museum exhibit from the past, but as a lived-in experience of the present.

This experience of a new *swadeshi samaj* relevant to the present times would, for Rabindranath, evolve a cultural space of its own – with its music, its dance and its theatre. His search for the new model of an Indian theatre, then, was part and parcel of the dream of a new cultural space imagined for the emergent nation. So, when it began in Santiniketan with the new dramaturgical structure of *Sarodotsav* (1908), for its staging he was relying upon *asram* inhabitants, trying to use the pleasurable experience of the theatre as an occasion for community participation. It may well be argued that he had already started to view the Santiniketan community as a platform for his imagined *swadeshi samaj*. With the Jorasanko tradition of using talents of family members for various home productions behind him,[13] and the ideological inspiration of a new *swadeshi samaj* before him, his theatrical experimentations at the *asram*-school now tried to involve as much of the Santiniketan community as possible. As one who combined in himself the roles of author, actor and producer, Rabindranath always kept in mind the accessibility of on-hand human resources within the Santiniketan community and planned his productions accordingly. The onstage cast as well as the backstage hands were from among the students and teachers of the school, and later of the university.

In the early days of the *asram*-school, since male students primarily comprised the student community, Rabindranath was seemingly handicapped in casting male actors for female characters. But he quickly changed this handicap into an advantage, casting the more talented boy students in the female roles. Sudhiranjan Das, who later became a vice-chancellor of Visva-Bharati, had already performed in some female roles[14] before the Poet cast him as Queen Sudarshana for the premiere show of *Raja* on 19 March 1911. Sudhiranjan has fond memories of Rabindranath's training process: "The poet would say, 'Dear Sudhiranjan, you are doing fine – just say the words with a little more feeling'; saying this, he would recite the words himself. When I was able to speak the lines according to his directions, he was very happy."[15] In this first production of *Raja*, Sushilkumar Chakraborty played Surangama and Narendranath Khan was Rohini.[16] In other productions, too, boys were made to play women's roles: so, Ajitkumar Chakavarty played Sudarshana in a subsequent production of *Raja* (May 1911); earlier, in the 1910 performance of *Malini*, Sudhiranjan Das was Malini and Narendranath Khan played the queen,[17] while in a 1910 *Prayaschitta* production, Biva was played by Jatindranath Mukhopadhyay.[18] This practice – though it may have been prompted by the exigencies of available human resources – gave credence to his theoretical enunciations made in the 1902 essay, "Rangamancha": "It is time we rid ourselves of such crude European barbarisms as demanding that a garden must be presented by an exact painting or *female roles acted by bona fide females.*"[19] The theoretical formulation and the theatrical practice, therefore, found a happy fusion, impelled by the material determinants of production and reception at Santiniketan.

Yet, even as female students came in increasing numbers to the *asram*-school, girls were given place in the dramatic performances. If *Sarodatsav* or *Phalguni* had been all-male-cast plays, now Rabindranath wrote all-female plays, *Lakshmir Pariksha* (initially written in 1899 and published in 1903, this was performed first in Santiniketan by the girl students in 1910) and *Natir Puja* (1926). Initially, as mixed casting (of girls and boys) was disapproved, the first performance of *Lakshmir Pariksha* at Santiniketan, in the monsoon of 1910, was presented as an all-women affair: "not only were the players only girls, even the audience were women only; no male teacher or student was allowed in."[20]. When the Women's Art Forum [*Mahila silpa samiti*], initiated by Hiranmoyee Devi, organized a national fair [*swadeshi mela*] from 14 to 18 September 1906, two days – 16 and 17 September – were earmarked for women only, and *Lakshmir Pariksha* was performed on both these days.[21] *The Bengalee* had advertised on 15 September 1906 that "Ladies will take part in the performance of Lakshmir Pariksha."[22] Again, there was the much-applauded all-female production of *Mayar Khela* (1927, at the Empire Theatre), mounted under the direction of Sarala Devi, with Amiya Tagore and Sati Devi in the roles of Promoda and Santa, and Santi Dutta playing Amar.[23]

Interestingly, though the production of *Lakshmir Pariksha* in the monsoon of 1910 saw the girls at Santiniketan actively engage in performance, when *Raja* was staged in 1911, first in March and again in May, for both performances an all-male cast was used. While Sudhiranjan Das played Queen Sudarshana in the March production, Ajitkumar Chakravarty played the same role in the May production. Perhaps, the Santiniketan community of 1911 was still not prepared for mixed cast productions. This suspicion proves correct when we find that in the context of still using boys for the female roles even in the subsequent 1919 staging of an abridged version of *Raja* at Santiniketan, the reason provided by Santidev Ghosh is that "many still objected to boys and girls acting together."[24] It was around 1921/22 that boys and girls of Santiniketan started appearing together for performances – not only in Santiniketan, but also in Calcutta and elsewhere. Santidev Ghosh identifies the 1921 *Varsha-mangal* production performed in the open-air behind the Vichitra house at Jorasanko as the first event in which boys and girls sang together.[25] Prabhatkumar Mukhopadhyay, however, holds that the 1922 *Varsha-mangal* production given at Madan Theatre and Alfred Theatre on 16 and 19 August was the first occasion for boys and girls to appear together on the public stage.[26] Both, of course, are of the opinion that *Varsha-mangal* was a musical recital, comprising songs and recitations; dances were yet to be accepted as entertainment fit for the 'refined' tastes of the *bhadralok* (polite) classes. There was even more hostile criticism of boys and girls appearing together when *Rinsodh* was performed in Calcutta the very next month – on 16 September at Alfred Theatre and 18 September at Madan Theatre (in 1922). Severe objections were voiced, for instance, by Lalitmohan Das, a Brahmo leader, and Krishnakumar Moitra, editor of *Sanjeevani*, raising the issue of girls of respectable families performing on the public stage. Rabindranath politely responded to their letters but decided to go ahead with the performances.[27] And in doing so, he was gradually working towards a change in the mindset of his audiences; the productions were increasingly being received with approval and appreciation, in Calcutta and elsewhere. So, with more talented female actors now at hand, Rabindranath was able to break the shackles of this conservatism and use mixed casting in his productions – of plays like *Visajan* (1923)[28], *Arupratan* (1924), *Tapati* (1929) or *Raja* (1935)[29], so, too for the dance dramas of his final phase.

While *Natir Puja* (1926) was composed as an all-female play, Rabindranath took the bold step of introducing a dance as the dramatic climax, and Gouri Bose, the daughter of Nandalal Bose, was cast in the role of Srimati, the court-dancer. After the initial performance at Santiniketan (the audience comprising local residents and some invited foreign dignitaries),[30] when it was decided to stage the production commercially in Calcutta (in 1927) to raise funds for Visva-Bharati, some among the Santiniketan residents were not comfortable with the idea of a respectable Bengali girl being made to dance in a dramatic performance in the public theatre. The Poet tried to resolve the issue by astutely creating a role for himself in the play. Though this seemed to take care of the problem, sections of the contemporary society were still too rigid to relent. They vented their ire through uncharitable remarks in different reviews: "Respected Rabindranath Tagore has grown old but his desire for pleasure has remained 'evergreen'. It is reported that he has started dancing classes for women at Santiniketan... What kind of education is he imparting to simple-minded inexperienced young girls!";[31] "He is the one who has first shown the way to raise funds through dance of women, and the consumerist society took his hint that more money may be generated if women are made to dance or act in plays."[32] Despite these controversies, the dance of Srimati itself made a stunning impact, at once aesthetically pleasing and emotionally moving. Abanindranath commented: "When she [Gouri] danced as the Nati [the dancer], it was an extraordinary dance. I never saw the like of it."[33] Parimal Goswami, who probably saw the Calcutta production, noted the novelty with which "the dance of Srimati was made into the dramatic climax ... that a dance could constitute an entire dramatic spectacle was beyond my imagination."[34] What was of significance is that the impact of the dance on the contemporary socio-cultural mindset was not all negative. There were encouraging responses from the more judicious among the spectators who comprehended the magnitude Rabindranath's experiment and realized that this would have a far-reaching and inspiring effect in the long run: "The upshot of the enactment of Natir Puja in the city was a supreme outcome of dramatic art ... We have witnessed nothing quite like this ... Its cadence has impacted our lives as well. A flow of beauty showered down from the dance and it watered our very lives with grace."[35] Rabindranath's success in this regard needs to be viewed not only as an aesthetic or cultural feat, but also as achieving a reform in the middle-class mindset of the contemporary society vis-à-vis received notions of propriety and impropriety. That songs and dances – and, to an extent, theatrical performances – were subsequently made available to girls of middle-class Bengali families (to the extent that these were soon considered as accomplishments for young girls) is because of the pioneering efforts of Rabindranath. Gouri Bhanja (née Bose) herself declared: "The bold and undaunted step that Gurudeva took through this performance [*Natir Puja*], brought social respectability to dance and song performed by women."[36]

However, despite this leap forward, it may be noted that for later productions of the dance dramas, which involved mixed casts, Rabindranath usually chose to make himself visible at one corner of the stage. An advertisement in *The Statesman*, announced that in *Chitrangada*, given at the New Empire Theatre in Calcutta on 11 March 1936:

RABINDRANATH TAGORE
PERSONALLY APPEARING
IN HIS IMMORTAL LYRIC
CHITRANGADA
ALONG WITH STUDENTS OF
SANTINIKETAN[37]

That Rabindranath had no role to play in the dance drama itself left many disappointed: "the poet himself took no active part in the play. Though he was on the stage throughout the performance and recited portions from the play."[38] Yet his very presence on the stage mattered much; it gave a kind of legitimation to the performance in which male and female performers acted, danced and sang together – many of them students of his *asram*-school/university. Keeping all possible censures firmly under wraps, from around this time Rabindranath usually made it a point to be seen on the stage during the performances of the dance dramas. When *Parishodh* (the original version of *Shyama*) was presented in Calcutta in October 1936, *The Statesman* noted with approval Rabindranath's onstage presence:

> He makes the stage human. Everyone else on the stage may be acting but he is not. He is reality. *Moreover he gives a dignity to the performance – nautch is transformed into dance.* The dancers are no longer to be exploited for our pleasure but are brothers and sisters, as the winds, and the stars are our brothers and sisters, joyously dancing and shining around us.[39]

What could have generated harsh criticism – and, in turn, could have dealt a hard blow to Rabindranath's experiments at Santiniketan – was transformed into a welcome mode of cultural communication. Sajanikanta Das, for instance, in reviewing *Shyama*, observed: "*I had misgivings about the propriety of the students of Visva-Bharati enacting this tale of physical love by*. In reality I found the touch of genius could make everything possible. The expressiveness of the soft bodily postures dissolved away the sense of the physical to recreate a world of cerebral perception."[40] Moreover, that the student performers of Santiniketan had been initiated into a new kind of experience, which they were inviting the viewers to participate in, seemed to have been made evident to the eyewitnesses: "Those who act feel themselves to be loved pupils. They know each other and feel at ease. Sometimes the Poet sings with them; sometimes the tune becomes so infectious that we should all like to get up and dance, as in Ai Ai go Ai."[41]

III

Not only the students, but even the teachers at the *asram*-school of Santiniketan were roped into theatrical performances – whether as onstage performers or as backstage designers/assistants. For instance, if the daughters, Gouri Bose and Jamuna Bose, played the roles of Srimati in *Natir Puja* and of Chitrangada in *Chitrangada*, their father, Nandalal Bose, along with Asitkumar Haldar and Surendranath Kar, teachers and eminent artists of Kala Bhavana, were given charge of stage and costume designs for various productions, done in Santiniketan and elsewhere.

With teachers often among the onstage cast with the students, the productions became truly collaborative ventures of the tutor and the taught. Jagadananda Roy, the erudite science teacher, whom the students both feared and revered, was often seen in comical roles like those of Laksheswar (*Sarodotsav*, 1908), Ramchandra (*Prayaschitta*, 1910), Mahapanchak (*Achalayatan*, 1914), Dada (*Phalguni*, 1915), and again in serious roles like Kanchiraj (*Raja*, 1911). Kalimohan Ghose, the *Adhyaksha* (Principal) of Sriniketan, played characters like Rammohan Mal (*Prayaschitta*, 1910) or the priest Bhargav (*Tapati*, 1929). Even the venerable Kshitimohan Sen was cast as Sannyasi in *Sarodotsav* (1908) or Thakurda/Guru in *Achalayatan* (1914). Among the students, who performed with this galaxy of teachers, were several who later became distinguished in their own fields – among them were Ajitkumar Chakravarty, Sudhiranjan Das, Santidev Ghosh, Sahana Bose, Amita Tagore, Amita Sen, Ranu Adhikari.

From beyond the *asram* proper, Rabindranath's nephews, especially the trio Gaganendranath, Samarendranath and Abanindranath, were often cast as onstage performers, especially when the plays were staged in Calcutta. It must be added here that Gaganendranath and Abanindranath also contributed immensely to the stage decor of various productions – if Abanindranath's stage setting for the 1917 *Dakghar* at Jorasanko is widely known, Gaganendranath's Cubist stage design for the 1923 *Visarjan* was extremely well received.

Dinendranath Tagore, the grandson of the Poet's eldest brother Dwijendranath, imparted music lessons at Santiniketan, and Rabindranath made him the "custodian" of his songs. When it came to participating in the theatrical performances, Dinendranath played a whole gamut of characters, ranging from Laksheswar and Thakurda (*Sarodotsav*, 1908), to Panchak (*Achalayatan*, 1914), to Raghupti (*Visarjan*, 1923, in which Rabindranath performed the young Joysingha). He was often cast in roles where his gifted singing could be made most of (like the Madman in *Raja*, 1911, or the Beggar's Companion in *Dakghar*, 1917–18, or even as part of the choric group in *Phalguni*, 1916). His nuanced singing in many of these roles is known to have moved the audiences:

> Dinendranath appeared as the Madman [in *Raja*], in rags and dishevelled hair, singing. There was no leap, no yell, no extra effort to depict madness; only a faraway look in search of the unattainable, and that song of yearning, "*Tora je ja bolis bhai, amar sonar horin chai* [Whatever you may say, I must have the golden deer]" ... the elderly gentleman (himself a talented actor), who sat next to me, grasped my hand firmly. I looked up to find tears rolling down his cheeks.[42]

Teachers and students collaborated in the staging of the plays, not only in onstage performance, but also for the backstage details of stage design, make-up and costume – often under the close supervision of the author himself. Overseeing the stage decor done for *Sarodotsav* by Abanindranath and a group of enthusiastic students, Rabindranath asked the "royal umbrella"[43] to be removed for the sake of keeping the stage clear and simple.[44] After the trio Nandalal Bose, Asitkumar Haldar and Surendranath Kar joined Kala Bhavana, the stage decor of the productions were designed chiefly by them, and executed by the students – sometimes under the caring eyes of Gaganendranath and Abanindranath. This helped a unique style of scenographic design to evolve that became recognizable as the distinctive signature of Santiniketan. Even costumes and make-up were in tune with this scenography. The costuming was often the responsibility of Nandalal Bose or Pratima Devi, the Poet's daughter-in-law.[45] Songs, whether sung in solo or in chorus, were meticulously supervised by Dinendranath, if not by the Poet himself. Though dance-like movements had been used sporadically, dances proper were introduced relatively late but flourished rapidly with the dance dramas. Rabindranath imported various dance forms from different climates and cultures, whether the Manipuri from North-East India, or the Bharatnatyam from South India, or even the Kandi Dance from Ceylon. Pratima Devi and Santidev Ghosh took the primary charge to mould out of these different forms an inclusive dance pattern suitable for the Poet's plays and dance dramas.

The *asram*-school at Santiniketan, thriving on the combined efforts of the residents, afforded Rabindranath with the necessary platform for experimentations and innovations, both in the writing and staging of plays, within a community that shared his commitment to shape up as a newfound *swadeshi samaj*. As suggested earlier, it was at Santiniketan that Rabindranath chose to implant the seed of his vision of the *swadeshi samaj*, so that the Santiniketan *samaj*/community would come to represent in an embryo what he dreamt of in the larger context of the nation. His theories and practices in the arena of the theatre helped him to achieve this in a significant way. On the one hand, his new crop of plays spoke of a new theatre semiology, a new style of production, and hence underscored his ideological impetus to create an alternative *swadeshi* model for the Indian theatre. On the other hand, his ability to engage the greater part of the Santiniketan community in such sociocultural activities as theatre performances indicated that the macro-vision of the *swadeshi samaj* was being situated within the micro-location of the Santiniketan *asram*-school. Jagadananda Roy, the venerable mathematics teacher at the school, who also acted in several of Rabindranath's plays, had an interesting observation to offer: "if for whatever reason there was any dissent brewing at the *asram*, arrangements for a theatrical performance usually dissipated the problem."[46] Rabindranath astutely used theatre to cement the societal bondings within the *asram* community to forge a cohesive organic unit.

Yet, a coda may not be out of place here. When it came to matters of theatre production, as a practising theatre-personality Rabindranath was flexible enough to keep in mind the material determinants of production and reception. He had his own theories about an Indian theatre (some of which will be discussed in the next chapter) but because he combined in himself the roles of author, actor and producer, his experiments on the stage were never constricted by rigidity of theories. More than a theorist, he was a theatre-practitioner, and so plays written for the Santiniketan situation could well be adapted to other venues, without any major distortion. Productions of *Sarodatsav, Raja, Dakghar, Phalguni* or *Natir Puja* – all staged later in Calcutta theatres or elsewhere – were just as well received, though presented under circumstances markedly different from those at Santiniketan. Yet, always stamped with the individuality of Rabindranath and the cultural markers of Santiniketan, they remained different from the usual run-of-the-mill stage productions then in circulation. This itself speaks volumes for the plasticity and comprehensive nature of Rabindranath's plays, as creations of a pragmatic man of the theatre.

Notes

1 The essay was first published in *Bangadarshan* on 30 December 1902, and later included in *Bichitra Prabandha* (1907). For detailed information, see Prasantakumar Pal, *Rabi Jibani* vol. 5 (Calcutta: Ananda Publishers, 1990), 103.
2 Ajitkumar Chakravarty, *Rabindranath o Kavya Parikrama*, rev. edn. (Calcutta: Mitra & Ghosh Publishers, 1998) 121; Chakravarty uses the Bengali term "*heynali*", which has been translated here as "enigmatic".
3 Ajitkumar Chakravarty uses the Bengali term "*adhyatma raser natya*" [mystical play] to describe *Raja*; he also uses the English appellation "soul drama" for the same play; see *Rabindranath o Kavya Parikrama*, 87, 93.

4 See Pramathanath Bishi, *Rabindra Natya-prabaha*, vol. 2 (Calcutta: Orient Book Company, 1958) 1–2; Bishi uses the Bengali term "*tattwa natya*" to brand these plays.
5 The earlier chapter has already noted how during this very period Rabindranath had invoked the cause of nation-building and had plunged into several programmes dedicated to that cause.
6 *My Reminiscences* (London: Macmillan, 1917) 238; emphases added.
7 The argument of Pramathanath Bishi is being followed here; see *Rabindra Natya-prabaha*, vol. 2, 6–11.
8 It is difficult to call them mere prose plays; the language in these is laced with a kind of poeticism that is a suitable vehicle for the larger vision they encapsulate. They have been also called 'symbolic drama', though Rabindranath was not always comfortable with this labelling: see his remarks in the explanatory note appended to *Raktakarabi*. As mentioned in n. 3 and 4 above, Ajitkumar Chakravarty classified these plays as "soul drama", while Pramathanath Bisi described this category as "*tattwa natya*" or thesis plays.
9 The English translation of the play (by Devabrata Mukherjea, with a preface by W.B. Yeats) was performed at the Abbey Theatre, Dublin, on 17 May 1913. Despite arrangements for a performance of the Bengali original at Santiniketan about eight months later, it was called off. The first performance of the Bengali play came as late as in 1917. For details, see Rudraprasad Chakrabarty, *Rangamancha O Rabindranath* (Calcutta: Ananda, 1995) 138–9; Prasantakumar Pal, *Rabi Jibani*, vol. 7 (Calcutta: Ananda, 1997) 291, 296; Biswajit Sinha, *Encyclopaedia of Indian Theatre – 5: Rabindranath Tagore*, Part I (Delhi: Raj Publications, 2003) 294.
10 See Prasantakumar Pal, *Rabi Jibani*, vol. 8, 276. In fact, no records seem to exist to show that this play was ever acted in Santiniketan within the Poet's lifetime.
11 *Visva-Bharati Quarterly*, ed. Rabindranath Tagore (14 April 1923) 1; this, in fact, was the very first number of the *Visva-Bharati Quarterly*, and this introductory announcement about Visva-Bharati, though left anonymous, may be presumed to have been written by Rabindranath himself, or, at most, by one under his close supervision. The same announcement was reprinted on the first page of the next number of *Visva-Bharati Quarterly*: July 1923 (ed. Surendranath Tagore).
12 Edward Thompson, *Rabindranath Tagore – Poet and Dramatist* (Delhi: Oxford University Press, 1948) 188; emphases added.
13 Not only the male members of the Tagore family (Satyendranath, Jyotirindranath, Gaganendranath, Abanindranath, Samarendranath, Arunendranath, Nitindranath), the women-folk of the Tagore household (Jnanadanandini, Mrinalini, Abhijna, Pratibha, Indira, amog them) also actively participated in the home productions at their Jorasanko residence.
14 According to Sudhiranjan Das, he was initiated into female impersonation with the role of Aparna (1909) and then also went on to do Malini (1910), though inadvertently he mentions *Malini* to have been performed in 1909. See Sudhiranjan Das, *Amader Santiniketan* (Calcutta: Visva-Bharati Granthalay, 1959) 84–5.
15 Sudhiranjan Das, *Amader Santiniketan*, 86–7.
16 Prabhatkumar Mukhopadhyay, *Rabindra Jibani*, vol. 2 (Calcutta: Visva-Bharati Granthalay, 1936) 315.
17 Sudhiranjan Das, *Amader Santiniketan*, 85.
18 See Rudraprasad Chakrabarty, *Rangamancha O Rabindranath: Samakalin Pratikriya*, 100.
19 "Rangamancha" ["The Theatre"] trans. Swapan Chakravorty, 99; emphases added.
20 Prabhatkumar Mukhopadhyay, *Rabindra Jibani*, vol. 2, 296.

21 See Prasantakumar Pal, *Rabi Jibani*, vol. 5, 156, 321 and 330. Unfortunately, details of the performance or the cast (of the 1906 staging) have not been located.
22 See Prasantakumar Pal, *Rabi Jibani*, vol. 5, 321 and Rudraprasad Chakrabarty, *Rangamancha O Rabindranath*, 103.
23 See Chitra Deb, *Thakurbarir Andarmahal* (Calcutta: Ananda Publishers, 1980), 263–4.
24 Santidev Ghosh, *Rabindrasangeet* (Calcutta: Visva-Bharati Granthalay, rev. edn. 1958; originally 1942) 230.
25 Santidev Ghosh, *Rabindrasangeet*, 229.
26 Prabhatkumar Mukhopadhyay seems to have made a slight error in the mention of the dates and venues. The 1922 *Varsha-mangal* was performed in Calcutta on 16 August at Rammohan Library Hall, on 17 August at Madan Theatre, and on 19 August at Alfred Theatre. See Prasantakumar Pal, *Rabi Jibani*, vol. 8 (Calcutta: Ananda, 2000) 221–2. However, Prabhatkumar's contention that boys and girls appeared together on the public stage may be acceptable on the grounds that the production in the previous year (referred to by Santidev Ghosh, see n. 26 above) was held within the precincts of the Jorasanko Tagore mansion, perhaps before a select audience.
27 See Prasantakumar Pal, *Rabi Jibani*, vol. 8, 226.
28 Ranu Adhikari played Aparna in *Visarjan*, with Manjushree Tagore playing Gunavati. In Arupratan, she mimed the role of Sudarshana while the Poet recited the dialogues; Sahana Devi sang the songs of Surangama.
29 Amita Tagore played Sumitra in *Tapati*, and was again cast as Sudarshana in *Raja*, where Nandita Devi played Surangama.
30 As reported in *Anandabazar Patrika* (13 May 1926); cited in Rudraprasad Chakrabarty, *Rangamancha O Rabindranath: Samakalin Pratikriya*, 207.
31 *Sanjeevani*, 12 Magh 1334 (B.S.) [January 1927]; cited in Dilipkumar Roy, *Rabindra samakale Rabindranataker Abhinoy* (Calcutta: Sramik Press, 1999) 159.
32 *Sanjeevani*, 17 Falgun 1334 (B.S.) [March 1927]; cited in Dilipkumar Roy, *Rabindra samakale Rabindranataker Abhinoy*, 159
33 Abanindranath Tagore, *Gharoa*, 129.
34 Parimal Goswami, *Smriti chitran* (Calcutta: Prajna Prakashani, 1958) 194; Goswami probably saw the Calcutta performance since he also mentions seeing Rabindranath play a role.
35 Nachghar, 3rd year, no. 3, 21 *Magh* 1334 BS (February 1927); cited in Dilipkumar Roy, *Rabindra samakale Rabindranataker Abhinoy*, 159
36 Gouri Bhanja, "Natir Puja 1333", transcribed by Alpana Roy Chowdhury, *Visva-Bharati News* (April 1978): 176–8; here quoted from 178.
37 *The Statesman*, of 9, 10, 11, 12 March 1936 carried this advertisement; cited in Rudraprasad Chakrabarty, *Rangamancha O Rabindranath: Samakalin Pratikriya*, 285–6.
38 *The Statesman*, 12 March 1936; cited in Rudraprasad Chakrabarty, *Rangamancha O Rabindranath: Samakalin Pratikriya*, 287.
39 *The Statesman*, 14 October 1936; cited in Rudraprasad Chakrabarty, *Rangamancha O Rabindranath: Samakalin Pratikriya*, 298; emphasis added.
40 *Anandabazar Patrika*, 8 February 1939; cited in Rudraprasad Chakrabarty, *Rangamancha O Rabindranath: Samakalin Pratikriya*, 301; emphasis added.
41 *The Statesman*, 14 October 1936; cited in Rudraprasad Chakrabarty, *Rangamancha O Rabindranath: Samakalin Pratikriya*, 298; emphasis added.
42 Jibanmoy Roy; cited in Ajitkumar Ghosh, *Thakurbarir Abhinay*, 71–2.
43 This was the '*rajchhatra*' or a kind of an umbrella held like a canopy over the heads of royal characters.
44 See Abanindranath Tagore, *Gharoa*, 133.

45 See, for instance, Biswajit Sinha, *Encyclopaedia of Indian Theatre – 5: Rabindranath Tagore*, Part I, 17.
46 Jagadananda Roy, "Smriti", *Santiniketan Patrika*, Birth Anniversary number, 1333 B.S., 1926; as cited in Pabitra Sarkar, "Abhinay, Projojona o Rabindranath", in *Manche Rabindranath*, ed. Ramkrishna Bhattacharya (Calcutta: Bharati Parishad, 1978) 19–35; here quoted from 33.

4 Theories of theatre

I

To reiterate what constitutes a primary argument of this study, if between 1900 and 1910 Rabindranath had started to imagine a new nation, he had also started to imagine a new theatre for that emergent nation. This period coincided with what seemed to be a pulling out of serious dramatic engagement for about eighteen years, between *Visarjan* (1890) and *Sarodotsav* [*The Autumn Festival*] (1908).[1] Yet, what appeared as a coincidence may be explained as a deliberate move, for, in private, Rabindranath at this point of time was rethinking his dramaturgical/theatrical configurations, rejecting the Western borrowings to which he himself had submitted in his early phase, and formulating new theories of theatre. One might even hypothesize that this temporary withdrawal from his usual hectic dramatic/theatrical activity was, in fact, a preparatory period to embark upon a new phase in his theatre career. Even as he was negotiating with new theories of nation-building, he was also theorizing about the writing and staging of plays. He was imagining a new dramaturgical model for modern Indian theatre – which, on the one hand, would break free from the appendages of the imported Western model; and, on the other, would invoke, though not replicate, the rich heritage of Indian theatre, available in both ancient classical and indigenous traditions. That his notions of an emergent nation were intertwined with his vision of a new theatre for that nation becomes evident with the publication of "Rangamancha" ["The Theatre"] in 1902,[2] where he first gives a cohesive shape to his theories of a new theatre. The significance of this date needs to be placed in proper perspective: Rabindranath sets up the *asram*-school at Santiniketan in 1901; he engages with the Bengal Partition movement in 1905; and he writes his early essays on nation-building during this period, with "Swadeshi samaj" appearing in 1904.

Unfortunately, Rabindranath has left us with only a handful of writings in which he enunciates his theories of theatre. The 1902 "Rangamancha" is, of course, his seminal tract on theatre. In this essay he criticizes the conventions of Western naturalistic theatre, especially the painted scenery, and promotes in its stead the staging principles of the Indian *jatra*, which employs a more suggestive performance idiom:

> I like our jatra for this very reason. Its performance does not maintain a strict distance between spectator and actor. They trust and help each other and the job is done well in a cordial setting. Assisted by performance, the poetry, which is the real thing, flows over the thrilled hearts of the spectators like a fountain. The gardener-woman roams her barren garden all day in search of flowers – you do not need to cart whole trees on to the stage to demonstrate that: the entire garden should spontaneously spring to life in the gardener herself. Or else what is so special about her, and what is the purpose of having spectators sit there like wooden dummies?[3]

Rabindranath's avowed preference for *jatra* is to be read as an attempt to move away from both the colonial and the urban nature of the contemporary Bengali theatre. He envisions a "parallel theatre" that would be free from the colonial borrowings and the urban cadences.

In the prologue that he later added to his play *Phalguni*, Rabindranath brings up the debate between the '*chitrapat*' (painted scenery) and the '*chittapat*' (scene of the mind) in the exchange between the King and the Poet (given the name 'Kabisekhar' in the Bengali original):

> Very well, Poet. Off with you. Make your stage preparations.
> No, King. We are going to act this play without any special preparations. *Truth looks tawdry when she is overdressed.*
> But, Poet, there must be some canvas for a background.
> No. *Our only background is the mind. On that we shall summon up a picture with the magic wand of music.* [4]

And when, in performance, Rabindranath himself played the role of the Poet, the self and the persona spoke in the same voice, underscoring his own position.

The rejection of the Western use of painted scenery is also to be found in the preface to *Tapati* (1929), the reworked version of the 1889 *Raja o Rani*. His criticism of the use of painted scenery in particular, and of overt realism in theatre in general, is reiterated here:

> In the modern European theatre, the painted scenery is a disturbing presence, a childish attempt to capture the eye. ... In *Sakuntala*, the notion of the *tapovan* is suggested in the poetry, and that is sufficient. Because there is no painted scenery, with its exacting specifications, the viewer's imagination may be easily engaged ... In our country, during the enactment of *jatra*, overcrowding may constrict the audience accommodation but there is no blatant scenery to constrain the audience's imagination.[5]

Interestingly, through this enunciation, he invokes both traditions of Indian theatre – the ancient classical (*Sakuntala*) and the indigenous folk (*jatra*) – and uses both to bolster his case against the Western model. However,

Sukumari Bhattacharji does not feel that Rabindranath really followed the path of classical Sanskrit drama; rather, he usually betrayed a propensity to move away from the conventions of Sanskrit dramaturgy: "Later, when he returned to some ancient conventions, he deliberately deviated from the essence of the convention, transforming it to suit his own exigency."[6] However, it is possible to argue here that Rabindranath's response to ancient Sanskrit drama did not encourage him merely to replicate, but rather to assimilate; as in other spheres of influences/borrowings, here, too, he was more interested in appropriation to suit his purposes, not to reproduce blindly. Therefore, much as he admired Kalidas and Sanskrit drama, he would rework the conventions, more often than not deliberately.

II

Though "Rangamancha" is chiefly remembered for Rabindranath's attack on the Western model of the realistic theatre vis-à-vis its use of painted scenery in particular, the essay also brings to the fore several of his other concerns regarding theatre. As an extension of his proposal of setting up an Indian model against the "crude European barbarisms" of the Western realistic stage, he voices his desire to discard the illusionistic tradition of gender-specific impersonation of characters. Though he does not elaborate much, he does make a pithy remark: "It is time we rid ourselves of such crude European barbarisms as demanding that a garden must be presented by an exact painting or *female roles acted by bona fide females.*"[7] In a subsequent chapter it will be discussed how, with male students coming to study at the *asram*-school in its early years, Rabindranath had at hand a group of young boys (and, by corollary, fewer girl students). So, when he decided to cast some of the more talented of these boys in the female roles of his plays, he was, in fact, putting his theory about female impersonation (by male actors) into practice. The theoretical formula was encouraged by this theatrical exigency within the Santiniketan set-up.

In "Rangamancha", Rabindranath also makes some brief but insightful observations with regard to the role of the audience. Not only does he endorse the model of a theatre where the imagination of the audience would not be circumscribed by overt realistic appendages of the stage ("is the spectator who has come to see you perform destitute of any resources of his own?")[8], but goes on to suggest that a viewer, who is not perceptive enough,[9] should not be allowed admission, even at double the price of the ticket ("Is he a child? Is he not to be relied on for anything? If that is the case, then you should not be selling him tickets even if he pays double the rate").[10] Analysing the process of the production and reception of performance, he elucidates:

> You are not in the courtroom that you have to swear to each word. Why go to such lengths to deceive those who have come to believe and to be entertained? They have not come leaving their imagination locked away

at home. You will explain some, they will make out the rest – you have a bargain of that sort with them.[11]

In this passage, Rabindranath raises several key issues. First, he emphasizes the mimetic nature of the performance, which should not be crudely realistic or illusionistic but rather allow adequate space for the interplay of imagination. Second, he does not see the actor and/or director as the sole authority in matters of production/reception. Third, he foregrounds the role of the spectator as an active agent, whose sensitive reception of the performance empowers him/her to "read" the performance perceptively. This would also seem to indicate that he is promoting the idea of a cultural meritocracy in place of the *nouveaux riches* strata – and hence the insistence upon the sensitive viewer (*"sahriday darshak"*). Finally, he alerts us to the collective nature of the theatre experience, where performer and viewer collaborate to generate the meaning(s) of the performance. Rabindranath, in this brief essay, though in a somewhat terse fashion, is already articulating, as early as in 1902, theories of production/reception that closely resemble subsequent theories of performance, including those of reader response and/or audience reception.

III

As has been discussed at various points, Rabindranath seems to have found his own distinctive voice as a dramatist and theatre-practitioner after his shift to Santiniketan. Though 1908 may be considered to be the starting point of this phase when *Sarodotsav* [*The Autumn Festival*] appeared, one should not lose sight of the 1884 *Prakritir Pratisodh* [literally *Nature's Revenge*, though translated as *Sanyasi or The Ascetic*]. Albeit an early and somewhat immature composition, its significance lies in marking out the parameters that he will follow in his later plays – both in content and in form. Probably because of this, he devotes an entire section to explaining this play in his life story:

> Nature took the Sanyasi to the presence of the Infinite, enthroned in the finite, by the pathway of the heart. In the *Nature's Revenge* there were shown on the one side the wayfarers and the villagers, content with their home-made triviality and unconscious of anything beyond; and on the other, the *Sanyasi* busy casting away his all, and himself into the self-evolved infinite of his imagination. When love bridged the gulf between the two, and the hermit and the householder met, the seeming triviality of the finite and the seeming emptiness of the Infinite alike disappeared.
>
> This was to put in a slightly different form the story of my own experience, of the entrancing ray of light which found its way into the depths of the cave into which I had retired away from all touch with the outside world, and made me more fully one with Nature again. This *Nature's Revenge* may be looked upon as an introduction to the whole of my literary work; or rather this has been the subject on which all my writings have dwelt – the joy of attaining the Infinite within the finite.[12]

80 *Rabindranath as dramaturge and theorist*

The plays from *Sarodotsav* onwards enact this very theme, represented usually by a quest or journey that takes one from the darkness of ignorance to the light of knowledge, and thereby to a fuller comprehension of life – *Achalayatan, Raja, Dakghar, Phalguni, Muktadhara, Raktakarabi, Tasher Desh*, all follow this trajectory (to be discussed more fully in the next chapter on "Preparing the playtext"). Following the same path, *Kaler Jatra* (1932) ends with a caveat that after the onward journey is completed there will be a shift in the reverse direction; so, the wheels of the chariot (of Time) will roll on relentlessly in quest for further change, further meaning.

These plays have undergone a refashioning both in their thematic concerns and in their dramaturgical structures. Rabindranath abandons the storytelling format of plays like *Raja o Rani* and *Visarjan*, or even of *Grihapravesh* and *Bansari*. A different dramaturgical/theatrical strategy is adopted to explore the inner recesses of the human heart that may yield a more inclusive perception of the meaning of life. Motifs, symbols, metaphors, images now become the staple of his dramatic narrative; this is in tune with his preference for folk idiom which makes liberal use of these. For instance, the motif of a dark enclosed space – a cave (*Phalguni*), a dark chamber (*Raja*), a quarantined room (*Dakghar*), a mesh enveloping the palace portals (*Raktakarabi*), a regimented kingdom (*Tasher Desh*) – is played off against the motif of an open space, usually a path or a grove, along which or to which characters come and go freely. With the help of these motifs, symbols, metaphors, he unravels the diverse tales of human interaction – with Divinity, with Nature, with Man. Following Pramathanath Bishi, one may postulate that by now Rabindranath was composing "thesis plays", which explored chiefly three kinds of human relationships – with Divinity (*Raja, Dakghar*), with Nature (*Sarodotsav, Phalguni*), with fellow humans (*Raktakarabi, Muktadhara, Tasher Desh, Kaler Jatra*).[13] In many ways, *Prakritir Pratisodh* marks the beginning of this different narrative style that Rabindranath adopts in his maturer plays – both in theme and in structure. He seems to indicate as much in that section on *Prakritir Pratisodh* in *Jibansmriti* [*My Reminiscences*].

Though approaches to acting is not be the concern of this chapter and would be discussed later (in Chapter 9: "Acting the role"), it may suffice to point out here that for the performance of these plays, so inscribed with motifs and symbols, Rabindranath had to evolve a nuanced style of his own, different from the acting styles available then. In his early years, he had relied on a naturalistic approach, as a legacy inherited from contemporary stage practices. He was also aware of the two traditions of acting style then dominating the Bengali theatre – the lyrical intensity of Girishchandra Ghosh, which promoted subjective empathy, and the non-lyrical detachment of Ardhendusekhar Mustafi, which advocated a non-illusory distancing. Yet, for his mature plays, Rabindranath had to rise above these known tracks, go beyond these binaries of lyrical/non-lyrical, illusory/non-illusory, affective/objective, and evolve an approach that would enable the actor to move from the external tangible reality to an inner cerebral (perhaps even spiritual) perception. It may be said that this cerebral/spiritual perception, which went beyond either Girishchandra's intensity or Ardhendusekhar's detachment, informs Rabindranath's impersonations in his mature plays – Sanyasi (*Sarodotsav*), the blind Baul (*Phalguni*), Thakurda/Fakir (*Dakghar*) or Thakurda (*Raja*) – where actor and role were merged in a unique blend. Edward Thompson's favourite was the role of the blind Baul in *Phalguni*: "The interpretation of the Baul reached a height of tragic sublimity which could hardly be endured. Not often can men have seen a stage part so piercing in its combination of fervid acting with personal significance."[14]

IV

Rabindranath took yet another bold step as he introduced dance as a medium of theatrical expression in *Natir Puja* (1926). The play culminates in the court-dancer Srimati's final offerings to the Lord Buddha performed through a dance (to the accompaniment of a song). His contemporaries were stunned by the novelty with which the "dance of Srimati was made into a dramatic climax ... [to] constitute an entire dramatic spectacle."[15] In the final years of his career, Rabindranath was increasingly convinced that "theatre has to be a kind of dance, the rhythm of which will go hand in hand with the rhythm of the poetic text. There is nothing more ridiculous than the Western style of reciting poetry along with gross realistic imitation of everyday gestures and postures."[16] From the Far East, he was imbibing a new spirit of the dance: "I went to see the Japanese dance. It seemed like melody expressed through physical postures ... The European dance is ... half-acrobatics, half-dance ... The Japanese dance is dance complete."[17] Of the dance of Java he observed: "In their dramatic performances [he uses the term *jatra*], there is dance from the beginning to the end – in their movements, their combats, their amorous dalliances, even their clowning – everything is dance."[18] This exposure to the dance languages of the Far East inspired Rabindranath to evolve what may be termed as his notion of "theatre as dance". This change in perception was, perhaps, the result of yet another ideological shift, for Rabindranath by now was not only focusing on the East and promoting it as a better alternative to the West, but was putting together a more inclusive concept of internationalism, as a confluence of East and West.

The result of this new concept of "theatre as dance" resulted in the crop of the dance dramas of the final phase. These were very different from the early experiments with the opera towards the beginning of his career. Though he had introduced the dance of Srimati at the climax of *Natir Puja*, this final phase may be said to have begun with *Shapmochan* (1931). Pratima Devi, his daughter-in-law and one of those in charge of implementing the use of dance, once remarked: "In the days of *Shapmochan*, we tried to bring into dance an element of dramatic narrative."[19] *Shapmochan* toured not only different parts of India[20] but also Ceylon where it drew rave responses: "The whole setting was a lavish simplicity – Greek in design, Javanese in execution" (*Forward*, 27

May 1934; originally in *The Daily News of Ceylon*).[21] The enthusiasm in Ceylon was so great that not only was the dance drama staged at Colombo's Regal Theatre for five evenings – probably 11, 12, 14, 16 and 18 May 1934 – but later performed in other parts of the island nation (between 19 and 25 May), and even after the troupe returned to Colombo, three more performances had to be arranged there.[22]

However, that Rabindranath was less interested in the form of a dance *per se* and more in deploying it as a language of the theatre is attested by the accounts given by Amita Sen, who played the first Kamalika, the female lead in *Shapmochan* (1931). The day after the rehearsal at Vichitra hall in the presence of Gaganendranath, Abanindranath and others, he called her to say that he was not quite satisfied with her rendition of the song "*Sakhi, andhare, ekela ghare*" [O friend, in this dark desolate room], and then went on to enact the sequence himself:

> With his head tilted to a side and his eyes cast faraway, he started to sing, "*Jeno kaar vani kabhu kane ane* [as though the tune of one comes floating to my ear]" – his ears straining to catch the tune coming from afar. And then, in despair, he sat down on the stool, almost breaking into tears with "*kabhu ane na* [and yet it comes not]".[23]

Again, in the final moment of *Chitrangada*, when the eponymous heroine, having resumed her former shape, declares her identity to Arjuna ("*Ami Chitangada, ami rajendranandini ...*": "I am Chitrangada, I am the daughter of the king"), Jamuna Devi, in performance, with a gesture of supreme authority, embodied the image of the empowered warrior-princess:

> *No rhythm-tapping of the feet, no sway of the body in dance*, but only a subtle blend of eminence and elegance presented the fullness of Chitrangada's female identity to Arjuna. Arjuna bowed his head in reverence and humbly accepted her, "I am deeply honoured."[24]

Both these instances cited here suggest that what was being offered was less of dance, more of theatre. And this is what Rabindranath seemed to have been aspiring to achieve through his concept of "theatre as dance", which finally evolved as the full-fledged dance dramas.

However, beginning with *Shapmochan* (1931), Rabindranath seems to have experimented further with "theatre as dance"; speech was reduced to a minimum in this amalgamation of dance and theatre. The novelty of the experiment did not pass notice:

> *Shapmochan* is indeed a new creation. It is different from the other plays of Rabindranath that we have seen. First, *much of the dramatic communication remains speechless*; that is to say, it is executed through tableau ... The poet narrates the story and the actors mime in tune with his narration.

This is punctuated with songs. Second, the play *Shapmochan, from its first word to its very last, is set upon an unceasing dance pattern* ... that is why the poet chooses to call it dance-enactment.[25]

The dependence on speech grows even less in the succeeding dance dramas, as songs take over from verbal dialogue. With each of the final trio – *Chitrangada* (1936), *Chandalika* (1938) and *Shyama* (1939) – Rabindranath was remodelling an earlier version into the subsequent dance drama form: *Chitrangada* had an antecedent in the verse drama of the same name (1892); *Chandalika* in the prose play *Chandalika* (1933); and *Shyama* in the poem *Parishodh* (1936). In each of these later renditions, dance becomes the vehicle of dramatic action, while songs provide the narrative, complete with the requisite scenography. In *Chitrangada*, verbal exchanges between characters in the form of dialogue were kept to a bare minimum; the rest of the interactions were through songs and dances. During the March 1936 production of *Chitrangada*, some were left disappointed as, contrary to expectations aroused by the advertisement in *The Statesman*, "the poet himself took no active part in the play. Though he was on the stage throughout the performance and recited portions from the play."[26] From his vantage position on the stage, he spoke the dialogues of the characters. What is important is that the novelty of the dance drama form was noted and critically acclaimed:

> The form of the dance-drama "Chitra" makes it embarrassing to label it by a class-name. It is a ballet yet rebelling against its accepted conventions; it is a pageant of dances, yet its theme, dramatic elements and continuous 'story' carry it on a plane higher than recitals of thematic dances; it is a drama, but the dialogue is reduced to a minimum, and its monuments are expressed not through events and happenings but through songs and dances.[27]

In performing the prose play *Chandalika* (1933), Rabindranath had followed the style of *kathakata* [28] and recited the lines as the sole *kathak*/narrator. Subsequently, for the dance drama *Chandalika*, [29] he retained much of the colloquialism as he set to tune the lines of the source prose play.[30] Commenting on this experiment, *The Statesman* wrote: "The technique of the dance-drama in 'Chandalika' is in many ways a revival of the ancient Indian form in which the dialogue is converted into songs as background music, and is symbolically interpreted by the characters through the dances."[31] The transformation of *Parishodh* into *Shyama* was complete by 1938, and when the full-fledged dance drama was presented before a Calcutta audience on 7 and 8 February 1939 at Sree Theatre, Sajanikanta Das wrote a long appreciative review in which he conceded:

> Those who had the good fortune of witnessing last evening at Sree Theatre the dance-drama form of "Parisodh", *Shyama*, will admit that

> *the language of the body is in no way less than the language of poetry.* In reality I found the touch of genius could make everything possible. *The expressiveness of the soft bodily postures dissolved away the sense of the physical to recreate a world of cerebral perception.* [32]

Interestingly, when the dance drama *Chandalika* was performed at the Chaya Theatre, Calcutta, in March 1938, the press preview in *Anandabazar Patrika* of 18 March declared:

> *Chandalika* was performed in Calcutta about five years ago.[33] There is a difference between the nature of that performance and the present one. The appeal then was chiefly 'poetic' – the quality of the present performance is mainly 'dramatic'. For this reason perhaps the poet, in giving a new shape to *Chandalika*, has called it a 'dance drama'. The verse and prose of the entire composition has been set to tune. The induction of additional characters has increased the audio-visual potential of the play. As the combination of 'ballet' and 'opera' in the Western theatre can generate novelty, that same unique fusion of form (*rup*) and emotion (*rasa*) would be available in this dance drama.[34]

Though both "ballet" and "opera" have been referred to in this extract – with, perhaps, a not too accurate suggestion of the two modes being combined in performance – yet, in the context of Rabindranath, it would perhaps not be incorrect to suggest that if the earlier experiments (*Valmiki Pratibha* or *Kal Mrigaya* or *Mayar Khela*) are closer to the form of the opera (hence "*geetinatya*" or song dramas),[35] the later dance dramas conform more to the style of the ballet (and are, therefore, "*nritya natya*" or dance dramas). Perhaps it is because he felt his dramatic/theatrical career coming to a full circle with these dance dramas that Rabindranath seems to have been prompted to transform into this form plays that he had written earlier in other versions – the operatic *Mayar Khela* (1888) became a dance drama in 1938; the tale of *Kush Jataka*, used as the source for the prose plays *Raja* (1910) and *Arupratan* (1926), was invoked again for the dance drama *Shapmochan* (1931);[36] the verse-play *Chitrangada* (1892) was remoulded into the dance drama *Chitrangada* (1936); the prose play *Chandalika* (1933) was reworked as a dance drama in 1938; the poem "Parisodh" (1900) was set to tune and first became the "*natyageeti*" ("dramatic song")[37] *Parisodh* (1936) and ultimately the dance drama *Shyama* (1939).

V

However, even while discussing Rabindranath's perception of theatre, one needs to bear in mind that, when it came to matters of actual performance, he was never rigid or inflexible. Because he combined in himself the roles of author, actor and producer, he was ever alert to the requirements of production and reception, kept adapting his staging principles accordingly, and thus allowed his theatre to be more inclusive. So, though he had once made boys play the roles of women, as if in confirmation of his theory in the essay "Rangamancha", with an increase in the number of girl students, they were also inducted into the productions – first only in all-women plays like *Lakshmir Pariksha*[38] (1910) and *Natir Puja* (1926), but later also in performances with mixed casts, starting with the 1921 *Varshamangal* and the 1922 *Vasanta* productions.[39] By this time, mixed casting had found its way into the staging of other plays as well (verse or prose dramas): Ranu Adhikari (later Ranu Mukherjee) played Aparna in *Visarjan* (1923) and mimed the role of Sudarshana in *Arupratan* (1924)[40]; Amita Tagore played Sumitra in *Tapati* (1929) and Sudarshana in *Raja* (1935).

Rabindranath's theories of theatre generated a new theatre semiology that was able to negotiate with varied possibilities and grew increasingly more inclusive. He retained his fondness for the indigenous resources (as late as in 1929 when he is writing the preface to *Tapati*), but he also accommodated the actual staging conditions at hand – particularly as actor and producer. As his early nationalist agenda was moderated by his subsequent espousal of internationalism and cosmopolitanism, his later theatrical/dramaturgical experiments, too, make it evident that he was working towards a more eclectic kind of theatre in which a non-realistic theatre semiology (like that of the *jatra*) could inflect productions even on a realistic proscenium stage. When he staged his plays in Calcutta – whether at the Vichitra hall of his Jorasanko residence, or any other auditorium – he accepted the structure of the proscenium playhouses designed in Western style; yet, whenever possible, he tried to inscribe the performances with signs of a non-realistic theatre semiology.

So, the 1923 production of *Visarjan* at the Empire Theatre used Gaganendranath's stage decor, in which "the blood-stained temple steps, designed in Cubist fashion, dominated the stage throughout, a lurid red light marked the entrance to the Temple itself, invisible in the darkness beyond the wings."[41] Amritalal Bose, a stalwart of the contemporary stage, who saw this *Visarjan* on 25 August, wrote a long appreciative review, in *The Daily News* (4 September 1923), in which he noted: "one looked on the neutral-linted cloth before one's eyes, and imagination did the rest."[42] This seemed to confirm Rabindranath's trust in the audience to use the imagination to interpret the performance, voiced two decades earlier in "Rangamancha".

Again, for the 1935 enactment of *Raja*, he used the proscenium stage of the New Empire Theatre but gave an overtly oriental bent to the stage decor, in tune with his predilection for using Indian cultural nuances: "At one corner of the stage, set with appropriate background of a blaze of colour – of blue, red and reddish brown – there is a gate of purely oriental conception supported by four pillars – this is the simple setting within which the play was enacted" (*Amritabazar Patrika*, 12 December 1935).[43]

Rabindranath, therefore, allowed the theatre-practitioner in him get the better of his theorist self; theory, then, was fitted to serve the needs of praxis. However, by way of concluding this chapter, it may be suggested that

Rabindranath, though accepting (and even adjusting to) the available conditions of staging, was not always entirely happy with the situation. He had definite reservations for the contemporary public theatre and was actually trying to create an alternative performative space where his kind of theatre could thrive. He was, in more ways than one, envisaging an alternative/experimental/parallel theatre. On 3 June 1927, in *Nachghar*, which Hemendrakumar Roy edited, he articulated his views, portions of which may be quoted here at some length:

> The manner in which the public theatre is conducting itself hardly holds any promise. One with refined tastes and aesthetic acumen can hardly bear to remain there for long.
>
> Can no alternative theatre be established in Bengal – not for the masses – but for them who would want to relish the subtler beauty of the fine arts?
>
> In the public theatre, performances are held on several days of the week; in this alternative theatre it would not be so.
>
> In the public theatre, artists are made to act the same role in the same play day after day. The human entity is not a machine. The true artist feels constricted by this drudgery of monotony. In the alternative theatre, no one play would be made to run for long.
>
> Of course, such an alternative theatre cannot take the help of the common people. For this, a few discerning patrons are required. Surely there would be at least two hundred such people willing to pay ten rupees every month as subscription/admission price. One could also turn to other spectators for aid. That would be sufficient for the alternative theatre.
>
> The alternative theatre need not be too large in size, because its patrons would be a select few. The arrangement for seating would be first grade. This would follow the model of the "little theatre" now operating in the West.
>
> Let the public theatre cater to the populace, the alternative theatre would have nothing to do with that. The plays selected for performance here would have a deep impact on the seasoned minds of the patrons. The plays of a superior quality, discarded as unfit for the common people in the public theatre, could easily be performed here.
>
> If such a theatre is established, our desire to witness performances and to compose plays would both be invigorated.[44]

This makes it evident that though Rabindranath's theatre did emerge with a more inclusive style of production, he was forced to adjust his production style to the playing conditions at hand – specially, perhaps, in the proscenium stages, when he brought his plays to Calcutta theatres (or took them to other metropolitan theatres). Obviously, the Santiniketan set-up could not be adequately simulated at these other venues. And that would mean that he had to – willy-nilly – resort to compromises. Perhaps an innate sense of dissatisfaction kept pushing him back to Santiniketan, his primary seat for theatrical experimentations, and even while performing at other places he

Theories of theatre 87

never stopped the experimental performances at Santiniketan. It is significant that not only most of his mature plays premiered at Santiniketan, but even after performances elsewhere they would be revived again at the *asram*-school for some subsequent event.

On yet another occasion,[45] when he was in conversation with Mani Bagchi, Rabindranath is known to have reiterated his aversion for the public theatre:

> The ambience in which I was nurtured had a distinct difference from that of the professional theatre. Sisirkumar had wanted to perform with me on the public stage; I could not agree precisely because of this ... The National Theatre that you speak of was the inspiration of a particular era, represented in the image of Girishchandra. Yet I always remained aloof from this, and was never able to come close to it.[46]

The writing penned for *Nachghar* or the conversation with Mani Bagchi foregrounds, on the one hand, Rabindranath's distaste for the contemporary public stage, and, on the other, his distinct vision of an alternative/experimental theatre. It might be tempting to read in his reservation for the public theatre a certain sociocultural elitism, but that would be countered by the fact that he not only encouraged Sisirkumar Bhaduri or Ahindra Chowdhury to stage his plays, at times even revising the texts to suit their needs, but also visited the public theatres on different occasions when his plays were being staged. It is possible to argue that he was trying to generate a new cultural imaginary for the contemporary audiences, which would be conducive to the different kind of sociocultural articulation that the emergent nation would/should be envisioning. He seems to have felt that this cultural imaginary could be achieved through new experiments in an alternative kind of performative space, distinctly different from what was available at the commercial theatres following the tradition of Girishchandra. These ideas were increasingly propelling him towards his ideas of an alternative/parallel theatre that he felt was necessary for the new model of a theatre for the emergent nation.

Yet, Rabindranath also knew that though he could continue with his theatrical experiments at Santiniketan – and, perhaps, to an extent at Jorasanko – he had to accept the trappings of the commercial theatre when he had to mount his productions at the New Empire Theatre or Alfred Theatre or Madan Theatre – all highly reputed theatres in Calcutta, but all conditioned by the material determinants of contemporary theatre architecture and/or staging principles. So, even though he had to submit to this reality of production/reception, he was acutely aware of the sharp differences between the kind of fare offered in the contemporary public theatres and the kind of theatre that he was trying to shape up. This is perhaps why he yearned for a smaller/alternative space where theatrical experiments could continue uninhibited – both in the writing and staging of plays. It is significant that he notes the inability/unwillingness of the public theatres to produce plays of a literary value and tendency to give in easily to the temptations of commercial success and cheap popularity. The commercial theatres hardly bothered to battle the cultural degeneration in which it was swamped, much less to construct that cultural imaginary which would nudge the audience to grow into the "*sahriday darshak*" (the sensitive/ perceptive viewer) that Rabindranath mentions in "Rangamancha". This concern for a cultural meritocracy is, in fact, not limited to Rabindranath alone. For that matter, even the proponents of the commercial theatre lamented the degenerate state of the public theatre. No less than Girishchandra (who otherwise did not seem to be favourably disposed towards Rabindranath's plays) was aware of how this cultural erosion was swamping the theatre: "Nowadays I do not write plays but only turn in some high-strung scenes."[47] Later actor-directors like Sisirkumar Bhaduri and Ahindra Chowdhury, faced with the same dilemma, tried to salvage the situation by staging Rabindranath's plays in the commercial theatre, but their attempts ended with disastrous returns at the box office. The more discerning viewers among their contemporaries were aware that a new vista could be opened up in the Bengali theatre with the plays of Rabindranath. So, when Ahindra Chowdhury staged *Grihapravesh* in 1925 at the Star Theatre, the reviewer of *Atmasakti* was all praise: "Even ten years ago who would have thought that… a play like 'Grihapravesh' could be performed on our stage and, however small in number, an enlightened section of spectators would gain so much delight?"[48] Yet, the larger section of the audience did not take favourably to the play, and it failed commercially. These experiments did not address the popular cravings of contemporary commercial theatre, and the audience expectation in mainstream Bengali theatre was not yet ready for the progressive elements latent in Rabindranath's drama.

Not only Rabindranath but also later theatre-practitioners – like Sisirkumar Bhaduri or Sombhu Mitra or Badal Sircar – tried to create spaces for more radical/revisionist experiments in Bengali theatres; but their efforts, too, more often than not met with limited success. Although the emergence of theatre movements like the "Group Theatre" and the "Third Theatre" did achieve alternative spaces for experimental theatre in Bengal to a certain degree, these movements, too, have with the passage of time shown signs of floundering. Badal Sircar's "Third Theatre" movement, for instance, despite its early enthusiastic reception among the Bengali playgoers, seems to have gradually diminished in stature, more so after the demise of Sircar. The sustained effects of such movements and whether they would be able to withstand the test of time is yet to be seen.

Notes

1 In between appeared a few comic plays and farces, and two verse-plays – *Chitrangada* (1892) and *Malini* (1896) – neither of which was produced by him.
2 "Rangamancha" was first published in *Bangadarshan, Pous* 1309 BS (December 1902–January 1903); since this issue was published on 30 December 1902, the date referred to here is 1902. The essay was later included in *Bichitra Prabandha* [Miscellaneous Essays] and published in *Gadyagranthabali* [Prose Anthology], vol. 1, 1907. For details, see Prasantakumar Pal, *Rabi Jibani* vol. 5 (Calcutta: Ananda Publishers, 1990)103, 361–2.

3 "Rangamancha" has been translated as "The Theatre" by Swapan Chakravorty in *Rabindranath Tagore, Selected Writings on Literature and Language*, ed. Sukanta Chaudhuri (Oxford, New York & New Delhi: Oxford University Press, 2001) 95–9; here quoted from 97–8. It had been previously translated by Surendranath Tagore as "The Stage".
4 "Introduction", *The Cycle of Spring*, in Rabindranath Tagore, *Collected Poems and Plays* (Delhi: Macmillan, 2001; 1st Indian reprint 1991; originally 1936) 439–519, here quoted from 461; emphases added.
5 *Rabindra Rachanabali* (Complete Works), Centenary edition, vol. 6 (Calcutta: West Bengal Government, 1961) 1033–4; subsequently referred to as *RR*.
6 Sukumari Bhattacharji, "Sanskrit Drama and Tagore", *Rabindranath in Perspective: A Bunch of Essays* (Calcutta: Visva-Bharati, 1989) 118–126; here quoted from 119.
7 "The Theatre" ["Rangamancha"], trans. Swapan Chakravorty, 99; emphases added.
8 "The Theatre" ["Rangamancha"], trans. Swapan Chakravorty, 97.
9 The original essay uses the term "*sahriday*" (literally, one with a heart); this would indicate that he has in mind a viewer who is able to receive the performance with sensitivity and perception.
10 "The Theatre" ["Rangamancha"], trans. Swapan Chakravorty, 97.
11 "The Theatre" ["Rangamancha"], trans. Swapan Chakravorty, 97.
12 Rabindranath Tagore, *My Reminiscences*, trans. Surendranath Tagore (London: Macmillan, 1917) 237–8; see also the original Bangla passage in *Jibansmriti, RR*, vol. 10, 109.
13 Pramathanath Bishi, *Rabindra Natya-prabaha*, vol. 2 (Calcutta: Orient Book Company 1958) 6–11.
14 Edward J Thompson, *Rabindranath Tagore: Poet and Dramatist* (Delhi: Oxford University Press, 1948) 254.
15 Parimal Goswami, *Smriti chitran* (Calcutta: Prajna Prakashani, 1958) 194; Goswami probably saw the Calcutta performance since he also mentions seeing Rabindranath play a role.
16 Romain Rolland notes in his diary that on 3 July 1926, when Rabindranath was visiting him, he expressed this view of theatre; this is reported in Abantikumar Sanyal, *Kabir Abhinay* (Calcutta: Rabindra Bharati University, 1996) 49–50.
17 *Japan jatri*, *RR*, vol. 10 (Calcutta; West Bengal Government, 1961) 519.
18 *Java-jatrir patra*, *RR*, vol. 10 (Calcutta: West Bengal Government, 1961) 636.
19 Pratima Devi, *Nritya* (Calcutta: Visva-Bharati, 1948; rpt. 1965) 21.
20 For instance, Lucknow (1933), Bombay (1933), Madras (1934), Waltair (1934); the performances in Madras and Waltair were given after the troupe's return from Ceylon. For details, see for instance Dilip Kumar Roy, *Rabindra samakale Rabindranataker Abhinoy* (Calcutta: Sramik Press, 1999) 173–5.
21 Cited in Rudraprasad Chakrabarty, *Rangamancha O Rabindranath: Samakalin Pratikriya* (Calcutta: Ananda, 1995) 255.
22 See Dilip Kumar Roy, *Rabindra samakale Rabindranataker Abhinoy*, 173–4.
23 Amita Sen, "Ananda Sarbakaaje", *Balaka* Special Issue: *Natya-byaktitwa Rabindranath* [Theatre-personality Rabindranath], ed. Dhananjoy Ghoshal, 19th year, no. 29 (November 2010) 17–26; here quoted from 22.
24 Amita Sen, *Santiniketane Asramkanya* (Calcutta: Tagore Research Institute 1977) 52; emphases added.
25 *Nabasakti Patrika*, 23 *Pous* 1338 BS (8 January 1932); cited in *Rangamancha O Rabindranath: Samakalin Pratikriya*, 247. The term '*nrityabhinaya*' used in the original Bengali has been translated here as 'dance-enactment', while 'dance drama' would be the translation for '*nritya natya*'.
26 *The Statesman*, 12 March 1936; cited in *Rangamancha O Rabindranath: Samakalin Pratikriya*, 267.

27 *The Statesman*, 17 March 1936; as quoted in Prabhatkumar Mukhopadhyay, *Rabindra Jibani*, vol. 4 (Calcutta: Visva-Bharati Granthalaya, 1956; rev. 1964) 53.
28 This was an indigenous form of performance in which the *kathak* (narrator) recited the whole narrative, impersonating different roles (using voice and gesture), with his own interventions as the ubiquitous *kathak* or narrator.
29 He composed a first version of this dance drama in 1938, and a second version in 1939; this second version is now the accepted text of the dance drama *Chandalika*.
30 It was the sheer genius of Rabindranath that could weave songs out of lines like "Oke chnuo na chnuo na,chi, O je Chandalinir jhi" ["Don't touch her, she is the daughter of a Chandal"] or "Kakhan chagal tui charabi?" ["When will you tend to the flocks?"].
31 *The Statesman*, 10 February 1939, after the performance at Sree Theatre in Calcutta (9 and 10 February); cited in *Rangamancha O Rabindranath: Samakalin Pratikriya*, 271–2.
32 *Anandabazar Patrika*, 8 February 1939; cited in *Rangamancha O Rabindranath: Samakalin Pratikriya*, 301; emphases added.
33 This is possibly a reference to the recital of the prose play *Chandalika* at Madan Theatre by Rabindranath in September 1933; the songs were sung by the chorus. This was in lieu of the original plan for a full-fledged performance; see Santidev Ghosh, *Rabindrasangeet*, 161.
34 Cited in *Rangamancha O Rabindranath: Samakalin Pratikriya*, 267.
35 Rabindranath, however, drew a distinction between his "geeti natya" (song drama) and the Western opera: "It (*Valmiki Pratibha*) is not what Europeans call an Opera but a little drama set to music. That is to say, it is not primarily a musical composition." Also, though grouped under the same class, he sets apart *Mayar Khela* from *Valmiki Pratibha* or *Kal Mrigaya*: "In this the songs were important not the drama ... this was a garland of songs with just a thread of dramatic plot running through": see *My Reminiscences*, 194, 196.
36 "The *Shapmochan* narrative ['*kathika*'] is premised upon the same Buddhist tale that was the source for the play *Raja*": "Introduction" to *Shapmochan* in *Rabindra Rachabali* [Complete Works] Popular edition (Calcutta: Visva-Bharati, 1990), vol. 11, 229.
37 See *Rabindra Rachabali* [Complete Works] Popular edition, vol. 13 (Calcutta: Visva-Bharati, 1991) 205.
38 For the first performance of *Lakshmir Pariksha* at Santiniketan, in 1910, "not only were the players only girls, even the spectators were women only; no male teacher or student was allowed entry." (Prabhatkumar Mukhopadhyay, *Rabindra Jibani*, vol. 2, Calcutta: Visva-Bharati Granthalay, 1936, 296).
39 "From around this time, girls were given an equal share with boys in singing and acting.": Santidev Ghosh, *Rabindrasangeet* (Calcutta: Visva-Bharati Granthalay, rev. ed. 1958; originally 1942) 229.
40 The dialogues were all recited by the Poet himself.
41 *Visva-Bharati Quarterly*, October 1923, 309.
42 *The Daily News*, 4 September 1923; as cited in *Rangamancha O Rabindranath: Samakalin Pratikriya*, 65.
43 Quoted in *Rangamancha O Rabindranath: Samakalin Pratikriya*, 113.
44 Translated; the Bengali original has been cited in "Natyamancha samparke Rabindra-chintan" ["Rabindranath's thoughts on the Stage"], *Gandharva, Rabindranatya sankha* [Number on Rabindranath's Theatre] 1368 BS (1961): 72–3.
45 The occasion was the performance of *Raktakarabi* by the Santiniketan Asramik Sangha at Natyaniketan, arranged by Prabodh Guha, at which Rabindranath was present; Mani Bagchi, who was nudged by Guha into conversation with the Poet, unfortunately did not remember the date.

46 As recorded by Mani Bagchi in "Peshadar Rangamancha O Rabindranather Natak" ["The Professional Theatre and Rabindranath's Plays"] in *Gandharva*, Rabindranatya sankha, 1368 [Number on Rabindranath's Theatre, 1961] 82–4; here quoted from 82–3.
47 As reported by Girishchandra's contemporary Apareshchandra Mukhopadhyay, who also regretted that Bengali plays often failed to show any literary merit and mostly declined to tedious melodrama merely to arouse the spectators to clap insensibly; cited in Ramenkumar Sar, "Sadharon rangamanche Rabindranath byartho", in *Balaka*, ed. Dhananjoy Ghosal, year 19, no. 19 (November 2010): 181–8; here quoted from 185.
48 Cited in *Rangamancha O Rabindranath: Samakalin Pratikriya*, 205.

Section 3
Rabindranath as theatre-practitioner

5 Preparing the playtext

I

As a dramatist, Rabindranath weaved his playtexts around ideas or themes drawn from varied sources, ranging from actual events to dreams and epiphanies. But whatever the nature of the source, it was always refashioned to cater to his individual needs. Some of the source materials could even have been chiselled to meet certain specific purposes. Many playtexts, therefore, moved through several phases of revisions/modifications/alterations, often prompted by the need to meet such purposes – social, cultural, ideological, even theatrical.

The theme of *Rajarshi*, the source novel for the play *Visarjan*, came to him in a dream, in which he seemed to see a young girl shuddering at the sight of sacrificial blood staining the white steps of the temple:

> At this sight, intense fright, immense sorrow played upon the girl's face. She repeatedly asked her father in a pitiful voice, Father, why so much blood? The father strove to stop her. Then the girl tried to wipe the blood stains with the trail of her own saree … The story was actually about the conflict between the aggressive celebration of power and the non-violent offerings of love.[1]

Though the novel moves on to engage with several other issues when he refashions it in a dramatic form as *Visarjan*, this theme defines the central concern of the play. In fact, the stage-copy for the 1923 production, not only has the characters of Hashi and Tata (apart from that of Aparna), but even mentions the former trying to wipe out the stains of blood spilled due to the animal sacrifice.[2] The English version, *Sacrifice* (published by Macmillan in 1917) updates the thematic concerns further in the context of the First World War by dedicating the play to "THOSE HEROES WHO/ BRAVELY STOOD FOR PEACE/ WHEN HUMAN SACRIFICE/ WAS CLAIMED FOR THE/ GODDESS OF WAR."[3] The dramatic text of this play, in fact, moves through several revisions/editions (as is discussed later in this chapter).

The idea of *Malini* also suggested itself in a dream. At Tarak Palit's house in London, when, tired after a dinner party while the others were still revelling, he retired for the night and dreamt of what looked like the enactment of a drama:

DOI: 10.4324/9781003110279-6

The subject was the conspiracy of a rebellion. Of the two friends involved, one, from his sense of duty, discloses the plan to the king. The rebel is caught and brought before the king. When his final wish is granted – to embrace his friend again – he strikes him on the head with the chains that bound his hands and kills him.[4]

Malini was the earliest of his dramatic compositions to engage with Buddhist theme and/or philosophy, which were close to his heart, and to which he would return time and again.

Chitrangada, on the other hand, germinated from a thought that struck him during a train ride from Santiniketan to Calcutta:

> It was perhaps the month of *Chaitra* (March-April). Beside the rail tracks were clumps of weeds, with yellow, purple and white coloured flowers. I suddenly remembered that within a few weeks the flowers, with their colourful hues, would vanish like the mirage under the blaze of the sun. Then, as the village groves will be laden with mangoes, nature would reveal her more permanent identity with her fruitfulness. And suddenly it struck me that if a beautiful young woman feels that she has enchanted her lover's heart only with her youthful charm then she would hold her beauty at fault for depriving her of her primary worth.[5]

In trying to express this idea, he turned to the Chitrangada story of the *Mahabharata*, infusing into it the god-gifted boon of a transfiguration, a detail that is absent in the original epic.

The genesis of *Raktakarabi* had intrinsic links with the image of the red flower which the Poet saw blossoming on a green shoot that had emerged from a pile of discarded iron scraps; it seemed to hail the very spirit of life, despite the odds heaped upon it. One may recall here the letter Pramathanath Bishi received from Kshitimohan Sen, mentioning Rabindranath's views on life and death a few days before his demise; describing the "epiphany" that prompted the final naming of the play, the Poet is reported to have said:

> In front of my room some rejected iron stuff had been stacked up. A small oleander plant had been buried under that heap. Its presence went unnoticed when the iron objects were piled upon it, and it could not be recovered even when some of the garbage was removed. All of a sudden one day, from under that mess of iron heap, a beautiful oleander sapling surfaced bearing a red flower. The harsh blow seemed to have made its heart bleed, with which it emerged, bearing a smile of cordial greetings. It seemed to say, I am not dead, you could not kill me. This stirred up a sense of pain in my heart. So I could not be contented with the name *Yakshapuri* or *Nandini* for the play, but renamed it *Raktakarabi* [*Red Oleanders*].[6]

That Rabindranath was overwhelmed with a sense of death while writing *Dakghar* is attested by several letters that he wrote around that time. A letter written in the same year that he wrote the play (1911) states: "For some time I had been feeling as though Death had struck me with its final arrow and it was time for me to depart from this world. But, Death and Deathlessness are manifestations of the same Entity – the Immortal has once again touched my soul."[7] He confesses that the visit to Shilaidah (from where this letter was written) has rejuvenated him. In fact, that his obsession with death had continued even after the play was written is to be found in a letter of 1915. He writes that he was prescribed the drug Aurium for certain ailments, but this had disastrous side effects; he lists the side effects of the drug mentioned in *Materia Medica* and confirms they matched with his own:

> Melancholy, with inquietude and desire to die. – Irresistible impulse to weep. Sees obstacles everywhere. Hopeless, suicidal, desperate. Great anguish. Excessive scruples with conscience. Despair of oneself and others. Grumbling, quarrelsome humour. Alternate peevishness and cheerfulness.
> All these symptoms mentioned in *Materia Medica* may be found in me. Night and day, an urge to die seems to haunt me.[8]

Ultimately, however, he seems to have found a catharsis for this fixation with death through the writing of the play, which left him with a sense of pleasurable relief. An address that he delivered at Santiniketan on 4 *Pous* 1322 BS (December 1915) points in this direction:

> When I was writing *Dakghar* my mind was swimming in a sea of emotions …. A huge urge arose in me: Come, come away; before you go, you have to circumambulate[9] the world, you have to acquaint yourself with the joys and sorrows of people living here. At that time I was busy with work related to the school. Yet, at two or three in the night, on the dark terrace my soul seemed to spread out its wings …. I felt as though something would happen, perhaps death. I was filled with a sense of pleasure at the thought of leaving the station in a quick leap. I felt I was going from here, I was being relieved. Since He had called me so urgently, I needed to have no qualms. This call to go elsewhere, this message of death … was articulated in *Dakghar* …. I will not remain, I will go, all are moving on in joy, all are calling out to me as they go, and will I stay behind? This sorrow, this urge has to be expressed. One unacquainted with this urge may be puzzled, but one who has felt this pain within will comprehend its meaning.[10]

Though at the end of *Dakghar* Amal falls asleep (an obvious metaphor of death), with the arrival of the royal physician carrying missives from the King, the play holds out a promise of fulfilment at the end of the journey. This is also echoed in the Introduction that W.B. Yeats wrote for the English version of the play:

> The deliverance sought and won by the dying child is the same deliverance which rose before his imagination, Mr. Tagore has said, when once in the early dawn he heard, amid the noise of a crowd returning from some festival, this line out of an old village song, "Ferryman, take me to the other shore of the river." It may come at any moment of life, though the child discovers it in death, for it always comes at the moment when the 'I', seeking no longer for gains that cannot be assimilated with its spirit is able to say, "All my work is thine".[11]

This movement from darkness to light, from blindness to vision, from ignorance to enlightenment, informs his major plays mostly composed in his Santiniketan phase. This movement, in fact, was first suggested in the 1884 *Prakritir Protisodh* [*Nature's Revenge*].[12] Though not among his mature writings, this early play carves out the trajectory of movement towards final fruition that the later plays were to follow. Notably, in his autobiography, Rabindranath has an entire chapter explaining the thematic significance of this play and its impact on his entire literary career:

> This [the narrative of the play] was to put in a slightly different form the story of my own experience, of the entrancing ray of light which found its way into the depths of the cave into which I had retired away from all touch with the outside world and make me more fully one with Nature again. This *Nature's Revenge* may be looked upon as an introduction to the whole of my literary work; or rather this has been the subject on which all my writings have dwelt – the joy of attaining the Infinite within the finite.[13]

As noted earlier, the theme of a journey from darkness/ignorance to light/enlightenment is at the core of the plays beginning with *Sarodotsav* (1908). This is the quest of Upananda (*Sarototsav*), Panchak (*Achalayatan*), Sudarshana (*Raja*), Amal (*Dakghar*), the group of young men (*Phalguni*), the oppressed subjects in the kingdom of Ranajit (*Muktadhara*), both the common miners and the King of Yakshapuri (*Raktakarabi*), the regimented card-people in card-land (*Tasher Desh*); in this quest, their more enlightened fellow-humans usually come to their aid – Sannyasi/Emperor Vijayaditya (*Sarodotsav*), Dadathakur (*Achalayatan*), Thakurda and Surangama (*Raja*), Thakurda/Fakir (*Dakghar*), the blind *baul* (*Phalguni*), Abhijit and Dhananjoy Bairagi (*Muktadhara*), Nandini and Bishu (*Raktakarabi*), the Prince (*Tasher Desh*).

With his adroitness to rework old themes in new formats, Rabindranath recast the idea of the revenge of nature to serve the requirements of the comedic genre in a play like *Chirakumar Sabha*. This comedy was originally serialized in *Bharati* as a farcical story (1901–3), which was subsequently published in *Rabindra Granthabali* (September 1904); then it was reworked into a novel, *Prajapatir Nirbandha* (1908), which exuded a dramatic flavour in the dialogues; finally, it was redone as a full-fledged comic drama, and its initial title reinstated (this final version being written in 1925 and published in 1926). If the hermit of *Prakritir Pratisodh* had transgressed the dictates of nature in isolating himself from the usual human ties, the bachelors' club of this comic play is similarly set up to evade marital bondings, in a gross violation of the ways of nature. This only helps to promote incongruities that ultimately cannot but surrender to the instinctive attraction between the sexes.

With *Sarodotsav* (1908), Rabindranath embarked upon a new phase of his dramaturgical career, both as playwright and practitioner; in this play not only did he eschew the Western modes of writing and staging plays, but he also introduced Nature as a major protagonist. It may be recalled here that his younger son, Samindranath, along with some enthusiastic friends, had, on 17 February 1907, staged a *Ritu Utsav* (a celebration of the seasons) at Santiniketan. Three students, including Samindranath, impersonated *Vasanta* (Spring), one student dressed as *Varsha* (Monsoon) and two others as *Sarat* (Autumn); plentiful use of flowers marked the stage decor, costumes and properties.[14] Rabindranath was away from Santiniketan then, but must have received reports of the event. According to Kshitimohan Sen, Rabindranath, on a rainy evening in 1908 (some eight/nine months after Samindranath's untimely demise in November 1907 at Munger) talked about the need to invoke the close bond between Man and Nature: "If we are able to experience each of the seasons of Nature within ourselves, we would be able to remove our failings and enrich our hearts … What would it be like if we were to celebrate each season in a new fashion?"[15] Prompted by his words, Kshitimohan and the other teachers at Santiniketan organized a *Varsha Utsav* (celebration of monsoon) with songs, readings and recitations in August 1908.[16] Unfortunately, during this programme, too, Rabindranath was not present in Santiniketan due to commitments at Shilaidah and Patisar. However, on returning to the school, he decided to arrange an event to celebrate the coming of autumn (*Sarat*). What started out as a series of songs soon congealed into the dramatic form of the new seasonal play *Sarodotsav* (translated later as *The Autumn Festival*).[17] To borrow the words of Kshitimohan Sen, "In the monsoons, the earth seeps in abundant waters from the skies; in autumn, decked in beauty and plenty, it repays its debts. This idea had then overwhelmed Gurudev and constituted the kernel of *Sarodotsav*."[18] The idea finds an echo in the name used for the reworked version of the play – *Rinsodh* [Debt Repayment] (1921). Interestingly, before the performance of *Sarodotsav*, Rabindranath wanted to add a Sanskrit invocation (*Nandi*), and requested Bidhusekhar Shastri for this. Charuchandra Bandyopadhyay, who was present, suggested that the dramatist himself should compose the invocation. Thereupon, excusing himself for half an hour, Rabindranath came back armed with a new poem and a new song, even set to tune ("Tumi naba naba rupey eso praane"), and these were used for the performance.[19] Another seasonal play followed in 1915 – *Phalguni* (The Cycle of Spring) – where the cycle of seasons and the cycle of human life were blended together. In fact, celebration of seasons soon became a regular feature at Santiniketan, whether as drama or in other performative/festive modes – *Varsha-mangal* [Benediction of the Rains], *Sesh*

Varshan [Farewell to Monsoon], *Vasantotsav* [Festival of Spring], *Rituranga* [Drama of Seasons], and even *Pous Utsav* [Festival of Winter]. The last-mentioned event had specific religious overtones because it commemorated the day of initiation (*diksha*) of his father, Maharshi Devendranath. But, with the other seasonal festivals, the purpose of celebration was increasingly becoming secularized. While on earlier occasions, people generally gathered together to observe religious festivals and rituals, Rabindranath was bringing people together through community celebrations of the seasons – largely secular in character. It is interesting to note how he was gradually effecting a change in this direction, which held significant socio-cultural nuances.[20]

II

For the stories and/or themes of his plays, Rabindranath is known to have rummaged diverse sources – ranging from the Indian epics, the *Ramayana* and the *Mahabharata*, to the Buddhist tales of *Jataka*, to popular beliefs and folk rituals concerning the vegetative myth and the cycle of seasons.

Buddhist sources figure prominently in several of his plays, providing primarily the narrative but sometimes also the spirit of non-violence and self-sacrifice. This is notably present in the early *Malini* (1896) and the late *Natir Puja* (1926), the latter being a dramatization of the poem "Pujarini" that appeared in *Katha* (1900); both exude the Buddha's teachings of love and sacrifice, and refer to characters related to Buddhist history, though not directly borrowed from the tales of *Jataka*. For many of the plays, a primary source was Rajendralal Mitra's *The Sanskrit Buddhist Literature of Nepal* (1882). From this source, he borrows the story of *Kusha-jataka* for *Raja* (1910)/*Arupratan* (1920) as well as the later dance-drama *Shapmochan* (1931). Kusha, whose ugly looks initially repel his queen, Sudarshana, is ultimately accepted and loved by her after his transformation through supernatural intervention that helps him to use a jewel to remove his ugliness and make him handsome. With Rabindranath, of course, the "jewel" becomes the jewel of inner worth, a comprehension of which removes all darkness/ugliness/ignorance; the significance is made more explicit in the title used for the revised version – *Arupratan*, "the Formless Jewel". For *Achalayatan* (completed in June 1911), he uses the "Story of Panchaka", included as part of the *Divyadanamala* in Rajendralal Mitra's book. However, using traces of the original tale, Rabindranath refashions it to posit a conflict between the need for regulations and the constricting effects these may produce if used in excess.[21] Again, for *Chandalika* (prose drama: 1933; dance drama: 1938) he goes back to *Sardulkarnavadana* available in Rajendralal Mitra. Here, the historical Ananda, a foremost disciple of Buddha, makes his appearance to enlighten the social outcast Prakriti with the message of love and equality. For the narrative poems "Pujarini" and "Parisodh", both included in *Katha* (1900), and their respective dramatic forms as the prose play *Natir Puja* (1926) and dance drama *Shyama* (1939), he delves into Buddhist sources again. Of the Indian epics, he resorts to various episodes of the *Mahabharata* for plays like *Chitrangada* (verse-drama:1892; dance drama: 1936) and playlets like *Gandharir Abedan* (1897), *Karna-Kunti Samvad* (1900)[22] or *Viday Abhishap* (1912)[23], while his creative genius reconstitutes the myth of the *Ramayana* into a modern myth relevant for contemporary concerns in *Raktakarabi* (1924).

What is most striking is the way Rabindranath makes use of the original sources to suit his personal/aesthetic requirements. His versions are always infused by the power of his own myth-making. Thus he takes liberties with the story of "Chitrangada", as available in the *Mahabharata*, and recreates a myth of his own. The original Chitrangada was a fair princess to start with, and Arjuna wanted her as his bride precisely for her beauty; he had only to acquiesce to her father's condition that his child by her would be the ruler of that land (Manipur). Chitrangada of the *Mahabharata* did not have to plead with the gods to transform her ugliness into fairness, even if temporarily, to gladden the eyes of Arjuna. With this twist, Rabindranath gives the narrative a different signification altogether, and out of the innocuous legend weaves a tale of carnal desire and eroticism that finally culminates into companionable love.[24]

The concept of a vegetative myth, based on the cycle of seasons, seems to be instilled into the theme of his seasonal plays, like *Sarodotsav* or *Phalguni*. If the primitive vegetative myth was based upon the idea of a vegetative god – supposedly born in spring, reaching primehood in summer, maturing in autumn, dying in winter, only to be reborn in the next spring – then Rabindranath's seasonal plays project a journey towards a realization of this order, not only encapsulated in the cyclic pattern of the seasons but even in the greater order that defines and regulates life. As has been suggested above, a ceaseless quest for the Eternal/Infinite/Truth informs not only the seasonal dramas but also plays like *Raja, Dakghar, Achalayatan, Muktadhara, Raktakarabi, Tasher Desh* or *Kaler Jatra*. This theme of a passage from darkness/ignorance to light/enlightenment works in most of these plays with the help of two major leitmotifs – one, an enclosed space; second, an open path or road. The enclosed space – a cave (*Phalguni*), a dark chamber (*Raja*), a walled-in institution (*Achalayatan*), a sick-room of the infirm (*Dakghar*), a net before the king's palace threatening to devour all (*Raktakarabi*), a regimented kingdom of the card people (*Tasher Desh*) – is hemmed in by the delimiting constrictions of ignorance and/or repression. By contrast, the path or road – with its expansive openness – promises a journey towards enlightenment and emancipation. The contrast between these two motifs informs the dramatic progression in all these plays, and was already made available in an embryonic form in the early *Prakritir Pratisodh*.

Rabindranath's myth-making potentials perhaps reach a crescendo in *Raktakatabi*, which, by his own accounts, looks back to the *Ramayana*. In the explanatory passages he has later added as appendices to the text of the play, there are repeated references to his reading of the *Ramayana* and his application of this reading to his own creation:

> We might suddenly feel that the Ramayana is an allegory, more so when we realise that the names Rama and Ravana signify opposite meanings.

Rama connotes comfort, peace, while Ravana is clamour, turbulence. In the one, there is the beauty of the green, the soft lilt of the foliage; in the other, there is the crazy siren of the demonic chariot speeding down the paved roadway.[25]

He elucidates the nature of power wielded by the King of Yakshapuri, and the acquisitive system of exploitation that he has unleashed:

There is a king in my drama. Writing in the present times, I did not have the courage to equip him with more than one head or two hands. Had I the nerve of the ancient poet, I would have done so. The powers of science and technology have added innumerable but invisible hands, feet and heads to the human entity. That the king of my drama extracts and devours by such excessive powers is indicated in the play.[26]

But he also goes on to hint at the schizophrenic schism within this power-system; the self-contradiction in the King pulls him in opposite directions that would bring about the inevitable collapse:

The ancient poet had no dearth of room in his seven chapters. So he allotted separate spaces to Ravana and Vivisana. Yet, he did hint that they were the same, brothers born of the same womb. The same locale has nurtured both sin and its destructive agent. In my terse play, the representative of Ravana is both Ravana and Vivisana, rolled into one; he destroys himself ultimately.[27]

Even as the myth of the ancient *Ramayana* is played out through the reconstituted myth of *Raktakarabi*, it also becomes inflected with significations derived from related mythical/legendary origins. Notably, the region is given the name of *Yakshapuri*.[28] The *Yaksha*, in Indian mythical sources, was a follower of *Kubera*, the god of acquisitive wealth, which was hoarded and accumulated, not fruitfully spent. The system of aggressive acquisition at *Yakshapuri*, initiated by the King and perpetrated by the Governors, re-invokes Rabindranath's image of the European Nation-State, constructed mainly in the negative. The exploitative and organized state power at Yakshapuri transforms humans into automatons, the "neatly impressed bales of humanity"[29] that Rabindranath referred to in a different context. When Nandini is horrified by the show of men reduced to mere shadows – "the King's leavings"[30] – the Professor clarifies the *modus operandi* of exploitation in Yaksha Town: "These small ones are consumed to ash, that the great ones may leap up in flame. This is the principle underlying all rise to greatness."[31] It is precisely against this oppression that Nandini and Ranjan (even through his absent-presence)[32] voice their protest, and finally persuade the King to tear apart his web and join in the fight against the system, which by then has gone beyond his control. The laws of *Kubera* are in sharp contrast to those of *Sree* or *Lakshmi*, the goddess of plenitude and abundance that breeds prosperity and welfare for all. His experiences of acquisitive capitalist societies had compelled Rabindranath to comment: "*Lakshmi* is of a kind, *Kubera* of another – the difference is vast. The inner essence of Kubera is acquisition, which leads to amassing of wealth."[33] This very contrariness between *Kubera* and *Lakshmi* informs the making of the playtext of *Raktakarabi*.

III

Rabindranath often kept coming back to the same story, though effecting changes in the narrative pattern. Some of the plays, therefore, move through multiple versions/editions, betraying his dissatisfaction with the last-rendered version. He kept revisiting the same work, making changes – of varying degrees – to the narrative. He reworked two of his novels, *Rajarshi* (1887) and *Bouthakuranir Haat* (1883) as tragic dramas, *Visarjan* (1890) and *Prayaschitta* (1909) respectively; of the former, multiple versions exist in several drafts and manuscripts, while the latter was further refashioned as *Paritran* (1929). The verse-drama *Chitrangada* (1892) and the prose drama *Chandalika* (1933) were reincarnated as dance dramas, the first in 1936, the other in 1938. He kept recycling the *Kushajataka* tale not only as *Raja* (1910), with its several renditions, but as its subsequent abridged "actable" version, *Arupratan* (1920), as well as in the form of the dance drama *Shapmochan* (1931). The fantasy in the short story, *Ekti Ashare Galpo*, was given a distinct sociocultural mooring in *Tasher Desh* (1933). In this context, we may recall what Rathindranath had to say about his father's penchant for revisions: "Father's creative mind could never find pleasure in repetition. Invariably he would make alterations and additions to the plays whenever they were about to be performed."[34] Admittedly, as Rathindranath suggests, often such revisions/modifications were made for theatrical exigencies. However, one is also left with the impression that there were times when the author in Rabindranath seemed to have been discontented and felt that a play was in need of further refashioning, for reasons not merely dramaturgical and/or theatrical. These factors – singly or even together – could be the cause for some of these plays running into several versions.

On several occasions, Rabindranath himself has made out cases for more "actable" structures through the revisions made. So, the preface of *Tapati* (1929) declares that the need to make *Raja o Rani* (1889) more "actable" through "abridgement and revision" resulted in the new play.[35] Similarly, *Arupratan* (1920) is supposed to be "a terser" and more "stageworthy" recension of *Raja* (1910), as again announced in the preface.[36] For similar reasons, *Achalayatan* (1912) became the shorter *Guru* (1918); *Sarodotsav* (1908) was reworked into *Rinsodh* (1921); *Prayaschitta* (1909), itself a dramatized version of the novel *Bouthakuranir Haat*, became *Paritran* (1929), though in between there appeared a radical reconstruction in *Muktadhara* (1922), where some of the thematic concerns and at least one major character (Dhananjoy Bairagi) had been retained. Presumably at the request of Sisirkumar Bhaduri, *Goray*

Galad (1892) was given an improved rendition in *Sesh Raksha* (1927); Sisirkumar produced the new version for Natyamandir on 14 September 1927.

Yet, theatrical necessities alone do not always explain Rabindranath's near-obsessive reworkings with the same play. The early *Raja o Rani*, despite being one of the most revised playtexts, still left the author with a sense of discontentment on several counts – the irrelevance of the Kumar-Ila subplot, the unwieldy length of the play, the dependence on the European model and the excessive lyricism of the blank verse used.[37] In the very second edition of the play (1894) Rabindranath discarded no less than thirteen scenes of the first edition of 1889. A third version, which found place among a collection of his works (1896), brought back all but three scenes, and became the base for the authorized text that appeared in Visva-Bharati's *Rabindra Rachanabali* [Complete Works] of 1939. There had also appeared an intermediary version as *Bhairaber Bali* (1929),[38] as well as the English translation *The King and the Queen* (1916). Still dissatisfied, Rabindranath chose to rewrite the play afresh, ridding it of many of the problems of the earlier version and replacing blank verse with prose; this resulted in what was virtually a new play, *Tapati* (1929).[39]

Again, *Visarjan* (based upon the earlier section of his novel, *Rajarshi*), though written first in 1890, moved through several major revisions that even went into print – in 1896, 1899 and 1926. When he decided to stage the play in 1923, he recast the text in a major fashion with performance in mind. A stage-copy, revised and edited by Rabindranath, and preserved at the Rabindra Bhavana archives, points to these revisions.[40] The several scenes of the original five-act structure were strung together to emerge as three dramatic phases (with suggestions for intermissions between the phases).[41] For instance, what constituted three separate scenes in the original text – Raghupati's aborted attempt, in collusion with Nakshatraroy, to sacrifice Dhruva before the goddess; the trial of Raghupati and Nakshatra by Govindyamanikya in his court; Raghupati's pleadings with Joysingha (at the temple) not to fail his cause – are run together as one scene in the revised version prepared for performance. Also, it has been said that there was a version in which Rabindranath omitted the role of Aparna and kept Gunavati as the only female character.[42] Again, as late as in 1936, he rewrote the play in simple prose and dispensed with all the women characters – presumably for a performance by young male students. And, for the English *Sacrifice* (1917), he replaced the blank verse with prose and condensed the five acts of the original into one continuous scene. Scholars are of the opinion that, "Tagore was trying his best in his advanced years to bring *Visarjan* in line with the style of his later works."[43]

Raja was written in 1910, the same year as *Gitanjali*, when he was relaxing at Shilaidah; he is believed to have started writing this play possibly at the request of the inmates of the *asram*-school.[44] What has been identified as the earliest draft is manuscript 143 at the Rabindra Bhavana archives at Santiniketan. Recent textual scholarship has revealed that "(t)he complexity of textual changes in ms 143 is such that at places one can find four to five different layers of deletion and insertion. The restlessness in the process of creation revealed through these changes suggests that this manuscript is the first draft."[45] Yet, this first draft (ms 143) was quickly revised, and the revised version has been identified as ms 148 (also available in Rabindra Bhavana archives). A major change was the transposition of the order of the first two scenes: the first draft (ms 143) begins with the Dark Chamber, while Thakurda, with his followers, appears in the second scene; in the second draft (ms 148), the order has been reversed, so that Thakurda comes in the first scene and the Dark Chamber becomes the second scene. The revised version (identified as ms 148) went into print in 1911, being published on 6 January 1911 in Calcutta by the Indian Publishing House, the Calcutta branch of the Indian Press, Allahabad.[46] However, he went back to the earlier draft and incorporated elements from the first manuscript – in particular, he transposed the order of the first two scenes (having reversed them once already from the first to the second draft). With the original scene order (of ms 143) restored (so, the first scene was the Dark Chamber; the second scene had Thakurda's entry with his followers), this later revised version became the text for the second edition that appeared in print first in *Kavyagrantha*, volume IX, in 1916, from Indian Press, Allahabad. He added to this edition an "Author's Note" which read:

> The first manuscript of this play, *Raja*, written in my notebook, was somewhat pruned and revised when it went into print. Suspecting that this could perhaps have caused some harm [to the play], the present edition is being printed based upon that original text.[47]

That he had misgivings about the reception of this symbolic play is evident from his remarks made to his contemporaries. A letter to Charuchandra Bandyopadhyay, dated 17 *Kartik* 1317 BS (3 November 1910), betrays some of his misapprehensions:

> It would be a bit strange – some would say "good", others "poor", while still others would not know how to respond, good or bad. Overall, three-fourths would conclude that Rabibabu's literary powers are declining with age. I do not deny the possibility. The quality of power is ever changing. If God wills to preserve the vigour, the change will be fruitful.[48]

Such anxieties may have prompted him to return to this play again and again, till he made a drastically shortened (and, arguably, a more "actable"[49]) version of it in *Arupratan* (1920). One of the primary concerns of this revision seems to have been to emphasize the formlessness of the King even further. By reassigning the dialogues of the King (in *Raja*) chiefly to Surangama in the revised text of *Arupratan*, even the vocal 'presence' of the King is reduced to a bare minimum. There were further attempts to rewrite *Arupratan*, in 1932 and again in 1935. The second edition, printed in 1935, is vastly different from the first edition, and this is the text of *Arupratan* currently in circulation.

Yet, that he could not ignore *Raja* entirely is made evident from a reprint of the 1916 second edition on 12 April 1921,[50] that is *after* the emergence of *Arupratan*.

106 *Rabindranath as theatre-practitioner*

In fact, that the 1921 version is a repetition of the 1916 version (published in *Kavyagrantha*, volume IX), complete with the "Author's Note" that had been affixed to the 1916 text, has been pointed out in recent textual scholarship.[51] That he was reworking on the play again is evident from the comments of various contemporaries. From the entry in the diary of Prasantachandra Mahalanobis (dated 5 August 1932) we get to learn that Rabindranath "is re-writing Raja, on an exercise book (of Japanese-made paper with two pages bound together). He has covered more than 80 pages, till the conversation between Sudarshana and Raja after the fire incident. On reading it, I found a lot of changes."[52] Sudhir Chandra Kar confirms that "the Poet had started writing the play Raja afresh" but the manuscript went missing from his desk; he cites Krishna Kripalani to suggest that the Poet himself might have gifted it to his daughter, Mira.[53] More interestingly, that he conflated *Raja* and *Arupratan* for the 1935 performance in Calcutta at New Empire Theatre is attested by a letter:

> A play has emerged combining *Arupratan* and *Raja*. I am busy now with its production related work. The performance will be in Calcutta, perhaps around 15 December. I shall perform on the stage as Thakurda. From the caverns of scarcity is echoing the need for material gains. So, in the guise of the thespian, I will have to hold out my bowl for alms.[54]

Though this conflated version does not seem to have gone into print, yet this was the playtext that Rabindranath had prepared for what was his final stage rendition – the 1935 Calcutta performance. Significantly, this performance was advertised in the dailies as a performance of *Raja*:

> THE FIRST PERFORMANCE IN CALCUTTA OF
> TAGORE'S FAMOUS PLAY
> IN AID OF VISVA-BHARATI
> RAJA
> AT
> THE NEW EMPIRE FOR TWO DAYS ONLY
> TO-DAY AND TOMORROW
> WEDNESDAY, the 11th Thursday, the 12 December
> Both Shows at 6 P.M...[55]

Also, the cast-list printed on this occasion, mentions on its cover-page:

> Raja
> By
> Students of Santiniketan
> New Empire Theatre
> Wednesday, The 11th and the 12th December Calcutta 1935.[56]

These evidences, therefore, contradict the generally held view that having reworked *Raja* as *Arupratan* (the later version of the play), Rabindranath did not ever return to the earlier version. The conflation of the two texts for this public performance (one of the very last in which he took part as actor and director) and its having been billed publicly as *Raja*, shows that Rabindranath was not able to either forget or abandon *Raja* and made a return to it as late as in 1935 for the New Empire performance.

The textual history of *Raktakarabi* (1926, though it was first serialized in *Probasi* in 1924) is no less fascinating. There are no less than ten extant manuscripts available.[57] Some of the author's correspondences seem to indicate that it was initially conceived as *Yakshapuri*,[58] but then briefly took on the name of *Nandini* in the fourth and fifth drafts[59], and finally – from the eighth draft[60] – became *Raktakarabi* when the red oleander flower became the central motif.[61] Earlier in this chapter the letter of Kshitimohan Sen has been mentioned in which he alluded to Rabindranath's reference to the red flower at the tip of the sapling that emerged from under the pile of iron scraps which inspired him to make the red oleander the primary symbol and rename/rework the play accordingly. Also, the first draft names the heroine as "Khanjani"; the second draft starts with this name but then cancels it to introduce the name "Nandini", while also toying with a third name "Sunanda". Subjected to a relentless process of revisions and modifications, the play exists now in no less than ten surviving versions,[62] apart from the English auto-translation, *Red Oleanders*.

Tasher Desh was the refashioning of the short story *Ekti Ashare Galpo* (1892) – almost fairy-tale in nature – reportedly at the request of Pratima Devi.[63] Originally composed in 1933, the play was radically revised by 1939.[64] After its early staging in Calcutta (on 12, 13 and 15 September 1933 at Madan Theatre), it was taken for performance (along with *Shapmochan*) to Bombay at the invitation of Sarojini Naidu. On 27 and 28 September 1933, when the play was given at the Excelsior Theatre of Bombay, the reception was cold; this was presumably because the prose dialogues failed to communicate adequately with the audience comprising primarily viewers who did not follow the Bengali language. On 30 November, Rabindranath wrote to Pratima Devi:

> On the third day was *Tasher Desh*. The thermometer dropped to subnormal. I felt disheartened. The problem was quickly addressed by introducing new songs and dances. ... The new *Tasher Desh* is more attractive than *Shapmochan*. The intermixing of romance and realism has done wonders in ensuring its success.[65]

It is believed that Sarojini Naidu advised the Poet to redesign the play with more songs and dances for the benefit of the Bombay audiences, and the Poet is said to have worked on the play overnight, adding more songs for the performance the next evening.[66]

Such additions of songs and reduction/revision of prose dialogues presumably continued till the revised second edition surfaced in 1938. But this change radically affected the character of the play with its customary presentation in subsequent stage history more as a dance drama, or at least a musical, with little or no importance given to the prose dialogues. Yet, on closer scrutiny, *Tasher Desh* appears to belong to the same category as Rabindranath's other prose plays like *Raja, Muktadhara* or *Raktakarabi*, where the interspersed songs not only add to the dramatic situation but often function as extensions of the dialogue as well. That it was originally envisaged as a prose play is further borne out by the fact that Rabindranath himself referred to it as a *"natika"* (play or playlet) in the dedication to Subhaschandra, prefixed to the revised version of 1939.[67] In the centenary edition of the Complete Works [*Rabindra Rachanabali*] published by the West Bengal Government, it has been published as a "prose play" in Volume 6. The Visva-Bharati Complete Works also groups it with other prose plays like *Chandalika* and *Bansari*, reserving the dance dramas (*Nrityanatya Chitangada, Nrityanatya Chandalika* and *Shyama*) for a different volume. Interestingly, the reviews of its early production in Calcutta in September 1933 refer to it as "a burlesque composition" (*Nabasakti*, 22 September 1933), "a sort of burlesque in which some serious ideas are dramatized in the form of a comedy" (*The Advance*, 12 September 1933), or even "a seemingly comic play, but in reality bearing the poet's harsh satire and whiplash of ridicule directed at the 'death-in-life' state of this land and society" (*Anandabazar Patrika*, 13 September 1933), but never as a musical or dance drama.[68] It may also be argued that, as in *Muktadhara* or *Raktakarabi*, the prose dialogues of this play, too, serve an important polemical purpose, which stands the risk of being subordinated – even blunted – by the overuse of songs and dances if the play is performed as a musical/dance drama. In fact, the political nuances of the play became even more pronounced when its second edition of 1939 was dedicated to Subhaschandra Bose: "You have undertaken the sacred vow to instil new life into the heart of the nation. Bearing that in mind, I dedicate the play *Tasher Desh* in your name."[69]

Around this time, he had written the second "Deshnayak" essay (1939),[70] which was addressed to Subhaschandra, and which started with these words: "I am a Bengali poet; on behalf of Bengal I bestow upon you [*"baran kori"*, in the original] the role of the *deshnayak* (leader/hero of the land)."[71] Continuing the stance of an address to Subhaschandra, the author makes an implicit call to his fellow-citizens to confer upon Subhaschandra this leadership: "Let the collective will of the Bengali people accept you as their leader; let that will mould you in the shape appropriate for that onerous responsibility."[72] Even as in the fictionalized world of the card-land, the card-people collectively chose to follow the leadership of the Prince, here, too, the *samajpati* is to be selected from among the people, by the collective will of the people. Rabindranath's narration of the nation had made a journey from "Swadeshi samaj" to "Deshnayak", via the fiction of *Tasher Desh*, and the critical discourse of "Rangamancha". The representation of the play as a mere musical or dance drama in present-day practice has done serious harm

Preparing the playtext 109

to its innate polemical potentials and blurred the political vision of the author.

This political vision, in fact, has often informed the making of Rabindranath's playtexts, particularly in his later career. If not overtly, there have been distinct attempts to anchor the writing of a play within a contemporary social/economic/political/cultural matrix. His increasing awareness of how the menace of materialist exploitation (often in the name of scientific/technological progress) ultimately leaves the human identity seriously impaired has been addressed in plays like *Muktadhara* (1922) or *Raktakarabi* (1924). After both *Muktadhara*, and its English translation *The Waterfall*, had been published, he wrote to Kalidas Nag in May 1922: "In your letter you have referred to a discussion on the machine; that machine plays a vital role in this play …. Those who use the machine to hurt others meet with disastrous consequences themselves because the humanity they assault is also in them; their very machines impair the human within themselves."[73] The *Ramayana* myth has been recycled in *Raktakarabi* to critically evaluate the modern acquisitive materialist society of *Yakshapuri*. As mentioned earlier, his experience of America had sharpened his awareness of the contrast between the worlds of Lakshmi and Kubera:

> For seven continuous months I had resided in the monstrous palace of wealth in America. I do not say 'monstrous' in a negative sense; perhaps in English one would say 'Titanic wealth' – the wealth of formidable power, immense magnitude. Every day I would sit at the window of the hotel, under the frown of the thirty thirty-five storied buildings. *And I would say to myself, Lakshmi is of a kind, Kubera of another – the difference is vast. The inner essence of Kubera is acquisition, which leads to amassing of wealth. There is no end to this amassing. Two into two is four, four into two is eight, eight into two is sixteen – the calculations leap on like a frog; and the range of the leaps keep growing.* [74]

Against this acquisitive world of Kubera (encapsulated in *Yakshapuri*), he posits the prosperity and plenitude of Lakshmi or *Sree* (grace/elegance), represented chiefly by Nandini in the play. The analysis given above has tried to underscore the ideological assumptions that underlie the play.

When, at the request of Pratima Devi, he took to reshape the poem "Pujarini" into a full-length play, *Natir Puja*, he was already disturbed by the uncontrolled communal violence and religious intolerance that had gripped Bengal and other parts of the country. In fact, the writing of the play provided him with an opportunity to articulate his anxieties and summon the spirit of peace and harmony in a world torn asunder by internecine fratricide. On 21 April 1926, at a prayer-meeting in Santiniketan, he lamented:

> We are supposedly a religious-minded race. Is this the reason why we see today bestial instincts raging all around in the name of religion? One is

killing another brutally, like wild animals, invoking the name of god. Is this the face of religion? Rather than such intoxicated fanaticism, it would be better to embrace all-out atheism. What we see around us today is a god-forsaken bestiality parading in the garb of religion. If India were to be truly born anew, she would need to consume to ashes such false religions and regain the true faith of her religious conviction. It seems that the only way open before us is to burn away all these false creeds in the flames of atheism and start afresh.[75]

While Rabindranath was deeply disturbed to find his country torn by such destructive fanaticism and fratricide, when he visited Russia (in 1930) he was excited to find constructive socio-economic-cultural changes there. Most importantly, he felt the changes had embraced all classes of the Russian society. Much of his responses were articulated in *Russiar Chithi* [*Letters from Russia*]. He was all praise for the Russian people for their success in dismantling age-old traditions: "Tradition occupies the inner recesses of the human mind in a thousand different ways with its labyrinthine chambers and close-guarded doors, levying taxes to increase its own coffers. They (the Russians) have uprooted it from its very base, without any fear or doubt or scruple."[76] He was particularly impressed to find that "those who were left totally immobile have sprung to motion",[77] so that even the downtrodden sections of the society, now empowered with education, were marching ahead: "Had I not seen with my own eyes I would have hardly believed that within a matter of ten years they have raised thousands from the lowest rungs of society, so long deprived of learning and dignity, not only to gain education but to be respected as humans."[78] He had already expressed his disgust for the materialist acquisitive system in plays like *Muktadhara* (1922) and *Raktakarabi* (1924). After his return from Russia, he refashioned out of his earlier plays the two new versions, *Rather Rashi* and *Kabir Diksha*, collated in *Kaler Jatra* [The March of Time] (1932), where he spoke of the deprived classes, more so in the Indian context of a caste-riddled society. The chariot of the deity refused to move despite the efforts of the upper classes; yet it rolled on smoothly when the *Sudras*, considered the lowest in the Hindu caste system, started to pull the rope of the chariot. Interestingly, this very incident was played out in real life in a village near Santiniketan. During the chariot festival (*Rathajatra*), the villagers were unable to move the deity's chariot, and sought help from some tribal people (the *Santhals*) who were passing that way. Though the *Santhals* are kept marginalized as belonging to the lowest rungs of both class and caste system, it was the effort of these people that helped the chariot to move. Pramathanath Bishi, who had witnessed this occurrence, not only recorded it in his memoir,[79] but even built a play around this (*Rathajatra*, 1923).[80] Rabindranath first proposed that he should send the play to *Probasi* for publication; when Pramathanath showed reluctance,[81] the Poet himself reworked the play, retained the name and, acknowledging his debt to Bishi, had it published in *Probasi* (November 1923).[82] This early version (*Rathajatra*) was later reworked as *Rather Rashi*, which was finally incorporated into *Kaler Jatra* (1932). The final form of the play, with underpinnings from his recent experiences in Russia, encapsulates the "march of Time", a movement in a new direction, which opens new horizons for the deprived. Rabindranath dedicated the play to Saratchandra Chattopadhyay, to whom he explicated in a letter:

> The bond between humans operates in all places at all times; this bond is the rope that pulls the chariot. That rope today is tied up in knots, making human relations untrue and unequal; so the chariot stands still. Those oppressed most by this untruth and inequality have today been invited by Time to drive its chariot. When their plight ends and there is a return to equality will the chariot move forward.[83]

It should also be noted here that some of the letters from Russia show that the Poet is aware of the possibilities of excesses in the Russian system and warns of a move in a reverse/different direction: "I am apprehensive that they have not understood the spheres within which the individual and the collective operate, which is where they betray some affinities with the Fascists. This is why their oppression of the individual in the name of the collective may cross limits."[84] He signs off those letters with a caveat: "Because the society once suffered at the hands individuals, there is now the *suicidal* proposal to repress the individual for the benefit of the collective."[85] And, towards the end of the play *Kaler Jatra*, the Kabi (Poet) similarly warns that one day, having reached a point of saturation, the direction will again change and the chariot will make a reverse turn: "And then on yet another day, in yet another age/ The time will come for the reverse move./ Once more, the high and the low of that new age will have to meet on their own terms."[86] And so the march of Time – *kaler jatra* – continues relentless. The first-hand experiences of a political change, viewed in a different community, are woven into an aesthetic expression to shape up the play, with his own distinctive ideological moorings.

Notes

1 Preface, *Rajarshi, Rabindra Rachanabali* [Complete Works] vol. 8 (Calcutta: West Bengal Government Centenary Edition, 1961) 114; subsequently referred to as *RR*.
2 *Bichitra: On-line Tagore Variorum*, School of Cultural Texts and Records, Jadavpur University, bichitra.jdvu.ac.in, RBVBMS_134 (i), 7 (image 7).
3 Rabindranath Tagore, *Collected Poems and Plays* (New Delhi: Macmillan, 2001; 1st Indian reprint 1991; originally 1936) 651.
4 Preface, *Malini, RR*, vol. 5, 485–6.
5 Preface, *Chitrangada* (verse-drama), *RR*, vol. 5, 438.
6 Pramathanath Bishi, *Rabindra Natya-prabaha*, vol. 2 (Calcutta: Orient Book Company, 1958) 157–8.
7 *Chithipatra*, vol. 2 (Calcutta: Visva-Bharati, 1942) 21.
8 *Chithipatra*, vol. 2, 27–32.
9 The Bangla word used ("*pradakshin*") usually connotes a religious sense of going around the idol in the temple.
10 As cited in Pramathanath Bishi, *Rabindra Natya-prabaha*, vol. 2, 101–2.

112 *Rabindranath as theatre-practitioner*

11 W.B. Yeats, "Preface" to Rabindranath Tagore, *The Post Office*, trans. Devabrata Mukherjea (London: Macmillan, 1914; rpt. 1961) v–vi.
12 Though *Nature's Revenge* is closer to the original Bengali title, its English version has been titled *Sanyasi or The Ascetic*.
13 Rabindranath Tagore, *My Reminiscences*, trans. Surendranath Tagore (London: Macmillan, 1917) 238–9; see also the original Bangla passage in *Jibansmriti, RR*, vol. 10, 109.
14 For details, see Prabhatkumar Mukhopadhyay, *Rabindra Jibani*, vol. 2 (Calcutta: Visva-Bharati Granthalay, 1936) 232–3.
15 Cited in Kshitimohan Sen, "Vedmantrarasik Rabindranath", *Visva-Bharati Patrika* (1943) 601–02; translated.
16 Kshitimohan Sen, "Vedmantrarasik Rabindranath", 602.
17 Kshitimohan Sen, "Vedmantrarasik Rabindranath", 603.
18 Kshitimohan Sen, "Vedmantrarasik Rabindranath", 602.
19 As mentioned by Charuchandra Bandyopadhyay, *Rabi-Rashmi*, vol. 2 (Calcutta: A. Mukherjee & Co., 1939) 107.
20 Further discussion of this issue is avoided here as this may go beyond the scope of the present chapter.
21 Interestingly, during the writing of *Achalayatan*, he was involved with the issue of framing rules for the school, while realizing the need to steer clear of unnecessary constraints that may be caused by too fastidious implementation of rules.
22 The first two playlets, whose Bengali originals appeared in *Kahini* of 1900, were translated as *Mother's Prayer* and *Karna and Kunti*, and included in *The Fugitive* (London: Macmillan, 1921); *Mother's Prayer*, however, had been published earlier from Calcutta in 1919.
23 *Viday Abhishap* appeared as an individual playtext in 1912, and was not a part of the original *Kahini* of 1900, which contained the other playlets. However, in *The Fugitive* (1921), its English version (*Kacha and Devajani*) was included along with the translations of the other verse playlets. Edward Thompson made a translation of this as *Curse at Farewell* in 1924.
24 Rabindranath was taken to task by Dwijendralal Roy precisely because of this: "In the Mahabharata ... Arjuna during his sojourn in Manipur was struck with the beauty of Chitrangada and married her with her father's consent. This tale was much too prosaic for Rabindra-babu; to seek for the consent of the father to marry the daughter is what all do. If Rabindra-babu does as much, then he would have to stoop to the level of Vyasdeva." (*Sahitya, Jaistha* 1316 BS, May–June 1909); cited in Rakhi Mitra, "Chitrangada Bitarka O Kabichitter Vibartan" ["The Chitrangada debate and the evolution of the Poet's Mind"], *Parikatha*, 14th year, no. 1, December 2011, 161–84; here quoted from 161.
25 *Raktakarabi* (Calcutta: Visva-Bharati, 1926) 110; this prose piece appeared first in *Probasi, Baisakh* 1332 (May 1925) and was later appended at the end of the playtext.
26 *Raktakarabi*, 107–8.
27 *Raktakarabi*, 108.
28 Many held that the play had initially been titled *Yakshapuri*, but none of the drafts found bear this name; some early manuscripts use the name *Nandini*, to be replaced by *Raktakarabi* from the eighth draft. The confusion probably arose because Rabindranath himself referred to the play as *Yakshapuri* in some letters, while he was in the process of composing it (for instance, letter to Ramananda Chattopadhyay, dated 19 *Bhadra* 1330 BS [1923], in *Chithipatra*, vol. 12, 1986, 86); for details, see Moloy Rakshit, *Raktakarabi: Path O Pathantarer Bhabnay* (Calcutta: Dey's Publishing, 2009) especially 49–50.
29 "Nationalism in the West", in *The English Writings of Rabindranath Tagore*, vol. 2, 420.
30 *Red Oleanders*, 95.
31 *Red Oleanders*, 98.

32 Ranjan's overwhelming presence throughout the play, though in absentia, is yet another masterstroke of dramaturgical innovation in this play. His corpse is discovered to view at the very end of the play.
33 "Sikshar Milan" (*Aswin* 1328 BS, 1921), *Siksha, RR*, vol. 11, 664–98; here quoted from 669.
34 Rathindranath Tagore, "Looking Back", in *Rabindranath Tagore: A Tribute*, ed. Pulinbihari Sen and Kshitis Roy (New Delhi: Sangeet Natak Akademi, 2006; originally 1961) 45–52; here quoted from 50.
35 Preface to *Tapati, RR*, vol. 6, 1034.
36 Preface to *Arupratan, RR*, vol. 6, 523.
37 See Preface to *Tapati, RR*, vol. 6, 1033–4. Some of these reasons are stated directly, others implicitly, in this preface.
38 The composition of *Bhairaber Bali* was over by 26 February 1929, and it was produced under the direction of Gaganendranath Tagore at the Empire Theatre on 27 April 1929; *Tapati*, the final product, was staged by Rabindranath at Jorasanko on 26, 28, 29 September and 1 October 1929 (because Empire Theatre was unavailable in end-September); it was also mounted by Sisirkumar Bhaduri for Natyamandir at Cornwallis on 25 December 1929. For details, see Rudraprasad Chakrabarty, *Rangamancha O Rabindranath: Samakalin Pratikriya* (Calcutta: Ananda, 1995) 229, 231–42.
39 In the Preface to *Tapati* he declares that, despite the revisions, he had realized that "unless this play was written anew, justice could not be done to it." (*RR*, vol. 6, 1033).
40 This stage-copy has the accession no. 134/1 in the Rabindra Bhavana archives.
41 This is also discussed in detail by Sekhar Samaddar in his *Visarjan: Rupe, rupantare* (Calcutta: Papyrus, 1992) 82–6. As for the requirements for intermissions (marked as "abakas" or respite), Samaddar is of the opinion that these were less intervals in the Western sense, more breaks in stage action to suggest shifts in scene/locale (82). He also suggests that in spite of Rabindranath's insertion of "Drop" in the stage-copy, these breaks were perhaps executed in performance with changes in lights (83).
42 This is reported by Satyaranjan Basu, as cited in Rudraprasad Chakrabarty, *Rangamancha O Rabindranath: Samakalin Pratikriya*, 69.
43 Ananda Lal, "Tagore in Kolkata Theatre: 1986–2010", in *Towards Tagore*, ed. Sanjukta Dasgupta, Ramkumar Mukhopadhyay and Swati Ganguly (Calcutta: Visva-Bharati, 2014) 515–48.
44 Several letters seem to indicate this – to Indulekha Choudhuri (*Shanibarer Chithi, Agrahayan* 1348, November 1941, 168).
45 Spandana Bhowmik, "Playwright versus Dramatist: Writing for Performance, Writing Raja", *Sangeet Natak*, vol. XLVI, nos. 1–4, 2012: Special issue on "Rabindranath's East-West Encounters: Performance and Visual Arts" (New Delhi: Sangeet Natak Akademi, 2013) 109–20; here quoted from 110.
46 See Prasantakumar Pal, *Rabi Jibani*, vol. 6 (Calcutta: Ananda, 1991) 182.
47 Rabindranath Tagore, *Raja, Kavyagrantha*, vol. IX (Allahabad: Indian Press, 1916) 3.
48 *Chithipatra*, vol. 14 (Calcutta: Visva-Bharati, 2000) 27–8.
49 This is the term ("abhinayjogya") used in the preface to *Arupratan*. However, he did not really arrange for the "acting" of *Arupratan* as a full-fledged stage performance, though there was a play-reading of the text at Alfred Theatre, Calcutta, on 15 Sep 1924. More details of the play-reading are given in Chapter 9: "Acting the role".
50 See Prasantakumar Pal, *Rabi Jibani*, vol. 6, 182.
51 See "Grantha Parichay", *Rabindra Rachanabali*, ed. Sankha Ghosh et al., vol. V: *Raja*, 683.
52 In *Rabindra-Biksha*, no. 28, 75 (as cited in "Grantha Parichay", *Rabindra Rachanabali*, vol. V: *Raja*, 683).

53 Sudhir Chandra Kar, *Kabi Katha* (Calcutta: Suprakasan, 1951) 41–2.
54 Letter to Amita Sen (Khuku), dated 23 November 1935, *Rabindrabiksha* no. 18 (Santiniketan: Rabindra Bhavana, Visva-Bharati, 1987) 32.
55 Advertisement in the dailies *Forward* (6, 7, 8, 9 and 11 December 1935) and *The Statesman* (11 and 12 December 1935); cited in *Rangamancha O Rabindranath: Samakalin Pratikriya*, 111.
56 This slim volume of eight pages is preserved in the Rabindra Bhavana archives and includes the summary of the play, both in English and Bengali, along with a mention of the scene divisions.
57 See Pranaykumar Kundu, *Raktakarabi: Pandulipi sambalita samskaran* (Calcutta: Visva-Bharati Granthan Vibhaga, 1998).
58 References to the name *Yakshapuri* are found in Rabindranath's letters, though not in the actual drafts; see earlier remarks.
59 The fourth draft is no longer in the Rabindra Bhavana archival holdings at Santiniketan; it was printed in the theatre journal *Bohurupee*, May 1986, and may be seen there. The fifth draft is on two exercise books, marked in the archives as ms 151 (i) and 151 (ii).
60 Identified in the archives as ms 151 (viii).
61 The red oleander flower does not appear in the first draft, is mentioned only twice in the second draft, and then becomes a central symbol of the play in the later drafts.
62 Except for the fourth draft, the others are available in the archives of Rabindra Bhavana, Visva-Bharati, Santiniketan.
63 Santidev Ghosh, *Gurudev Rabindranath O Adhunik Bharatiya Nritya* (Calcutta: Ananda, 1983) 65.
64 For details of textual and stage history of the play, see "Grantha Parichay", *RR*, vol. 16, 773–86.
65 *Chithipatra*, vol. 3 (Calcutta: Visva-Bharati, 1942; rpt. 1994) 130.
66 See Santidev Ghosh, *Gurudev Rabindranath O Adhunik Bharatiya Nritya*, 90–1.
67 See "Dedication" to *Tasher Desh*, in *RR*, 6, 1161.
68 Quoted in Rudraprasad Chakrabarty, *Rangamancha O Rabindranath: Samakalin Pratikriya*, 275–6.
69 "Dedication" prefixed to *Tasher Desh*, *RR*, vol. 6, 1161.
70 The first "Deshnayak" essay had been written in 1906, two years after "Swadeshi samaj".
71 "Deshnayak", *Kalantar, RR*, vol. 13, 387–90; here cited from 387.
72 "Deshnayak", *Kalantar, RR*, vol. 13, "Deshnayak", *Kalantar, RR*, vol. 13, 389.
73 As cited in Prasantakumar Pal, *Rabi Jibani*, vol. 8 (Calcutta: Ananda, 2000) 167.
74 "Sikshar Milan" (Aswin 1328, 1921), *Siksha, RR*, vol. 11, 664–98; here quoted from 669; emphases added.
75 This address was transcribed by Kshitimohan Sen, revised by the Poet, and published as "Dharma o Jorota" ["Faith and Inertia"] in *Probasi, Ashar* 1333 BS (June 1926); as cited in Debjit Bandyopadhyay, *Natir Puja* (Calcutta: Signet Press, 2019) 1.
76 Letter no. 3 (dated 25 September 1930), *Russiar Chithi* [*Letters from Russia*], *Rabindra Rachabali*, Popular edition, vol. 10 (Calcutta: Visva-Bharati, 1989) 558.
77 Letter no. 8 (dated 4 October 1930), *Russiar Chithi* [*Letters from Russia*], *Rabindra Rachabali*, Popular edition, vol. 10, 579.
78 Letter no. 9 (dated 5 October 1930), *Russiar Chithi* [*Letters from Russia*], *Rabindra Rachabali*, Popular edition, vol. 10, 582.
79 See Pramathanath Bishi, *Purano sei diner katha* (Calcutta: Mitra & Ghosh, 1958) 178.
80 Pramathanath read this before his schoolmates in Santiniketan on 26 July 1923.
81 See Pramathanath Bishi, *Purano sei diner katha* (Calcutta: Mitra & Ghosh, 1958) 178–9.

82 Rabindranath acknowledges in the footnotes that he had been inspired to write this play by a composition of Pramanath Bishi, his beloved student. For details, see Prasantakumar Pal, *Rabi Jibani*, vol. 9, 33–4; also Pramathanath Bishi, *Purano sei diner katha* (Calcutta: Mitra & Ghosh, 1958) 178–9.
83 As cited in Prabhatkumar Mukhopadhyay, *Rabindra Jibani*, vol. 3 (Calcutta: Visva-Bharati Granthalay, 1959; rev. 1961) 151.
84 Letter no. 13 (dated 9 October 1930), *Russiar Chithi* [*Letters from Russia*], *Rabindra Rachabali*, Popular edition, vol. 10, 590.
85 "Uposamhar", *Russiar Chithi* ["Conclusion" to *Letters from Russia*], in *Rabindra Rachabali*, Popular edition, vol. 10, 602.
86 *Kaler Jatra*, in *Rabindra Rachabali*, Popular edition, vol. 11 (Calcutta: Visva-Bharati, 1990) 277. The reverse move is described in the original as "*Ultorather pala*", referring to the Hindu ritual of the chariot of *Jagannath* (literally, Lord of the World; supposedly a form of Vishnu) moving in a reverse direction to return home, seven days after the main ritual of *Rathajatra* [Chariot procession] that had taken him away from home.

6 Selecting the cast

I

The radical changes in Rabindranath's dramaturgical and theatrical structures were made possible on two counts: first, his shift to Santiniketan with the emergence of the *asram*-school there; second, his ability to combine in himself the roles of the playwright and the practitioner. The writing and staging of plays always kept in view not only the open-air ambience of Santiniketan (exploited to the fullest perhaps in his seasonal plays) but also the logistics of the human resources available in and around the residential *asram*-school. With his eagerness to stage his plays at the earliest given opportunity, he would often have a potential cast in mind (from among the existing resources) while he wrote them, and would then proceed to have them performed. Though his relocation to Santiniketan enabled him to access the local resources in giving shape to his new concepts of theatre, yet even before he moved to Santiniketan, the early Rabindranath had already seen how for their family plays the members of the Tagore household were inducted. This trend, already available at the Jorasanko residence, would develop further in the subsequent years, for which he was largely indebted to staging principles practised within his family.

A constant factor in all his theatrical ventures, whether in early experiments (*Valmiki Pratibha* or *Visarjan*), in maturer dramas (*Raja, Phalguni* or *Natir Puja*), or in later dance dramas (*Chitrangada, Chandalika* or *Shyama*) is Rabindranath's consistent attempts to make use of human resources available at hand. In fact, the tradition of the Tagore family had been to employ the abilities of its different members for the various household productions at Jorasanko, and this had been the norm even before Rabindranath took charge of his own productions. Not only the male members of the Tagore family (Satyendranath, Jyotirindranath, Gaganendranath, Abanindranath, Samarendranath, Arunendranath, Nitindranath), but even the women (Jnanadanandini, Mrinalini, Abhijna, Pratibha, Indira) had actively participated in these home-productions. When Rabindranath's *Raja o Rani* was performed in 1889, directed by his second brother, Satyendranath, Rabindranath played King Vikramdev to Jnanadanandini's Queen Sumitra, while his wife Mrinalini was cast as Narayani, the wife of Devadatta, the character enacted by Satyendranath.[1] Rathindranath later commented on Mrinalini's stage appearance: "My mother was persuaded to take the part of Narayani, in *Raja-o-Rani*, the first and only time she appeared on the stage."[2] Despite eyebrows being raised at such pairing of brothers-in-law and sisters-in-law as onstage couples,[3] the Tagores continued undeterred, impervious to such unwarranted aspersions. Among other family members and friends drawn into the casting were Abanindranath, Pratibha, Akshay Majumdar and Pramatha Chowdhury. This tradition of falling back upon existing talents within the family or its close associates, along with the practice of using mixed casting for performances, were already available to Rabindranath from his Jorasanko days. This assumes greater significance in view of the fact that women of respectable families were yet to find a foothold on the Bengali stage; the Tagore family was a major exception.[4]

Interestingly, in several of the family performances, male members enacted female roles in keeping with the *jatra* convention: Jyotirindranath's impersonation of the Nati in *Nabanatak* is known to have drawn much applause;[5] Rabindranath himself might have played a couple of female roles, perhaps in Swarnakumari Devi's *Vibaha-utsav* or in Harishchandra Haldar's *Muktakuntala*.[6] This early exposure to the *jatra* practice could have inspired him, in "Rangamancha" (1902), to take a stand against the European illusionistic mode of having "female roles acted by bona fide females",[7] and, later, to put this theory into actual practice in casting young male students in female roles in the early Santiniketan productions.

Even after he shifted base to Santiniketan, there were occasions when Rabindranath would depend upon the histrionic flair of family members in Calcutta and would rework plays to induct them. After adding a prologue to *Phalguni*, for the Calcutta performance in January 1916 in aid of the Bankura famine, he included his nephews Gaganendranath, Samarendranath and Abanindranath in the cast and went on to play the Poet, Kabisekhar, himself. In fact, Rathindranath felt that one of the reasons to append this prologue to the play was that "he wished to draw upon the histrionic talents of his nephews Gaganendra, Samarendra and Abanindranath. The parts seemed to have been specially designed to suit their talents."[8] Gaganendranath as the King and Abanindranath as Shrutibhusan are known to have excelled in their roles. Gaganendranath won accolades for his regal onstage presence from, among others, Hemendrakumar Roy: "Before him, I had seen many kings, but none of them came across as a real king in the way Gaganendranath did."[9] Satyendranath Dutta, in his review of the *Phalguni* production in Calcutta, had much the same to say about Gagendranath's king: "If one has not seen a king in real life one would have done so that day [in Gaganendranath's impersonation]."[10]

Again, when *Dakghar* was presented in Calcutta a number of times between October 1917 and January 1918, Gaganendranath was cast as Madhavdutta, while Abanindranath played both the Physician (Kaviraj) and the Headman (Morol); among other family members impersonating other roles were Dinendranath, Soumyendranath, Nabendranath, Rathindranath and Surupa, Abanindranath's daughter, who played Sudha. Ashamukul Das, who played young

Amal, had already appeared in the role in a production of Brahmo Samaj given on 3 May 1917 at Mary Carpenter Hall in Calcutta. He was introduced to the Poet by Prasantachandra Mahalanobis, and, after an audition and some initial grooming, he was selected for the role.[11] Gaganendranath Tagore, with his sedate looks, was usually cast in serious roles, like that of Madhavdutta in *Dakghar* (1917), but was particularly applauded for his performances as kings in different plays like *Visarjan* (1890), *Sarodatsav* (1922, in Calcutta), *Phalguni* (1916, in Calcutta). Abanindranath, on the other hand, was adept at comical roles and type characters, and was notorious for improvising on the stage. He played six roles in *Raja o Rani*, changing costume for each; one of the dacoits in *Valmiki Pratibha*; Tinkori (to Rabindranath's Kedar) in *Baikunther Khata*; Kabiraj and Morol (both characters antagonistic to Amal, but with a comical edge) in *Dakghar* (1917).[12]

After he moved to Santiniketan, Rabindranath continued in his attempts to engage the whole community there. With his comprehensive approach to education,[13] he was consciously trying to deploy the potentials of the students and teachers (of Visva-Bharati) in different ways, including performances of dramas and dance dramas. With the practice of using talents of family members as his inheritance, and the shaping up of the local community as a model for his imagined *swadeshi samaj* as his dream, Rabindranath tried to draw the Santiniketan-Sriniketan community into the collective participation of theatrical performances. The inherited family tradition, now engrafted onto the new ideological vision of a *swadeshi samaj* where each member of the community needed to contribute to the greater welfare of the entire society,[14] attempted to find a concrete shape in this practice at Santiniketan. The productions of Santiniketan evolved in this manner, drawing upon the talents of the local community, comprising students, teachers and residents. If Nandalal Bose, a noted artist and a leading teacher at Kala-Bhavana, was engaged in stage design, his daughter, Gouri, was cast as Srimati (in *Natir Puja*). While Kalimohan Ghosh served as a reputed teacher and competent *Adhyaksha* (Principal) at Sriniketan, his son, Santidev (the name Santimoy was changed by Rabindranath) became a chief exponent of dances, importing dances from other cultures with Rabindranath's enthusiastic support. Teachers and students performed together in these theatrical events. So, students found themselves playing roles with reputed teachers like Jagadananda Roy (a noted scientist and science teacher), Dinendranath Tagore (in charge of music lessons), Kalimohan Ghosh (Principal of Sriniketan) or even the august Kshitimohan Sen (both teacher and administrator). Satyendranath Dutta's review of the Calcutta production of *Phalguni* (1916) underscores how various layers/age groups of the Santiniketan community had been used for the cast of this production:

> The five and six year old children sang, danced and chattered with the blissful ease of birds. ... Then came a group of ten and twelve year olds. ... Some of them acted with such natural grace that could put to shame the performance of many a renowned player of the city. ... Above

them, was a group of twenties and thirties ... among whom special mention must be made of the musical expert Dinendranath Tagore – he is the repository of Rabindranath's musical genius, there is none second to him. ... Commendable performances were given by the scientist Jagadananda Roy, the artist Asitkumar Haldar, the professor Kshitimohan Sen and the foreign student at Bolpur Narbhup Rao. [The Poet's son] Rathindranath Tagore was also natural in his impersonation of Winter and Spring. ... And finally came the group of seniors, comprising Rabindranath, Gaganendranath, Samarendranath, Abanindranath and Professor William Pearson.[15]

II

At the *asram*-school in Santiniketan, efforts were made right from the start to stage plays and keep the students engaged in performance. So even before Rabindranath ventured as a producer with a new play at Santiniketan, some of his earlier plays – in particular *Visarjan* and the farces of *Hasyakautuk* – were enthusiastically staged by the students, with able support not only from the Poet but also from Dinendranath, Santoshchandra Majumdar, Nayanmohan Chattopadhyay and others. Much of it was amateurish, even half-ready, yet Rathindranath felt, "despite the childishness, the performances went off well. If nothing else, Father discovered a few among us who had the flair for acting."[16] This would help Rabindranath in selecting the cast for his subsequent plays, and ultimately even develop a kind of a theatre troupe, comprising both students and teachers of the school.

It was with *Sarodotsav* [Autumn Festival] (1908) that Rabindranath took up the business of doing plays at Santiniketan in all earnestness. As mentioned in the earlier chapter, after his remarks upon the close communion between Man and Nature, the inmates of the school decided to celebrate the rains with songs and readings (though done in the absence of Rabindranath). The success of this programme set Rabindranath thinking about a celebration of the advent of autumn. He began composing songs for the proposed event, but soon a dramatic structure weaved itself around the songs, and *Sarodotsav* emerged. For the 1908 Sarodotsav performance, he first cast Kshitimohan Sen as Thakurdada. However, because he lacked a singing voice, the role passed on to Ajitkumar Chakraborty. Kshitimohan Sen played Sannyasi/Vijayaditya, and the songs of this character were sung by Rabindranath himself from off-stage. Lakheswar was played by Dinendranath, and Upananda by the student Narendranath Khan. Rabindranath was the prompter for this performance.[17]

In those early days of the residential school, when male students primarily comprised the student community, there could have been a major setback when it came to casting actors for the female characters. But Rabindranath, using his theoretical pronouncements of "Rangamancha", tried to convert this disadvantage into an advantage: "It is time we rid ourselves of such crude European barbarisms as demanding that ... female roles [must be] acted by bona fide females."[18] Accordingly, he made boy students impersonate roles of women, among them Sudhiranjan Das, who later became a vice-chancellor of Visva-Bharati. According to Sudhiranjan's reminiscences, his impersonation of female roles began with the character of Aparna in *Visarjan*. [19] Prasantakumar Pal is of the opinion that this was probably staged on 7 *Pous* 1316 BS (22 December 1909).[20] Sudhiranjan not only mentions Aparna as his first female role but also recalls how he played Malini for the reception of Rathindranath and his newly wedded bride after they arrived with the Poet in Santiniketan on 8 February 1910.[21] He had, therefore, already made a 'name' for himself as a player of female roles when the Poet selected him to play Sudarshana for the premiere of *Raja* (March 1911). Sudhiranjan recalls how Rabindranath trained him and the other young boys for their roles; not only did he boost their confidence with his unfailing words of encouragement but also took extra care to prepare them for the performance, even serving them with eggnog to keep their voices mellifluous.[22] Among other boy actors inducted to play female characters were Sushilkumar Chakraborty playing Surangama (*Raja* 1911); Narendranath Khan enacting Gunavati (*Visarjan* 1909), the Queen (*Malini* 1909) and Rohini (*Raja* 1911); Jatindranath Mukhopadhyay playing Biva (*Prayaschitta* 1910).[23] In the May 1911 performance of *Raja*, Ajitkumar Chakravarty played Sudarshana (replacing Sudhiranjan Das). It appears, then, that with a group of capable young boys at hand (and, by corollary, a dearth of girls), Rabindranath was putting his theory about female impersonation by male actors into practice. The theoretical formula and theatrical praxis, therefore, went hand in hand in those early days of the *asram*-school.

Subsequently, with an increase in the number of girl students at the *asram*-school, they were also made part of the dramatic performances. In fact, Rabindranath also wrote plays exclusively for the girls, like *Lakshmir Pariksha* and *Natir Puja*. Yet, mixed casting (including both girls and boys) seems to have been discouraged in those early years, so that during the first performance of *Lakshmir Pariksha* at Santiniketan, in 1910, "not only were the players only girls, even the audience were women only; no male teacher or student was allowed to enter."[24] Earlier, in 1906, at the *swadeshi mela* (national fair) arranged by the *Mahila silpa samiti* (a women's art organization) held from 14 to 18 September, two days – 16 and 17 September – were reserved for women spectators only. *Lakshmir Pariksha* was performed on both these days, but details of the performance or the performers have not been found. *The Bengali* had advertised on 15 September that "Ladies will take part in the performance of Lakshmir Pariksha."[25] In 1919, even after girls had been drawn into performances, an abridged version of *Raja* was staged at Santiniketan with boys in the female roles because "many still objected to boys and girls acting together."[26] Santidev Ghosh informs us how mixed casting was gradually introduced into the productions:

> In the 1921-performance of *Varshamangal* in Calcutta, many of the girls joined the boy-students. In 1922, in the musical drama *Vasanta*, girls mimed to the accompaniment of songs. From around this time, girls were given an

equal share with boys in singing and acting. The use of dances had just begun; this increased more from the performance of *Natir Puja*.[27]

Mixed casting was gradually introduced for other plays as well (verse or prose dramas), whether at Santiniketan or in Calcutta or in other cities: so, Ranu Adhikari (later Ranu Mukherjee) played Aparna in *Visarjan* (1923) and Sudarshana in *Arupratan* (1924); in the 1935 production of *Raja* at the New Empire Theatre in Calcutta, Amita Tagore played Sudarshana and Nandita Devi (Kripalani) enacted the role of Surangama.[28]

It would not be out of place to mention here that Rabindranath's fastidiousness as director and producer was at work right from the selection of the cast. As an author-actor-producer, he was supposedly at an advantage, for he could foresee some of the prospective players for particular roles – Gaganendranath for the roles of kings, Abanindranath for comic characters, Dinendranath for singing roles, Jagadananda Roy for roles either comic (Lakheswar in *Sarodotsav*) or formidable (Kanchiraj in *Raja*). Though these available resources often helped him, there were characters about whose portrayal he was more choosy, perhaps more exacting. The role of Sudarshana in *Raja* offers an instance of this. When he was preparing *Raja* for the early performances in Santiniketan, he was particularly anxious about the representation of Queen Sudarshana. We know that, with having to cast boy students in the women's roles in the early years of the school, he had to look for the best talent available among the boys then studying in the school. So, for the first performance of *Raja* at Santiniketan (March 1911), he chose Sudhiranjan Das to play Sudarshana and took special care to train him for the role: "When I was able to speak the lines according to his directions, he was very happy …. To keep our voices mellifluous, he even personally made us have egg whisked in warm milk."[29] However, despite his efforts, Sudhiranjan Das must have failed to impress the Poet enough as Sudarshana. For, he cast Ajitkumar Chakravarty in the role for the next performance of *Raja* (May 1911), also at Santiniketan. To his daughter, Mira Devi, he wrote in a letter:

> Perhaps you will have a good laugh to know that Ajit will play Sudarshana. With proper make-up, complete with wig, he will have to be made to manage the role. The dark scenes are not a problem – but I am not sure of the effect in the lighted scenes. But there is no alternative. *There is no other boy to play Sudarshana.*[30]

This remark once again indicates the kind of precision that Rabindranath brought to bear upon himself as a director, and, by corollary, upon his actors. He could not cast Ajitkumar Chakravarty in the first performance, as the latter had been away then, but with his subsequent return to the school, Rabindranath lost no opportunity to use him for Sudarshana. Ajitkumar was somewhat handicapped by his age; Sudhiranjan as a young student could be more easily passed off in a female role, while Ajitkumar was already a fullgrown adult. Moreover, Sudhiranjan Das had by then played quite a few female roles in different plays at Santiniketan – Aparna in *Visarjan* (1909)[31] and Malini in *Malini* (1910)[32] and, in 1912 – that is a year after the first two performances of *Raja* – would go on to play Queen Sumitra in a production of *Raja o Rani*.[33] Yet, for the second *Raja* production at Santiniketan, the Poet decided in favour of Ajitkumar because he had more faith in his acting capabilities and stage interpretation – as is evident in the letter to Mira Devi cited above.

For that matter, even as late as in 1935, when female actors had already been accommodated into Rabindranath's theatrical repertoire, for the roles of Sudarshana and Surangama he was just as selective. Though Ranu Adhikari and Sahana Bose had mimed Sudarshana and Surangama in the 1924 *Arupratan* production at Alfred Theatre in Calcutta, he did not cast them for these roles for the *Raja* of 1935, staged at New Empire, Calcutta. He preferred to fall back upon the proven talent of Amita Tagore (daughter of Ajitkumar Chakravarty) for Sudarshana; she had excelled in the role of Queen Sumitra in *Tapati* (1929).[34] In a letter to Nirmalkumari Mahalanobis, dated 29 November 1935, he writes:

> Amita having arrived here, I caught hold of her to do Sudarshana. She has not been keeping too well lately, which is some cause for concern. This play is not so easy that in case she is unable to perform, someone else may be asked to step in.[35]

And for Surangama he had faith in the abilities of his grand-daughter, Nandita; he wrote to her in a letter:

> The role of Surangama is not too difficult; I can teach you that bit. Go through the lines carefully. *I tried out a couple of girls here – it was a miserable failure*. If you could be given a few days of thorough training, I am sure you would do fine.[36]

It may be mentioned here that Rabindranath had definite intentions of staging *Raktakarabi*. He had requested Ramananda Chattopadhyay to delay the publication of the play in *Probasi* till he had staged it: "I do not wish to have it published before its performance."[37] He had also read the play several times in private circles, presumably to test its worth.[38] But, because he did not find anyone adequately equipped to play Nandini, his own plans of doing the play finally remained unfulfilled. These instances bear witness to his alertness as a director and his unwillingness to compromise on quality, as far as practicable.

III

For *Natir Puja* [The Worship of the Dancing Girl] (1926), Rabindranath had the dramatic climax precipitated through the final dance of Srimati. For this role of the dancing girl (*nati*) turned into the devotee of Buddha, he selected Gouri Bose, the daughter of the famous artist Nandalal Bose. On 8 May

1926, on the occasion of the Poet's birthday, the performance was given at Santiniketan before an audience consisting of local residents and distinguished visitors (among them the consuls of the Italian and French Embassies as well as Dr. Cousins).[39] Gouri, though apprehensive at first,[40] put her heart and soul into the role of the *nati* (the dancing girl) and gave shape to a memorable performance, particularly with her soulful rendition of the culminating dance that created history. As his biographer remarks: "after seeing Gouri's dance, the Poet had no qualms that in the field of dance, too, Santiniketan had something significant to offer."[41]

Yet, when it was proposed to take the production to Calcutta to raise funds for Visva-Bharati, there was a sense of unease even among the residents of Santiniketan. That a prudishness was at work in the Santiniketan community, particularly in the early days of the *Brahmacharyasram*, is recounted by his biographer: when young students were given to read from the Poet's works, the verse-play *Chitrangada* or a poem like *Parisodh* (presumably for their celebration of the erotic) would either be omitted from the textbook, or teachers would stitch the pages together to make them inaccessible to the students; Prabhatkumar holds that even if Rabindranath was not directly involved, he would not have been totally unaware of such measures.[42] This prudishness again reared its head at the possibility of *Natir Puja* being staged in Calcutta. This would possibly be the first time that a girl from a respectable Bengali family would dance in a dramatic performance on the public stage before an audience that had paid for its rights of admission. Not all were comfortable with the idea. When Rabindranath went to seek the opinion of Gouri's parents, they told the Poet that the responsibility (for consequences, whether favourable or otherwise) lay squarely with him: "We reside in this *asram*, under your wings. So, you may please decide on our behalf. Whether praise or censure, it will all be yours."[43] To tide over the problem, Rabindranath created the only male character of Upali and played the role himself. In a subsequent interview, Gouri Bhanja (nee Bose) commented: "Girls from Santiniketan singing and dancing on the stage may have provoked criticism; to prevent that, the Poet involved himself in the production."[44] But the dance of the *nati* so touched the hearts of the viewers "with its controlled display of devotion (*bhakti*) and unsullied purity"[45] that much of the misgivings were dispelled. Still, it was not all smooth sailing. It has been noted earlier how the contemporary middle-class mindset unleashed its fury and dismay through some adverse – even repugnant – comments: "Respected Rabindranath Tagore has grown old but his desire for pleasure has remained 'evergreen'. It is reported that he has started dancing classes for women at Santiniketan... What kind of education is he imparting to simple-minded inexperienced young girls!"[46]; "Beneath a cartoon of Rabindranath wearing a *ghagra*[47] it was written, What is happening to our country? Girls from respectable families are dancing in public. Rabindranath, by making girls dance, is making us droop our heads in shame."[48] Still, undeterred by such revolting insinuations, Rabindranath continued with his innovations and slowly but steadily won for himself, and his students, a more liberal and liberating cultural space. Gouri Bhanja (nee Bose) realized the important role played by the *Natir Puja* production in this endeavour: "The bold and undaunted step that Gurudeva took through this performance [*Natir Puja*], brought social respectability to dance and song performed by women."[49] In fact, *Natir Puja* proved to be such a path-breaking experience for women that soon there were other groups of women staging their own productions of the play, complete with the dance: "Last evening at the University Institute some girls of respectable Hindu families performed Rabindranath's verse drama *Natir Puja*. Rabindranath himself was invited and stayed through the entire duration of the performance."[50] Hemendrakumar Roy observed:

> That the dance form could be born anew in Bengal has now been made evident to all ... To witness "Natir Puja" with their own eyes and judge the truth for themselves, people rushed in hordes to the ticket counter. Within a few days it was found that Bengali girls were enthusiastically trying out the dance of "Natir Puja" within their own household precincts.[51]

At a later phase, immediately before he toured Ceylon with *Shapmochan*, the Poet, in a letter to Amiya Chakravarty, referred to the special role played by Visva-Bharati in this context: "The waves of dance, song and painting that we now see spreading from Bengal through the whole of India had its origins here; this fact has to be acknowledged."[52] Amiya Chakravarty himself, functioning as the Poet's secretary, once wrote in a letter (in response to queries about the practice of songs and dances in Santinketan): "Dr. Tagore believes that through dancing and music the highest spiritual gifts of man can be expressed and therefore by neglecting them we shall be crippling our essential personality."[53] It may not be out of place to recall here the words with which Rabindranath welcomed Uday Shankar, the renowned dancer, when the latter visited Santiniketan on 12 July 1933:

> A country which has no dance often forgets that dance is not merely for entertainment. Dance is vibrant, lively and pure where the human spirit is energetic. The land which celebrates the splendour of the human self expresses itself through spirited dance. The monsoon clouds dance in lightning, with thunder for company. Where there is decadence, dance disappears or loses its robustness and vigour, often to dwindle into *nautch* .... Its [dance] purpose is not to entice the mind but to arouse it.[54]

That Rabindranath envisaged a more meaningful role for dance than mere entertainment becomes manifest in this address. His conscientious efforts gradually impacted the contemporary social perception and his achievements in this sphere were ultimately appreciated not only for providing aesthetic pleasure but also for etching a deep influence upon the sociocultural milieu.

To ensure this change in the contemporary attitude towards songs and dances, Rabindranath also fell back upon certain strategies. If for the 1927 *Natir Puja*, he created for himself the onstage role of Upali, for the 1936 *Chitrangada* given at the

New Empire Theatre in Calcutta, he "was on the stage throughout the performance and recited portions from the play."[55] Because *The Statesman* (9, 10, 11, 12 March 1936) had advertised: "RABINDRANATH TAGORE/PERSONALLY APPEARING/IN HIS IMMORTAL LYRIC/CHITRANGADA/ALONG WITH STUDENTS OF/ SANTINIKETAN",[56] it raised expectations that he would be performing on stage, and many were disappointed when it did not exactly happen as they had expected. Rabindranath was seen sitting on the stage in full view of the audience, but at a distance from the performers, and he only recited the dialogues from his removed position. Yet, for others in the audience, his very presence on the stage created a powerful impact, even as he looked upon, and participated in, a performance in which men and women were engaged in collaborative participation. His onstage presence, therefore, not only signalled his approval of the performance, but even won for it a social ratification. To reiterate a point made elsewhere, to ensure this approval (and the smooth conduct of events), for subsequent productions, too, Rabindranath usually made it a point to be seen on the stage during performances. When *Parisodh* (the original version of *Shyama*) was staged in Calcutta in October 1936, *The Statesman* noted with approval the Poet's onstage presence: "He makes the stage human. Everyone else on the stage may be acting but he is not. He is reality. *Moreover he gives a dignity to the performance – nautch is transformed into dance.*"[57] Sajanikanta Das's analysis of the performance of *Shyama* in Calcutta on 7 and 8 February 1939 offers a similar view:

> All those who had the good fortune to witness *Shyama*, the dance drama version of *Parisodh*, last evening at Sree Theatre, will agree that *the language of the body is in no way less than the language of poetry.* I had misgivings about the propriety of the students of Visva-Bharati enacting this tale of physical love by. In reality I found the touch of genius could make everything possible. *The expressiveness of the soft bodily postures dissolved away the sense of the physical to recreate a world of cerebral perception.* [58]

Not only was the controversy of the days of *Natir Puja* and *Varsha-mangal* firmly put behind, but the aesthetic beauty of the productions was widely appreciated and elicited respectful appreciation from the Calcutta audiences. Rabindranath, and his actors from the Santiniketan community, had finally arrived with a new crop of plays in the Bengali theatre.

Notes

1 This was Mrinalini's only stage appearance, and that, too, under the persuasions of Satyendranath. For details, see Prabhatkumar Mukhopadhyay, *Rabindra Jibani* vol. 1 (Calcutta: Visva-Bharati Granthalay, 1933, rev. 1960) 349; Abanindranath Tagore, *Gharoa* (Calcutta: Visva-Bharati Granthan Vibhaga, 1941; rpt. 1983) 104–6. Khagendranath Chattopadhyay, however, suggests that Mrinalini also participated in certain performances arranged by the woman organization, Sakhi Samiti, founded by Swarnakumari Devi and Sarala Roy; see *Rabindra Katha* (Calcutta: Parul Prakasani, 2015; originally1941) 213.

126 *Rabindranath as theatre-practitioner*

2 Rathindranath Tagore, "Looking Back", in *Rabindranath Tagore: A Tribute*, ed. Pulinbihari Sen and Kshitis Roy (New Delhi: Sangeet Natak Akademi, 2006; originally 1961) 45–52; here quoted from 46.
3 Mentioned in Indira Devi, *Rabindra-smriti* (Calcutta: Visva-Bharati, 1961) 36.
4 Though admission rates may not have been charged in the early days, not all performances were restricted within the family circle. Distinguished members of the society, both Indian and foreign, were often invited to the performances.
5 *The National Paper*, 9 January 1867; as cited in Brajendranath Bandyopadhyay, *Bangiya Natyasalar Itihas, 1795–1876*, 7th edn. (Calcutta: Bangia Sahitya Parishad, 1998; originally 1933) 65.
6 See Rudraprasad Chakravarty, *Rangamancha O Rabindranath: Samakalin Pratikriya* (Calcutta: Ananda, 1995) 21–2; Chakravarty alerts us to the controversies regarding these performances.
7 "Rangamancha" ["The Theatre"], trans. Swapan Chakravorty, 99; emphases added.
8 Rathindranath Tagore, "Looking Back", 81.
9 Cited in Ajitkumar Ghosh, *Thakurbarir Abhinay* (Calcutta: Rabindra Bharati Society, 1988) 63.
10 Satyendranath Dutta, "Sahare Phalguni", *Bharati*, 39th year, no. 11, Phalgun 1322 (1916), 1110.
11 See Asitkumar Haldar, *Rabitirthe* (Calcutta: Anjana Prakashani, 1958) 104–5.
12 For details, see Ajitkumar Ghosh, *Thakurbarir Abhinay*, 65–9.
13 The motto of Visva-Bharati, as spelt out in the first volume of *Visva-Bharati Quarterly* (1923), was "To study the Mind of Man in its realization of different aspects of truth from diverse points of view."
14 This is the thrust, for instance, of the essay "Swadeshi Samaj", 1904.
15 Satyendranath Dutta, "Sahare Phalguni", *Bharati*, 39th year, no. 11, *Phalgun* 1322 BS (1916), 1104–5.
16 Rathindranath Tagore, *Pitrismriti* (Calcutta: Jijnasa, 1966) 132; in an English rendition of this, Rathindranath writes: "It at least helped Father to pick out some promising material from amongst the amateur actors." ("Looking Back", *Rabindranath Tagore: A Tribute*, 47).
17 For details, see Prabhatkumar Mukhopadhyay, *Rabindra Jibani*, vol. 2 (Calcutta: Visva-Bharati Granthalay, 1936) 235, n. 3.
18 "Rangamancha" ["The Theatre"], trans. Swapan Chakravorty, 99; emphases added.
19 See Sudhiranjan Das, *Amader Santiniketan* (Calcutta: Visva-Bharati Granthalay, 1959) 81, 84.
20 See Prasantakumar Pal, *Rabi Jibani*, vol. 6 (Calcutta: Ananda, 1991) 137.
21 Sudhiranjan Das, *Amader Santiniketan*, 81, 84–5. Probably through inadvertence, he mentions the date of *Malini* as 8 February 1909, and yet claims Aparna (in *Visarjan*), played in December 1909, to be his first female role.
22 Sudhiranjan Das, *Amader Santiniketan*, 87.
23 See Prabhatkumar Mukhopadhyay, *Rabindra Jibani*, vol. 2, 315; Sudhiranjan Das, *Amader Santiniketan*, 85; Prasantakumar Pal, *Rabi Jibani*, vol. 6, 137, 140; Rudraprasad Chakrabarty, *Rangamancha O Rabindranath: Samakalin Pratikriya*, 70–1,100.
24 Prabhatkumar Mukhopadhyay, *Rabindra Jibani*, vol. 2, 296.
25 *Rangamancha O Rabindranath: Samakalin Pratikriya*, 103.
26 Santidev Ghosh, *Rabindrasangeet* (Calcutta: Visva-Bharati Granthalay, rev. edn. 1958; originally 1942) 230.
27 Santidev Ghosh, *Rabindrasangeet*, 229.
28 See *Rangamancha O Rabindranath: Samakalin Pratikriya*, 61; 108–9; 111.
29 Sudhiranjan Das, *Amader Santiniketan* (Calcutta: Visva-Bharati Granthalay, 1959) 86–7.

30 *Chithipatra*, vol. 4 (Calcutta: Visva-Bharati, 1943) 17; emphases added.
31 See Sudhiranjan Das, *Amader Santiniketan*, 81. The date of the performance remains somewhat uncertain; see Prasantakumar Pal, *Rabi Jibani*, vol. 6, 137.
32 See Sudhiranjan Das, *Amader Santiniketan*, 84.
33 See Prabhatkumar Mukhopadhyay, *Rabindra Jibani*, vol. 2, 345.
34 In fact, Amita Tagore was chosen to play Sumitra only after a few others had been tried out but had all failed to impress the Poet (see Sekhar Samaddar, "Rabindranather Natyabhavna", 265)
35 Letter to Nirmalkumari Mahalanobis, dated 29 November 1935, *Desh*, 23 Agrahayan 1386 BS (December 1979) 503.
36 *Chithipatra*, vol. 4 (Calcutta: Visva-Bharati, 1943) 202; emphases added
37 Letter to Ramananda Chattopadhyay, dated 5 September 1923, in *Chithipatra*, no. 12 (Calcutta: Visva-Bharati Granthan Vibhaga, 1986) 86.
38 For instance, he read *Raktakarabi* before the Santiniketan inmates on 19 October 1923, on the day of Vijaya Dasami; see Prasantakumar Pal, *Rabi Jibani*, vol. 9 (Calcutta: Ananda, 2003) 84.
39 As reported in *Anandabazar Patrika* (13 May 1926); cited in *Rangamancha O Rabindranath: Samakalin Pratikriya*, 207.
40 Gouri Bose was particularly afraid that she would falter with the dialogues and her Sanskrit diction, but the Poet assured her that he would see her through. See Gouri Bhanja, "Natir Puja 1333", transcribed by Alpana Roy Chowdhury, *Visva-Bharati News* (April 1978): 176–8, specially 177; reported also in *Rangamancha O Rabindranath: Samakalin Pratikriya*, 207.
41 Prabhatkumar Mukhopadhyay, *Rabindra Jibani*, vol. 3 (Calcutta: Visva-Bharati Granthalaya, 1952, rev. 1961) 242.
42 Mentioned in Prabhatkumar Mukhopadhyay, *Rabindra Jibani*, vol. 4 (Calcutta: Visva-Bharati Granthalaya, 1956; rev. 1964) 52.
43 Gouri Bhanja, "Natir Puja 1333", 177.
44 Quoted in *Rangamancha O Rabindranath: Samakalin Pratikriya*, 207–8; see also Bishnu Basu, *Rabindranather Theatre*, 99.
45 Review in *Anandabazar Patrika*, 13 Magh 1333 BS (28 January 1927); as cited in Prabhatkumar Mukhopadhyay, *Rabindra Jibani*, vol. 3, 270.
46 *Sanjeevani*, 12 *Magh* 1334 BS (January 1927); cited in Dilipkumar Roy, *Rabindra samakale Rabindranataker Abhinoy* (Calcutta: Sramik Press, 1999) 159.
47 A dancing skirt.
48 Mentioned by Kumaresh Ghosh in *Jashthi-Madhu*, Baisakh 1385 BS (May 1978) 47; as cited in Debjit Bandyopadhyay, *Natir Puja* (Calcutta: Signet Press, 2019) 23.
49 Gouri Bhanja, "Natir Puja 1333", transcribed by Alpana Roy Chowdhury, *Visva-Bharati News* (April 1978): 176–8; here quoted from 178.
50 *Anandabazar Patrika*, 25 April 1927 (12 *Baisakh* 1334 BS). There was yet another production, given at the University Institute Hall, on 6 April 1931, and at Corinthian Theatre on 27 April 1931 (as reported in *Anandabazar Patrika*, 24 April 1931); cited in Debjit Bandyopadhyay, *Natir Puja*, 35–6.
51 Hemendrakumar Roy, *Jader Dekhechi*, as cited in Debjit Bandyopadhyay, *Natir Puja*, 25.
52 Letter to Amiya Chakravarty, dated 29 April 1934, in *Chithipatra*, vol. 11 (Calcutta: Visva-Bharati, 1974) 109.
53 Letter dated 8 January 1933; as cited in Prabhatkumar Mukhopadhyay, *Rabindra Jibani*, vol. 3, 469, n. 1.
54 This was initially delivered as an address and later published in *Probasi, Bhadra* 1340 BS (August 1933); as cited in Prabhatkumar Mukhopadhyay, *Rabindra Jibani*, vol. 2, 445.
55 *The Statesman*, 12 March 1936; cited in *Rangamancha O Rabindranath: Samakalin Pratikriya*, 267.

128 *Rabindranath as theatre-practitioner*

56 *The Statesman*, of 9, 10, 11, 12 March 1936 carried this advertisement; cited in Rudraprasad Chakrabarty, *Rangamancha O Rabindranath*, 285–6.
57 *The Statesman*, 14 October 1936; cited in *Rangamancha O Rabindranath: Samakalin Pratikriya*, 298; emphasis added.
58 *Anandabazar Patrika*, 8 February 1939; cited in *Rangamancha O Rabindranath: Samakalin Pratikriya*, 301; emphases added.

7 Rehearsing the play

I

Having prepared the playtext and selected the cast, Rabindranath moved into the next phase as producer/director – rehearsing the play. Though details about rehearsals remain relatively sparse and scattered, some amount of information may be gleaned from accounts in memoirs and reminiscences of his contemporaries. However, because many of these accounts came from those who were in Rabindranath's company, but who did not necessarily understand the finer nuances of theatre, the theatrical import of Rabindranath's experiments may sometimes have been missed or glossed over.

Valmiki Pratibha was first presented before the members of "Vidyajjan Samagam" [The Assembly of Intellectuals] on 26 February 1881. The invitation card was sent out in the name of Dwijendranath Tagore, Rabindranath's eldest brother.[1] The twenty-year-old Rabindranath, perhaps, was not in sole charge of the production. Jyotirindranath we know had set to tune several of the songs; Akshoychandra Chowdhury also helped with some of the musical compositions.[2] It has even been suggested that the major responsibility for the production, at least initially, lay with Jyotirindranath; Rabindranath was merely the actor of Valmiki.[3] When the play was given before Lady Lansdowne and Sir Charles and Lady Elliott at the Jorasanko Tagore residence (1890), Satyendranath insisted that the dacoits, in place of their earlier bare-chested appearance, be dressed properly in deference to the distinguished visitors; so, Kabuli costumes were tailored for them.[4] Again, *Raja o Rani* of 1889 was staged under the stewardship of Satyendranath at his Birjitala residence. During the final rehearsals Satyendranath expressed his strong disapproval of Akshaykumar Majumdar's exaggerated comic acting in the role of Trivedi, and that almost led to a disaster, till the latter was placated with a gift of a shawl and fifty rupees.[5]

It seems that from the time of the production of *Visarjan* (1890),[6] the reins passed slowly but steadily into the hands of Rabindranath. Prabhatkumar Mukhopadhyay mentions October 1890 as the date of the earliest performance of the play,[7] but this seems unlikely because Rabindranath did not return from Europe till November 1890. Abanindranath mentions the rainy months of 1890,

DOI: 10.4324/9781003110279-8

when Rabindranath handed over the completed play for a proposed performance.[8] However, the date of the first performance of *Visarjan* remains uncertain. Sekhar Samaddar mentions what he considers were the three earliest performances, one in 1893, two in 1900 (16 and 27 December).[9] Yet another source mentions two performances in 1890 (at Park Street and Jorasanko), one in 1893 (at Park Street), one in 1900 for Sangit Samaj (possibly on 16 December 1900), one in 1901 (again at Park Street) and yet another in 1902 at Santiniketan.[10] Whatever the dates of the first few performances, the dramaturgical structures of both *Visarjan*, and the previous play, *Raja o Rani*, make it evident that he was then inspired by Western traditions of playwriting. Also, prior to the days of *Visarjan*, when Rabindranath was visiting England (22 August to 4 November 1890), he saw Henry Irving in the production of Scott's *The Bride of Lammermoor* at the Lyceum Theatre; though he did not like Irving's mannerisms and affected diction, he praised Ellen Terry's acting and seems to have been generally impressed by the production.[11] Moreover, since the style of production in contemporary Bengali theatre was, anyway, inflected with Western borrowings, it is likely that the early stagings of *Visarjan* were inscribed with Western designs. A photograph of an early performance shows Rabindranath as Raghupati bent over the dead body of Joysingha (Arunendranath), with the stage decor suggesting use of realistic details including a leopard-skin. Abanindranath mentions that an image of the Goddess Kali was placed at one corner of the stage; Rabindranath (as Raghupati) was supposed to push it towards the wings, but, carried away by his histrionics, he lifted it up and sprained his back.[12] If in stage design this *Visarjan* still remained largely realistic, when it came to the style of acting, Rabindranath seemingly was trying to move away from overt effects of verisimilitude. Amita Tagore recalls:

> During the rehearsal of *Visarjan*, Arunendranath as Joysingha, after stabbing himself in the chest, lay on the floor showing signs of tremor in both legs. Seeing this, Rabindranath asked, "Why are you shaking your legs?" Arunendranath's reply was, "If one killed oneself with a stab in the chest, would there not be slight shivers in the body?" To which Rabindranath responded, "No, no, there is no need for this. We do not want such acute realism in performance."[13]

The later performance of *Visarjan* in 1923 (in which the sixty-two-year-old Rabindranath played the young temple attendant, Joysingha) was, of course, significantly different.

Rabindranath's abilities as a director were particularly noticed when he took charge of the production of *Goray Galad*, mounted for the Sangit Samaj. One of the performances (not the first, but perhaps the one given on 24 February) was reported in *Indian Daily News* on 28 February 1900.[14] On this occasion, the Poet is supposed to have told a friend:

> The educated people in our land are not always able to act with a proper understanding of the wit and humour in a play. To place oneself totally in

the situation of a dramatic character and enact the role accordingly is difficult. There are mannerisms in individuals that need to be observed, else the impersonation may become lifeless. … At the Sangit Samaj performance of "Goray Galad", I had given the actors some minor by-play. Someone twirled his moustache while he chatted; someone tore a piece of paper, rolled it up and tickled his ear with it, etc. These little details make the actor more natural, otherwise the acting becomes all too obvious.[15]

This telling comment reveals Rabindranath's awareness of the effects of mannerism and by-play in extracting humorous/incongruous elements in comic acting. The aim was to "get rid of all artificiality and adopt an easy everyday style in speaking, vocal intonation, pronunciation, even movements and gestures."[16] As director, Rabindranath put in a lot of effort behind this production, often walking back home after rehearsals, as late as 1.30 or 2.00 at night. In this context, Rabindranath is reported to have narrated an amusing anecdote to the other members: "When I returned home late last night, I entered like a thief stealthily by the back-door. In the dim light I went upstairs to my bedroom, changed my clothes and sat down to eat. I found the dinner had gone cold, while my wife was in a boiling rage."[17]

Contemporary accounts show how the perfectionist in Rabindranath repeatedly came to the fore when he put on the mantle of the director. When he was directing *Visarjan* for the Sangit Samaj in 1900, "he spent the afternoon correcting the diction of those who spoke in an affected manner, catching hold of them either at their houses or at the premises of the samaj; again in the evenings he guided them to recite their lines, to the accompaniment of appropriate gestures and postures."[18] This meticulousness was a distinctive feature of his rehearsal process. His contemporaries recall the Poet's rigorous training during rehearsals: "The rehearsal period for any play would not be less than two months. He would meticulously observe if anyone was going wrong anywhere and why, and the training would continue till the fault was rectified";[19] "He would never approve anything to be staged that was just about acceptable; *everything had to be perfect*."[20] Amita Sen, writing about the rehearsals of *Natir Puja* (1926), remembers how the Poet insisted upon correct and clear enunciation of words: "Right from the early readings, he paid particular attention to diction. Everyone's pronunciation had to be correct."[21] Again, as late as in 1935, as director of *Raja*, he was so fastidious about correct pronunciation that he even replaced words in the original play to avoid possibilities of mispronunciation due to the faulty diction of the actors.[22] Not only diction or intonation, he even alerted his actors about the technicalities of vocal acting. Since there were no microphones available then, he saw to it that the voices should be audible for the spectators in the last row. He knew that voices tended to drop in volume towards the end of the sentence, and warned the actors against this. His advice to the players during the early days of *Goray Galad* has been reported:

> If the lines are not memorised sufficiently, the voice throw remains feeble and if proper attention is not given to diction right from the start, later it

becomes difficult to rectify mispronunciations. Social drama depends on the quick repartee of dialogues; so if the audience misses a few words due to faulty diction, the play loses its impact. When we speak, we usually tend to run out of breath towards the end of the sentence and blur the words; it becomes necessary, therefore, to give extra stress on the final words so that they may be heard right till the end of the auditorium. Even if this entails a slight artificiality, this may be used judiciously, though without exaggeration.[23]

Recalling the later rehearsals at Santiniketan, Amita Sen writes in a similar vein: "He would keep a close watch on this and instruct us repeatedly, 'Your voices should not drop. Utter the last word at a high pitch'. So even without microphones, every word would be distinctly audible from the rear of the auditorium."[24] Also, that he could be strict and exacting as a director is attested by this account of the rehearsals of *Natir Puja*. When he was teaching the specificities of rustic intonation of a village girl, the girls were in fits of laughter, which left him disappointed and angry: "He was so incensed by our behaviour that he sharply admonished us all and walked out of the rehearsal. We were left petrified and all our glee vanished in a trice. We never repeated such slackness before him again."[25]

Several eyewitness accounts mention how Rabindranath tirelessly acted out roles for those who needed some guidance, so that the best possible effect could be achieved in performance. For instance, Sahana Devi, in her memoir, writes: "During the rehearsals, if the Poet felt someone needed help he would act out the role himself, or if someone had to be rectified he would do so, not through verbal explaining but through actual performance", or again, "I always felt that to watch Rabindranath's style of direction was itself a lesson. *From the little I have seen, I gathered that the Poet preferred to train through actual acting, less through verbal explanation. He would repeat as many times as required, with immense patience. He could become one with the character he was demonstrating.*"[26] When Gouri Basu was selected to play the *nati* (the dancing girl) of *Natir Puja*, she was somewhat diffident because she thought it would be difficult for her to master the dialogues, and in particular the Sanskrit *slokas*. The Poet reassured her and took charge of preparing her for the role.[27] And when the production was taken to Calcutta in 1927, the girl playing Malati was down with high fever just a day before the performance and had to be replaced. Rabindranath immediately caught hold of Surupa, the youngest daughter of Abanindranath, for the role; she had earlier played Sudha in *Dakghar*, and so the Poet now relied on her proven abilities. Surupa Devi reminisces:

The more I pleaded, "Please let me go, I cannot manage within such a short time, please find someone else", the more was he insistent, "You will do it, I will teach you". With what enthusiasm he tutored me for the role through the entire afternoon. On the day of the performance, though terror-struck, I acted the role of Malati, sang a few lines, and ultimately felt that I had managed. At the end of the performance Rabi-dada called me to the balcony of the upper floor, lovingly put a garland on my neck and said, "This is your prize."[28]

That the Poet had confidence in the talents of the more accomplished among his players is borne out by incidents like these. As a judicious director, he knew he could depend upon the likes of Gaganendranath or Abanindranath or Dinendranath to deliver as expected. The roles which required onstage singing were specially reserved for Dinendranath, and the latter gave some excellent portrayals, both in the singing and acting of these roles. Particular mention may be made of his cameo appearance as the Madman in *Raja*:

> Dinendranath appeared as the Madman, in rags and dishevelled hair, singing. There was no leap, no yell, no extra effort to depict madness; only a faraway look in search of the unattainable, and that song of yearning, "*Tora je ja bolis bhai, amar sonar horin chai*" ["Whatever you may say, I must have the golden deer"] … the elderly gentleman (himself a talented actor), who sat next to me, grasped my hand firmly. I looked up to find tears rolling down his cheeks.[29]

That Dinendranath was a finished actor, and left his mark in other (non-singing) roles as well, is attested by Amritalal Bose, who wrote in his review of the 1923 *Visarjan*:

> Few actors know how to make their entrances and exits. Babu Dinendra Nath Tagore, as the high priest of the Holy Mother's temple, entered and, before he uttered a single word, we knew the genius of an actor was in him. He looked the haughty Brahmin, proud of his "paita" [the sacred thread], conscious of his authority, intriguing, designing, yet never losing his native dignity, no convention, no mannerism, no stiffness.[30]

It was because Rabindranath had full faith in his histrionic abilities that he gave Dinendranath the charge of not only training the young students for onstage singing but even of honing their acting skills, as in the case of Ashamukul Das, who was prepared by Dinendranath for the role Amal (as discussed below).

With his female leads like Amita Tagore or Nandita Kripalani, too, Rabindranath was on surer ground. He knew they could present what he expected of them. After Amita's brilliant portrayal of Sumitra in *Tapati* (1929), he recruited her for the role of Sudarshana in *Raja* (1935): "Amita having arrived here, I caught hold of her to do Sudarshana."[31] And he coaxed Nandita into accepting the role of Surangama (for the same production) as he had faith in her capabilities: "The role of Surangama is not too difficult; I can teach you that bit …. If you could be given a few days of thorough training, I am sure you would do fine."[32]

These incidents may give us some idea of Rabindranath's astuteness as a director; he would be more particular with actors who needed help, but with those on whose abilities he could trust he would perhaps be more flexible and allow some liberty. If he felt that Ashamukul Das, Amita Sen or Ranu Adhikari needed close supervision, he also felt that Dinendranath and Abanindranath, Amita Tagore and Nandita Kripalani could be relied upon for their proven histrionic capabilities. Yet, all the while, he wanted to maintain a control of the productions with his meticulousness and precision. In fact, his advice to any other aspirant director was much the same: "Do not leave the rehearsals in their hands; train them yourself."[33] Envisaging a new approach to staging, Rabindranath aimed for a certain quality and aesthetic standard that would be a marker of his productions and give them a unique identity of their own.

It was against this high standard of quality and precision that Ashamukul Das was found to fall short when he was tried out for Amal for the proposed 1917 performance of *Dakghar* at Jorasanko. Though Ashamukul had already played the role earlier in a Calcutta production of the play,[34] Rabindranath was left sorely disappointed by his affected tone, and entrusted Dinendranath Tagore and Asitkumar Haldar with the task of rectifying his deficiencies. Only after these two had adequately tutored Ashamukul for the role of Amal, to the satisfaction of Rabindranath, was he finally selected to play the character.[35] In the final stages, Rabindranath seems to have taken over and trained Ashamukul himself.[36] Ranu Adhikari played Aparna in the 1923 *Visarjan* to Rabindranath's Joysingha (at Empire Theatre, Calcutta) and mimed the role of Sudarshana, with the Poet reciting the lines, in the 1924 *Arupratan* production (at Alfred Theatre, Calcutta). In either case, Rabindranath trained her for the roles with tender care. Sahana Devi records that for the role of Aparna, each little detail was repeatedly demonstrated by Rabindranath step by step, right from her very entry to every detail of her impersonation, till the player of Aparna could master it;[37] and Ranu Adhikari herself has mentioned how she was taught to mime the role of Sudarshana by the Poet himself.[38] Sahana Devi played Surangama in this 1924 *Arupratan*, miming the role and also singing the songs; she gives a graphic account of how exacting the Poet was even in the minute use of gestures:

> what remains unforgettable is the way he taught me to act in *Arupratan*, though I did not really have much to perform. I particularly remember his showing beautifully how with a slight twist of the wrist the garland held in the hand should be placed on the platter. He held my hand and took me through the process, saying, "Why do you keep your hand so stiff? Stretch it out with natural grace and ease." He would stretch out his own hand so beautifully, and then, with that subtle twist of the wrist, would keep the garland – it was a sheer delight to watch. I realised from his demonstration how even a small matter could be rendered so aesthetically pleasant.[39]

In fact, for the rehearsals of the musical *Punarvasanta*, Rabindranath is reported to have even "taught dancing steps to the girls, with his drape wrapped around his waist, clapping his hands."[40] And, during the rehearsals of *Navin*, when Amita Sen's dancing was unable to express the mood of fatigue (as required by the accompanying song) Rabindranath said, "Could you dance so rhythmically if you were tired? Through the rhythm of the feet, the posture of the body, you need to convey that fatigue." And he took up the *ektara* [41] in his own hands and showed her how to do this.[42] Amita Sen has also recalled how she rehearsed as Kamalika, the heroine of *Shapmochan,* under the Poet's close supervision. Dissatisfied with her rendition of a particular situation, Rabindranath went on to enact it himself, showing how with a slight tilt of the head she should strain to listen to a tune from afar, and then, realizing it all to be mere fancy, collapse upon the stool in despair, almost dissolving into tears.[43] Because Santidev Ghosh was down with measles after the first few rehearsals, Harry Timbers, then working at Sriniketan, was cast as the king, Aruneswar. Since he did not know the Bengali language, Rabindranath made the extra effort of clarifying to him the meaning of every word, every song: "He was explaining to the king the meaning of the lines and the songs, even enacting them – not once, but several times. And we experienced this rare sight with all our heart."[44] This capacity to extract out of his players what was required for the performance is something that was a hallmark of Rabindranath's directorial capabilities. Before the final enactment of *Raja*, he was meticulously conducting the rehearsals at Uttarayan in Santiniketan, not only preparing the roles but even nudging the players to dance when the dramatic situation so required:

> For the scene of the wayfarers he insisted that singing was not enough, there should also be dancing. The nimble few responded immediately, but the less agile were finding it difficult to shed their inhibitions. But the Poet was persistent. He left his own seat, and, with the song on his lips, he started to demonstrate the dance – the dance of the rustic folk celebrating a festival. With the merriment and gaiety prevailing, the others also joined their movements following rhythms of dance. Nothing escaped his eyes, though strict vigil was hardly required. His cheerful presence was enough to infuse jollity into the others and to inspire them to dance and sing.[45]

If this is from the days of preparation for the final performance of *Raja* (1935), the Poet was then in his seventy-fourth year.

When *Chandalika* was being rehearsed on the occasion of Mahatma Gandhi and Kasturba's visit to Santiniketan, Rabindranath again displayed how exacting he was as a director: "He personally supervised the rehearsal and even delayed the programme by a quarter of an hour till he was satisfied when at one stage he almost jumped to the edge of his seat and broke out into musical interpolation to provide the cue when the performers seemed to have lost it."[46] Santidev Ghosh attributes the huge success of his productions to the immense effort that Rabindranath put behind them:

> The audiences have enjoyed the performances thoroughly, but it was difficult for them to imagine how the tremendous endeavours of one person

could make this possible. He had to labour day after day to prepare his team of players. He never worked with professional actors or actresses. He fell back upon resources available to him – the students, teachers and staff who came to Santiniketan, who often had no exposure to theatre – and with them he created successful productions. He trained them painstakingly for the different roles. He took them through each detail repeatedly – the precise stress on the words, the varied inflections of the voice. He even extracted performance out of one who nobody thought could utter a word on the stage. To avoid any kind of inhibition in the actors, he worked out the precise movements, gestures and postures that would be in tune with what the performance demanded. He paid close attention to every detail.[47]

Not only acting, but every detail related to the production had to be agreeable, meeting the standard that he had set for his new theatre. Early in his career, during the staging of *Sarodotsav* in Santiniketan (1908), he was unhappy with Abanindranath's use of a mica-sprinkled royal umbrella as a stage property, and had it removed summarily.[48] For *Phalguni* (1916 production), he gave detailed instructions to Gaganendranath about costuming ("When Sardar emerges from the cave, he should carry a bow and arrows in his hand ... Sardar should be more elaborately dressed. The others should use coloured scarves and turbans to create an effect. The Baul should be in white, from top to toe") and even went on to specify the fabric of the white gown for the Baul, which he was playing himself ("The white gown that you will design for me should be fitted with long loose sleeves – if the cloth is muslin, the whiteness will appear splendid").[49] When the dance drama *Chitrangada* was being prepared for production, he advised his daughter-in-law Pratima Devi: "Too much of dance ... looked tiresome. Manipuri needs to be curtailed to ensure a decent reception. The whole performance should be fast-paced and balanced. This play is more dramatic than lyrical."[50] For a performance of the dance drama *Chandalika*, he sent elaborate instructions to Santidev Ghosh to incorporate extra stage business: "For this new song, it would be good if, while Mamata makes gestures of selling flowers, Anita and Hashi enter and gesticulate as though they are buying flowers to decorate their ears or hair."[51] During the staging of *Tapati* (in 1929), he meticulously supervised every aspect of the performance, as has been reported by Amita Tagore, who played Sumitra to his Vikramdev in this production. In an interview given on 6 July 1991, she mentions how Rabindranath was not happy with the white colour of Sumitra's costume for the fire scene; also how he discouraged the wearing of any "glossy dress or shiny crown or ornament on the head lest its radiance eclipsed the facial expression".[52] She also narrated at a gathering, where the writer of this book happened to be present, an amusing anecdote regarding Rabindranath appearing as Vikram in black hair and beard. She told the Poet that since everyone knew he was playing the role, there was hardly any need for him to blacken his hair and beard every evening and again go through the tedious process of removing the colour after the performance.

Rabindranath's reply had been that if he played Vikram in his white hair and beard, everyone would say that the Queen ran off because her husband was old – a miserable interpretation that would utterly ruin the play. Abanindranath informs us how he solved the problem by covering Rabindranath's original white beard with black gauze.[53] Perhaps a similar technique may have been employed for his dual roles in *Phalguni* – though there is no first-hand account of this. These details indicate that not only was he thinking through all the nitty-gritty of a production, but was also trying to invest the Bengali stage with a new/modern approach to theatrical performance that would redefine categories like realism and verisimilitude, and in all that was striding far ahead of his times.

II

Despite such painstaking efforts and meticulous rehearsals, there were still moments when the production could/would veer off in unforeseen directions. Such indeterminacies would be caused primarily by mistakes and errors on the part of the actors, but sometimes were also the result of improvisations on the part of the director – for which Rabindranath had a particular propensity.

The most common kind of mistake that actors would be prone to was, of course, lapse of memory. But as a producer/director, Rabindranath was against the use of prompters; he felt that dependence on the prompter resulted in docile acting, feeble voice throw and inhibited movements. Elaborating on this, a contemporary writes: "He was annoyed if a single word was missed from the song or dialogue. There was no provision for prompting in his productions. He would be present in the theatre making it impossible for the actors to prompt each other."[54] Yet, despite his exacting control over the other actors, the Poet himself sometimes fell prey to the quirks of memory. Abanindranath mentions how during the performance of *Baikunther Khata*, Rabindranath once forgot the lines of Kedar, and when Abanindranath (playing Tinkori) provided him with the cue, he deftly managed the situation.[55] The rehearsals of *Sarodotsav* proved to be another major hurdle for the Poet when it came to remembering his lines. In a letter to Ranu Adhikari, somewhat jocularly, he confesses:

> The rehearsals of *Sarodotsav* have made me fidgety. Every afternoon Bibhuti makes me go through the whole text; like a small boy, I have to memorise my lines. Yet, such is my idiocy, that during rehearsals I keep forgetting – even the little boys and girls laugh; my sorry state hardly bears mentioning.[56]

Abanindranath devised an ingenious method to aid the Poet's (as well as his own) failing memory. He had two prompters covered from head to foot in bluish black *burquah*-like gear, with slits for the eyes and mouths. They moved across the stage, behind the players, holding in their hands rods with discs covered in silver and golden foil, with the scripts attached to the inner side: "The two prompters with these rods in hand moved from two sides following the stage actors and prompting the lines. It suited us immensely; no more memory lapses and the performance was smooth."[57] The strategy not only worked effectively but also elicited readings from the spectators that were more than expected. Abanindranath reports the response of one eyewitness who said that nobody realized that the two figures were prompters, but took them to be "mysterious" even "monster-like" presences that were a part of the play's larger scheme: "we thought those monsters were meant to remain at the back while the rest of you performed in the front stage."[58] Pramathanath Bishi, who was one of the prompters, corroborates such responses from the audience: "The spectators did not understand the real fact but regarded the two (figures) as symbols of some idea."[59] Though introduced as a tactic to ward off memory lapses, the device, while posing a major challenge to the expectations of verisimilitude, passed off easily as a symbolic feature. This worked specially in the performance of a play like *Sarodotsav* which was trying to refashion the notions of theatrical representation. The audience responses were particularly significant as they indicated the willingness in the audience to suspend disbelief and accept the newness that was being offered through the performance.

However, that Rabindranath worried about remembering the lines on other occasions as well is documented in his letter to Pratima Devi, dated 1 October 1910, when he complains of this problem, having been pressed into playing the role of Dhananjoy Bairagi in *Prayaschitta*:[60] "The day of our performance is approaching near, and I am worried that I have not been able to memorise my lines yet. How does one memorise? Day and night, one has to meet with so many people. Some come all the way from Calcutta to bother me here."[61] Not only the dialogue, memory lapses plagued the Poet in other ways as well. It is Abanindranath, again, who provides us with the information that for a particular *Valmiki Pratibha* staging, Rabindranath entered to blow the conch shell but had forgotten to remove his spectacles; on being warned, he turned his face aside and neatly took them off.[62]

At times, the excitement of acting appears to have swept Rabindranath off his feet – more so in his younger days. We may again recall here Abanindranath's account of how, as Raghupati (in *Visarjan*, 1890), the Poet forgot that in the final scene he had merely to give a shove to the idol of the goddess kept on the stage; cords were attached to it with which the others, waiting in the wings, would pull it away. Instead, he lifted up the heavy clay idol and somehow managed to put it down near the wings; as a result of this, he sprained his back.[63] Again, according to an eyewitness report, during the performance of *Visarjan* for Sangit Samaj on 16 December 1900, Rabindranath as Raghupati was seemingly so overwhelmed with emotion that it might have been perilous for the young boy playing Dhruva: "he became so involved that he forgot how sharp the scimitar really was; if the other actors, realising his state, had not quickly removed Dhruva [Aswini], there might have been a terrible disaster."[64] However, because in the play Raghupati does not actually get to use the scimitar and is apprehended by the King and his men before he can reach Dhruva, it seems unlikely that the boy was really in any real danger.

Also, it is possible to explain this as merely a simulation of emotion on the part of a seasoned actor like Rabindranath, which others might have mistaken for real. But it is also true that indeterminacies and unforeseen situations always have a part to play in theatrical performances. When Rabindranath was playing the young Joysingha at the age of sixty-two, for a particular dramatic situation, he was required to kneel before Dinendranath playing Raghupati. During the actual performance, having knelt down, he was unable to rise on his feet till Dinendranath helped him up, ad libbing some words to suit the situation. After their exit, Rabindranath is supposed to have told Dinendranath that he had saved the day by helping him up, to which the latter replied that because he had realized the plight of the Poet he had lifted him up.[65] In fact, in that same production Dinendranath's string of beads (*rudraksha*) snapped accidentally, but, unperturbed, he flung the beads towards the spectators as a part of the performance.[66] During rehearsals, Rabindranath is reported to have complained that Dinendranath, a heavily-built man, who as Raghupati was required to throw himself upon the body of Joysingha, often forgot that the Poet – acting the dead Joysingha – was not really dead.[67]

The excitement of performance, resulting in unforeseen situations, affected not only the Poet, but other actors too. This could be even truer when performers of different age groups were engaged. Parimal Goswami reports one such instance when, during the staging of *Navin/Vasanta* at New Empire in 1932, a little girl was becoming impatient to dance, while the Poet was still reciting a passage. His reading was to be followed by a dance with the song "*Ora okarone chanchal*" ["They are restive for no reason"], in which the girl was to perform: "the little girl was becoming impatient to dance, and could hardly wait for the Poet's reading to end. Every time she was about to start dancing, the Poet held on to her dress and prevented her. What a coincidence with the spirit of the song: they were indeed impatient for no reason!"[68]

III

Innovations and/or improvisations by the author/producer/director could also account for performances to go beyond the set parameters of rehearsals. Rabindranath had a penchant for this, and is known to make additions/alterations to the script till the penultimate hour. In Rathindranath's words:

> Father's creative mind could never find pleasure in repetition. Invariably he would make alterations and additions to the plays whenever they were about to be performed. Such modifications would continue till the last day of the rehearsals and even in between successive nights of the performance much to the consternation of the actors.[69]

Often multiple versions of the same play have evolved as a result of Rabindranath's continuous interventions into the text in search for newness and his reluctance to repeat himself – both as playwright and theatre-practitioner. So, there are several existing versions of a play like *Visarjan*; in fact, one version dropped Aparna and retained only Gunavati among the women,[70] while yet another did away totally with the female characters.[71] *Raja* was revised many times, and ultimately was majorly reworked as *Arupratan*; yet, for the 1935 production in Calcutta, he returned to *Raja* and collated it with the later version of *Arupratan*.[72] The dance drama *Shapmochan* also used the same source tale of *Kusha-jataka*, though thematically did not quite address the deeper resonances of *Raja*. What was envisaged first as *Yakshapuri*, and then as *Nandini*,[73] finally emerged as *Raktakarabi*, to be instantly followed by the English auto-translation, *Red Oleanders; Raktakarabi*, however, was never produced by him. And the early *Raja o Rani* (1989), moving through the intermediary version of *Bhairaber Bali* (1929), ultimately developed into the "actable version"[74] of *Tapati* (1929). The changes in the dramatic structure made by Rabindranath as a dramatist have been discussed in the earlier chapter "Preparing the playtext"; the following section will be concerned with the changes made for staging purposes, determined by theatrical exigencies and/or his predilection for improvising.

As mentioned above, Rabindranath, nudged by Abanindranath, agreed to allow the disguised prompters to enter the stage for the *Sarodotsav* production to avoid memory lapses. One must concede, however, that this innovation was more the brainwave of Abanindranath, and, had the fear of faltering memory not plagued him, the perfectionist in Rabindranath might not have permitted this stratagem. Of course, there were moments when onstage improvisations became necessary. As described earlier, during the performance of the 1923 *Visarjan*, Dinendranath's Raghupati helped Rabindranath's Joysingha to rise to his feet, when the sixty-two-year-old poet, having knelt before the former, had difficulties in getting up on his own. Also, Dinendranath's string of beads (*rudraksha*) having snapped, he tossed it towards the audience as an extension of his theatrical gesture.

There is a particularly interesting account of how, when a fire started backstage one evening during the performance of this play, Rabindranath as Joysingha held Ranu Adhikari (Aparna) firmly by the hand to prevent her from escaping in the middle of the scene, and went on reciting improvised lines till the fire was doused. Charuchandra Bhattacharya, who attended the evening's performance (yet had no inkling of what had happened backstage), reports how Rabindranath provided the details in a conversation he had with him the day after; this may be cited here at some length because it provides interesting clues about Rabindranath's level-headed pragmatism as actor and producer:

> I went upstairs and asked him, "What happened yesterday?"
> "Which row were you seated in?"
> "Seven or eight rows behind (the first row)."
> "Yet you didn't understand anything even from there! Let me tell you what happened. During Joysingha-Aparna's dialogue, I noticed a fire had started backstage. Ranu was bent on fleeing. *If that happened, there would*

have been utter chaos. *The spectators would all want to escape; if not by fire, people would be killed in a stampede.* By then efforts were already on to extinguish the flames. The sounds of the fire brigade could also be heard. I held Ranu firmly by the hand, and turning her around so that she did not have to face the fire, went on speaking my lines. I finished, it was Ranu's turn to respond, but she could not utter a word. So I went on speaking. *The prompter stood still. After six or seven minutes of such reciting, the fire was doused and we left the stage.* You understood nothing of this?"

"Nothing at all."

"*I went on adding lines not in the text* and yet you could not catch it?"

"Not in the least. But one has to recite quite a lot to cover six to seven minutes. There was a fire inside, your co-actor was ready to escape, under such circumstances how could you provide appropriate words in blank verse for Joysingha?"

"My dear sir, it was ultimately my writing, so what was so difficult?"

I was left wondering – indeed, what was so difficult![75]

What struck Charuchandra Bhattacharya was Rabindranath's ability to improvise blank-verse lines to suit the situation and continue the scene (holding firmly by the hand a frightened co-actor) till the fire was extinguished. It was the Poet's pragmatism and quick thinking that saved the day and brought to the fore his alertness as actor-producer-director.

Rabindranath was also known for sudden incursions into the performance, which may or may not have been premeditated, and could have taken others by surprise. For the 1917 *Dakghar*, he once passed over the rear stage disguised as a *baul*, singing a song, and again, from behind the curtains he broke out into another song.[76] There was an English synopsis made of the play,[77] which includes a stage direction: "*Enter GAFFER in the road disguised as a beggar. He signs to the boy and passes on, followed by the curd-seller.*"[78] Evidently, by the time this English synopsis was prepared, his entry as a beggar/wandering minstrel (*baul*) had become an established stage practice, though not marked as such in the early written versions of the play. Again, for the 1917 *Achalayatan* at Santiniketan, when the chorus songs were becoming rather listless, he suddenly joined in one, startling the audience but bringing back the desired life into the performance.[79]

Revisions/alterations/innovations often had to be made for theatrical exigencies. For instance, to minimize the possibilities of mispronunciation by actors, Rabindranath revised texts and altered words which could otherwise prove to be stumbling blocks for them. When *Tasher Desh* was being rehearsed, eyewitness accounts mention how Rabindranath tried to address the problem of faulty diction by altering the original words:

There were flaws in pronunciation. The melody of the songs can conceal the errors, but they jar on the ears in the spoken dialogues. I believe this

142 *Rabindranath as theatre-practitioner*

is the reason why the Prince and the Merchant have been given a bare minimum to speak. The King of Diamonds [Sarojranjan Chowdhury] though rebuked as a *Bangal* [80] from Srihatta could not rectify his "*e*" of "*megh*". His "*k*"-s have been aspirates. So, dialogues had to be curtailed, words had to be altered.[81]

As late as in 1935, for the final production of *Raja*, to resolve the problem of faulty diction of some of the actors, he again replaced words in the original text:

> For them, the original language of the text has to be changed: "*phanki*" is replaced by "*banchana*"[82]; "*haan kore thaka*" by "*abak hoye thaka*";[83] the word "*kebal*" has been removed from the entire text and "*sudhu*" used instead; thankfully there is no "*megh*"[84] in the text, or I would have to use "*kuasha*" though that would have clouded the language.[85]

Though *Dakghar* originally had no female role, for a particular performance at Santiniketan, lacking an adequately skilful male actor for Madhavdutta, he introduced the role of Madhavdutta's wife (for a lady resident of the *asram* who was known for her histrionic abilities), and made necessary revisions in the text: "He was told about the acting talents of a particular lady of the *asram*. As a result, he introduced Madhavdutta's wife, and curtailed drastically the dialogues of Madhavdutta."[86] In fact, with other female actors also available in the *asram* by then, he inducted a female companion for Thakurda with the name of Khanjanayani, and even made the curd-seller a woman.[87] Though, unfortunately, this production of *Dakghar* ultimately could not be staged, this attempt speaks volumes for his ability to play around with the fixity of gendered roles (as given in the playtext) to suit the requirements of the situation at hand. In the early days of the school, when girl students were few in number, he would cast the boys in the female characters; in this particular incident, lack of adequate accomplished male actors made him take a reverse turn and induct women where no such roles were provided in the original text.

Rabindranath's masterstroke at improvisation probably came with the memorable use of Sahana Devi for the 1923 *Visarjan*. When she was available almost in the final stages of preparation, he drafted her in the performance and made her enter at several points in the play singing songs; cast in the role of a detached observer, her songs served to elucidate the immediate dramatic situation. Sahana Devi mentions how Rabindranath inducted her into the performance with ten songs for her to sing: of these, three had been already written for *Visarjan*, two were earlier works, and five more were composed for this occasion.[88] The performance started with one of these songs. The stage-copy for this production mentions "*Jhunu* [89] / *Janani tomar aruna charanakhani/ Pronam o prasthan –/ Sankha ghanta ityadi/ Rajar prabesh –*" ["Jhunu/ Mother, your glowing feet/ Bows and leaves –/ Conch, bells, etc./ Enter the king –"].[90] Sahana Devi, however, cites a different song: "The play would begin with my singing '*Timir duar kholo eso eso nirob charaney*' ['Open the gates of darkness and come silently']"[91]; one might surmise that there was a shift from what was intended in the stage-copy and what was actually performed. The enactment was punctuated with her songs almost in the manner of choric commentary. On the one hand, this looked back to the tradition of introducing characters like Fate (*Niyoti*) or Conscience (*Vivek*) to comment on the action/characters as practised in the public theatre and/or *jatra*; on the other, by conceptualizing her role as that of *Visva-Mata* (World-Mother), Rabindranath was adding an extra dimension to the play which deliberates upon the nature of the goddess viewed as the Eternal Mother. In fact, the press release which appeared prior to the performance indicated as much:

> a new female character – if it can be so called – [has been] introduced. This new character is an entirely novel conception. She will appear on the stage at intervals and sing a song interpreting in a way the clash of actions and emotions and furnishing them with a proper background. She is as it were, *the spirit of the play personified*. Her songs have been specially composed by the poet.[92]

That Sahana Devi's inclusion bolstered the production considerably is evident from the rave reviews that followed:

> But no notice of the play will be complete without a mention of the valued contribution Mrs. Sahana Bose made to its success. She played the part of chorus and interpreted the piece and supplied the connecting links with the aid of beautiful solos – the melody of their language and that of her voice casting a rare spell on the house.[93]

Evidently, Rabindranath's inspiration to use Sahana Devi was an ingenious piece of innovation that added an extra dimension to the production: "Mrs. Sahana Bose's songs were punctuated with tremendous cheers from every direction of the hall",[94] or, "The musical part of the play was well rendered by Mrs. Sahana Bose",[95] or again, "Another feature of the play was the songs by Mrs. Shahana Bose who kept the house spell bound by her beautiful voice."[96]

Sometimes certain decisions – even not so palatable ones – have to be taken on the spur of the moment in the larger interests of the performance. Even Rabindranath was not spared this. He who had made out a case for the freedom of the reader/viewer to interpret the performance text in the theatre (in "Rangamancha") could not restrain himself from taking a step to control an over-enthusiastic crowd during a performance of *Navin/Vasanta* at New Empire, Calcutta, in 1932. According to an eyewitness report:

> During the performance, before particular dance sections could end some among the audience burst out clapping, perhaps to show their appreciation. More readings and musical sequences were to follow. But the long

duration of applause was interrupting the performance. At times the applause was crossing the limit. Rabindranath was putting up with all this, but only up to a point. Before the second half began, he came in front of the stage and with folded hands made an appeal: "Please do not clap in the middle of the performance. That is done to mock the performance. If you like it and would want to clap, please do so at the end. As this nature play is a complete whole, no one portion can be either good or bad; it is a composite creation, not discrete individual scenes. So, it is my humble request, please do not spoil its wholeness by clapping in the middle." While he was speaking, his face was flushed, and it was clearly evident that he was agitated. His hands remained folded, but there was such a stern note in his voice that those who had been clapping hung their heads in shame.[97]

The audience that had assembled needed to be "educated", and Rabindranath took the somewhat harsh decision to intervene to ensure the smooth conduct of the production. Again, when *Shapmochan* was given at the Andhra University at Waltair (in 1934), the audience, unable to follow the language, grew restless, and was reprimanded by the Poet: "During the performance, a section of the audience who could not follow the language of the play did not maintain silence and the poet rebuked them."[98] Perhaps goaded by such experiences, he took the decision to declare on the back cover of the programme note clear instructions for the audience not to clap before the performance ended: "You must have noticed the programme of Rabindranath, where there is a direction on the back cover that nobody should clap before the end of the performance."[99] Rabindranath's remark (made at the New Empire in 1932, as cited above) that the performance "is a complete whole, no one portion can be either good or bad; it is a composite creation, not discrete individual scenes" reminds us that this spirit of wholeness underlies not only his dramaturgical practices or theatrical performances but his entire aesthetic and philosophical principles of life. To comprehend this wholeness, the audience has to be made adequately aware, educated, or, 'sensitized' (to use a term that looks back to his appeal to the *"sahriday darshak"* [sensitive/amiable/perceptive spectator] in "Rangamancha", 1902). An audience, sensitive and genial, was a pre-text for the proper reception of his theatre. Such interventions, then, even if unforeseen and unfortunate, often became a necessity not only in the interests of the performance but for what the Poet was trying to achieve through his theatre.

Notes

1 Cited in Rudraprasad Chakrabarty, *Rangamancha O Rabindranath: Samakalin Pratikriya* (Calcutta: Ananda, 1995) 26.
2 See Rudraprasad Chakrabarty, *Rangamancha O Rabindranath: Samakalin Pratikriya*, 25.
3 See Sekhar Samaddar, "Rabindranather Natyabhavna", in *Punascha Rabindranath*, ed. Sabyasachi Bhattacharya and Bratin Dey (New Delhi: National Book Trust, India, 2012) 215–83; specially 219.

4 See Abanindranath Tagore, *Gharoa* (Calcutta: Visva-Bharati Granthan Vibhaga, 1941; rpt. 1983), 117.
 5 For details, see Abanindranath Tagore, *Gharoa*, 105–6.
 6 *Visarjan* was written in 1890, presumably after his return from the tour of Europe between August and November 1890. But there are controversies regarding the date(s) of its first few performance(s).
 7 Prabhatkumar Mukhopadhyay, *Rabindra Jibani*, vol. 1 (Calcutta: Visva-Bharati Granthalay, 1933; rev edn. 1960) 318. See also n. 6 above.
 8 Abanindranath Tagore, *Gharoa*, 22; however, that Abanindranath's report may be inaccurate has been pointed out: see Prasantakumar Pal, *Rabi Jibani*, vol. 3 (Calcutta: Ananda Publishers, 1987) 131; also, Rudraprasad Chakrabarty, *Rangamancha O Rabindranath: Samakalin Pratikriya*, 50.
 9 Sekhar Samaddar, "Rabindranather Natyabhavna", 280, n. 16, 17 and 18.
10 See *Manche Rabindranath*, ed. Ramakrishna Bhattacharya (Calcutta: Bharati Parishad, 1978) 99.
11 He mentions this in his reminiscences in *Europe Jatrir Diary*, in *Rabindra Rachanabali* (Complete Works) Centenary Edition, vol. 10 (Calcutta; West Bengal Government, 1961) 399.
12 Mentioned in Abanindranath Tagore, *Gharoa*, 110.
13 Amita Tagore, "Rabindra Prasanga" (1988) in a collection of essays published on the occasion of the 125th birth anniversary of Tagore; cited in Rudraprasad Chakrabarty, *Rangamancha O Rabindranath: Samakalin Pratikriya*, 54.
14 Mentioned in Rudraprasad Chakrabarty, *Rangamancha O Rabindranath: Samakalin Pratikriya*, 77.
15 Jatindranath Basu, "Shilaidahe Rabindranath", *Sahitya*, Ashar 1307 BS (June 1900) 148; as cited in Rudraprasad Chakrabarty, *Rangamancha O Rabindranath: Samakalin Pratikriya*, 76.
16 Khagendranath Chattopadhyay, *Rabindra Katha* (Calcutta: Parul Prakasani, 2015; originally 1941) 189.
17 Khagendranath Chattopadhyay, *Rabindra Katha*, 186.
18 Prabhatkumar Mukhopadhyay, his biographer, mentions this in the context of a letter written to his wife, in *Rabindra Jibani*, vol. 1, 346.
19 Bijanbehari Bhattacharya, *Lipibibek* (Calcutta: Bookland, 1962) 87.
20 Amita Tagore in her unpublished memoir, as cited in Rudraprasad Chakrabarty, "Abhineta o Nirdeshak Rabindranath", in *Korok Sahitya Patrika: Anya Rabindranath*, ed. Tapas Bhowmik, pre-Autumn issue (2000): 181–90; here quoted from 189; emphases added.
21 Amita Sen, "Natir Pujar Pujarini", in Debjit Bandyopadhyay, *Natir Puja* (Calcutta: Signet Press, 2019) 59–70, here quoted from 61; originally in *Desh: Sahitya Sankhya* (1978) 177–80.
22 See letter to Nirmalkumari Mahalanobis, dated 29 November 1935, in *Desh*, 23 *Agrahayan* 1386 BS (December 1979) 503.
23 Khagendranath Chattopadhyay, *Rabindra Katha*, 196.
24 Amita Sen, "Natir Pujar Pujarini", in Debjit Bandyopadhyay, *Natir Puja*, 61.
25 Amita Sen, "Natir Pujar Pujarini", in Debjit Bandyopadhyay, *Natir Puja*, 63.
26 Sahana Devi, *Smritir Kheya* (Calcutta: Prima Publications, 2011; originally 1978) 125, 130; emphasis added.
27 Gouri Bhanja, "Natir Puja 1333", as transcribed by Alpana Roy Chowdhury, *Visva-Bharati News* (April 1978): 176–8, here quoted from 177; also cited in Debjit Bandyopadhyay, *Natir Puja* (Calcutta: Signet Press, 2019) 71–4.
28 Surupa Devi, "Sudhar Smriti", in *Balaka: Natya-byaktitwo Rabindranath*, ed. Dhananjoy Ghoshal, no. 19, November 2010: 27–30; here cited from 30; originally published in *Rabindra Bharati Patrika*, January–March 1979.
29 Jibanmoy Roy, cited in Ajitkumar Ghosh, *Thakurbarir Abhinay*, 71–2.

30 *Indian Daily News*, 25 August 1923; cited in Rudraprasad Chakrabarty, *Rangamancha O Rabindranath: Samakalin Pratikriya*, 64; also in Ajitkumar Ghosh, *Thakurbarir Abhinay*, 73–4.
31 Letter to Nirmalkumari Mahalanobis, dated 29 November 1935, *Desh*, 23 *Agrahayan* 1386 BS (December 1979) 503.
32 *Chithipatra*, vol. 4 (Calcutta: Visva-Bharati, 1943) 202.
33 This was his advice to Sourindramohan Mukhopadhyay; see Sourindramohan Mukhopadhyay, *Rabindra Smriti* (Calcutta: Sisir Publishing House, 1957) 196.
34 Prasantachandra Mahalanobis, who was aware of Ashamukul's performance as Amal at the Brahmo Samaj in Calcutta, introduced him to Rabindranath.
35 See Asitkumar Haldar, *Rabitirthe* (Calcutta: Anjana Prakashani, 1958) 104–5.
36 See Prasantakumar Pal, *Rabi Jibani*, vol. 7 (Calcutta: Ananda Publishers, 1997) 290.
37 See Sahana Devi, *Smritir Kheya*, 131.
38 Mentioned in Rudraprasad Chakrabarty, *Rangamancha O Rabindranath: Samakalin Pratikriya*, 109.
39 Sahana Devi, *Smritir Kheya*, 113.
40 As cited in Ajitkumar Ghosh, *Thakurbarir Abhinay* (Calcutta: Rabindra Bharati Society, 1988) 32.
41 A single-stringed musical instrument, usually used by the *bauls* (wandering minstrels).
42 Amita Sen, *Ananda sarba kaaje* (Calcutta: Tagore Research Institute 1983) 137.
43 See details in Amita Sen, *Ananda sarba kaaje*, 153.
44 Amita Sen, *Ananda sarba kaaje*, 146.
45 Sudhirchandra Kar, *Kabi Katha* (Calcutta: Suprakasan, 1951) 125.
46 Reported in *Harijan*, 9 March 1940; cited in Rudraprasad Chakrabarty, *Rangamancha O Rabindranath: Samakalin Pratikriya*, 274.
47 Santidev Ghosh, *Rabindrasangeet* (Calcutta: Visva-Bharati Granthalay, rev. ed. 1958; originally 1942) 210.
48 See Abanindranath Tagore, *Gharoa*, 133.
49 Letters to Gaganendranath in Pulinbehari Sen collections; as cited in Pabitra Sarkar, *Natmancha Natyarup* (Calcutta: Proma Publications, 3rf edn. 1999) 160.
50 Cited in Santidev Ghosh, *Rabindrasangeet* (Calcutta: Visva-Bharati Granthalay, rev. ed. 1958) 222.
51 Santidev Ghosh, *Rabindrasangeet*, 222. A similar instruction came during the rehearsals of *Shyama* to quicken the rhythmic pace of the first dance to express the mood of mirth (Santidev Ghosh, *Rabindrasangeet*, 213).
52 Cited in Rudraprasad Chakrabarty, *Rangamancha O Rabindranath: Samakalin Pratikriya*, 240.
53 Abanindranath, *Gharoa*, 139.
54 Bijanbehari Bhattacharya, *Lipibibek*, 88.
55 For details, see Abanindranath Tagore, *Gharoa*, 113–4.
56 Letter no. 51, dated 18 *Bhadra* 1329 BS (September 1922), *Bhanusingher Patrabali*, in *RR*, vol. 11, 314.
57 Mentioned in Abanindranath Tagore, *Gharoa*, 130–2. Pramathanath Bishi, who was one of these prompters, also reports this incidence in his memoirs: see *Rabindranath o Santiniketan* (Calcutta: Visva-Bharati, 1959; rpt. 1975) 76, and *Purano sei diner katha* (Calcutta: Mitra & Ghosh, 1958) 158–9.
58 Abanindranath Tagore, *Gharoa*, 132.
59 Pramathanath Bishi, *Purano sei diner katha*, 159.
60 This was the third performance of *Prayaschitta* at Santiniketan; the Poet had not acted on the two previous occasions (earlier in the same year).
61 *Chithipatra*, vol. 3 (Calcutta: Visva-Bharati, 1942), 6.
62 Abanindranath Tagore, *Gharoa*, 121.
63 Abanindranath Tagore, *Gharoa*, 110.

64 Hemendraprasad Ghosh, "Sangit Samaj" in *Masik Basumati, Ashar* 1360 BS (June–July 1953) 576; also cited in Prasantakumar Pal, *Rabi Jibani*, vol. 4 (Calcutta: Ananda Publishers, 1988) 306.
65 Mentioned in Ajitkumar Ghosh, *Thakurbarir Abhinay*, 74–5.
66 See Ajitkumar Ghosh, *Thakurbarir Abhinay*, 75.
67 Mentioned in Ajitkumar Ghosh, *Thakurbarir Abhinay*, 74.
68 Parimal Goswami, *Smriti chitran* (Calcutta: Prajna Prakashani, 1958) 227.
69 Rathindranath Tagore, "Looking Back" in *Rabindranath Tagore: A Tribute*, ed. Pulinbihari Sen and Kshitis Roy (New Delhi: Sangeet Natak Akademi, 2006; originally 1961), 45–52; here quoted from 50.
70 See Satyaranjan Basu, *Asram smriti, Rabindranath o Tripura* 1368 BS (1961) 246–7; cited in *Rangamancha O Rabindranath: Samakalin Pratikriya*, 69.
71 See Pramathanath Bishi, *Rabindranath O Santiniketan* (Calcutta: Visva-Bharati, 1975) 75. These changes were made usually for theatrical exigencies.
72 "A play has emerged combining *Arupratan* and *Raja*. I am busy now with its production related work. The performance will be in Calcutta, perhaps around 15 December." (Letter, dated 23 November 1935): *Rabindrabiksha*, no. 18, 1987, 31.
73 Though he initially refers to the play as *Yakshapuri* in some of his letters, none of the drafts preserved at the Rabindra Bhavana archives mentions this name. The earliest name there is *Nandini*, later renamed as *Raktakarabi*.
74 Preface to *Tapati, RR*, vol. 6, 1033.
75 Charuchandra Bhattacharya, *Kabi Smarane* (Calcutta: Basudhara Prakashani, 1961) 38–40; specially 39; emphases added.
76 See Sita Devi, *Punya Smriti*, 127.
77 The English synopsis could have been occasioned by the visit of Gandhi, Tilak, Anne Besant and Malavya, who saw the play at the Vichitra Hall at Jorasanko on 4 January 1918.
78 Cited in Sekhar Samaddar, "Rabindranather Natyabhavna", 249.
79 See Sita Devi, *Punya Smriti*, 19.
80 One who hails from East Bengal, and hence speaks in one of the dialects of that region. The Poet supposedly had difficulties with the *Bangal* dialect of the likes of Sarojranjan Chowdhury or Anil Chanda.
81 Bijanbehari Bhattacharya, *Lipibibek*, 86.
82 Possibly to avoid the Bengali '*ph*' to be pronounced as '*f*'.
83 The nasal pronunciation of the word ('*haan*') was perhaps eluding the actors.
84 For '*kebal*', the problem must have been in pronouncing '*e*' (as in 'd*e*sk') as '*a*' (as in 'c*a*t'); the same problem would have persisted with '*megh*', had the term occurred in the text. This was a fault more usually found in someone hailing from East Bengal, who would be commonly referred to as "Bangal". See also n. 80 above.
85 Letter to Nirmalkumari Mahalanobis, dated 29 November 1935, *Desh*, 23 Agrahayan 1386 BS (December 1979) 503.
86 Santidev Ghosh, *Rabindrasangeet*, 231.
87 Some of these revisions are found in versions available at the Rabindra Bhavana; Rudraprasad Chakrabarty mentions having seen a revised copy in the custody of Santidev Ghosh: see *Rangamancha O Rabindranath: Samakalin Pratikriya*, 149–50. It is also reported that Rabindranath tried out Nilima Sen (who had come to the asram-school as a six-year old in 1934) in the role of Amal, but perhaps this production also did not happen. See Nilima Sen, "Amar Chelebela" in *Durer Nilima*, ed. Arundhati Deb, 2nd edn. (Calcutta: Thema, 2018) 173-8; here referred to 175.
88 Sahana Devi, *Smritir Kheya*, 124.
89 This was Sahana Devi's nickname.
90 See *Bichitra: On-line Tagore Variorum*, School of Cultural Texts and Records, Jadavpur University, bichitra.jdvu.ac.in, RBVBMS_134 (i), 1 (image 4).
91 Sahana Devi, *Smritir Kheya*, 129.

92 *Indian Daily News*, 25 August 1923; cited in *Rangamancha O Rabindranath: Samakalin Pratikriya*, 60; emphasis added.
93 *Indian Daily News*, 27 August 1923; cited in *Rangamancha O Rabindranath: Samakalin Pratikriya*, 62.
94 *The Statesman*, 26 August 1923; cited in *Rangamancha O Rabindranath: Samakalin Pratikriya*, 62.
95 *The Englishman*, 27 August 1923; cited in *Rangamancha O Rabindranath: Samakalin Pratikriya*, 63.
96 *The Bengalee*, 26 August 1923; cited in *Rangamancha O Rabindranath: Samakalin Pratikriya*, 63.
97 Parimal Goswami, *Smriti chitran*, 227–8.
98 *The Madras Mail*, 6 November 1934; cited in Rudraprasad Chakrabarty, *Rangamancha O Rabindranath: Samakalin Pratikriya*, 261–2.
99 Harindranath Dutta, "Rangalaye Rabindranath: Smriticharan", in *Manche Rabindranath*, ed. Ramakrishna Bhattacharya, 14.

8 Setting the stage

I

> No, King. We are going to act this play without any special preparations. *Truth looks tawdry when she is overdressed.*
> But, Poet, there must be some canvas for a background.
> No. *Our only background is the mind.* On that we shall summon up a picture with the magic wand of music.
>
> (*The Cycle of Spring*)[1]

In the prologue that he later added to his play *Phalguni* (rendered into English as *The Cycle of Spring*), Rabindranath Tagore has the Poet (Kabisekhar) interact thus with the King. The voice of the dramatist and that of the created character seemed to be collapsed together – more so when, in performance, Rabindranath played the role of Kabisekhar, foregrounding his oft-made declarations regarding the theatre and the language that it needs to adopt. His contribution to the sphere of scenographic design and stage-setting has to be understood in the context of the alternative mode of performance he was conceptualizing for his "new" theatre that would be conducive to a meaningful articulation in our contemporary cultural milieu.

Though discussed in some of the earlier chapters, certain factors need to be kept in view, even at the risk of repetition, to understand the trends in Bengali theatre and Rabindranath's responses to these mainstream trends. First, the colonial legacy as well as the urban character of the nineteenth-century Bengal theatre; second, the increasing marginalization of the indigenous forms of entertainment even as the urban theatre thrived; third, the close contact between the Tagore family and the contemporary theatre traditions, both urban and folk; and finally, Rabindranath's relocation to Santiniketan which, while coinciding with his engagement with nation-building, also helped to crystallise his vision of a new theatre.

With the influx of the contemporary stage practices (that emulated Western traditions) into his own family productions, it was not surprising that, even in matters of scenography and stage-setting, the performances of his early compositions were inscribed with overt realistic stage norms, as was then available in the public theatre – first, in the operatic experimentations in *Valmiki-Pratibha*

DOI: 10.4324/9781003110279-9

(1881), *Kal Mrigaya* (1882) and *Mayar Khela* (1888), and, then, in his Shakespearean five-act tragedies, *Raja o Rani* (1889) and *Visarjan* (1890). The painted scenery, in which the likes of Dharmadas Soor had specialized, was the accepted convention. Bengal Theatre had introduced horses on stage, which was plastered with clay to simulate actual forests.[2] Keeping abreast with this fashion, the Tagore household performances also used similar stage designs, with Harishchandra Haldar initially in charge of this department. Nitindranath Tagore did the stage décor for the 1890 staging of *Valmiki-Pratibha* at Jorasanko[3] (on 24 December 1890), of which Abanindranath gives a graphic description. Not only was the illusion of a forest created with actual trees planted on a clay-layered stage, but because the wood nymphs (*banadevi*) were required to dance in the rain, "It must actually rain on the stage. So, from the first-floor balcony pipes were directed onto the stage."[4] In *Mayar Khela*, the fairies (*mayakumari*) held wands fitted with electric bulbs "in imitation of European fairies. To imitate everything European was in vogue."[5] Before he started work on *Visarjan*, Rabindranath had visited England (August to November 1890),[6] and the scenography that he saw on the British stage may have influenced the mounting of this play. This seems to be attested by the photograph of Rabindranath as Raghupati bent over the dead body of Joysingha (Arunendranath), with the stage strewn with realistic stage properties. It is further corroborated by Abanindranath's report of the onstage use of a clay image of the Goddess Kali which Rabindranath was supposed to shove aside during a dramatic crescendo towards the end of the play.[7] For the earlier production of *Raja o Rani*, the severed head of Kumar was presumably brought on to the stage, as a wax model of the head of Pramatha Chowdhury (playing Kumar) had been made.[8] This sensational detail was added perhaps in emulation of similar stage effects in the public theatre – Dara's severed head displayed in Dwijendralal Roy's *Shahjahan* or Basanta Roy's cut-off head exhibited in *Raja Basanta Roy*, the dramatized version of Rabindranath's novel, *Bouthakuranir Haat*.

Between *Visarjan* of 1890 and *Sarodatsav* of 1908, while engaging in several nation-building projects (including setting up of the *asram*-school at Santiniketan as an alternative model of pedagogical training: 1901; writing several essays that defined his notion of Nation: 1893–1908, protesting against Curzon's Partition policy: 1905; being a member of the National Council of Education: 1906), he also penned a seminal tract on theatre, "Rangamancha" in 1902.[9] In this essay he postulated his vision of a new theatre, which would be significantly different from the colonial mimicry then practised on the public stage. Here, he expresses his impatience with the Western illusionistic style of stage-setting then practised in the public theatres, and suggests a return to our indigenous cultural roots for a more imaginative use of the performance codes to reinvigorate the contemporary Bengali theatre with a fresh lease of life:

> I like our jatra for this very reason. …. Assisted by performance, the poetry, which is the real thing, flows over the thrilled hearts of the spectators like a fountain. The gardener-woman roams her barren garden all day

in search of flowers – you do not need to cart whole trees on to the stage to demonstrate that: the entire garden should spontaneously spring to life in the gardener herself. Or else what is so special about her, and what is the purpose of having spectators sit there like wooden dummies?[10]

Rabindranath's endorsement of *jatra* indicates his disapproval of both the colonial and the urban elements of the contemporary Bengali theatre. In the preface to *Tapati* (written as late as in 1929) he reiterates his criticism of pictorial realism in theatre, particularly the use of painted scenery, and argues in favour of Indian traditions – both classical and folk:

> In the modern European theatre, the painted scenery is a disturbing presence, a childish attempt to capture the eye.... In *Sakuntala*, the notion of the *tapovan* is suggested in the poetry, and that is sufficient. Because there is no painted scenery, with its exacting specifications, the viewer's imagination may be easily engaged … In our country, during the enactment of *jatra*, overcrowding may constrict the audience accommodation but there is no blatant scenery to constrain the audience's imagination.[11]

In the prologue added to *Phalguni* (for the performance in 1916), he introduced the debate between the '*chitrapat*' (painted scenery) and the '*chittapat*' (imagined scenery, or scenery of the mind), with his obvious preference for the latter.[12] This debate also finds its way into the English translation of the play (*The Cycle of Spring*), and the relevant passage has been quoted right at the start of this chapter.

As in other theatrical features, so also in matters of scenography, Rabindranath was, on the one hand, veering away from unnecessary colonial borrowings and urban inflections, and, on the other, reminding his fellow countrymen of the rich repository of traditional Indian roots. He was, in fact, conceptualizing a "parallel theatre", which would draw upon but not replicate indigenous theatre, to create an alternative theatrical mould for the emergent nation. With this "parallel theatre" in mind, he was also reminding producers and performers that audience reception was not delimited by the "crude European barbarisms" of the Western realistic stage and, therefore, was not to be underestimated: "is the spectator who has come to see you perform destitute of any resources of his own?"[13]

II

When he moved to the open-air environs of the *asram*-school in Santiniketan, Rabindranath was able to put into practice his notions about a 'new'/'parallel' theatre – particularly in the productions of seasonal plays like *Sarodotsav* and *Phalguni*. For certain initial performances in Santiniketan, before Rabindranath took full charge (like that of *Visarjan*, staged in 1902),[14] painted scenery seems to have been deployed, as reported by Rathindranath:

an artist from Calcutta was requisitioned to paint the scenes. He had a facile brush and could wield it to produce bizarre effects, not unlike the painted rags used for scenes, the stock-in-trade of professional touring theatres. The man was something of a character and was universally known by his Bengali initials "Ha-Cha-Ha".[15]

This "Ha-Cha-Ha" was Harishchandra Haldar, who had also been entrusted with the stage design of many a production at the Jorasanko Tagore residence. It seems likely that he was brought over from Calcutta to Santiniketan to help with setting the stage for the early performances at the *asram*-school.

It was with the 1911 *Sarodotsav* production (in which Rabindranath played the Sannyasi) that a definitive change in the approach to stage design was adopted; the students are reported to have "decorated the stage with lotus flowers, *kash*, [16] leaves and foliage".[17] Rabindranath allowed only a blue backcloth to stand in for the sky, and made Abanindranath remove the "royal umbrella"[18], sprinkled with mica to create a shiny effect: "Rabikaka did not like it, and asked, 'Why the royal umbrella? The stage should remain clear and fresh'; so saying, he had the umbrella removed."[19] The bare stage was the appropriate setting for the two scenes of this play: the first located on the road; the second, on the banks of the River Betashini. For a later performance at the *asram*-school (in 1928), when the play was renamed *Rinshodh*, Nandalal Bose used a suggestive backdrop which "from a distance gave the impression of white foamy waves on a sea of green.... In Bengal, the fields in autumn do look like green seas with foamy waves [with the *kash* in bloom]. This overall impression cannot be conveyed by depicting each individual detail."[20]

The dramaturgical structure of the other seasonal play, *Phalguni* (1915), collapses together topographic and psychic spaces: "Beginnings: the Street" (Scene 1), "Search: the *Ghat*2 (Scene 2), "Doubt: the Field" (Scene 3), "Revelation: the Cave-mouth" (Scene 4). This duality is underscored in the dialogue as well. This flavour of the Bengali text spills also into the English translation done by C.F. Andrews and Nishikanta Sen, probably in collaboration with the author:

> Do you feel as though something was in the air?
> The sky seems to be looking into our face, like a friend bidding farewell. This little stream of water is trickling through the *casuarina* grove. It seems like the tears of midnight.[21]

During the first performance at Santiniketan (25 April 1915), the stage décor was in tune with this poetic structure of the play. As Sita Devi reminiscences, "the stage was strewn with leaves and flowers. On the two sides were two swings on which two small boys swung gleefully to the accompaniment of the song."[22] Indira Devi, referring to a 1916 Jorasanko performance (a charity show for the Bankura famine), comments: "In place of the previous incongruous Western imitation, a blue backdrop had been used; it is still used now.

Against it, was a single branch of a tree, with a single red flower at its tip, under a pale ray of the moonshine."[23] Though Sita Devi missed the natural gusto of the Santiniketan production, the performance in Calcutta was also highly applauded. Appreciating the use of a new theatrical idiom, inscribed in the innovative scenography, Satyendranath Dutta wrote: "A tinge of green on the blue backdrop – as though the sky and the forest had fused together into an oneness. This is stage-setting as it should be."[24] Edward Thompson was similarly moved: "The songs were of ravishing beauty, and far more important than the words of the dialogue. There were boys, almost babies, rocking in leafy swings under shining branches."[25] The reviewer of *The Statesman* (1 February 1916) noted: "'Phalguni' is a feast of colour and sound and joy."[26] Further details are provided by Asitkumar Haldar who was involved with the 1916 Calcutta staging of the play, when it began with the newly added prologue set in the royal court: "The royal court was made in an ornate Ajanta-style, complete with crowns and ornaments. Next to it was a large dark blue curtain, on which were stitched white lotus designed on white cloth placed within red circular cloth-patches."[27]

Around this time, Rabindranath also wrote what have been considered his mature prose plays – *Raja* (1910), *Dakghar* (1917), *Muktadhara* (1922), *Raktakarabi* (1924) and *Tasher Desh* (1933). In each of these he experimented considerably with the dramaturgical structure, but the performances of the two seasonal plays in the open-air ambience of Santiniketan exuded a freshness that would not/could not be available in any other ludic space. Though Rabindranath never got to produce *Muktadhara* or *Raktakarabi*, other plays like *Achalayatan* or *Raja* or *Natir Puja* were performed both in Santiniketan and in other metropolitan venues, whether in Calcutta or in other cities. But many felt that when these were performed in Santiniketan they were invested with a uniqueness that could not be replicated elsewhere. Perhaps, the major difference was provided by the natural ambience of the place. For, instead of the usual proscenium stage in a walled-in auditorium, at the *asram*-school "(t)he ramshackle shed behind the Library, used as the dining hall, was selected for the stage and auditorium…. for the making of the stage there were only a few rickety bedsteads."[28] Even, with such make-shift arrangements, Sita Devi preferred the 1915 Santiniketan production of *Phalguni* to the one done in Calcutta in 1916 for the Bankura charity show, which, nevertheless, won huge critical acclaim. One significant dissenting voice was that of Jitendralal Banerjee whose report of the 1916 *Phalguni* production in Calcutta was, in the main, adverse. Yet, on this occasion, he fondly recalled his earlier spectating experience of *Raja* at Santiniketan:

> The performance took place in a large barn-like structure. With a crudely improvised stage and amidst scenery and surroundings of quite a primitive character. Dress, equipment, stage furnishing – there was an air of improvisation over the whole thing; and yet, all of it was in wonderful congruity and harmony.[29]

154 *Rabindranath as theatre-practitioner*

Towards the end of the report, he even suggested that the appropriate venue for the performance of Rabindranath's drama was Santiniketan/Bolpur: "Thus it was in the past, and so it might be again at the proper place and with a proper audience. But from the charm, freshness and simplicity of Bolpur, it is a far cry to the crowded atmosphere of Calcutta."[30]

III

This "simplicity" took on a well-crafted look when artists like Nandalal Bose, Asitkumar Haldar, Surendranath Kar and Mukulchandra Dey took charge of the stage design for the productions of Visva-Bharati. As Rathindranath observed: "Draperies came at a later stage, when attempts to introduce artistic effects became more conscious on the part of those who took up the responsibility of stage-decoration."[31] Sometimes even Gaganendranath and Abanindranath made their contributions, notably in the 1917 *Dakghar* and the 1923 *Visarjan* productions, both given in Calcutta. In fact, with the school evolving into the university, this new phase in formulating a modern Indian approach to the arts and aesthetics became palpably available at Santiniketan, particularly under the aegis of Nandalal Bose and the other eminent artists then working at Kala Bhavana. This had its impact upon stage performances as well, chiefly in matters related to stage décor, costume and make-up. This new band of creative minds jointly gave shape to the Poet's dreams of a theatre inscribed with Indian motifs. The stage now was usually fitted with a dark blue backcloth, with the wings draped in earthy colours – red, brown, yellow ochre or saffron, and the fly overhead of the same/similar shade. On these were often pasted/stitched cloth-pieces with ethnic designs. Low seats were used, covered with similar patterned cloth. A brass lamp, or a copper platter, or a wicker basket would be introduced to usher in both variety and a touch of ethnicity. Door frames or arches, if used, would be of Indian architectural designs. The stage setting of *Raja* (at New Empire, Calcutta, in 1935) was described in *Amritabazar Patrika* on 12 December 1935:

> At one corner of the stage, set with appropriate background of a blaze of colour – of blue, red and reddish brown – there is a gate of pure oriental conception supported by four pillars – this is the simple setting within which the play was enacted.[32]

The costumes were noted as being "rich golden red and black of vigorous colour harmony"[33] as well as "gorgeous".[34] Regarding the 1923 *Visarjan*, Ranu Adhikari (later Mukherjee), who played Aparna, mentions that "for costume, make-up and stage designs, Abanindranath or Gaganendranath had to make coloured sketches and get them approved by Rabindranath."[35] Amita Tagore, who played Queen Sumitra in *Tapati* (1929), has said that not only was the Poet finicky about the white colour of the dress that Sumitra should wear in the fire scene but also had distinct reservations about any "glossy dress or shiny crown or ornament on the head lest its radiance eclipsed the facial expression."[36] This eye for detail is what marks out the "modern" approach that Rabindranath brought to the Bengali theatre.

IV

Yet another move in the direction of the "modern" in theatre was Rabindranath's induction of dance as a medium of theatrical expression in his play *Natir Puja* (1926). It has been mentioned how contemporary spectators were left amazed in the way the "dance of Srimati[37] was transformed into a dramatic climax … that a dance could constitute an entire dramatic spectacle was beyond my imagination."[38] His exposure to the Asiatic dance-languages of Japan, Java, Bali and Ceylon as well as inspiration drawn from dances of other parts of India (Manipuri, Kathakali, Bharatnatyam) coalesced with his own notion of 'theatre as dance'. This resulted in the dance dramas of the final phase that commenced with *Shapmochan* (1931) and achieved greater heights with *Chitrangada* (1936), *Chandalika* (1938), and *Shyama* (1939). Reworked upon an earlier text,[39] each of these is now reconstructed as dance drama, where the dramatic narrative is played out by the dances in accompaniment of songs, and the setting is effortlessly built into this narrative of dance-and-song structure. The sparseness – and the subtlety – of the stage design of these performances were much appreciated on several occasions. For that matter, even the 1929 performance of a somewhat less notable song-and-dance tableau like *Sundar*, celebrating the spirit of spring, left the audiences impressed: "The whole thing was conceived with the spirit of the performance."[40]

When the dance drama *Chandalika* was performed at Sree Theatre, Calcutta, on 18, 19 and 20 March 1938, it was hailed as "a revival of the oldest form of Indian play acting."[41] That the production achieved a blend between the dances and the stage designs was highly appreciated: "The settings, light-effects and stage accoutrements heightened the illusion and subtle charm of the dance compositions, some of which were strictly conventional and followed traditional form, while others were original compositions inspired by the mood and the theme."[42] For a later performance of *Chandalika* (9 and 10 February 1939, also at Sree Theatre) *Amritabazar Patrika* applauded the modest but tasteful stage setting: "The simplicity and economy of stage-paraphernalia have been observed almost to bareness. The costumes are all 'dulce et decorum', interpreting the personalities they clothe."[43] Similarly, when the dance drama *Chitrangada* was performed at Allahabad (19 March 1936), a reviewer gushed: "The dance-drama was a feast of exquisite beauty. But what simplicity side by side with such artistic skill! … Simple again, but effective was the colour arrangement alike in costumes and light thrown from time to time on the stage in various shades."[44] And after a performance at Regal Theatre, New Delhi, on 26 and 27 March 1936, the local dailies remarked: "The setting was brilliant yet simple; the actors danced to express their love, their sorrow or their joy, but all without extravagance" (*The Statesman*, Delhi, 27 March 1936) and "Wholly oriental in style and fully expressive of the spirit underlying the play, the presentation through dancing and songs, was grand in setting, marvellous in rhythm, exquisite in harmony and brilliant in the richness of colour" (*Forward*, 28 March 1936).[45] And the performance of *Shyama* before the Calcutta audiences on 7 and 8 February 1939 proved that "the language of the body is in no way less than the language of poetry."[46]

By this time, with "(t)he expressiveness of the soft bodily postures"[47] taking over, much of the scenographic requirements were subsumed in the songs and dances. The external trappings of scenic appendage were almost made redundant under these new circumstances. The language of the body engaged in dance, and the language of the songs expressing the words defined the requisite audio-visual settings for these dance dramas. As the Allahabad reviewer noted of the minimalist stage design of *Chitrangada*: "Nor was an elaborate stage-setting required, when the whole drama was vividly expressed in dance."[48]

V

Though Rabindranath, in realizing his alternative language for the theatre, eventually moved in the direction of the dance drama, yet it must be remembered that when it came to matters of actual performance he was never rigid or inflexible. Because he was both author and producer of his plays, he was ever alert to the requirements of production and reception, kept adapting his staging principles accordingly and thus allowed his theatre to be more inclusive. This is why his new theatre semiology negotiated with varied possibilities and grew increasingly more wide-ranging and expansive. He retained his fondness for the indigenous resources but also – particularly as producer – conceded to the actual staging conditions at hand.

Rabindranath's later experiments in the theatre (as actor and producer) indicate a movement towards a more eclectic kind of theatre, so that even when performing in a realistic proscenium playhouse, non-realistic theatre semiology (usually drawn from indigenous cultures) was made to bear upon the performance. So, when playing either at the Vichitra hall of his Jorasanko residence, or any other proscenium theatre in Calcutta (New Empire Theatre or Madan Theatre or Alfred Theatre), he conceded to the Western architectural design of the proscenium playhouse but tried to build into the performance elements from non-realistic/anti-illusionistic resources, so that what ultimately emerged was a more nuanced performance-text. And this was true not only for productions of his major plays/dance dramas but even for relatively minor ones. For instance, for the 1929 performance of the song-and-dance tableau, *Sundar*, the proscenium stage at the Jorasanko residence was so decorated with anti-illusionistic décor that it exuded a refreshing novelty: "There was nothing of the common place here. The whole thing was conceived with the spirit of the performance. It was all foliage and flowers artistically placed."[49] The spectators were again pleasantly surprised with the performance of *Vasanta* (in 1931) and dubbed it as "entertainment of a class that is unfortunately all too rare even in a big city like this."[50]

The 1923 production of *Visarjan* at the Empire Theatre deployed a stage design by Gaganendranath, in which "the blood-stained temple steps, designed in Cubist fashion, dominated the stage throughout, a lurid red light marked the entrance to the Temple itself, invisible in the darkness beyond the wings."[51] In "Rangamancha", the Poet had entrusted the audience with the task of interpretation by invoking their imagination. Amritalal Bose – an eminent theatre-personality of the day, who was present among the audience (on 25 August) – was able to do precisely this, as is evident in the long favourable review he wrote for *The Daily News* (4 September 1923): "one looked on the neutral-linted cloth before one's eyes, and imagination did the rest."[52] Yet, realistic details were not wholly discarded. So, the stage copy of this performance mentions not only stage properties to be used ("articles for worship, flowers, basket, piece of cloth, lamp and stand", "copper plate", "spears, shields, axes", "knife", "crown, garland") but also the time for each dramatic sequence, ("dawn", "morning", "Afternoon", "evening", "sunset"; or the more specific "8 Am", "12 A.M."; or even a combination of both, "Night 9 P.m."). Presumably these were shorthands for light effects which become more obvious in requirements for "midnight (moon)" or the direction for "red tinge" (between "dawn" and "morning").[53]

For the Jorasanko production of *Dakghar*, performed several times between October 1917 and January 1918, Rabindranath permitted detailed realism in Nandalal Bose's stage design[54] – a cottage abundantly decorated with motifs related to Indian village life – but Abanindranath's introduction of the empty birdstand was a master stroke that encapsulated the symbolic nuances of the play.[55] Despite the use of realistic details, there was a certain Indian/Bengali flavour that informed the whole presentation, as recorded by an eyewitness, who applauded the "adaptation of western technique to eastern drama; everything we saw was true to reality. The dress of the actors, their speech, their gestures, the furnishing and appearance of the room, were 'true to life'. Yet the whole play was Indian through and through."[56] The realism used here was given so overt an Indian/Bengali makeover that, far from being mired in Western mimicry, it alerted the spectator to the indigenous ethos of the performance. The same trend was repeated in the 1935 enactment of *Raja*, when Rabindranath overlaid the proscenium architecture of the New Empire Theatre with a distinctive oriental touch in the stage décor, dominated by "a gate of purely oriental conception supported by four pillars."[57] The story of acculturation started in the Bengali theatre by Madhusudan Dutt seems to have come a full circle.

Rabindranath returned to his early blank-verse play *Raja o Rani*, rewriting this first as *Bhairaber Bali* (February 1929) and finally as *Tapati* (August 1929). In the preface to *Tapati*, he explained his urge to enact this new version: "Having rewritten an old drama anew, to overcome the older memories and establish the new identity, performance is necessary."[58] *Tapati* was staged in September 1929 at Jorasanko, in which Rabindranath himself gave a memorable performance as King Vikramdev, and Amita Tagore offered able support in the role of Queen Sumitra. Amita Tagore, in an interview given on 6 July 1991, has provided valuable first-hand information about the production, where, among other details, she gives interesting accounts of his fastidiousness with matters related to make-up and stage appearance.[59]

Late in the same year (on 25 December 1929), Sisirkumar Bhaduri, despite the warnings of his friends, decided to stage *Tapati* in the professional theatre. Sisirkumar himself played King Vikramdev that pleased, among others, Abanindranath, who promised to convey to "Rabikaka" that Sisirkumar's performance was no less than his and that he should come and see the performance for himself. Queen Sumitra was played by Prabha Devi, the foremost actress of the professional theatre then, of whom it was reported that she tackled the role adroitly: "Srimati Prabha in the role of Sumitra has reached the pinnacle of her stage career, because all her other roles pale before this" (*Nachghar*).[60] Unfortunately, however, Sisirkumar's friends were proved right; his *Tapati*, though an artistic success, could not deliver as a commercial success.

It is a misfortune that Rabindranath has been increasingly transfigured into a cultural icon, but has not been made relevant to our everyday living. Even in theatre, despite such efforts from foremost theatre-personalities like Sisirkumar Bhaduri or Ahindra Chowdhury, Rabindranath's attempt to create an alternative idiom for the Bengali drama/theatre – both in writing and in performance – has hardly gained the appreciation it deserves, whether in the academia or in the theatre. Consequently, Rabindranath's model of a "parallel theatre" has remained "parallel", perhaps even marginalized, for it has never really become mainstream theatre.

In the post-1947 situation, first the Indian People's Theatre Association (IPTA) and then some of the theatre troupes that emerged with the Group Theatre movement did try their luck with Rabindranath. But except for *Bohurupee*, which doggedly kept up its engagement with Rabindranath,[61] there was no consistent effort to grapple with his plays. The earlier spate of dance drama performances – centring around the birth anniversary celebrations primarily but often continuing the year round – became overdone after a while, when quality made way for quantity. More recently, particularly during the sesquicentennial year, the trend has been towards an interest in reading contemporary issues through the enactment of the plays. So *Visarjan* or *Tapati, Dakghar* or *Raktakarabi, Chandalika* or *Shyama* have all been inspirations for recent recensions with sociopolitical contemporaneity. But whether these explorations have truly won for Rabindranath his rightful place in Bengali theatre is yet to be seen.

Notes

1 Rabindranath Tagore, *Collected Poems and Plays* (Delhi: Macmillan, 2001; 1st Indian reprint 1991; originally 1936) 461; emphases added.
2 See Sekhar Samaddar, "Rabindranather Natyabhavna", in *Punascha Rabindranath*, ed. Sabyasachi Bhattacharya and Bratin Dey (New Delhi: National Book Trust, India, 2012) 215–83; specially 219.

3 The first performance of *Valmiki Pratibha* was given on 26 February 1881 at Jorasanko.
4 Abanindranath Tagore, *Gharoa* (Calcutta: Visva-Bharati Granthan Vibhaga, 1941; rpt. 1983) 117.
5 Indira Devi Chaudhurani, "Rabindrasmriti" (1961), in *Smriti Samput*, vol. 3, ed. Anathnath Das (Santiniketan: Rabindra Bhavana, Visva-Bharati, 2001) 23.
6 During this visit he saw Henry Irving in *The Bride of Lammermoore* at the Lyceum, but found Irving's acting much too loud for his liking; see *Europe Jatrir Diary, Rabindra Rachanabali* (Complete Works) Centenary Edition, vol. 10 (Calcutta; West Bengal Government, 1961) 399. The Complete Works will be subsequently referred to as *RR*.
7 Mentioned in Abananindranath Tagore, *Gharoa*, 110.
8 Mentioned in Sekhar Samaddar, "Rabindranather Natyabhavna", 226.
9 The essay was first published in *Banga-darshan* (30 December 1902), and later included in *Bichitra Prabandha* (1907).
10 Though there was an earlier translation of the essay by Surendranath Tagore ("The Stage"), the translation used here is "The Theatre" done by Swapan Chakravorty in *Rabindranath Tagore, Selected Writings on Literature and Language*, ed. Sukanta Chaudhuri (Oxford, New York & New Delhi: Oxford University Press, 2001) 95–9; here quoted from 97–8.
11 *RR*, vol. 6, 1033–4.
12 See, "Suchana", *Phalguni*, in *RR*, vol. 6, 454.
13 "The Theatre", trans. Swapan Chakravorty, 97,
14 Mentioned by Rathindranath Tagore in Rathindranath Tagore, "Looking Back" in *Rabindranath Tagore: A Tribute*, ed. Pulinbihari Sen and Kshitis Roy (New Delhi: Sangeet Natak Akademi, 2006; originally 1961) 45–52; the reference here is from 46.
15 Rathindranath Tagore, "Looking Back", 47.
16 A kind of long white grass that grows in autumn.
17 Prabhatkumar Mukhopadhyay, *Rabindra Jibani*, vol. 2 (Calcutta: Visva-Bharati Granthalay, 1936) 235.
18 This was the "*rajchhatra*" or a kind of an umbrella held like a canopy over the heads of royal characters.
19 Abanindranath Tagore, *Gharoa*, 133.
20 Parimal Goswami, *Smriti chitran*, 143.
21 *The Cycle of Spring*, Act IV, in Rabindranath Tagore, *Collected Poems and Plays* (New Delhi: Macmillan India Limited, 2001; 1st Indian reprint 1991; originally 1936) 503.
22 Sita Devi, *Punya Smriti* (Calcutta: Probasi, 1942) 73.
23 Indira Devi Chaudharani, "Rabindra Smriti", 26.
24 Satyendranath Dutta's "Sahare Phalguni" appeared in *Bharati*, ed. Monilal Gangopadhyay and Sourindramohan Mukhapadhyay, 39th year, no. 11, *Phalgun* 1322 (1916), 1098–110; here quoted from 1104.
25 Edward Thompson, *Rabindranath Tagore – Poet and Dramatist*; cited in Ajit Kumar Ghosh, *Thakurbarir Abhinay* (Calcutta: Rabindra Bharati Society, 1988) 55.
26 Cited in Rudraprasad Chakrabarty, *Rangamancha O Rabindranath: Samakalin Pratikriya* (Calcutta: Ananda, 1995) 125–6.
27 Asitkumar Haldar, *Rabitirhe* (Calcutta: Anjana Prakashani, 1958) 104.
28 Rathindranath Tagore, "Looking Back", 47.
29 "RABINDRANATH'S/PHALGUNI/ (Notes and Impressions by/Jitendralal Banerjee)", *The Bengalee*, 29 January 1916; as cited in Rudraprasad Chakrabarty, *Rangamancha O Rabindranath: Samakalin Pratikriya*, 129.
30 *Rangamancha O Rabindranath: Samakalin Pratikriya*, 129–30.
31 Rathindranath Tagore, "Looking Back", 50.

32 *Amritabazar Patrika*, 12 December 1935; as cited in *Rangamancha O Rabindranath: Samakalin Pratikriya*, 113.
33 *Rangamancha O Rabindranath: Samakalin Pratikriya*, 113.
34 *The Statesman*, 12 December 1935; also cited in *Rangamancha O Rabindranath: Samakalin Pratikriya*, 113.
35 Unpublished; courtesy: Sankha Ghosh; cited in *Rangamancha O Rabindranath: Samakalin Pratikriya*, 61.
36 Cited in Rudraprasad Chakrabarty, *Rangamancha O Rabindranath: Samakalin Pratikriya*, 240.
37 Through this dance, Srimati (the dancer) makes her last offerings to the Lord Buddha, as she sings the song, "*Amay kshamo hey kshamo*" ["Forgive me, O Unparalleled One, it is in remembrance of you that my soul overflows thus in the rhythm of dance"].
38 Parimal Goswami, *Smriti chitran* (Calcutta: Prajna Prakashani, 1958) 194; Goswami probably saw the Calcutta performance since he also mentions seeing Rabindranath play a role.
39 *Shapmochan* went back to the tale of *Kusha-Jataka*, already used in *Raja* (1910) and *Arupratan* (1920); *Chitrangada* was a reworking of the verse-drama *Chitrangada* (1892); *Chandalika* of the prose play *Chandalika* (1933); and *Shyama* of the poem *Parishodh* (1936).
40 *Forward*, 27 January, 1929; cited in *Rangamancha O Rabindranath: Samakalin Pratikriya*, 201.
41 *The Statesman*, 19 March 1938; as cited in *Rangamancha O Rabindranath: Samakalin Pratikriya*, 267.
42 *Amritabazar Patrika*, 19 March 1938; as cited in *Rangamancha O Rabindranath: Samakalin Pratikriya*, 268.
43 *Amritabazar Patrtika*, 10 February 1939; cited in *Rangamancha O Rabindranath: Samakalin Pratikriya*, 272.
44 *The Leader*, 20 March 1936; as cited in *Rangamancha O Rabindranath: Samakalin Pratikriya*, 290.
45 Cited in *Rangamancha O Rabindranath: Samakalin Pratikriya*, 291.
46 Sajanikanta Das, reviewing in *Anandabazar Patrika*, 8 February 1939; cited in *Rangamancha O Rabindranath: Samakalin Pratikriya*, 301.
47 These terms are also used by Sajanikanta Das in the above-mentioned review ("The expressiveness of the soft bodily postures dissolved away the sense of the physical to recreate a world of cerebral perception"): see *Rangamancha O Rabindranath: Samakalin Pratikriya*, 301.
48 *The Leader*, 20 March 1936; as cited in *Rangamancha O Rabindranath: Samakalin Pratikriya*, 290.
49 *Forward*, 27 January, 1929; cited in *Rangamancha O Rabindranath: Samakalin Pratikriya*, 201.
50 *Liberty*, 21 March, 1931; cited in *Rangamancha O Rabindranath: Samakalin Pratikriya*, 189.
51 *Visva-Bharati Quarterly*, October 1923, 309.
52 *The Daily News*, 4 September 1923; as cited in *Rangamancha O Rabindranath: Samakalin Pratikriya*, 65.
53 See *Bichitra: On-line Tagore Variorum*, School of Cultural Texts and Records, Jadavpur University, bichitra.jdvu.ac.in, RBVBMS_134 (ii). The directions for time have usually been marked in red in the left margin.
54 Perhaps this was done under Abanindranath's supervision.
55 See Abanindranath Tagore, *Gharoa*, 136.
56 C. Jinaraja Das, "The Future Indian Drama", *New India*, 12 January 1918.
57 *Amritabazar Patrika*, 12 December 1935; quoted in *Rangamancha O Rabindranath: Samakalin Pratikriya*, 113.

58 *RR*, vol. 6, 1033.
59 Cited in *Rangamancha O Rabindranath: Samakalin Pratikriya*, 240.
60 Cited in *Rangamancha O Rabindranath: Samakalin Pratikriya*, 243.
61 *Bohurupee* offered the Bengali audiences some memorable performances of Rabindranath's works, among which were *Char Adhyay, Raktakarabi, Visarjan, Raja, Dakghar, Muktadhara, Ghare Baire, Malini.*

9 Acting the role

I

Years before Rabindranath himself appeared on the scene, the Tagore family had forged close associations with the theatre of Bengal. His grandfather, Dwarakanath Tagore, was one of the early patrons of the nineteenth-century Calcutta theatres. Dwarakanath was enlisted as the only Indian member of the Amateur Dramatic Society formed by the local British residents and contributed handsomely towards the setting up of at least two English theatres in Calcutta – the Chowringhee Theatre in 1813 and the Sans Souci Theatre in 1840.[1] Closer to his times, Rabindranath's elder brothers and cousins – all keen theatre enthusiasts – were in close contact with the public stage of their generation. His cousins Ganendranath and Gunendranath, his brother Jyotirindranath, and their brother-in-law Saradaprasad Gangopadhyay took the initiative of setting up a theatre at their Jorasanko residence, referred to as the Jorasanko Natyasala or Jorasanko Theatre. His brothers, chiefly Satyendranath and Jyotirindranath, were instrumental in honing the dramatic interests of the young Rabindranath. It may be guessed that such an atmosphere at home so favourable to theatre and such encouraging support from the elder members of his family helped Rabindranath's abilities, both as actor and author, to blossom.

There is some controversy regarding his earliest appearance as an actor. In *Galpa-salpa*, written late in his life, in a fictive mode he mentions how he played the eponymous heroine, in Harishchandra Haldar's play, *Muktakuntala*. He writes that to play the character he borrowed some vermillion from his sister-in-law, possibly Kadambari Devi, the wife of Jyotirindranath: "Nothing in particular struck me when putting on the vermillion in the parting of the hair. But I had forgotten to rub off the mark before going to school. That had the boys rolling in laughter. I was unable to show my face for a few days after that."[2] Though an amateur production, largely produced as a pastime within the household, this was perhaps his first attempt at impersonation of a dramatic character on the stage.

Rabindranath seems to have been particularly close to his brother Jyotirindranath, who had written several plays for the public stage – serious plays like *Purubikram-natak, Sarojini*[3], *Asrumati*, as well as farces like *Hathat Nabab* and

DOI: 10.4324/9781003110279-10

Emon Karma Aar Korbo Na (later renamed as *Aleekbabu*, after Rabindranath's inspired acting in the lead role).[4] There are reports that he acted as Vasanta in Jyotirindranath's play, *Manmoyee*, with Jyotirindranath as Indra and Kadambari as Urvashi; that he fought a stage duel with Jyotirindranath in Swarnakumari Devi's *Vasanta-Utsav*; and again with Jyotirindranath[5] debated (through songs) on the advantages and disadvantages of marriage in *Vivaha-Utsav*.[6] While Sajanikanta Das reports Gaganendranath having reminisced how Rabindranath first acted in *Manmoyee*, Prasantachandra Mahalanobis recalled that the Poet himself refuted this.[7] Again, according to Sarala Devi, Swarnakumari Devi's *Vasanta-Utsav* was performed when Rabindranath was in England.[8] There are, therefore, conflicting reports about his having taken part in some of these productions. As such, Aleekbabu is usually considered to be his first major stage role, which is corroborated by Rabindranath's own statement: "Before appearing in public on the stage, I acted as Aleekbabu in Jyoti-dada's farce *Emon Karma Aar Korbo Na. That was my first acting.*"[9] We are told that Rabindranath once performed in an in-house production with Ardhendusekhar Mustafi, the renowned professional actor of the period, but felt that acting with such a "stage free" actor demanded a kind of constant alertness that affected his own style of acting.[10]

In many of his own early plays, too, Rabindranath played lead roles with great success – notable among these were the roles of Valmiki in *Valmiki Pratibha* (first performed 1881),[11] King Vikramdev in *Raja o Rani* (1889) and Raghupati in *Visarjan* (1890). These early performances were, more often than not, marked by overt realistic details – whether the operatic *Valmiki-Pratibha* (1881), or the Shakespeare-inspired tragedies *Raja o Rani* (1889) and *Visarjan* (1890). To cite an instance already mentioned, for the 1890 staging of *Valmiki-Pratibha* at Jorasanko (probably on 24 December 1890), Nitindranath, in charge of the stage décor,[12] layered the stage floor with clay, planted trees to create the forest, and directed pipes from the first floor onto the stage to sprinkle water to simulate actual rain.[13]

Before the performance of *Visarjan*, Rabindranath had visited England (August to November 1890), and had seen Henry Irving's production of *The Bride of Lammermoor* at the Lyceum Theatre.[14] Though he did not much care for Irving's acting, he seems to have preferred – at least around this time – a heightened style of acting; he confesses he was inspired by the poetry of Shakespeare, Milton and Byron, and "Romeo-Juliet's love-madness, Lear's agony of futile regret, Othello's destructive fire of jealousy" are specially mentioned.[15] His opinion, around this time seems to have been that "in acting a certain degree of spiritedness, even over-acting, is preferred, for that helps remove the self-inhibitions of the actor, and appeals to the audience."[16] In fact, Abanindranath recounts how Rabindranath (as Raghupati in *Visarjan*), overpowered by emotion, forgot to shove aside the idol of the Goddess Kali (which was then to be dragged within), and instead lifted it up, spraining his back.[17] This would seem to bear out his (early) inclination towards high-pitched histrionics. And Hemendraprasad Ghosh's account also seems to refer to Rabindranath's highly charged impersonation of Raghupati: "While acting as Raghupati in *Visarjan*, he became so involved that he forgot how sharp the scimitar really was; if the other actors, realising his state, had not quickly removed Dhruva [Aswini], there might have been a terrible disaster."[18] The photographs of this performance – particularly the one in which, as Raghupati, he is bent over the body of the dead Joysingha (Arunendranath) – point to the intensity with which he infused the role he played. However, it may certainly be possible to explain this intensity as a simulation of emotion; a seasoned actor like Rabindranath would know the distinction between affective empathy and objective detachment when it came to stage impersonation.

In fact, in his formative years, Rabindranath may have been exposed to the contrary styles of acting already available in the Bengali public theatre, one associated with Girishchandra Ghosh, the other with Ardhendusekhar Mustafi.[19] Girishchandra had introduced a style of lyrical acting, in the belief that for expression of deep emotions a kind of lyrical tunefulness is required of the actor. As a writer, actor and producer he believed that dramatic conversation should be conducted in a rhythmic language. So, he replaced the colloquial prose with a stylized verse pattern that has since been named after him ("Gairish chhanda"). He wrote: "The critic perhaps feels what is written in prose is natural. That is far from the truth; prose is not natural. We speak in a rhythmic language, so rhyme is natural. We express our emotions in tune, so tune is natural."[20] Girishchandra believed in emotional empathy and was dubbed the "Garrick" of Bengal, excelling in tragic roles executed through lyrical mellifluous declamation. By contrast, his contemporary, Ardhendusekhar Mustafi was more inclined towards a non-lyrical style of acting – which might have been prompted by the fact that he usually played comic/farcical roles. He seems to have brought a more detached, objective (proto-Brechtian) approach to his style of acting: "In the theatre, I play Sirajuddullah. I lose my kingdom, my treasures, my kinsmen, my family, ultimately even my life to the assassin's blow. There is no end to my sorrows. But how does it affect me? At the end of it all, I am the same Narahari. That is acting."[21] Rabindranath would have been aware of both these styles. If he used the Girishchandra-like intensity and lyricism for his roles in *Valmiki Pratibha*, *Raja o Rani* or *Visarjan*, for the comedies and farces – from *Aleekbabu* to *Baikunther Khata* and *Goray Galad* – he would perhaps have recalled the non-lyrical objective approach in Ardhendusekhar's satirical sketches.

II

With his shifting base to Santiniketan, Rabindranath's notions of theatre and histrionics seem to have undergone significant changes, with major reconfigurations in his theatre career – dramaturgical, theatrical, even ideological. Much of these changes were articulated briefly but poignantly in the essay "Rangamancha" (1902),[22] where he advocated a rejection of Western approaches and a return to indigenous cultural traditions, even in matters of acting the role. The open-air ambience of Santiniketan enabled him to realize much of his imagined 'new' theatre through the productions at the *asram*-school, best encapsulated perhaps in the seasonal plays like *Sarodotsav* and *Phalguni*. These plays – along with the other mature plays like *Raja, Dakghar, Raktakarabi* written during this period – seem to have required a different approach to performance, perhaps more subtle, more nuanced.

For the first performance of *Sarodatsav* (24 September 1908), Rabindranath served as the prompter[23], but in the 1911 *Sarodatsav* production, he played the Sannyasi; he was in his usual dress with only a saffron-coloured cloth wrapped around his head.[24] When the play was given in Calcutta in September 1922 to raise funds for Visva-Bharati,[25] not only was the production warmly received, but the Poet's style of acting was critically acclaimed. The drama critic of *The Englishman* (20 September 1922), though finding it difficult to follow the Bengali text, appreciated the performance and remarked: "It is rare to see an author act his own play or a composer sing his own songs. Rabindranath did both and the memory of it is one to treasure."[26] But *Indian Daily News* (18 September 1922) went a step further and astutely observed:

> The poet's acting was, of course, of another order. It was something uplifting and ennobling, bringing out subtle inner meaning of the play, making it plain to the least intelligent among the audience and imparting to the whole performance a wonderful dignity and charm.[27]

It may be argued that, from around this time, Rabindranath seems to have developed a style of acting (at least for himself) that allowed effortless transitions between the actor and the role. He would both immerse himself in a role, and yet get out of it to indulge in remarks that directly related to the "thesis" of the play. The implications of this will be elaborated further later in the chapter.

The first performance of *Phalguni* at Santiniketan (25 April 1915) used a stage décor in tune with the poetic structure of the play: "the stage was strewn with leaves and flowers. On the two sides were two swings on which two small boys swung gleefully to the accompaniment of the song."[28] Even the 1916 Jorasanko performance, a charity show to help the distressed due to the famine in Bankura, was widely appreciated for its novelty. It was, in fact, a huge success, both aesthetic and commercial: people were ready to pay one hundred rupees even to stand and view the performance; several hundred rupees were collected from the sale of the programme notes; and eight thousand rupees were ultimately donated as aid for the famine.[29] The drama critic of *The Statesman* (1 February 1916) remarked:

> "Phalguni" is a feast of colour and sound and joy.... I have never seen more spirited acting. All alike, whether children of six or the grey headed seer of 50, acted as the birds sing – because of the happiness they feel; and as the flowers grow, because the spring is in their veins.[30]

In this performance of *Phalguni*, Rabindranath played double roles, eliciting tributes and accolades. *Amritabazar Patrika* noted how his "magnetic personality in the double role of the poet gay and the ministerial grave made the oratorio a complete success which it so eminently deserved."[31] His biographer filled in the details: "The young Rabindranath of twenty years ago seemed to present himself in a new form. How agile, how lively that form! Then he came back as the old blind *baul*,[32] a picture of peace and serenity."[33] *The Bengalee* (of 30 January 1916), in assessing Rabindranath's impersonation of the blind *baul*, observed:

> Specially when the blind singer comes out with his stately figure a sudden thrill is sent through the audience. The dramatic motif crystallizes at the appearance of the blind singer. The author has taken upon himself the most difficult role of the opera. The music of the blind singer shows extraordinary original powers of the author and the capacity and volume in the voice is marvellous.[34]

Obviously, these characters needed a mode of representation far removed from that used for Vikramdev (*Raja o Rani*) or Raghupati (*Visarjan*). Neither the affective style of Girishchandra nor the objective detachment of Ardhendusekhar were adequate any longer to plumb the depths of a more muted and suggestive style of acting, resonating with the philosophical enquiry that these characters were invested with. The subtler shades of dramaturgical characterization on the page were etched out through the nuanced theatrical representation on the stage. This shift in his approach to acting finds expression in an essay written in 1912:

> Though acting seems to indulge in imitation more than other forms of art, it is not plain mimicry. It draws aside the veil of naturalism to reveal the inner play (*leela*) ... If instead of *depicting* truth, one would want to *imitate* truth one would resort to excesses like the false witness. One's faith in moderation is, then, lacking. Our theatre regularly indulges in such physical acrobatics of false testimony.[35]

This style of acting, which was required to "reveal the inner play", where truth was depicted rather than merely imitated, seems to have been promoted in the plays that he wrote and experimented with after moving to Santiniketan. In most of the productions following *Sarodatsav*, Rabindranath played characters that appeared, more often than not, as his spokespersons. These characters, almost archetypal in representation, played pivotal roles as poet, prophet, seer, philosopher, or many/all of these often rolled into one, and they often used songs as a medium of heightened expression. There was also a recurrence of the Sage-King figure in several of his plays, collapsing together the ideals of the king and those of the sage.[36] Just a year before writing the above-quoted lines in "Antar bahir" of *Pather Sanchay*, he played both the offstage Raja/King[37] and the onstage Thakurda/Gaffer in *Raja*, for the first two performances at Santiniketan (March and May 1911). It was evident that the style of acting had already moved in a different direction. Sita Devi, recapitulating the May 1911 performance, records: "Rabindranath acted as Thakurda, and also played the role of the King from off-stage", and "The boys sang exquisitely. And the Poet dancing as Thakurda amidst them was a moving sight. He could dance remarkably well. Those who have seen him only in his mature years have missed much."[38] In fact, in what was a not too friendly account of the 1916 *Phalguni* that appeared in *The Bengalee* of 29 January 1916, Jitendralal Banerjee compared this production of *Phalguni* with the May 1911 *Raja* performance at Santiniketan, showing a definite preference for the latter, and underscoring the novelty of its theatrical style: "Dress, equipment, stage furnishing – there was an air of improvisation over the whole thing; and yet, all of it was in wonderful congruity and harmony. Besides, the play made atonements for all – it was 'Raja' first and greatest of the poet's new series of symbolical plays."[39] Though the natural setting of Santiniketan ("The performance took place in a large barn-like structure"[40]) was a far cry from the proscenium stage of the New Empire Theatre in Calcutta, where *Raja* was staged in December 1935, the freshness of Rabindranath's approach still remained unmistakable in in the later production. The press reviews were lavish with praise both for the production and for the Poet's histrionic abilities, particularly as the onstage Thakurda:

> He was so natural in his part, so intensely human that the appeal was universal, the success of his performance was great because he was merely showing on the stage what he had shown throughout his life – the desire to awaken the youth of the country, and thus within his heart remain evergreen.[41]

Or, again:

> the poet, though approaching his seventy-fifth year, moved acted and sang on the stage with the energy and freshness of youth and one heard a clear and unmistakable personal note as he [the poet] represented the character of the ever jovial grand-papa.[42]

These reviews of *Raja*, together with the ones cited earlier for the productions of *Sarodatsav* ("The poet's acting was, of course, of another order. It was something uplifting and ennobling, bringing out subtle inner meaning of the play": *Indian Daily News*, 18 September 1922) and *Phalguni* ("I have never seen more spirited acting. All alike, whether children of six or the grey headed seer of 50, acted as the birds sing – because of the happiness they feel; and as the flowers grow, because the spring is in their veins": *The Statesman*, 1 February 1916)[43] all point towards a new style of acting/staging at which Rabindranath now seemed to have arrived. With its subtleties, its suggestive approach and its nuanced representations, this was significantly different from the usual fare then on offer in the public theatres.

Moving forward to the days of *Natir Puja* (1926), we may recall the controversy stirred up, even among the local residents of Santiniketan, that a girl from a respectable family (Gouri Bose, Nandalal's daughter, had played the *nati*, Srimati) would dance on the public stage in Calcutta. We have discussed how Rabindranath resolved the problem by creating the only male character of Upali and played the role himself. Yet, giving the lie to all misgivings, Srimati's dance not only left everyone pleasantly surprised ("the dance of Srimati was made into the dramatic climax.... So ennobling a scene is hardly seen on the stage"[44]) but also proved to be most telling in its affective import ("The performance created so heart-wrenching an effect with its controlled display of devotion (*bhakti*) and unsullied purity that many were moved to tears"[45]). Subsequently, when Rabindranath went on to explore further into the potentials of dance as a theatre idiom, in the dance dramas *Shapmochan* (1931), *Chitrangada* (1936), *Chandalika* (1938) and *Shyama* (1939), he appears to have been regularly present on the stage during the performances, even if he did not actively participate. This may have been a deliberate 'strategy' adopted to prevent any further objections about mixed casting performances. His onstage presence not only scotched any possibilities of demur but, in fact, had a positive impact upon the performances: "He makes the stage human. Everyone else on the stage may be acting but he is not. He is reality. *Moreover he gives a dignity to the performance – nautch is transformed into dance.*"[46] One may also submit (in continuation of the discussion above) that while he thus won dignity and social respectability for the dance dramas, his onstage presence both in *and* out of the performance underscored his simultaneous involvement *and* detachment, which, in turn, would have inscribed the performance with the dual presence of illusionism and anti-illusionism.

III

What one always needs to keep in view is the fact that Rabindranath was never rigid or inflexible in his ideas of performance. He was a playwright churning out new plays; he was a theorist formulating new concepts of theatrical performance; but he was also a producer of his plays, ever alert to the material determinants of a theatrical performance. To appreciate the range of the vast arena that he gave himself in the context of performance, one may consider two excerpts from his writings. The first is from a letter written to Indira Devi Chaudhurani, dated 24 November 1894:

> The plain ground is most suitable for all manner of ordinary activity, but performance needs a stage; to descend to the level of the audience to perform disallows the requisite illusion. Performance needs to be highlighted by segregating its space, illuminated by lights, aided by scenography and music. Only then can it, in a comprehensive and unique manner, etch itself upon the imagination.[47]

The second excerpt is from the essay "Antar bahir", written in 1912 (also quoted earlier):

> Though acting depends more upon imitation than the other arts, yet it is not plain mimicry. It draws aside the veil of naturalism to reveal the inner play within.[48]

While separated by several years, these two excerpts help us envisage the conciliation that Rabindranath was often making between the two trends. Though the gap between the two extracts almost coincides with the gap between his early drama and his experimental plays at Santiniketan, though the two passages may suggest a certain evolution in his notions about theatrical representation, yet it is also a fact that, despite major conceptual changes, he did not reject outright everything that he had imbibed from his early days. Therefore, on the one hand, he could demand a privileged ludic space to underscore the illusion of the theatre; and, on the other, he could discard the kind of exaggerated realism that was often practised in the name of theatrical illusion. For him, a certain degree of illusionism is necessary, though not a total surrender to overt attempts at verisimilitude. Though he was borrowing from the folk theatre idiom, he was not creating folk theatre *per se*, but rather a kind of experimental mix and match, which would, more often than not, be performed before an urban clientele. He was, in fact, evolving a prototype of what recent scholars have defined as the "urban folk"[49]. Precisely because of this flexibility, Rabindranath was able to shift easily between different cultural registers – urban and folk, Eastern and Western. It was this flexibility that allowed him to adapt his style of writing and style of acting, his dramaturgical structure and staging principles, to the immediate requirements of production and reception. His dramatist and/or theorist self always allowed the theatre-practitioner in him to have the final say when it came to matters of production.

So, the later production of *Visarjan* at the Empire Theatre, Calcutta (25, 27 and 28 August, 1923) replaced the 1890 illusionistic scenography with a more suggestive stage décor, designed by Gaganendranath, but did not entirely do away with appendages of the proscenium stage: "the blood-stained temple steps, designed in Cubist fashion, dominated the stage throughout, a lurid red light marked the entrance to the Temple itself, invisible in the darkness beyond the wings."[50] Rabindranath, then sixty-two, played the young Joysingha; his nephew, Dinendranath, acted as Raghupati; his son Rathindranath was the king, Govindamanikya. Sita Devi observed that he "could be easily mistaken for a youth, so bold was his gait, so resonant his voice".[51] Sahana Devi's memoir also gives a detailed analysis of Rabindranath's impersonation of Joysingha, moving through the different phases of faith, dilemma, conflict to the final resolution through self-sacrifice.[52] There were near-euphoric responses in the press: "As Joy Singh, his [Rabindranath's] every utterance and gesture drew applause from the vast and admiring audience"[53], or, "His vacillation when picturing the struggle between obedience to his preceptor (the priest) and adherence to his ideal of love was a masterpiece of histrionic skill."[54] Unlike the carefree representation of the different Thakurda-s in various earlier plays (where he could afford to retain his usual look)[55], for the role of the young Joysingha he evidently took a lot of care about his stage appearance. This was noted – and appreciated – by the critics:

> He looked so young when he first appeared. The make up completely disguised the 60 years old poet, the long hair and the blowing beard were all gone – the gray yielding place to a very natural dark ... the poet looked at least forty years younger... some of his poses were the acme of histrionic art and the last scene – the scene of self-immolation ... will for long be remembered by the house or, perhaps, be indelibly impressed on the tablet of its memory.[56]

He is also known to have taken extra care about his appearance for certain other roles as well, which would seem to dispel the notion that in his later years he had totally discarded stage-illusionism. When he appeared in double roles in *Phalguni* – as the younger poet in the prologue, and the old blind *baul* in the later part of the play – he made deliberate attempts to distinguish the one from the other, not only through his acting but also the details of his onstage looks. His biographer gives a detailed account of this:

> Having done his own make-up, he emerged from his own chamber. I remember I was startled to see him near the dressing-room, and when he entered the stage the audience cheered loudly. It was as though the young Rabindranath of thirty years before had returned anew. His was a lively frisky self. Then came the old blind *baul*. That again was so calm, so serene an appearance.[57]

For the younger poet, his beard and hair were made black, while as the old *baul* he appeared in white hair and white beard:

> As Kabisekhar, his black beard was folded short and his hair was tucked beneath a turban. It reminded one of the poet's appearance in his younger days. Again, the old *baul*, in a robe, with his white hair and beard flowing as he moved in circles singing with the *ektara*[58] in hand is an image that one vividly remembers.[59]

Even as King Vikramdev in *Tapati* (performed in 1929), considered yet another milestone in his acting career, Rabindranath is known to have blackened his hair and beard.[60] Returning to his early blank-verse play *Raja o Rani*, he rewrote this play first as *Bhairaber Bali* (February 1929) and finally as *Tapati* (August 1929); this final version was staged in September 1929 at Jorasanko. Rabindranath's memorable performance as King Vikramdev found adequate support from Amita Tagore's Queen Sumitra. *Nachghar*, in its 1929 autumn issue, made some discerning remarks in a review of the performance:

> The incongruities in the contemporary political scenario that disturb Rabindranath have been articulated in this symbolic drama, *Tapati*.... The rich dramatic content to be found in the tragedy of Tapati is rare not only in Bengal but in world drama. Unfortunately, our public theatres

lack the ability to give shape to this intense drama. Because Rabindranath was all too aware of this, he arranged for the staging of the play himself at his own residence.[61]

Liberty on 28 September 1929 heaped praises on the production, in general, and on Rabindranath's performance, in particular: "The poet in the role of Vikram was self-incandescent in his blaze of his own glory."[62] Amita Tagore, in interviews and eyewitness accounts, has provided some vital first-hand information about the production.[63] His predicament of blackening his hair and beard for every evening's performance (to appear as a more robust and youthful Vikramdev) was finally put to rest by Abanindranath, who solved the problem by covering Rabindranath's original white beard with black gauze.[64] The striking stage presence and authoritative acting of Rabindranath as King Vikramdev is recorded in several eyewitness accounts: "Enter the sixty-eight year old Rabindranath as the young king of Jalandhar. What an appearance! His erect frame exuding power, black hair, black beard, band on head, a *zaree* cloak draped around his body. And his acting? All were left spellbound"[65]; "The aged Rabindranath in the role of the youthful king. Yet his vocal and physical acting belied his age. It leaves one amazed to think of the extent of expertise in make-up that could create such a stage presence"[66]; "The seventy-year old Rabindranath, with his spirited acting, puts to shame twenty-four year-old youths when, with a strong arm raised high, he gives vent to his umbrage."[67] And that he was a gifted actor, not only in vocal but even in silent moments, is reported by his co-actor, Amita Tagore – which is reserved for a later section in this chapter.

IV

What all this makes evident is the wide range spanned by Rabindranath's histrionic talent. As mentioned before, from the earlier preference for a heightened manner of expression, he moved increasingly towards a more restrained style. This was not only more suited to the sage-like characters he impersonated in his later career, but also gave a different perspective when he returned to his earlier plays later in life. So, when a play like *Visarjan* (in 1923) or a reworked version of *Raja o Rani* as *Tapati* (1929) are brought back on the stage – with decades intervening between the early and later performances – his approach to acting and production had undergone significant changes. Many contemporaries have held that he had a naturally tuneful voice. Harindranath Dutta, in his reminiscences, recalls:

> his acting was entirely tuneful acting …. And Rabindranath's voice was loud and sharp and like the flute would reach right up to the rear of the galleries: when he performed at Empire (now Roxy) [it] would reach the first and second floors, right till the last row of the audience seats. So sharp was his voice. I had seen him perform in Visarjan both as Raghupati and Joysingha. I personally felt his style of vocal acting was more suited to the role of Joysingha than that of Raghupati.[68]

172 *Rabindranath as theatre-practitioner*

As has been mentioned earlier in this chapter, Girishchandra Ghosh, the doyen of nineteenth-century Bengali theatre, was also partial towards a mellifluous intonation for speaking dramatic dialogues. Rabindranath, too, favoured a tuneful intonation in vocal acting, but his style of theatrical enunciation was markedly different from the lengthened recitation of words then in vogue in the public theatre.[69] He seems to have followed the tradition of tuneful vocal acting, but infused into it his own individuality. Unfortunately, there is no adequate audio-visual documentation of his stage acting, but the few specimens of elocutionary pieces that survive attest to this. For instance, for a powerfully emotive poem like "Jhulan", he uses an effusive tuneful style of elocution, but in reciting the shorter poems from *Sishu*, like "Veerpurush"[70] or "Chotoboro",[71] he adopts a more prosaic, even colloquial, diction, sometimes even simulating the persona of a child. Nilima Sen mentions Rabindranath's reading of "Veerpurush" while recalling how, when trying her out for the role of Amal (*Dakghar*), he effortlessly adopted the natural voice of a child to read out the lines.[72] Parimal Goswami has given a vivid description of the moving effect that Rabindranath's voice could create; not only was the recitation "powerful" but could excite strong responses in the listeners, as he did with his invocation of Death for the ultimate union ("*Koho milaner eki riti ei/ Ogo moron, hey mor moron*" ["The heart was dancing in excitement; it was as though, if the call came, one could leap into the arms of death"]).[73]

Similar comments, stray but insightful, have been made about Rabindranath's vocal acting. He was in the habit of reading aloud a newly composed play to a select audience, before it was mounted. After he completed the final version of the comedy *Chirakumar Sabha* (completed in 1925, published 1926)[74], he read it before a gathering at Jorasanko. Though he was never able to produce three of his major plays, *Muktadhara* (1922), *Raktakarabi* (1924) and *Kaler Jatra/Rather Rashi* (1932), there are reports of his having at least read the first two before audiences, both in Santiniketan and in Calcutta. Hemendrakumar Roy, who was present on several occasions when Rabindranath read aloud his plays, has commented on the Poet's skilful vocal acting in his accounts of these different readings. About the reading of *Chirakumar Sabha*, he writes:

> Rabindranath started to read. A comic play, so his voice was suitably jocular and his facial expressions also betrayed signs of flippancy. I have not had the chance to see him perform in a comic role on the stage, but the reading was proof enough that he was a comic actor of high order .... He impersonated the roles of all the characters and we sat speechless enjoying with rapt attention the remarkably variegated reading/acting.[75]

And in his recollection of Rabindranath's reading of *Raktakarabi* [76] on 12 October 1923 before a Calcutta gathering, Hemendrakumar observes:

> When Rabindranath started to recite, every detail of the play began to blossom forth. To my mind, recitation is more difficult than acting. On the stage, the actor is helped by his gestures and movements, his co-

actors, the stage decor, the light effects, and so on. But the elocutionist has to depend solely on his voice. Rabindranath possessed a gifted voice, which could articulate any manner of emotion – a talent often lacking in the best of actors .... I have never heard anyone – in the theatre or literary circle of Bengal – to recite like Rabindranath.[77]

Hemendrakumar was moved by the amazing range of Rabindranath's vocal acting; he marvelled that the Poet's voice alone could achieve so much. When Rabindranath appeared as Thakurda/Fakir in *Dakghar* (performed in 1917 in Calcutta), Hemendrakumar appreciated his remarkable vocal inflections: "If voice be the chief implement of theatre, then one would unhesitatingly class Rabindranath's voice as matchless .... The varied intonations in his voice would be fitting for any first grade actor."[78] He makes an even more perceptive remark as he recounts the Poet's ability to impersonate the incorporeal persona of the King of the Dark Chamber through a masterful use of the voice alone during the 1935-Calcutta performance of *Raja*:

It hardly needs to be stressed how much command over one's voice is required to represent the essence of this particular character. The King is in control of the entire action; so that character must possess a unique personality and that too manifested through the deft use of the voice only. It is a near-impossible task like casting the shadow of a disembodied spirit. Rabindranath, weaving the magic of his remarkable and variable vocal powers, was able to achieve just this.[79]

Even others had observed the range of Rabindranath's vocal acting. For instance, after the 1916 *Phalguni* production in Calcutta, the drama critic of *The Bengalee* (29 January 1916) had noted: "*The excellent elocution and the irresistible force of delivery at once betrays the author in the court Poet* in spite of his make-up to hide himself from the audience."[80]

That Rabindranath had the ability to get his play across merely with the use of his voice is borne out by two readings of *Arupratan* (the revised version of *Raja*). On 15 September 1924, at the Alfred Theatre, Calcutta, all the roles of *Arupratan* were recited by Rabindranath, with adequate musical support from Dinendranath and the Visva-Bharati singing troupe: "Dr. Rabindranath Tagore recited and a number of boys and girls of his school sung the song of his new drama Arup-Ratan .... But the piece of the evening was probably the dumb show of Miss Tagore, a grand daughter of Bengal's beloved poet."[81] The critic seems to have erred in identifying the mime actor, as it was Ranu Adhikari (Mukherjee) who mimed Sudarshana; she has given an account of this herself: "The year after *Visarjan*, I played the queen in *Arup Ratan*. But it was a dumb acting. Rabindranath himself had tutored me in this. Sahana Devi would sing the songs from within."[82] Though according to Ranu Adhikari, Sahana Devi only sang from within, Sahana Devi's own reminiscences indicate that she had mimed the role of Surangama, and sang her songs.[83]

174   *Rabindranath as theatre-practitioner*

This is most likely, as the drama depends much upon the interaction between Sudarshana and Surangama, which demands the onstage presence of both characters. Again, just a year before his death, when attempts to mount another *Arupratan* failed, Rabindranath decided to read the play aloud to the *asram* community. The *Visva-Bharati News* gives a detailed report of this:

> Gurudeva gave readings from his own drama Arupratan (King of the Dark Chamber), and for a whole hour and a half kept his audience spellbound by the magic charm of his voice. He made the whole drama living and real, with characters, dialogue, and situations unfolding themselves into a harmonious pattern until the solemn grandeur of the final scene was reached.[84]

Yet, at the height of his acting career, when he appeared in the role of Vikramdev in *Tapati* (staged in September in 1929), for the dramatic climax Rabindranath eschewed the potent effects of his resonant voice and took recourse to silent acting. Amita Tagore, playing Queen Sumitra in the production, gives a vivid description of Rabindranath's silent acting in the final scene after Sumitra has entered the lit pyre:

> In the last scene after my entry into the fire, I stood beside the wings and watched with rapt attention Gurudev's [Rabindranath] unforgettable silent acting, which is almost impossible to recount in words. Imagine the scene. Sumitra has entered the lit fire; suddenly the royal drums are heard off-stage; King Vikramdev enters the temple; the drums stop; the glow of the lit fire still filters onto the stage; Vikramdev enters, looks at the flames and stands astounded; he strikes the ground with his sceptre and lifts his head to face the fire. A mixture of intense surprise, despair, anguish and pain play upon his face in a manner that can hardly be expressed in language.[85]

This brief but graphic account speaks volumes for the powerful histrionic talent of Rabindranath, even in moments of silent acting.

V

This assessment of Rabindranath's histrionic capabilities, particularly displayed through his impersonation of a character, assumes significance in the light of remarks made by contemporary eyewitnesses. On the one hand, there have been accounts that have time and again pointed out that he was always himself, even while acting a role. On the other, there have been reports which suggested that his acting could move through a gamut of widely different roles, each individuated with its own specificity. This was more often than not available in the rehearsal room when the Poet painstaking acted out a vast range of characters, one unlike another. This may lead us back to the point raised earlier about his increasing mastery of the art of amalgamating presentation and re-presentation; empathy and detachment, so that the final product was an impersonation, delicately nuanced and suggestive of a deeper comprehension of Life.

The first group, which holds that the Poet's own self shone through his dramatic impersonations, would include contemporaries like Sita Devi. Recounting the May 1911 performance of *Raja* at Santiniketan, for instance, she comments:

> Whenever I saw his acting I always felt whatever be the role it was impossible for us to forget that it was Rabindranath. Though he was an excellent actor of the first grade, it was hardly possible for him to remain incognito. Just as the sun cannot be made to take on the guise of a star, it was impossible to disguise him as any other self.[86]

In this production of *Raja*, for the role of Thakurda, Rabindranath "used the saffron garment he is usually dressed in, and simply wore a garland of flowers when he entered the stage",[87] though when the character appeared as the commander of the King's army, "there was a change in costume. He wore a white silk dress, with a broad red waistband."[88] It seems when Rabindranath acted as Thakurda, he merely retained his usual self, but in the role of the King (which he played from offstage, simultaneously with the onstage role of Thakurda), he conveyed the King as an invisible intangible presence only through his voice, as is required in this play. Others, too, have noted how whenever Rabindranath performed, "the roles would be coloured by his personality."[89]

In the 1917 Jorasanko *Dakghar* performance, he again played Thakurda without many external appendages, only having wrapped a saffron cloth around his head;[90] he was again Thakurda in a 1935 performance of *Sarodotsav* at Santiniketan. Describing the latter event, he wrote to Hemantabala Devi in a letter: "A few days ago,[91] *Sarodotsav* was performed here, in which I played Thakurda. The heavens have already dressed me in the external garb of Thakurda, and so the cost of a wig was saved."[92] By corollary, this implies that he merely had to be himself for this role. And Soumyendranath is reported to have observed: "Whatever role he played, Rabindranath remained Rabindranath. His exceptionally conscious self did not allow a total merger with the self of the character enacted."[93]

There was another group among his contemporaries who held that the Poet could, like a chameleon, effortlessly slide from one role into another. This particularly became evident during rehearsals when he preferred to act out rather than verbally explain the characters. Sahana Devi, for instance, had happened to see him at close quarters preparing his actors for the 1923 *Visarjan* production and was amazed by his immense range of character impersonation:

> I always felt that to watch Rabindranath's style of direction was itself a lesson. From the little I have seen, I gathered that the Poet preferred to train through actual acting, less through verbal explanation. He would repeat as

many times as required, with immense patience. He could become one with the character he was impersonating. At times, he had to demonstrate several characters to several actors one after another. I would be amazed to see how quickly he transformed himself from one to another. He could even change the dramatic ambience just as effortlessly.[94]

Though Rabindranath increasingly limited himself to roles of the poet/sage/ hermit/beggar/minstrel (generally viewed as his spokespersons), as an actor he really could not be straitjacketed within a type figure. That his histrionic ability straddled a substantial range – as hinted by Sahana Devi – was made evident when, after having played roles like Sannyasi (*Sarodotsav*, 1908), Thakurda and the King (*Raja*, 1910), Kabisekhar and blind *baul* (*Phalguni*, 1916), or Thakurda/Fakir (*Dakghar*, 1917), late in his life he took up the relatively younger roles of the conflict-riddled young Joysingha (*Visarjan*, 1923) and the love-obsessed King Vikramdev (*Tapati*, 1929).

Because Rabindranath's style of performance encompassed a vast array of theatrical possibilities, he did not fight shy of resorting to effects of verisimilitude, if required, with the help of illusionistic strategies. Often these could be coalesced with more non-realist stage effects, to create an effect of suggestive realism. The use of the Cubist steps and the "lurid red light" cast upon the "entrance to the Temple itself invisible in the darkness beyond the wings" in *Visarjan* (1923 production),[95] or the red glow on the white backdrop to simulate the blaze of the lit pyre in *Tapati* (1929)[96] may be cited as instances. Again, while the stage copy of the 1923 *Visarjan* mentions the use of stage properties like bells and conch shells, it also indicates Sahana Devi's appearance as *Visva-mata* [World-Mother], a role loaded with the nuanced implications of the functions of the goddess as Eternal Mother.[97]

Rabindranath was particularly fastidious about his own onstage physical appearance. Sita Devi recounts how he was bothered about whether he should use a headgear for his role of Adinpunya in *Achalayatan* (performed 1917), and kept asking Dinendranath and Kamala Devi about this.[98] He dictated the details of his costume for the 1916 *Phalguni* in a letter to Gaganendranath: "Keep the sleeves very loose in the white robe you are designing for me. The effect of white would work best on muslin."[99] The stage appearance of the character mattered so much to Rabindranath that he took great pains to adopt the right look and demeanour for the role. As early as in 1897, for his portrayal of Kedar in *Baikunther Khata*, he is reported to have used "in costume and get-up, posture and movement, make up and mannerism, such a callous attitude and a mock humility that the inner core of the character was easily discernible."[100] When at sixty-two he played the young Joysingha (*Visarjan*, 1923), his "make up completely disguised the 60 years old poet, the long hair and the blowing beard were all gone – the gray yielding place to a very natural dark ... the poet looked at least forty years younger"[101]; the acting matched the appearance, he "could be easily mistaken for a youth, so bold was his gait, so resonant his voice".[102] We have discussed earlier how for Kabisekhar in *Phalguni* or Vikram in *Tapati* he took

Acting the role 177

similar steps to "look" the character. Rabindranath, ever evolving, never inflexible, kept adapting his style of acting and his staging principles to the requirements of the production at hand. His own style of acting kept varying as he quickly moved through a whole gamut of characters – if the old *baul* of *Phalguni* (1916)[103], or Thakurda/Fakir of *Dakghar* (1917), or Thakurda of *Raja* (1935) needed a more presentational/anti-illusionistic style, the roles of Joysingha (*Visarjan*, 1923) and Vikramdev (*Tapati*, 1929) certainly demanded a more representational/illusionistic approach. Rabindranath explored all possibilities of the art of theatrical representation for all it was worth – whether through illusion or anti-illusion, mimetic or anti-mimetic, affective empathy or objective detachment.

It would perhaps be apt to conclude this discussion on Rabindranath's acting talent by referring to the observations of an eminent contemporary, himself a playwright, actor and producer. After the 1923 production of *Visarjan*, the *Indian Daily News*, on 4 September 1923, carried an elaborate report of the staging, written by the noted theatre-personality, Amritalal Bose, who had seen the performance on 25 August. This report (titled "Visarjan – an appreciation") needs to be quoted at some length for its insightful observations about Rabindranath's talent as an actor, that too coming from a contemporary theatre celebrity:

> The style of acting changes every twenty years, if not sooner, and Kemble's Hamlet on the Irving-stage would be out of date today. So Irving and Matheson Lang would be two perfect yet different Hamlets. So here also the Tagore "troupe" were up-to-date.
>
> Bengal has not yet discovered for herself a distinct national type of acting. And as long as we cannot find this, we must be content to borrow as much as suits us from the English stage, since any action is better than no action.
>
> Taking all this for granted, the performance of "Visarjan" was, begging the captious critic's pardon, an unqualified success ….
>
> After the officers have proceeded [he was evaluating Dinendranath's Raghupati and Ranu Adhikari's Aparna] comes the General. The Rabindranath. Born great, he has achieved greatness and greatness courts him too. "The great poet is a great actor", almost a master of the technique of stagecraft. But, young aspirants to histrionic fame, beware of the great master! As in poetry one must drink at the fountain of Rabindranath's mind and not simply borrow his words, so, on the stage, one should imbibe the spirit of his acting and not imitate him in action, attitude, gesture or pose. They are all his own, and the copy-right is not to be infringed.
>
> In endowing Rabi Babu with a great mind, Providence seems to have prepared a special mould to cast the golden casket in which that mind was to find its home. There is, in the masculine frame of Rabindranath, such a judicious admixture of the feminine, that the product almost

approaches the Divine. He sighs, murmurs, wails, kneels, claps his hands, draws out his long vowels and we feel that the woman peeps out without making effeminate the poetry of his presentation.[104]

Amritalal's observations are most perceptive on several counts. First, in the context of the changing style of acting, he notes the "up-to-date" approach of the Tagore troupe. Second, the admission of the lack of a "national style" of acting is telling in the context of Rabindranath's own search for a 'new' Indian theatrical idiom. One wonders if any specific element in the *Visarjan* production (hailed by him as "an unqualified success") put Amritalal in this frame of mind. Third, he identifies the unique histrionic talent of Rabindranath, which he realizes may tempt young aspirants to imitate, but cautions them against any such attempt. Fourth, he locates in Rabindranath's genius an androgynous self, also available in his acting as elsewhere in his creative corpus. This is a fitting tribute from one who was himself so closely involved with the business of playwriting and play production.

Admittedly, as a practising artist, Rabindranath's views of theatre and mode of performance did not remain the same throughout. For instance, his appraisal of Henry Irving's style of acting (seen during his visit to England in 1890) has not remained uniform. Though he did not like Irving's style of performance, the criticism (made in 1891) came somewhat haltingly: "Irving's acting was also good, but such mannerism, such unclear diction, such revolting gestures! Still, it was a good performance."[105] Later (in 1912), he is more forthright in his assessment: "Irving's tremendous display left me dumbfounded. Such exaggeration mars the inner clarity of the performance. This merely stirs up the outside, but poses impediments to gain access within."[106] At a mature phase in his career, he offered some interesting observations on theatre and the style of acting. By then, Rabindranath seems to have arrived at an idea of acting that amalgamated the intense and the detached approaches to reveal further possibilities towards an inward exploration for the actor. One may cite at some length from the essay "Antar bahir" (1912), which has already been referred to earlier, even at the risk of repetition:

> Though acting seems to indulge in imitation more than other forms of art, it is not plain mimicry. It draws aside the veil of naturalism to reveal the inner play (*leela*). If there is too much stress on the natural, then the inner truth is blurred. In the theatre, we often find actors making use of exaggerated vocal and physical histrionics to demonstrate human emotions in an inflated manner. If instead of *depicting* truth, one would want to *imitate* truth one would resort to excesses like the false witness. One's faith in moderation is, then, lacking. Our theatre regularly indulges in such physical acrobatics of false testimony ...
>
> Art, above all, requires restraint, for moderation is the gateway to that inner world ... The pursuit (*sadhana*) of Art is the quest for the Ultimate One. Therefore, the real goal of Art cannot be to intoxicate the heart with

excessive thrusts. Its aim is to transport us to that innermost depth through the practice of moderation. To blindly imitate or exaggerate with crude emphases will only result in child's play.[107]

Rabindranath, then, whether in writing or in acting of his plays, moved in a different direction – from the outer world of tangible/material reality to the inner world of cerebral (perhaps even spiritual) perception. Though it cannot be denied that a profound sense of mysticism informs most of Rabindranath's works, yet this spiritual perception may also be seen as pointing towards a deeper quest of his innate Romantic spirit – the quest for the Other, which may or may not be defined as merely religious or mystical. In certain respects, this interplay between inside and the outside (the "antar-bahir"), the Self and the Other, helps to form the identity of the Romantic artist. In the case of Rabindranath, too, he seems to have been under its influence, even while engaging with the theatre. One may even argue that in his impersonation of stage characters, Rabindranath attained a oneness with the role through a cerebral/spiritual perception that went beyond either the kind of intensity practised by Girishchandra or the kind of detachment advocated by Ardhendusekhar. As has been suggested early in this chapter, Rabindranath was evolving a style of acting that enabled an effortless transition between the actor and the role. This is what had been noticed in his depiction of the roles of Sanyasi (*Sarodotsav*), the blind *baul* (*Phalguni*), Thakurda/Fakir (*Dakghar*) or Thakurda (*Raja*). Those who witnessed his performances have commented repeatedly on how he would merge himself with the impersonated roles, so that actor and character were blended in total unison in the quest for that deeper realization of the Other.[108] Edward Thompson singled out the role of the blind *baul* in *Phalguni* for special mention: "The interpretation of the Baul reached a height of tragic sublimity which could hardly be endured. Not often can men have seen a stage part so piercing in its combination of fervid acting with personal significance."[109] And when Rabindranath performed in the strikingly different role of King Vikramdev (in *Tapati*, 1929), his silent acting communicated the inner struggles felt at that climactic moment: "Vikramdev enters, looks at the flames and stands astounded; he strikes the ground with his sceptre and lifts his head to face the fire. A mixture of intense surprise, despair, anguish and pain play upon his face in a manner that can hardly be expressed in language."[110]

What has been said in the context of his seasonal plays in particular may well be applicable to most of the plays of his mature years: "He reforms performance to effect a change in the roles of the actor and the spectator. The actor is like the performer of a ritual, the priest of a service. And the spectators are the patrons participating in the occurrence."[111] The acting/performance/ritual goes beyond the immediate theatrical event and expands into a wider perception of Life where contraries meet – winter melts into spring (*Phalguni*); external darkness dissolves away as an inner light dawns from within (*Raja*); the constricted confines of a quarantined room expands into a vast measureless space to prepare for the welcome of the royal guest (*Dakghar*). Most of these themes relate to Rabindranath's faith in the wholeness of Life, for which we need to look beyond its discrete and disparate forms. In his scheme of things, even Death appears not to signal an end but a continuation of Life, of an existence where contraries coexist in a harmonious blend. Because this conviction informed every sphere of his activities, when his grandson, Nitindranath, passed away in his thirties in 1932, he did not let the performance of *Varsha-mangal* be hampered; he called together the shocked and dejected *asram*-residents and told them: "I have suffered a personal loss, the blow has shattered my doors, but for that why should the celebrations of the *asram* cease? ... Such celebrations are above loss, sorrow, pain or distress; in this world of sorrows, through much agony and suffering, has bliss (*ananda*) arrived."[112] The style of acting and the mode of performance that Rabindranath was evolving increasingly foregrounded this inner realization and his deep-seated faith in the flow of Life, where pain and pleasure, joy and sorrow, were blended together in blissful harmony. To convey this harmony, this inner perception of order, he needed a different approach to playwriting, as well as a different style of performance. Sankha Ghosh, commenting upon this development in Rabindranath's performance style, writes:

> Like Rabindranath, Girishchandra would also remark, "Acting is not quite natural; it is 'as if natural'." But to give expression to this 'as if natural', to transcend the boundaries of the natural, Rabindranath's performance was inflected with a different aspect, which, to avoid linguistic debates, one may identify as rhythm. A middle path would emerge out of the merger of the older pattern and the new one, of the exaggerated and the natural; this harmonious blend would generate a rhythmic elegance.[113]

This "rhythmic elegance", this different melody that Rabindranath's plays demand has baffled our received notions of dramaturgical structure and/or theatrical performance.[114] With our lack of understanding, we have tended to brand his plays as plays of ideas (*bhav*) and have relegated them to the margins as not being stageworthy enough.

Notes

1 Mentioned, for instance, in Subroto Ghosh, *Rabinataker Natyakatha* (Calcutta: Signet Press, 2017) 35–6.
2 "Muktakuntala", in *Galpa-Salpa, Rabindra Rachanabali* [Complete Works] vol. 7 (Calcutta: West Bengal Government Centenary Edition, 1961)1056–8; here quoted from 1057; the Complete Works will be referred to as *RR* in subsequent references.
3 This play was also performed in the *jatra* form.
4 See Indira Devi Chaudhurani, *Rabindra Smriti (*Calcutta: Visva-Bharati, 2010; originally 1960) 31–2; also Bishnu Basu, *Rabindranather Theatre* (Calcutta: Pratibhas, 1987) 19–20.

5 The married Jyotirindranath sang against marriage, while the bachelor Rabindranath argued in favour of marriage.
6 Following Prabatkumar Mukhopadhyay, *Rabindra Jibani*, vol. 1 (Calcutta: Visva-Bharati Granthalay, 1933; rpt. 1960) 95; Indira Devi Chaudhurani, *Rabindra Smriti*, 26–8; Hemendrakumar Roy, "Jyotirindranath" in *Prabandha Samkalan [Collected Essays]*, compiled by Deviprasad Ghosh (Calcutta: Agami, 1990) 12; also Ajitkumar Ghosh, *Thakurbarir Abhinay* (Calcutta: Rabindra Bharati Society, 1988) 14–16. However, according to Khagendranath Chattopadhyay, in *Manmoyee* Rabindranath played Madan, Hemendranath was Indra and his wife Neepmoyee Devi was Sachi; and in *Vivaha-Utsav* Rabindranath impersonated a woman when arguing in favour of marriage: see Khagendranath Chattopadhyay, *Rabindra Katha* (Calcutta: Parul Prakasani, 2015; originally 1941) 168–9.
7 See Sajanikanta Das, *Shanibarer Chithi*, December 1939 (*Pous* 1346 B.S.) 445–6.
8 Sarala Devi Choudhurani, *Jibaner Jharapata* (Calcutta & Allahabad: Rupa, 1975) 29.
9 *Jibansmriti, RR*, vol. 10, 91; emphases added.
10 See Khagendranath Chattopadhyay, *Rabindra Katha*, 205. In this context, Khagendranath also reports that the Poet was not against naturalism, but to express more insightful thoughts he preferred a certain degree of stylization in voice and diction; else the dialogue would not convey the inner spirit of the play to the audience.
11 For this performance on 26 February 1881 among the audience were present Bakimchandra Chattopadhyay, Gurudas Bandyopadhyay, Haraprasad Shastri, and others; see Abantikumar Sanyal, *Kabir Abhinay*, 18.
12 Earlier, the stage design would be mostly done by Harishchandra Haldar: see Indira Devi Chaudhurani, *Rabindra Smriti*, 35; also mentioned in Sekhar Samaddar, "Rabindranather Natyabhavna", in *Punascha Rabindranath*, ed. Sabyasachi Bhattacharya and Bratin Dey (New Delhi: National Book Trust, India, 2012) 219.
13 See details mentioned in Abanindranath Tagore, *Gharoa* (Calcutta: Visva-Bharati Granthan Vibhaga, 1941; rpt. 1983) 117.
14 See *Europe-jatrir diary, RR*, vol. 10, 399; also "Antar bahir", *Pather Sanchay, RR*, vol. 10, 896.
15 *Jibansmriti, RR*, vol. 10, 84.
16 Mentioned in Khagendranath Chattopadhyay, *Rabindra Katha*, 195; see also Pabitra Sarkar, "Abhinay, Projojona o Rabindranath", in *Manche Rabindranath*, ed. Ramkrishna Bhattacharya (Calcutta: Bharati Parishad, 1978) 26–7.
17 Mentioned in *Gharoa*, 110.
18 Hemendraprasad Ghosh, "Sangit Samaj", in *Masik Basumati, Ashar* 1360 B.S. (June–July, 1953) 576; also cited in Prasantakumar Pal, *Rabi Jibani*, vol. 4 (Calcutta: Ananda Publishers, 1988) 306.
19 I am indebted to Sekhar Samaddar for drawing attention to this point in his "Rabindranather Natyabhavna", specially 222–3.
20 Girishchandra Ghosh, "Abhinay o abhineta", *Girish Rachanabali*, ed. Debipada Bhattacharya, vol. 3 (Calcutta: Sahitya Samsad, 1946) 829–41; here quoted from 839.
21 See Mani Bagchi, "Girish Juger Theatre", *Sisirkumar O Bangla Theatre* (Calcutta: Jijnasa, 1960) 76–7.
22 The essay was first published in *Banga-darshan* (30 December 1902), and later included in *Bichitra Prabandha* (1907).
23 Prabhatkumar Mukhopadhyay, *Rabindra Jibani*, vol. 2 (Calcutta: Visva-Bharati Granthalay, 1936) 235.
24 Sita Devi, *Punya Smriti* (Calcutta: Probasi, 1942) 38.
25 He wrote in a letter to Ranu Adhikari: "I will have to play the Sanyasi. This has no other purpose than to raise funds" (*Bhanusingher Patrabali, RR*, vol. 11,

313). In the original, he jestingly plays upon the two senses of the Bengali term "*artha*": "purpose/meaning", and "funds/money".
26 Cited in Rudraprasad Chakrabarty, *Rangamancha O Rabindranath: Samakalin Pratikriya* (Calcutta: Ananda, 1995) 92.
27 Cited in Rudraprasad Chakrabarty, *Rangamancha O Rabindranath: Samakalin Pratikriya*, 91.
28 Sita Devi, *Punya Smriti*, 73.
29 See Rathindranath Tagore, "Looking Back", in *Rabindranath Tagore: A Tribute*, ed. Pulinbihari Sen and Kshitis Roy (New Delhi: Sangeet Natak Akademi, 2006; originally 1961) 50; also Sekhar Samaddar, "Rabindranather Natyabhavna", 246.
30 Cited in Rudraprasad Chakrabarty, *Rangamancha O Rabindranath: Samakalin Pratikriya*, 125–6.
31 Cited in Rudraprasad Chakrabarty, *Rangamancha O Rabindranath: Samakalin Pratikriya*, 125.
32 The wandering minstrel who moves around singing songs in rural Bengal.
33 Prabhatkumar Mukhopadhyay, *Rabindra Jibani*, vol. 2, 535.
34 Cited in Rudraprasad Chakrabarty, *Rangamancha O Rabindranath: Samakalin Pratikriya*, 127.
35 "Antar bahir", *Pather Sanchay, RR*, vol. 10, 893–7; here quoted from 896; emphases added.
36 As has been suggested in the chapter "Theatre and Nation", these characters seem to encapsulate Rabindranath's search for a model leader, one who could merge in himself the principles of the king and the sage.
37 With Rabindranath categorically stating that his "Raja" will never be visible on the stage, this gives us perhaps the earliest, if not the only, example of a central character of a play being represented only through voice – a disembodied yet overpowering presence, whose very 'invisibility'/'formlessness' gives meaning to the play. The revised version was named *Arupratan* [The Formless Jewel].
38 Sita Devi, *Punya Smriti*, 19
39 "RABINDRANATH'S/PHALGUNI/ Notes and Impressions by/Jitendralal Banerjee", in *The Bengalee*, 29 January 1916; cited in Rudraprasad Chakrabarty, *Rangamancha O Rabindranath: Samakalin Pratikriya*, 129.
40 Cited in Rudraprasad Chakrabarty, *Rangamancha O Rabindranath: Samakalin Pratikriya*, 129.
41 *The Statesman*, 12 December 1935; as cited in Rudraprasad Chakrabarty, *Rangamancha O Rabindranath: Samakalin Pratikriya*, 112.
42 *The Forward*, 12 December 1935; also cited in Rudraprasad Chakrabarty, *Rangamancha O Rabindranath: Samakalin Pratrikiya*, 113.
43 These reviews, along with others, are cited in n. 27 and n. 30.
44 Parimal Goswami, *Smriti chitran* (Calcutta: Prajna Prakashani, 1958) 194.
45 Review in *Anandabazar Patrika*, January 1927; as cited in Prabhatkumar Mukhopadhyay, *Rabindra Jibani*, vol. 3 (Calcutta: Visva-Bharati Granthalay, 1952; rev. 1961) 270.
46 *The Statesman*, 14 October 1936; cited in Rudraprasad Chakrabarty, *Rangamancha O Rabindranath: Samakalin Pratikriya*, 298; emphasis added.
47 *Chinnapatrabali*, letter no. 176, dated 24 November 1894, in *RR*, vol. 11, 195.
48 "Antar bahir", *Pather Sanchay, RR*, vol. 10, 896.
49 See, for instance, Aparna Bhargava Dharwadker, *Theatres of Independence: Drama, Theory and Urban Performance in India since 1947* (Oxford: Oxford University Press, 2005; rpt. 2008) 317–31.
50 *Visva-Bharati Quarterly*, October 1923, 309.
51 Sita Devi, *Punya Smriti*, 242.
52 Sahana Devi, *Smritir Kheya*, 5th edn. (Calcutta: Prima Publications, 2011; originally 1978) 132–4.

53 *The Statesman*, 26 August 1923; cited in Rudraprasad Chakrabarty, *Rangamancha O Rabindranath: Samakalin Pratikriya*, 62.
54 *The Englishman*, 27 August 1923; cited in Rudraprasad Chakrabarty, *Rangamancha O Rabindranath: Samakalin Pratikriya*, 63.
55 Sita Devi in *Punya Smriti* recounts how he appeared in his everyday self, often wearing his usual dress, for the roles of Sanyasi in *Sarodatsav* (38), Thakurda in *Raja* (19), or Adinpunya in *Achalayatan*, (19).
56 *Indian Daily News*, 27 August 1923; cited in Rudraprasad Chakrabarty, *Rangamancha O Rabindranath: Samakalin Pratikriya*, 62.
57 Prabhatkumar Mukhopadhyay, *Rabindra Jibani*, vol.2, 535.
58 *Ektara* is the instrument used by *bauls*, usually fitted with a single string.
59 Phanindranath Roy, "Amar dekha Rabindranath", *Jugantar Patrika*, Sunday, 9 May 1971; cited in Rudraprasad Chakrabarty, *Rangamancha O Rabindranath: Samakalin Pratikriya*, 135.
60 Rabindranath is reported to go through the tedious task of blackening the beard for every evening's performance and then having the dye removed again after performance. Abanindranath solved the problem by covering the Poet's original white beard with black gauze: see *Gharoa*, 139; also cited in Rudraprasad Chakrabarty, *Rangamancha O Rabindranath: Samakalin Pratikriya*, 238.
61 Quoted in Rudraprasad Chakrabarty, *Rangamancha O Rabindranath: Samakalin Pratikriya*, 235.
62 Quoted in Rudraprasad Chakrabarty, *Rangamancha O Rabindranath: Samakalin Pratikriya*, 235.
63 See, for instance, Rudraprasad Chakrabarty, *Rangamancha O Rabindranath: Samakalin Pratikriya*, 240–1.
64 Abanindranath, *Gharoa*, 139. One may assume that a similar technique may have been deployed for his dual roles in *Phalguni*; however, there is no first-hand account of this.
65 Sujanendranath Tagore, *Ja Dekhechi*, Tapati Regent Estate Ladies' Club, 14 December 1985; cited in Rudraprasad Chakrabarty, *Rangamancha O Rabindranath: Samakalin Pratikriya*, 238.
66 Sourindramohan Mukhopadhyay, *Rabindra Smriti* (Calcutta: Sisir Publishing House, 1957) 214.
67 Amita Sen, *Santiniketan Asramkanya* (Calcutta: Tagore Research Institute, 1977) 73.
68 Harindranath Dutta, "Rangalaye Rabinbranath: Smriticharan", in *Manche Rabindranath*, ed. Ramkrishna Bhattacharya (Calcutta: Bharati Parishad, 1978) 13–18; here quoted from 13.
69 See Ajitkumar Ghosh, *Thakurbarir Abhinay* (Calcutta: Rabindra Bharati Society, 1988) 35.
70 The poem begins "*Mone koro jeno bidesh ghure*" ["Imagine as though I have travelled through foreign lands"] and moves into a world of fantasy as the child imagines an encounter with dacoits to save his mother.
71 This poem, starting with "*Ekhono to boro hoi ni ami*" ["I have not yet grown up"], also recounts childhood dreams.
72 Nilima Sen, "Amar Chelebela" in *Durer Nilima*, ed. Arundhati Deb, 2nd edn. (Calcutta: Thema, 2018) 173-8; here referred to 175.
73 Parimal Goswami, *Smritichitran* (Calcutta: Prajna Prakashani, 1958) 98–9. Goswami cites the lines from Poem no. 45 of *Utsarga* to explain the overwhelmimg effect of the Poet's recitation.
74 Though first published in *Bharati* (*c*.1904) as a farce with the title *Chirakumar Sabha*, when it was published as a single text it assumed a form mid-way between a novel and a play and was named *Prajapatir Nirbandha* (1908); then it

was reworked again as a full-fledged comic drama and renamed *Chirakumar Sabha* (1925).
75 Hemendrakumar Roy, *Soukhin Natyakalay Rabindranath*, (Calcutta: Indian Associated Publishing Co. Pvt. Ltd., 1959) 96.
76 The play was still in its nascent stage and was called then *Nandini*; it would later be named *Raktakarabi*.
77 Hemendrakumar Roy, *Soukhin Natyakalay Rabindranath*, 124–5.
78 Hemendrakumar Roy, *Soukhin Natyakalaye Rabindranath*, 112.
79 As cited in Ajitkumar Ghosh, *Thakurbarir Abhinay*, 30–1.
80 Cited in Rudraprasad Chakrabarty, *Rangamancha O Rabindranath: Samakalin Pratikriya*, 126; emphases added.
81 *The Statesman*, 16 September 1924; as cited in Rudraprasad Chakrabarty, *Rangamancha O Rabindranath: Samakalin Pratikriya*, 108.
82 Cited in Rudraprasad Chakrabarty, *Rangamancha O Rabindranath: Samakalin Pratikriya*, 109.
83 Sahana Devi, *Smritir Kheya*, 113.
84 *Visva-Bharati News*, May 1940, 86.
85 Cited in Rudraprasad Chakrabarty, *Rangamancha O Rabindranath: Samakalin Pratikriya*, 238.
86 Sita Devi, *Punya Smriti*, 19.
87 Sita Devi, *Punya Smriti*, 19.
88 Sita Devi, *Punya Smriti*, 19.
89 Pramathanath Bishi, *Rabindranath O Santiniketan* (Calcutta: Visva-Bharati, 1975) 72.
90 Sita Devi, *Punya Smriti*, 126.
91 The performance was given on 29 September 1935.
92 Letter to Hemantabala, dated 14 November 1935, in *Chitipatra*, vol. 7 (Calcutta: Visva-Bharati, 1964) 307.
93 Cited in Ajitkumar Ghosh, *Thakurbarir Abhinay*, 36.
94 Sahana Devi, *Smritir Kheya*, 130–1.
95 *Visva-Bharati Quarterly*, October 1923, 309.
96 See review in *Nachghar*, Autumn issue, 1929; cited in Rudraprasad Chakrabarty, *Rangamancha O Rabindranath: Samakalin Pratikriya*, 235–6.
97 See *Bichitra: On-line Tagore Variorum*, School of Cultural Texts and Records, Jadavpur University, bichitra.jdvu.ac.in, RBVBMS_134 (i), p. 1 (image 4). Also Sahana Devi, *Smritir Kheya*, 129.
98 Sita Devi, *Punya Smriti*, 19.
99 *Rabindra-biksha*, no. 14 (Santiniketan: Visva-Bharati, 1985) 41.
100 Khagendranath Chattopadhyay, *Rabindra Katha*, 191.
101 *Indian Daily News*, 27 August 1923; cited in Rudraprasad Chakrabarty, *Rangamancha O Rabindranath: Samakalin Pratikriya*, 62.
102 Sita Devi, *Punya Smriti*, 242.
103 The dates mentioned are dates of performances, all given at different venues in Calcutta.
104 Cited in Rudraprasad Chakrabarty, *Rangamancha O Rabindranath: Samakalin Pratikriya*, 64–5.
105 *Europe Jatrir Diary*, in *RR*, vol. 10, 399.
106 "Antar bahir", *Pather Sanchay*, in *RR*, vol. 10, 896.
107 "Antar bahir", *Pather Sanchay*, in *RR*, vol. 10, 896. The words *leela* and *sadhana*, used in the Bengali original, have been indicated in parentheses as they have specific sociocultural nuances in the Indian context; also, emphases have been added.
108 See, for instance, the remarks of Sita Devi, Indira Devi Chaudhurini or Hemendrakumar Roy quoted earlier.

109 Edward J. Thompson, *Rabindranath Tagore: Poet and Dramatist* (Delhi: Oxford University Press, 1948) 254.
110 From the accounts of Amita Tagore, as cited in Rudraprasad Chakrabarty, *Rangamancha O Rabindranath: Samakalin Pratikriya*, 238.
111 Pabitra Sarkar, *Natmancha Natyarup* (Calcutta: Proma Prakashani, 3rd edn., 1999) 126.
112 As cited in Pabitra Sarkar, *Natmancha Natyarup*, 162.
113 Sankha Ghosh, *Kaler Matra o Rabindra Natak*. 3rd edn. (Calcutta: Dey's, 1985; originally 1969) 128.
114 These notions, moreover, are borrowed from the West under the colonial influence. Rabindranath, in fact, was closer to certain notions of the Indian performance traditions.

10 Theatricalizing cultures

I

As one of the most eclectic figures among the founding fathers of modern India, Rabindranath displayed a similar propensity towards eclecticism in his career as a creative artist in fashioning a new cultural space for the emergent nation. His dreams of a new theatre were equally informed with this spirit of eclecticism, so that his receptivity to cultures of different parts of the globe helped him arrive at the model of a theatre that was inclusive, yet distinct for its own kind of identity.

In what constituted the initial stages of his career, living through a turbulent phase of anti-colonial nationalism, Rabindranath himself felt the sway of an infectious patriotic zeal, though he never really participated in active politics. All the while, however, he remained alert to the Reformist-Revivalist debates that shaped the ways of thinking in the Bengal Renaissance. Also, he never lost sight of the syncretic structure of the Indian civilization. For him, the term "Hindu" denoted less a religious community, more an inclusive sociocultural concept that accommodated several races, religions, cultures.[1] This vision of an all-encompassing Indian ethos was encapsulated, for instance, in poems like "Bharat-tirtha"[2] or "Jana Gana Mana".[3] At a later phase in his career, he chose to dissociate himself from all extreme brands of nationalism, whether in the East or in the West, including in his own land. He was sharply critical of the rise of such tendencies, which, he felt, were exclusionist and self-destructive. The motto of Visva-Bharati, the university that evolved out of the school he founded, is "where the world makes its home in a single nest"; this motto, too, points in the direction of his vision of a more comprehensive concept of internationalism. Unfortunately, in the wake of a xenophobic brand of patriotism then gripping not only India but other parts of the globe as well, Rabindranath's agenda of internationalism and citizenship of a world community was grossly misunderstood, both in his own country and elsewhere.

While Rabindranath's notions of an emergent nation passed through these various phases, his literary career (including his dramatic/theatrical oeuvre) evolved and matured, continuously interacting with various cultures, Indian and foreign. His emphasis on the need to keep all windows open to allow easy rapport with other cultures did not contradict his concept of Indianness,

DOI: 10.4324/9781003110279-11

precisely because he envisioned India as an all-inclusive socio-politico-cultural entity. He did not endorse the shunning of other cultures – even that of the colonizer – in the name of Indian nationalism. His theory of India as "a country of No-Nation",[4] though primarily asserting the distinction between the Indian and European contexts, is not opposed to his later inclination towards the idea of a world community, precisely because his vision of Indianness was always an all-inclusive comprehensive concept. He was acutely conscious of the ground reality where several factors were at work. First, India herself as a multilingual, multiracial, multicultural entity thrives on a rich diversity of languages and cultures. Second, because the colonial influence cannot be entirely rejected, it has to be accepted and assimilated in the right spirit.[5] Third, alternative modes of cultural expression were available in other parts of Asia, with which India needed to connect. These multiple cultural templates, available in the East and in the West, left their variegated impressions upon his artistic genius and inflected his own cultural articulations. While on the sociopolitical plane this awareness helped the formulation of his notions about what the emergent nation should address to acquire an inclusive identity, on the cultural front he was imagining a cultural space (hence, also a theatre) where this openness to multiple cultures would be one of the primary guiding principles.

So, to recapitulate discussions made earlier, in the world of drama/theatre, Rabindranath started out with the Western model – the operatic experiments in *Valmiki-Pratibha* (1881), *Kal Mrigaya* (1882) or *Mayar Khela* (1888), and the Shakespearean five-act structure in *Raja o Rani* (1889) and *Visarjan* (1890). He went on to conceptualize an alternative model of theatre in "Rangamancha" (1902), which he put into practice at Santiniketan – both in writing and staging – starting with *Sarodotsav* (1908) and continuing through the other major plays of this period. Finally, he embarked upon his concept of "theatre as dance", sculpting the dance dramas of the final phase. These three phases, in turn, reflect his early emulation of Western theatrical traditions (in keeping with the Reformist zeal of the Bengal Renaissance); his championing of the indigenous resources of theatre (when he was responding to the anti-colonial ideological imperatives); and his widening of the scope of theatre to include cultural resonances from other parts of the globe (to encapsulate the more expansive cosmopolitanism and international fraternity that he was then envisaging). In veering away from the European tradition, he upheld both the rural *jatra* and the classical Sanskrit drama as exemplary forms[6] – to be followed, not replicated.[7] This quest for an "Indianness", rooted in tradition yet relevant to the contemporary situation of an emergent nation, while providing the ideological foundation for his creative output, is concurrently alert to the possibilities of multicultural transactions – between Orient and Occident, local and global, rural and urban. This perception seems to have informed his entire career – whether as a creative artist, or an innovative educationist, or a philosophical thinker, or even as a visionary yet pragmatic theatre-practitioner.

188 *Rabindranath as theatre-practitioner*

It is for this reason that, though Santiniketan offered a space suitable for his new theatrical experiments, Rabindranath did not shy away from opportunities of performing on proscenium stages at various urban venues, whether at Jorasanko or at the New Empire, Madan or Alfred theatres in Calcutta, or again the Excelsior Theatre in Bombay or the Regal Theatre in Colombo. On the one hand, this attests to his eagerness to deploy all available resources of production and reception; on the other, it underscores his prioritizing of theatrical exigency, disallowing theory to stand in the way of practice. As such, despite his avowed preference for the scenery of the mind (*"chittapat"*), he did, at times, permit other modes of presentation (as in the realistic stage-setting for the 1917 *Dakghar*, designed by Abanindranath and others) and, at other times, sought to overlay them with signs of non-naturalistic theatre semiology (as in the stage décor of the 1935 *Raja* given at the New Empire Theatre, with "a gate of pure oriental conception"[8] making amends for the proscenium setting). It may be argued that the expanse of an open uninhibited ludic space returned with the dance dramas, where setting was largely contained in the song-dance narrative. The scenes became more 'person-scenes' than 'place-scenes'; the characters entered ushering in the scene, which is reconstructed more through the song-dance narrative without resorting to realistic stage appendages to designate locales, and with their exit they took away the scene with them.

II

Rabindranath's visits to the Far East (to Japan in 1916, and again in 1924; to Java and Bali in 1927) and to Ceylon (in 1934) exposed him to the dance forms of other Asian cultures,[9] and helped him to evolve his notion of "theatre as dance", which, in turn, gave shape to the dance dramas of the final phase – *Shapmochan* (1931), *Chitrangada* (1935), *Chandalika* (1938) and *Shyama* (1939). Though dance as a mode of theatrical expression was introduced earlier in the climax of *Natir Puja* (1926), the experiment with dance becoming theatre reached a culmination in these dance dramas. Alongside the full-fledged dance dramas, there were compilations of songs and dances around a particular theme, usually seasonal – if the coming of monsoon was greeted joyously in *Varsha-mangal* (1921), *Sesh Varshan* (1925) bid farewell to the rains; the mirthful spirit of spring occasioned *Vasanta* (1923), *Sundar* (1925)[10] and *Navin* (1931); and the entire cycle of the seasons was celebrated in *Nataraj-Riturangasala/Rituranga* (1927).

Just prior to *Rituranga*, Rabindranath had toured Java, and the impact of Javanese dance was perceptible in the dances used for this presentation. This finds support in Pratima Devi's statement:

> He brought with him pictures and descriptions of different Javanese dances, along with an urge to use their artistic expertise. This helped our boys and girls to learn Javanese dance styles. The Javanese influence was perceptible in the performance and costuming of *Rituranga*; Javanese

architecture, too, was suggested through the stage design of Surenbabu [Suren Kar].[11]

Yet another source seems to indicate that, in fact, in this production the style of Javanese dance was infused with the styles of Indian dances from Manipur (in North-East India) and South India.[12] It has also been said that for the dances by girls, Manipuri was mixed with the Gujrati folk dance, Garba.[13] In fact, when visiting Sylhet in November 1919, Rabindranath was so impressed by Manipuri dance that he wanted to introduce this dance form in Santiniketan. At the Poet's request, the King of Tripura sent a few Manipuri artistes to Santiniketan to teach the dance form; among them was Buddhimanta Singh. Eventually, Manipuri became one of the primary dance forms practised at Santiniketan, and widely used in his dance dramas.

When *Shapmochan* toured different cities, including the 1934 tour of Ceylon, Manipuri seems to have been the staple for the dance drama. There were descriptions of how the young dancers "transformed the simple rustic Ras-leela dance of Manipuri into a delightful dream of rhythmic perfection".[14] But, that it was not only Manipuri but an eclectic mix of several cultural styles was also noted approvingly in reviews and press reports: "The gestures with the hands excelled those of the dances in Bali, Nepal and Travancore in grace and expressions; the movements of the bodies were pliant, fluent and harmonious",[15] or again, "The whole setting was a lavish simplicity – Greek in design, Javanese in execution."[16]

For *Chitrangada* (1935), Manipuri dance was the obvious choice, as the dramatic locale was, anyway, set in Manipur. But the more discerning among the spectators detected blends of other dance styles as well: "The dramatic cubism of Kathakali gloriously wedded to the sensitive lyricism of the Manipuri and occasionally punctuated with folk feelings breathe an aroma of dreamland interspersed with haunting melody and silvery moonlight."[17] That the costume design also experimented with different cultural codes found appreciation: "A word of commendation is due to the designer of the costumes. He borrows ideas from the repertories of the continental Asiatic stage – from the Javanese and Cambodian dancers, from the Burmese Pwe, as well as the Indian nautch girl and exploits old models with effective innovations."[18]

For the performance of the prose play *Chandalika* (1933) Rabindranath was often the sole narrator of the performance and followed the style of *kathakata*.[19] When he transformed the text into dance drama *Chandalika*,[20] he retained much of the conversational mode of the prose play version so that the colloquial lines of that source text could be easily set to tune.[21] *The Statesman* remarked: "The technique of the dance-drama in 'Chandalika' is in many ways a revival of the ancient Indian form in which the dialogue is converted into songs as background music, and is symbolically interpreted by the characters through the dances."[22] That the choreography presented a judicious admixture of several styles was noted approvingly by several reviewers: "The dances followed the traditional styles of Kathakali with snatches and catches from

190 *Rabindranath as theatre-practitioner*

Monipuri, both the styles being harmoniously blended";[23] "suggestive Manipuri dance and gestural South Indian dance – the two separate approaches were merged together. To this was added some bits of mirthful rural Kandi dance";[24] "The conception of the dance interpretations is based principally on the Monipuri system of Assam and the Kathakali of South India";[25] "In general the symbolism of the Manipuri school was followed but the blending of South Indian styles and in one or two of the dances Buddhist dances of the Tibetan type, with it gave the dances a variety and added richness."[26]

For a performance of *Parisodh/ Shyama* (in 1937 at Santiniketan), five different kinds of dance styles were used to individuate the characters: Bharatnatyam (for Bajrasen, played by Mrinalini Swaminathan), Manipuri (for Shyama, by Nandita Kripalani), Jaypuri Katthak (for Uttiya, by Asha Ojha), Kathakali (for Prahari/Guard, by Kelu Nair) and Kandi dance (for Kotal/ Law Officer, by Anangalal).[27] What was particularly interesting in this performance was the parallel use of so many different dance styles which suited the expertise of each of the dancers and allowed each role to be etched with a distinct individuation, yet creating a cohesive whole. Admittedly, this cohesiveness was the more usual thrust, aiming for a harmonious blend of different cultural templates, while retaining the separate characteristics of the different dance patterns, so that one syncretic whole would emerge. So, in a later production of *Shyama* (on 7 and 8 February 1939 at Sree Theatre), Kelu Nair danced Bajrasen in a "gesture-inflected rendition of Kathakali"; the Japanese dancer Maki as the Guard and Anangalal as the Friend energized their dances with the verve of masculinity; while Nandita Kripalini as Shyama used a more pliant style like Manipuri or Bharatnatyam.[28] Interestingly, Uttiya in this performance was not played by Asha Ojha (who had danced in Kathak in 1937) but by Mrinalini Swaminathan (who had played Bajrasen then). That the total effect was an effortless synthesis of discrete patterns was much appreciated:

> Their dramatic dancing, where the actor or actress is required to put every part of the body and mind into a full expression, has variety, dignity and power of evoking sublime sentiments. Their command of intricately difficult movements is suggestive, illuminative and puissant. Their fluency of improvisation on the different events, grace and suppleness of form, facility in varying the poses, the capacity to harmonise different emotions – all seemed to be remarkably effortless.[29]

In this context, it may be helpful to recall some of the comments made in contemporary accounts and reviews that stressed the novelty of these dance dramas. Hailing *Shapmochan* as "a new creation ... different from the other plays of Rabindranath", it was observed:

> First, much of the dramatic communication remains speechless; that is to say, it is executed through tableau …. Second, the play *Shapmochan*,

from its first word to its very last, is set upon an unceasing dance pattern ... that is why the poet chooses to call it dance-enactment.[30]

And when, in March 1938, the dance drama *Chandalika* was staged at the Chaya theatre in Calcutta, a press preview underlined that the new dance drama belonged to a different category from the prose play of 1933:

There is a difference between the nature of that performance and the present one. The appeal then was chiefly 'poetic' – the quality of the present performance is mainly 'dramatic'. For this reason perhaps the poet, in giving a new shape to *Chandalika*, has called it a 'dance drama'.[31]

The preview went on to declare: "As the combination of 'ballet' and 'opera' in the Western theatre can generate novelty, that same unique fusion of form (*rup*) and emotion (*rasa*) would be available in this dance drama."[32] Though one might disagree with the suggestion of ballet and opera being intermingled, the reference to these Western performance modes, while locating the *Chandalika*-performance within the Indian traditions of "*rup*" (form) and "*rasa*" (emotion), is in itself interesting.

III

In introducing dance into his plays, in evolving theatre itself as dance in his final dance dramas, and in selecting the cast from available resources at Santiniketan (comprising primarily students and teachers of his institution), Rabindranath was making major advances with each step. Prior to this, it was unthinkable that female members of respectable families would sing and dance on the stage. Though he had behind him his own family tradition of home productions where male and female members of the family took part in plays, songs and dances, these were given generally before more select audiences. In the early days of the *asram*-school he had refrained from using mixed casting and had relied on boys to play the female roles; of course, girl students were still few in numbers, but social conditions were not favourable either. To justify his practice, he evolved a theoretical formulation for female impersonation in "Rangamancha" (1902). Still, controversy erupted in Santiniketan when *Natir Puja* was being prepared for performance in Calcutta (in 1927). To recall the words of Gouri Bhanja (née Bose), who played Srimati the *nati*: "Girls from Santiniketan singing and dancing on the stage may have provoked criticism; to prevent that, the Poet involved himself in the production."[33] We know how Rabindranath resolved the problem not only for *Natir Puja* but also for the subsequent dance dramas that used mixed casting. For these later dance dramas, he usually made it a point to be seen on the stage in what seems to have been a bid to give legitimation to the performances through his onstage presence. This finds corroboration in the photograph from the 1936 performance of *Chitrangada* at New Empire, now widely available in the public domain. Even earlier, for the *Shapmochan* performance in Colombo (March 1934), it was remarked: "Through it all Rabindranath Tagore himself sat on a side of the stage nearest the audience looking on the great pageant of music dance rhythm fragrance flowers and flames like an artist looking at a picture of his own creation."[34] Again, *The Statesman* noted with approval the Poet's onstage presence during a performance of *Parishodh* (the earlier version of *Shyama*) in October 1936: "He makes the stage human. Everyone else on the stage may be acting but he is not. He is reality. *Moreover he gives a dignity to the performance – nautch is transformed into dance.*"[35] Sajanikanta Das, witnessing a performance of *Shyama* (in February 1939), was moved to discover that

> *the language of the body is in no way less than the language of poetry. ...* I found that the touch of genius could make everything possible. *The expressiveness of the soft bodily postures dissolved away the sense of the physical to recreate a world of cerebral perception.* [36]

That Rabindranath was exploring new grounds and offering a fresh cultural space to his audiences was realized by some of the more perceptive members among them. More importantly, he was expanding the sociocultural horizon of the middle-class mindset to ensure respectable acceptance of dance as a valid mode of cultural articulation. He seems to indicate as much when he writes to Amiyachandra Chakravarty:

> This may perhaps be considered as one of the primary tasks of Visva-Bharati ... Today as wave after wave of dance, song and painting spreads from Bengal to the rest of India, it has to be admitted that its place of origin was here.[37]

Winning this battle for his theatre, songs and dances, Rabindranath was able to accommodate a whole range of diverse traditions, Western, Asiatic, Indian. His theatrical experimentations moved back and forth between different cultural registers, achieving a synthesis of disparate cultural codes – Oriental and Occidental, urban and rural – and, in turn, evolved as a more syncretic model, though firmly anchored in the Indian ethos. His explorations in the world of theatre – as in other idioms of performing and visual arts, like music, dance, theatre, or painting – testify to this basic impetus that marks out his uniqueness as a creative genius. It was this cultural space – composite and comprehensive, local yet global – that Rabindranath was trying to offer as a model for the emergent nation. If he had imagined a new Indian nation, he had also imagined for it this new cultural space.

Notes

1 "Hindu is a racial consequence (*jatigata parinam*) of Indian history": "Atmaparichay" (1912–13), *Rabindra Rachanabali* [Complete Works] vol. 12 (Calcutta: West Bengal Government Centenary Edition, 1961) 175.

Theatricalizing cultures 193

2 This poem, later set to tune, sings of the coming together of multiple races – Aryans and non-Aryans, Brahmins and Sudras, Muslims and Buddhists, and even the English – on the occasion of the anointment of Mother India, and each contributes its offerings to the celebrations; that is what makes this nation a site for pilgrimage ("tirtha").
3 This poem, also set to tune later, extols the Guide ("*Adhinayaka*") of the minds of the peoples ("*jana gana mana*") of this land unique for its multilingual, multiracial, multicultural identity. Its first stanza was subsequently adopted as the national anthem of independent India.
4 "Nationalism in the West", in *The English Writings of Rabindranath Tagore*, ed. Sisir Kumar Das, vol. 2 (New Delhi: Sahitya Akademi, 2004) 434.
5 "Nowadays we get to hear in our land that there is evil in the knowledge of the West, so we have no need for it. I do not say so. I do not hold that because power is destructive, powerlessness should be our goal." ("Palliprakriti" (6 February 1928) in *Rabindra Rachabali* [Complete Works] Popular edition, vol. 14, (Calcutta: Visva-Bharati, 1991) 362–7; here quoted from 367).
6 See "Rangamancha", prologue to *Phalguni* and preface to *Tapati* – all of which have been mentioned earlier.
7 His own theatrical experiments bear this out. He used the idiom of folk theatre to rejuvenate his theatrical practices, but did not create a *jatra* or a Sanskrit drama *per se*.
8 *Amritabazar Patrika*, 12 December 1935; as cited in Rudraprasad Chakrabarty, *Rangamancha O Rabindranath: Samakalin Pratikriya* (Calcutta: Ananda Publishers, 1995) 113.
9 He considered the Japanese dance as "dance complete", as distinct from the "half-acrobatics, half-dance" of Europe (*Japan jatri, RR*, vol. 10, 519) and in Java he found "in their movements, their combats, their amorous dalliances, even their clowning – everything is dance" (*Java-jatrir patra, RR*, vol. 10, 636).
10 "The playlet [*Sundar*] contained sixteen well chosen songs of the season set to music of an exquisite character which represented the yearning of the poet for the realization of the ideals associated with the spring, its advent and the departure of winter." (*Amritabazar Patrika*, 29 January 1929; as quoted in Rudraprasad Chakrabarty, *Rangamancha O Rabindranath: Samakalin Pratikriya*, 200–1).
11 Pratima Devi, *Nritya* (Calcutta: Visva-Bharati, 1948; rpt. 1965) 12.
12 See Amita Sen, *Ananda Sarba Kaaje* (Calcutta: Tagore Research Institute 1983)118–19.
13 See Dilipkumar Roy, *Rabindra samakale Rabindranataker Abhinoy* (Calcutta: Sramik Press, 1999) 204.
14 *Forward* (27 May 1934) quoted extensively from reports that appeared in *The Daily News of Ceylon*; as cited in Rudraprasad Chakrabarty, *Rangamancha O Rabindranath: Samakalin Pratikriya*, 253–5.
15 Andreas Nell, reviewing one of the performances in Ceylon, in *Amritabazar Patrika* (3 June 1934); as cited in Rudraprasad Chakrabarty, *Rangamancha O Rabindranath: Samakalin Pratikriya*, 255.
16 *Forward* (27 May 1934); as cited in Rudraprasad Chakrabarty, *Rangamancha O Rabindranath: Samakalin Pratikriya*, 255.
17 Amritabazar Patrika; as cited in Pronoykumar Kundu, *Rabindranather geeti-natya o nritya-natya*. (Calcutta: Orient Book Co., 1965) 376.
18 *The Statesman*, 17 March 1936; as quoted in Prabhatkumar Mukhopadhyay, *Rabindra Jibani*, vol. 4 (Calcutta: Visva-Bharati Granthalaya, 1956; rev. 1964) 53.
19 This was an indigenous form of performance in which the *kathak* (narrator) recited the whole narrative, impersonating different roles (using voice and gesture), with his own interventions as the ubiquitous *kathak* or narrator.
20 He composed a first version of this dance drama in 1938, and a second version in 1939; this second version is now the accepted text of the dance drama *Chandalika*.
21 It was the sheer genius of Rabindranth that could weave songs out of lines like "Okey chnuo na chnuo na,chi, O je Chandalinir jhi" ["Don't touch her, she is the

daughter of a Chandal"] or "Kakhan chagal tui charabi?" ["When will you tend to the flocks?"]
22 *The Statesman* (10 February 1939), after the performance at Sree Theatre in Calcutta (9 & 10 February); cited in Rudraprasad Chakrabarty, *Rangamancha O Rabindranath: Samakalin Pratikriya*, 271–2.
23 *Amritabazar Patrika* (19 March 1938), as cited in Rudraprasad Chakrabarty, *Rangamancha O Rabindranath: Samakalin Pratikriya*, 268.
24 *Jugantar* (10 February 1939), as cited in Rudraprasad Chakrabarty, *Rangamancha O Rabindranath: Samakalin Pratikriya*, 270.
25 *Hinusthan Standard* (9 February 1939); as cited in Rudraprasad Chakrabarty, *Rangamancha O Rabindranath: Samakalin Pratikriya*, 272.
26 *The Statesman* (10 February 1939); as cited in Rudraprasad Chakrabarty, *Rangamancha O Rabindranath: Samakalin Pratikriya*, 271–2.
27 Santidev Ghosh cites a letter to provide this information in *Rabindrasangeet* (Calcutta: Visva-Bharati Granthalay, rev. edn. 1958; originally 1942) 193. This is also mentioned in Dilipkumar Roy, *Rabindra samakale Rabindranataker Abhinoy*, 198; and in Mandakranta Bose, "Nrityanatya, Rabindranath o Bangasamskritir nutan diganta", in *Balaka, Special issue: Natyabyaktitwa Rabindranath*, year 19, no. 29 (November 2010): 56–68; here referred to 63.
28 Details given in *Jugantar* (8 February 1939); as cited in Rudraprasad Chakrabarty, *Rangamancha O Rabindranath: Samakalin Pratikriya*, 302–3.
29 *Amritabazar Patrika* (8 February 1939); as cited in Rudraprasad Chakrabarty, *Rangamancha O Rabindranath: Samakalin Pratikriya*, 304.
30 *Nabasakti Patrika*, 23 *Pous* 1338 B.S. (8 January 1932); cited in Rudraprasad Chakrabarty, *Rangamancha O Rabindranath: Samakalin Pratikriya*, 247. As the term *"nrityabhinaya"* has been used in the original Bengali review, it has been translated here as "dance enactment", though "dance drama" is the usual translation for what is described as *"nritya natya"*.
31 *Anandabazar Patrika* (18 March 1938); as cited in Rudraprasad Chakrabarty, *Rangamancha O Rabindranath: Samakalin Pratikriya*, 267.
32 Cited in Rudraprasad Chakrabarty, *Rangamancha O Rabindranath: Samakalin Pratikriya*, 267.
33 Quoted in Rudraprasad Chakrabarty, *Rangamancha O Rabindranath: Samakalin Pratikriya*, 207–8; see also Bishnu Basu, *Rabindranather Theatre*, 99.
34 *Forward* (27 May 1934); as cited in Rudraprasad Chakrabarty, *Rangamancha O Rabindranath: Samakalin Pratikriya*, 255.
35 *The Statesman* (14 October 1936); cited in Rudraprasad Chakrabarty, *Rangamancha O Rabindranath: Samakalin Pratikriya*, 298; emphasis added.
36 *Anandabazar Patrika*, 8 February 1939; cited in Rudraprasad Chakrabarty, *Rangamancha O Rabindranath: Samakalin Pratikriya*, 301; emphases added.
37 Letter to Amiya Chakravarty (29 April 1934), written prior to the departure for Ceylon, in *Chithipatra*, vol. 11 (Calcutta: Visva-Bharati, 1974; rpt. 2010) 109.

11 Translating the playtext

I

This discussion on Rabindranath's translation of playtexts will begin by referring to his views on translation, in general; then, briefly invoke the context of his translation of *Gitanjali* (through which the Western readership first came to know of him); and finally, consider how he went about the task of translating his plays, negotiating with the translation/transcreation of the dramaturgical and/or theatrical elements in them. It may be recalled here that only a handful of his works – like *Sadhana* (1914), *Personality* (1917), *Nationalism* (1917), *The Centre of Indian Culture* (1919), *Creative Unity* (1922), *Talks in China* (1924), *Letters from Abroad* (1924; later revised as *Letters to a Friend*, 1928), *The Religion of Man* (1931), *The Child* (1931)[1] or *East and West* (1935) – were written at first in English. The only playlet he wrote in English was *The King and the Rebel* (1913), perhaps as an aid to the students' mastery over the English language; it was performed by the students of the school. All his other English writings are translations of Bengali compositions. A couple of volumes, like *Thought Relics* (1921) or *Fireflies* (1928), included original English poems along with English translations of Bengali versions.[2]

There was, however, a sizeable number of translations done by his friends and associates, usually working under his supervision, sometimes in collaboration with him. For instance, he depended largely, though not exclusively, upon his nephew, Surendranath Tagore, for translations of his novels and short stories. Other translators also contributed regularly. For instance, *Mashi and Other Stories* (1918) contained translations by W.W. Pearson ("Mashi" [originally "Seser Ratri"]), Edward Thompson ("Castaway" ["Apad"]), Jadunath Sarkar ("The River Stairs" ["Ghater Katha"], "The Supreme Night" ["Ek Ratri"]), Prabhatkumar Mukhopadhyay ("Skeleton" ["Kankal"], "The Trust Property" ["Sampatti Samarpan"], "The Riddle Solved" ["Samasya Puran"]), Debendranath Mitter ("The Post Master"), Anath Nath Mitra ("Elder Sister" ["Didi"]), Keshab Chandra Bandyopadhyay ("Raja and Rani" ["Sadar o Andar"]). Again, there were occasions when Rabindranath decided to translate a work anew rather than use an existing translation; for the collection *Hungry Stones and Other Stories* (1916), he translated "Jay-parajay" as "The Victory", using it in place of Jadunath Sarkar's earlier translation of the same story as "Victorious in Defeat".[3] However, for whatever reason – lack of foresight/tact/ adequate communication on the part of the author, or eagerness/astuteness on the part of the publisher to cash in on Rabindranath's English writings as a marketable commodity after the Nobel award[4] – the translations were published in Rabindranath's name, as though he were the sole translator. This was repeated in the translation of drama also, as will be discussed later in this chapter.

Rabindranath's views on translation of his Bengali originals into English have remained immensely flexible, shifting with varying circumstances of production and reception of the translated texts. For instance, in a letter to his friend, Jagadishchandra Bose, dated 12 December 1900, he has betrayed rather strong reservations about translation:

> You have ventured to present before the world my writings that are like a goddess to me.[5] But stripped of her garment of the Bengali language, would she not, like Draupadi, be publicly disgraced?[6] That is the great problem with literature – the way she expresses herself to her close ones in private spaces is lost the moment any attempt is made to drag her outside.[7]

The image of the publicly humiliated Draupadi used here to describe translation stripped of its original language is particularly striking. And in an essay of 1905, commenting on Charuchandra Basu's translation of *Dhammapadam*, he suggests:

> the translation should be a word for word, literal one. Where the meaning turns abstruse, there is no harm in explaining with the help of a note. It is unfair if a translation takes the form of analysis in places, because the translator may well err in his analysis. To keep the translation and the analysis apart leaves room for the reader to use her judgement. Those words in the original the meanings of which are not sufficiently clear, we deem it our duty to leave them in place ... in some instances, the original meaning should be left unaltered .... It does no harm to place the additional words, solicited for the sake of lucidity, within brackets.[8]

Even as late as in 1935, he wrote to Sturge Moore (in a letter dated 11 June 1935): "Translations however clever can only transfigure dancing into acrobatic tricks, in most cases playing treason against the majesty of the original."[9]

Yet, when it came to his own attempts at translation, Rabindranath, more often than not, veered away from this rigid stand. The ball was set rolling, of course, by the translation of *Gitanjali* done, as he mentioned himself, during a period of convalescence. In a letter to his niece, Indira Devi, dated 6 May 1913, Rabindranath tried to explain the English translation of *Gitanjali* (*The Song Offerings*) as a chance accident, the fruits of his "unpremeditated thought", undertaken while recovering from illness (due to which the March 1912 tour of England had to be called off); not having the urge for strenuous creative work, he had apparently turned to render into English the Bengali poems of *Gitanjali*:

Then I went to Shelidah to take rest. But unless the brain is fully active, one does not feel strong enough to relax completely; so the only way to keep myself calm was to take up some light work.

It was then the month of *Chaitra* (March–April), the air was thick with the fragrance of mango-blossoms and all hours of the day were delirious with the song of birds. When a child is full of vigour, he does not think of his mother. It is only when he is tired that he wants to nestle in her lap. That was exactly my position. With all my heart and with all my holiday I seemed to have settled comfortably in the arms of Chaitra, without missing a particle of light, its air, its scene and its song. In such a state one cannot remain idle. It is an odd habit of mine, as you know, that when the air strikes my bones, they tend to respond in music. Yet I had not the energy to sit down and write anything now. So I took up the poems of *Gitanjali* and set myself to translate them one by one. You may wonder why such a crazy ambition should possess one in such a weak state of health. But believe me, I did not undertake this task in a spirit of reckless bravado. I simply felt an urge to recapture through the medium of another language the feelings and sentiments which had created such a feast of joy within me in the days gone by.[10]

But in these translations he took major liberties to deviate from the originals, so much so that they mostly became new creations. This process involving translation/transcreation is described through a curious analogy of the reception of the bride after the wedding in a letter written by him to Ajitkumar Chakravarty from Urbana, Illinois, on 13 March 1913. This merits to be cited at length:

it is the translating of my poems which pleases me most – it simply seizes me like an intoxication. To transfer to a different language what I myself had once composed is an aesthetic enjoyment of a kind. To me it is the reception of the bridal pair following the ceremony of marriage. The marriage has been ritualised but the bride has to be introduced to the larger community. When the guests accept refreshments at the hands of the bride the union of man and wife becomes an accepted fact of the world. When I wrote the poems originally in Bengali it marked the union of the poet and his poetry; at that moment I had no clear awareness of any other motive. *But when I translate the same, I virtually extend an invitation to others to come and partake of something at the bride's hand. It is happiness of another kind. The enthusiasm for arranging such a big affair has completely occupied my mind. Repeatedly, and repetitively I am erasing and striking out, brushing up and chiselling – acting as if in a frenzy.* Nobody here would accept that these are translations – none would hear that these were originally written in Bengali and written better. As for myself, I too cannot quite dismiss this opinion as entirely unjustified. *In fact, one cannot quite translate one's own works …. I intend to carry the essential substance of my poetry into the English translation and this means a wide divergence from the original. You may not even be able to identify a poem of mine unless I do it for your benefit .... The English language has a beauty and a splendour of its own and my poems will also attain a class if they achieve the rebirth by being invested with the virtues of the English language.*[11]

When it came to translating his own works, Rabindranath viewed the transition from the Bengali version to the English as something more than mere lingual transposition. For the Bengali equivalence of 'translation', he increasingly moved towards the term *tarjama* rather than use *anubad, rupantar* or *bhasantar: tarjama*, more than the other terms, conveys a sense of 'rendition', even 'interpretation'. As late as in 1935, he wrote in a letter to Amiyachandra Chakravarty who was then engaged in the translation of *Char Adhyay* (*Four Chapters*):

in my writings language is the prime vehicle. That is, the sense cannot be communicated through the meaning of the word alone, much depends upon the semantics of the language. Without that, it is made so much poorer and untidy that I am unwilling to present it before a foreign audience. Had I made the translation myself, I would have written it afresh.[12]

Rabindranath in his own translation projects, then, behaved less as a translator, more as a transcreator. However, not every critic/translator would agree with this view. Some have expressed dismay at the "gulf ... between the originals and their English versions",[13] resulting from the revisions/reworkings of the source text, often so severely truncated that we are left with only "a whimpering foreshortened shadow"[14]; they have regretted Rabindranath's habit of "tampering with the original".[15] Others, on the other hand, have applauded Rabindranath's translation methodology as "creative regeneration"[16] or "a parallel creative process",[17] which enriched his literary corpus further with "rewritings and recastings, rearrangements and cross-matings, exegesis and fresh interventions making up a concurrent, counterpoising creative process, a commentary on the Bengali line, uniquely valuable as being from the poet's own pen".[18] And yet others have interpreted the tendency as "the swing back and forth, a kind of love-hate relationship [that] Tagore had all through experienced with regard to translating".[19]

II

It must also be remembered here that when Rabindranath decided to translate his Bengali compositions into English, it was a voluntary choice of the colonizer's language, which was not his natural medium for literary creation. On the one hand, this necessitated the rewriting of the English works more as interpretations/transcreations rather than as mere translations (*tarjama* more than *anubad/bhasantar*). On the other, this involved a "dilemma of linguistic choice" which Sisir Kumar Das views as "part of a larger problem involving a power relation between the major and minor languages."[20] In his use of the terms "major" (for English) and "minor" (for the Indian regional languages), Das alerts us to the "political, economic, ideological" determinants that condition the "power relations" between the languages of the colonizer and the colonized. In fact, Das goes so far as to state: "An Indian writer, that is a writer who writes in an Indian language either by choice or accident, is fated to be unknown to the rest of the world irrespective of his literary accomplishments *unless he is translated into a major language.*"[21]

Rabindranath's awareness of such "power relations" between "major"/"minor" languages may have conditioned the apologies offered for his lack of mastery over the English language. He repeatedly sought the help of Englishmen, mostly poets, to revise, edit, even correct his English renditions. To W.B. Yeats he once wrote: "I am so absolutely ignorant of the proprieties of your language ... I do hope you will take the trouble of once going over the proofs of the second edition and make all the restorations you think necessary" (26 January 1913).[22] To Ernest Rhys he confessed: "You know my English needs brushing up" (31 May 1913).[23] He elaborated further in a letter to Ezra Pound:

> I am not at all strong in my English grammar – please do not hesitate to make corrections when necessary. Then again I do not know the exact value of your English words. Some of them may have their souls worn out by constant use and some others may not have acquired their souls yet. So in my use of words there must be lack of proportion and appropriateness perhaps that could also be amended by friendly hands (5 January 1913).[24]

Even later, in 1935, when efforts were being made to publish a collected edition of his poems and plays, he was advising Amiya Chakravarty (who was initially entrusted with the responsibility) to take help from either Sturge Moore (letter dated 12 April 1935) or Ernest Rhys (letter dated 11 July 1935) or even work in tandem with C.F. Andrews (letters dated 7 October, 28 December, 1935).[25] In the letter he wrote to his niece, Indira Devi, on 6 May 1913, Rabindranath confessed:

> That I cannot write English is such a patent fact, that I never had even the vanity to feel ashamed of it. If anybody wrote an English note asking me to tea, I never felt equal to answering it. Perhaps you think that by now I have got over that delusion. By no means. That I have written in English seems to be the delusion.[26]

In trying to explain the genesis of the English *Gitanjali* as a chance event occasioned by a period of convalescence from illness, he wrote:

> I did not undertake this task in a spirit of reckless bravery; *I simply felt an urge to recapture, through the medium of another language, the feelings and sentiments which had created such a feast of joy within me in past*

days. The pages of a small exercise-book came gradually to be filled, and with it in my pocket I boarded the ship.[27]

To Stopford Brooke also he wrote in a similar vein: "It was a mere accident that set me translating these poems into English and it was a sudden caprice that urged me to cross the sea and come to England" (5 January 1913).[28]

Despite this impression that Rabindranath sought to create, the truth probably was that the decision to translate *Gitanjali* – and subsequently other works – was a deliberate one taken on several counts. For one, translations of some of his works by other translators (Sister Nivedita, Ananda Coomaraswamy, Jadunath Sarkar, Lokendranath Palit, Ajitkumar Chakravarty, Pannalal Basu and Roby Dutt among them) were already in circulation, most read by Rabindranath but many not liked by him.[29] Second, through the enterprise of some of his friends and well-wishers, Rabindranath was being discussed in England even before the *Gitanjali* translations were made available there; it is reported that by May 1912 (that is prior to the Poet's arrival in Britain in June 1912) the Oxford University was already mulling the idea of conferring upon him an honorary degree, which was scuttled by Lord Curzon, the then-Chancellor of the university.[30] Third, despite such 'official' set-backs, his young admirers, firmly believing that Rabindranath should be introduced to the English cultural elite, had already undertaken the task of translating some of his poems to acquaint the English readers with his works.

It is in this context that Rabindranath's decision to translate his Bengali works into English needs to be viewed. Despite his early boyhood dread of the English language, by 1912 the Poet himself seems to have been eager, almost anxious, for a favourable reception of his English translations in the West. His fervent pleas to the different English poets to edit/revise his translations betray this anxiety. Added to this was his idealization of the "great English", pitted against his awareness of "an abnormal relationship" between the colonizer ("small English") and the colonized.[31] While Rabindranath could be faulted for what may be read as the colonized subject's attempts to put on the white mask in a bid to find acceptability among the colonizers, to be fair to him, this attempt needs to be historicized within that dialectical relationship that informed cultural transactions between the colonizing British and the colonized Indians since the days of the Bengal Renaissance.[32] It could perhaps be argued that in his subsequent years, his urge to translate was sited in the larger context of his pleas for an international cosmopolitanism. By then, Rabindranath was increasingly disengaging from any narrow brands of sectarian nationalism and, at the risk of being misunderstood, was upholding the need for universal fraternity: "The awakening of India is a part of the awakening of the world ... From now onward, the anxiety that each country has for its own safety must embrace the welfare of the world."[33]

If Rabindranath believed that both the West and the East had much to offer to each other, in his specific case, what seemed to have been foregrounded was his particular image as the Indian mystic poet enshrined, for instance, in the English *Gitanjali (Song Offerings)*. This perception was further fomented by the "Introduction" that Yeats wrote for the volume: "Mr. Tagore, like the Indian civilization itself, has been content to discover the soul and surrender himself to its spontaneity",[34] as well as in his eulogy of Rabindranath in a letter (dated 7 September 1931) that was subsequently included in *The Golden Book of Tagore*: "That [Asiatic] form I found first in your works ... What an excitement it was that first reading of your poems which seemed to come out of the fields and the rivers and have their changelessness."[35] On 1 July 1912, Rothenstein had invited Bernard Shaw to come and meet Tagore: "I want you to meet Rabindra Nath Tagore ... He represents all that is religious, literary, democratic, scholarly and aristocratic in Bengal."[36]

Scholars have seen in Rothenstein's early enthusiastic responses the setting out of the parameters that would define the European reception of Rabindranath "as a compendium of all civic and cultural values, an unofficial ambassador, and an embodiment of a kind of mystical perfection rendered impossible by the Western pursuit of material things. Above all, he was to be regarded as saint and seer."[37]

Admittedly, this perception of Rabindranath appears as a prototype of the notion of Orientalism propagated by Edward Said, according to which the West constructs the image of the East that it would desire to see: the English reception of the Indian poet was creating for itself, and for its own requirements, the image of an Eastern magus/sage.[38] Yet, it is also true that some among his English readers were quick to discern in the English translations elements that rose above regional/cultural boundaries and pointed towards a wider confluence of cultures. The anonymous reviewer of *The Times Literary Supplement* considered Rabindranath's poems "not ... curiosities of an alien mind, but ... prophetic of the poetry that might be written in England if our poets could attain to the same harmony of emotion and idea" (7 November 1912), and *The Nation* found them "not, as some have imagined, a thing strange and remote from us, but, on the contrary, something so near – so closely interwoven with the stuff of our spirits – that we cannot stand away from it" (16 November 1912). Lascelles Abercrombie, writing in *The Manchester Guardian*, was even more insistent: "Rabindra Nath seems to be an Oriental profoundly influenced by European thought ... we should rather say that the European influence has been completely Orientalised in him."[39] And Stopford Brooke felt that the *Gitanjali* poems exuded "the strange unity of the East and West".[40] Yeats, too, had made this point in his "Introduction" to *Song Offerings* (the English *Gitanjali)*:

> A whole people, a whole civilization, immeasurably strange to us, seems to have been taken up into this imagination: and *yet we are not moved because of its strangeness, but because we have met our own image,* ... or heard, perhaps for the first time in literature, our voice as in a dream.[41]

Rabindranath himself, responding to the warm reception he received in Britain, said (on 10 July 1912): "East is East and West is West – God forbid that it should be otherwise – but *the twain must meet in amity, peace and understanding*; their meeting will be all the more beautiful *because of their differences*, it must lead both to holy wedlock before the *common altar of humanity*."[42] This cultural difference that informed the reception of Rabindranath in the Anglophone world, however, was anything but unproblematic; it was riddled with Western assumptions of and/or expectations from a poet of the East. According to Alex Aronson, though the initial projection of Rabindranath as an Eastern mystic (particularly in the English *Gitanjali*) seemed to offer to the West an escape route from the plaguing realities of the contemporary world, the later translations did not necessarily live up to this demand for an exotic Oriental mysticism. This would explain the subsequent lukewarm reception of Rabindranath's later English writings, leaving Aronson to conclude that "many readers considered Rabindranath an anti-climax, in short, not sufficiently 'Eastern'".[43]

The additional factor of contemporary politics may have compounded the complications further.[44] As long as Rabindranath could be accommodated within the received notion of an Eastern magus, he did not pose any threats. But problems came to a head with his renunciation of the knighthood conferred upon him by the British Empire, which many an Englishman considered an act of impertinence.[45] Further, his attempts to find acceptance in Europe or even across the Atlantic did not go down well with many of his English friends. Consequently, during his next visit to England in 1920, his reception was somewhat lukewarm. While Bridges turned down the invitation to chair a session in Oxford ("I do not feel able to accept the invitation, which I have just received, to speak at the meeting in Oxford on Friday")[46], even Rothenstein was uncharitable in some of his remarks: "Tagore has just gone off to accept the homage of the neutral countries .... Alas, that the strong wine of praise, and the weak wine of worship, should have gone to this good man's head. It is a misfortune for a poet to be too handsome; ... Perhaps adulation is a habit – I mean the receiving of it."[47] And with the British Parliament's refusal to condemn the actions of British officials, like Dyer, guilty of the Jallianwalla Bagh massacre, in August 1920, Rabindranath left England a sorely disappointed man ("The result of the Dyer debates in both Houses of Parliament makes painfully evident the attitude of mind of the ruling class of this country towards India ... The unashamed condonation of brutality expressed in their speeches and echoed in their newspapers is ugly in its frightfulness.")[48]

The translator in Rabindranath, then, did a kind of tightrope walking, even as the tension generated by equal and opposite pulls of the two cultural registers conditioned most of his attempts at cultural transactions. This was evidently magnified because of the problematic of his historical situation: a colonized poet trying to communicate his feelings in the language of the colonizer, and his justification of this through his classification of what he saw as a duality in that colonizing identity as the 'great' and the 'small'. Only after shattering experiences of British atrocities as in the Jallianwala Bagh genocide or of the outbreak of the Second World War, which threatened to push human civilization to the brink of collapse, did he find his earlier faith in the 'great' English crumbling: a counter-discourse was gradually taking shape through his changed perception of the West. A play like *Raktakarabi/Red Oleanders* (1924–25) or a prose lecture like *Sabhyatar Sankat/Crisis in Civilisation* (1941) attests to this altered perception. In a letter to Amiya Chakravarty, written on 18 September 1939, he anticipates many of the misgivings he was to express in *Crisis in Civilisation*. In that letter, Rabindranath writes: "I had deep faith in the Western civilisation. I had forgotten that civilisation has come to mean the deft expertise in materialistic usage." He quotes from a poem of his in *Balaka*, indicating that he had sounded the alarm in that poem, and adds: "If I had the voice, I would have recited this poem before the whole human world. I have nothing more to add.... You have probably forgotten this poem of mine; if not, you would have said that I have done my bit." In the final paragraph, he adds: "The poem I am speaking of has a weak rendition (*tarjama*), possibly included in *Fugitive*, but you will hardly hear my real voice there."[49]

III

If the discussion above has so far mentioned chiefly the English *Gitanjali*, that is because it was *the* translation through which the West first came to know Rabindranath. A study of the translations of the plays requires a similar, yet somewhat different, approach. Two factors need to be spelt out at the very start. First, as with the other genres, the English translations of the dramatic works were not always done by him, though they have been published in his name. Second, in his own translation of his plays – as of his poems – he has taken liberties as a creative artist to such an extent that the final product has often emerged less as translation, more as transcreation.

Though most translations of the plays were done with Rabindranath's approval, and appeared in his name, not all the plays were translated by him. Translations of at least two major plays went into print despite the author's reservations – *The Post Office*, a translation of *Dakghar* by Devabrata Mukherjea, done in 1912 and published in 1914,[50] and *The King of the Dark Chamber*, a translation of *Raja* by Kshitishchandra Sen, also translated in 1912 and published in 1914.[51] *The Post Office* not only carried an "Introduction" by W.B. Yeats but also premiered at the Abbey Theatre, Dublin, on 17 May 1913,[52] even prior to Rabindranath's own production of the play in Bengali in 1917. Among his translated plays performed overseas *The Post Office* seems to have been an all-time favourite,[53] closely followed by *Chitra*.[54] Rabindranath had reservations about the quality of the translation but, nevertheless, allowed its publication – a fact which many recent scholars/translators regret.[55] Kshitishchandra Sen's translation of *Raja* at first carried the title *King*, which was later expanded as *The King of the Dark Chamber* by Rabindranath himself. This translation poses even greater problems, as analysed by Shyamal Kumar Sarkar in his research paper, "*The King of the Dark Chamber*: Text and Publication".[56] Rabindranath revised

Kshitishchandra's draft thoroughly – he added the longer title, made changes in the sentences, abridged some of the dialogues, and even added eleven songs. He repeatedly made changes in the translated text.[57] When he moved to America in October 1912, he left a typed copy of the first revision with Rothenstein and carried the other copies with him to the US. He was working further on the translation, and what is now the fourth draft in the Rabindra Bhavana archival holdings was printed by the Chicago-based theatre journal, *The Drama*, in May 1914. Returning to India, he made yet another fresh draft, with the help of Andrews, which retained only fourteen scenes and six songs from the original.[58] Unaware of these subsequent developments, Rothenstein sent the typed copy he had with him to Macmillan, when they asked for new manuscripts of Tagore,[59] and this went into print as *The King of the Dark Chamber*.

In an earlier letter to Macmillan (dated 2 April 1913), in response to publishing the play in *The Nation*, Rabindranath wrote: "As to the offer of fifteen pounds to publish 'The King of the Dark Chamber' *I do not think this play lends itself for publication in a magazine. I shall send the manuscript of the above play as soon as I have done the revision.*"[60] However, Macmillan did not wait for the revised version but published the play from the typed copy sent by Rothenstein, mentioning on the title page "Translated into English/by the Author". Rabindranath rued this hasty move in a letter to Rothenstein: "the worst of it is that I am not the translator."[61] Despite Rabindranath's telegraphic message to Macmillan to correct the name of the translator, the publishing house paid no heed, and that unrevised, and unapproved, translation has remained in print till date, though there have been several reprints. Ananda Lal quips: "we have in *The King of the Dark Chamber* the ironic – if not unique – case of an unauthorized publication issued by the writer's authorized publisher."[62]

On the one hand, a translation like that of *Phalguni* done in 1917 as *The Cycle of Spring* by C.F. Andrews and Nishikanta Sen was so thoroughly checked and revised by Rabindranath that it almost amounted to a work of collaboration; this was also published by Macmillan, London. On the other, *The Curse at Farewell*, a translation of *Viday Abhishap* (1893), may have been done independently by Edward Thomson (published in 1924 by Harrap & Co., London); this seems to have been the case as there was an already existing translation of the poem as *Kacha and Devayani*, possibly an auto-translation, which appeared among the poems of *The Fugitive* (in 1921). Other playlets (each an auto-translation) also included in *The Fugitive* were *The Mother's Prayer* (*Gandharir Abedan*, 1897), *Ama and Vinayaka* (*Sati*, 1897), *Somaka and Ritvik* (*Narakavasa*, 1897), and *Karna and Kunti* (*Karna-Kunti Samvada*, 1900). Incidentally, these five translated playlets were staged at Wigmore Hall, London, on 28 July 1920, organized by the Union of East and West. Sarojini Naidu summarized the contents of the plays before each was enacted. The dumb-show before *Kacha and Devjani* was much appreciated.[63]

That Rabindranath's plays have been considered worthy of translation is attested by the fact that translators have unceasingly been drawn to try their hands at them; several translated versions of his plays have appeared – and continue to appear – even after his death. Marjorie Sykes presented her translations of *Muktadhara, Natir Puja* and *Chandalika* as *Three Plays* (Bombay: Oxford University Press, 1950). *A Complete Translation of Tagore's Chitrangada* was an English translation of the verse-play *Chitrangada* (1892) done by Birendranath Roy (Calcutta: Sri Bhumi Publishing Co, 1957). *Natir puja* was given yet another English rendition as *The Court Dancer* by Shyamasree Devi (Calcutta: Writers' Workshop, 1961). A significant contribution in this area is *Rabindranath Tagore, Three Plays* translated by Ananda Lal, containing translations of *Raktakarabi, Tapati* and *Arupratan* and prefixed with an insightful introduction (Calcutta: MP Birla Foundation, 1987; published subsequently by Oxford University Press, 2nd edition, 2001). Ananda Lal recently published a translation of the dance drama *Chandalika* (in *Shades of Difference: Selected Works of Rabindranath Tagore*, ed. Radha Chakravarty, New Delhi: Social Science Press, 2015: 94–115). There has been a fresh translation of *Raktakarabi* as *Roktokorobi* by Rupendra Guha Majumdar in *The Essential Tagore*, ed. Fakrul Alam and Radha Chakravarty (Cambridge, Mass. & London: Harvard University Press, 2011: 376–450). There had been an earlier translation of *Tasher Desh* done by Krishna Kripalani as *Kingdom of Cards* in *Visva-Bharati Quarterly*, New Series 4 (February 1939): 264–89. In more recent times, this play has been translated by William Radice as *Card Country* (Calcutta: Visva-Bharati, 2008) and again by this author as *The Kingdom of Cards* in *The Essential Tagore* (eds. Fakrul Alam and Radha Chakravarty, Cambridge. Mass.: Harvard University Press, 2011: 450–87).

IV

To return to Rabindranath's own translations, what is most conspicuous in them is his penchant for radical departures from the originals to an extent that is far beyond what has been usually attempted – if at all – by other translators of his plays. Such departures are in tune with his preference for the term *tarjama* over others like *anubad* or *rupantar*, with the element of rendition, interpretation or even recreation being foregrounded. While other translators have usually tended to remain loyal to the original version, as a creative artist he could afford to take liberties with the originals, often remodelling them as new works. As mentioned above, he had once remarked in his letter to Ajit Chakravarty: "In fact, one cannot quite translate one's own works …. I intend to carry the essential substance of my poetry into the English translation and this means a wide divergence from the original. You may not even be able to identify a poem of mine unless I do it for your benefit."[64] His auto-translated plays, therefore, emerge – more often than not – as new/ transcreated playtexts. Sukanta Chaudhuri makes a case for the "self referentiality" that emerges as a consequence of this; his observations in this regard merit to be quoted at length:

> His works pick up one another's threads, refer back and forth among themselves, extend one another's meaning. They are endlessly various, divergent, contradictory; yet they intermesh in striking ways …

the English 'translations' radically rework the Bengali, not only to simplify or impoverish (though often that too, alas) but to work genuine variations and expansions ...

As with all auto-translation, the 'afterlife' of the work, in Walter Benjamin's perceptive term, becomes part of its integral or essential life.[65]

It is interesting to note that, as with his lyrical poems, so with his verse-dramas, Rabindranath discarded verse and chose a prose medium, though admittedly infused with a measure of poeticism. Because the work was shorn of its lyrical effusiveness, it was often sharply abridged. This is notably available in the translations of the shorter verse-plays that had mostly appeared in *Kahini* (1900), and which, as has been mentioned earlier, were compiled in *The Fugitive* (1921): *The Mother's Prayer* (*Gandharir Abedan*, 1897), *Ama and Vinayaka* (*Sati*, 1897), *Somaka and Ritvik* (*Narakavasa*, 1897), and *Karna and Kunti* (*Karna-Kunti Samvada*, 1900).[66] To the same group belongs *Kacha and Devyani* (also included in *The Fugitive*), though the original, *Viday Abhishap*, had appeared not in *Kahini* but as a separate playtext in 1912. *The Mother's Prayer* does not include the role of Bhanumati, the wife of Duryodhana, with whom Gandhari interacts towards the end of the drama in the original. *Kacha and Devyani* ends with the curse of Devyani, and omits Kacha's final words with which he blesses the aggrieved woman with blissful forgetfulness. Both omissions needlessly prune some fine-nuanced statements of the characters that hardly indicate any improvement upon the originals. Ultimately, these translations of the verse-playlets leave the impression of being drastically truncated renditions of the original dramas, shorn of much of their beauty.

Among the longer verse-plays, *Chitra* (1913), though terser in the English rendition, uses nine scenes in prose, replacing the eleven in the original *Chitrangada*. It also shows the author's tendency to use morphed forms of Indian names for their English equivalences: if *Chitra* follows the truncated name of the eponymous heroine (who is Chitrangada in the original), in *The King and the Queen* Shila and Ajit are the morphed versions of Shiladitya and Yudhajit of the Bengali *Raja o Rani*, and Govindamanikya, the king in *Visarjan*, becomes Govinda in *Sacrifice*. These other verse-plays, also deploying prose, are more radically reduced than *Chitra*. The five-act structure of *Raja o Rani* becomes *The King and the Queen* (1916) of two acts, using two locales – "The Palace Garden [of King Vikram]" and a "Tent in Kashmir", and moves faster through the medium of prose. *Malini*, originally composed in four scenes, in the translated version (1917) has two acts – more sharply chiselled – set in "The Balcony of the Palace facing the street" and "The Palace Garden". Also, though the early drafts[67] begin with the interaction between Malini and Kashyap, as in the source text, in the later drafts and the final print version, the character of Kashyap is dropped altogether. For some inexplicable reason, the name of the antagonist "Kshemankar" (in the Bengali text) becomes "Kemankar" in the final printed version in English, though all the six drafts mention the character as "Kshemankar". One wonders if the change occurred due to some editorial/publishing oversight, as this seriously distorts the pronunciation of the name. *Visarjan*, the other five-act tragedy emulating the Shakespearean model, is drastically shortened into the English *Sacrifice* (1917) [68] so that it comprises just one long scene with continuous run-on action, located before "A temple in Tippera". Even the duration of action is more condensed. So, while in the original, Joysingha has two days to bring the royal blood as offering to the goddess ("the last night of the month of Sravana"), in *Sacrifice*, he is bound by the oath to "bring kingly blood to the altar of the Goddess before it is midnight"; he later repeats before Raghupati, "If the Goddess thirsts for kingly blood, I will bring it to her before to-night."[69] Thus, the time frame is circumscribed within a single day in the translation. Many are of the opinion that these trimmings in the translation help the text to gain in dramatic texture.[70] In general, the English translated versions not only make use of prose, discarding the lyrical mellifluousness of the original verse, but are also briefer and terser in structure.

Because many of these plays are derived from Indian mythical/classical sources, Rabindranath seems to have felt the need to acquaint the target readers (of his translations) with details that may help them to follow the narrative. These details, appearing in the introductory remarks, were not required for the original readership. *The Mother's Prayer* opens with the comment: "Prince Duryodhana, the son of the blind Kaurava King Dhritarashtra, and of Queen Gandhari, has played with his cousins the Pandava Kings for their kingdom, and won it by fraud"; while *Karna and Kunti* explicates: "The Pandava Queen Kunti before marriage had a son, Karna, who, in manhood, became the commander of the Kaurava host. To hide her shame she abandoned him at birth, and a charioteer, Adhiratha, brought him up as his son." In *Somaka and Ritvik* (*The Fugitive* III, no. 25), though not elaborate, an expository comment is offered: "On the road to heaven. The shade of King Somaka, being borne to heaven, in a chariot and the shades of former high priest, Ritvik, and others at the roadside." For the exposition of the drama leading up to the curse of Devjani, *Kacha and Devyani* is introduced thus: "Young Kacha came from Paradise to learn the secret of immortality from a Sage who taught the Titans, and whose daughter Devayani fell in love with him."[71] The Bengali original, *Viday Abhishap*, has an equivalent introduction, which even mentions Devyani's father, Sukracharya, by name. Significantly, in Indian mythology, the tussle is between the gods (*devatas*) and the demons (*daityas/asuras*); Vrihaspati is the *guru* (teacher) of the gods and father of Kacha, while Sukracharya is the guru of the *asuras* and father of Devyani. Rabindranath did not feel it necessary to go into these details for his translated version and omitted the names of the respective fathers. Interestingly, he translocated the fight between the Indian *devatas* and the *asuras* into the corresponding Greco-Roman myth of the tussle between the Olympians and the Titans, with which the Western readers would be more familiar.

The exposition for *Chitra* is lengthier, elucidating the context of the dramatic episode. It is interesting that the introduction does not mention the particular way in which Rabindranath reworks the original story (both in the original and translated versions):

208 *Rabindranath as theatre-practitioner*

> In the course of his wanderings, in fulfilment of a vow of penance, Arjuna came to Manipur. There he saw Chitrangada, the *beautiful* daughter of Chitravahana, the king of the country. *Smitten with her charms*, he asked the king for the hand of his daughter in marriage. Chitravahana asked him who he was, and learning that he was Arjuna the Pandava, told him that Prabhanjana, one of his ancestors in the kingly line of Manipur, had long been childless. In order to obtain an heir, he performed severe penances. Pleased with these austerities, the god Shiva gave him this boon, that he and his successors should each have one child. It so happened that the promised child had invariably been a son. He, Chitravahana, was the first to have only a daughter Chitrangada to perpetuate the race. He had, therefore, always treated her as a son and had made her his heir. Continuing, the king said:
> "The one son that will be born to her must be the perpetuator of my race. *That son will be the price that I shall demand for this marriage.* You can take her if you like, on this condition."
> *Arjuna promised and took Chitrangada to wife*, and lived in her father's capital for three years. When a son was born to them, he embraced her with affection, and taking leave of her and her father, set out again on his travels.[72]

This introduction, following the *Mahabharata*, merely reports the special stipulation for a male ruler for Manipur, and Arjuna's compliance with the condition laid down by Chitrangada's father to marry her. There is no hint here of the transformation, through divine intervention, of her plain/unattractive looks into an alluring beauty to attract Arjuna. In fact, the passage mentions that Chitrangada was the "beautiful daughter" of Chitravahana and that Arjuna was "(s) mitten with her charms"; *in what manner* and *to what extent* he was "smitten" is what Rabindranath's tale engages with. There is another note appended before the actual text of *Chitra* begins, which has some significant bearing on its textual as well as dramaturgical structure. This note reads:

> The dramatic poem "Chitra" has been performed in India without scenery – the actors being surrounded by the audience. Proposals for its production here having been made to the author, he went through this translation and provided stage directions, but wished these omitted if it were printed as a book.[73]

This "Note", however, was appended to the text of *Chitra* by Thomas Sturge Moore, who was helping to prepare the manuscript for publication. Sturge Moore was under the mistaken impression that the play had been performed in India by "Mr Tagore's pupils at Bolpur" (as he had written originally) and, then, gathering some more information,[74] "thought it best to substitute 'India' for the words quoted above".[75] Evidently, in performance Rabindranath wished to see *Chitra* presented in the Indian mode without the appendages of Western stage-setting; the original Bengali verse-play *Chitrangada* (1892) makes no mention of any scenographic requirement. So, though *Chitra* in translation accommodated dramaturgical interventions (like, directions for stage arrangements),[76] Rabindranath would have preferred to have these removed, so that the play appeared as one consolidated whole, leaving the theatrical details to the imagination of the reader/viewer.[77] Interestingly, when a performance of *Chitra* was staged in England by Stockport Garrick Society on 10 March 1916, the author's wishes seem to have been honoured:

> No scenery is used; the exquisite poetry of the Hindoo masterpiece needs no artificial aids to assist the imagination. Cool and restful dark green curtains, a couple of vague formless green seats, warm soft lighting effects, with at times the plaintive music of Samisam and tom-tory and the distant chiming of temple bells, seemed to create an atmosphere of mysticism eminently suitable to the story of "Chitra".[78]

Among the other auto-translated plays, the transmutation of *Raktakarabi* into *Red Oleanders* presents a particularly interesting case study, and may warrant a discussion here at some length. Rabindranath is believed to have started work on the Bengali play during his Shillong sojourn in 1923,[79] but the idea of the play could have been suggested even earlier, particularly with his first-hand acquaintance with the acquisitive/capitalist structures of America and Japan, during his visits in 1916.[80] Some of his responses to the materialist exploitative system seem to have filtered into the preceding play, *Muktadhara* (1922), the translation of which was also done at a rapid pace.[81] As for *Raktakarabi*, he probably started work on the play in 1923 and the Bengali version was first published in *Probasi* in 1924 (the *Aswin* issue of the Bengali year 1331). The first book of the third draft[82] – ms. 151 (iii) – on pages 19, 27 and 49 mentions four English words in the margins: "release", "desire", "aspiration" and "appropriate"; the fifth draft – ms. 151 (i) and 151 (ii) – again has quite a number of English terms noted in the margins.[83] The jotting down of these English terms in the two drafts suggests that he was already thinking of a translation. While usually years, even decades, elapsed before any of his Bengali originals was given an English rendition,[84] *Raktakarabi* seems to have been translated almost immediately after its composition. With the Bengali text first published in *Probasi* in September–October (*Aswin*) 1924, the English *Red Oleanders* was available in print, first in *Visva-Bharati Quarterly* (vol. II, no. ii, Special *Sharadiya*/Autumn number, 1924),[85] and then as a published playtext in 1925; this, then, appeared before the Bengali original was published as an individual playtext in December 1926 (12 *Pous* 1333 B.S.) by Visva-Bharati Granthalaya. This swift passage from *Raktakarabi* to *Red Oleanders* makes one wonder whether Rabindranath had even been working on the two versions almost simultaneously. He seemed to have been making an extra effort to have this play (in its English rendition) made available to an overseas readership as quickly as possible. The only other play, in translating which he appears to have displayed an equal haste, was *Muktadhara* – the Bengali original and the auto-translated *Waterfall* both appeared in 1922[86]; however, *Waterfall* did not seem to have enjoyed the same degree of either authorial attention or popular circulation among readers as did *Red Oleanders*. Rabindranath's particular anxiety about the global reception of *Red Oleanders* is further attested by the fact that by October 1925 an English essay, "*Red Oleanders*: Author's Interpretation" appeared in *Visva-Bharati Quarterly*, October 1925. The Poet, during his 1924 visit to Argentina, had verbally analysed *Raktakarabi/Red Oleanders* for Victoria Ocampo. Elmhirst, who was present as his secretary and travel-companion, made a transcript of this analysis, which now appeared in the October issue of *Visva-Bharati Quarterly*, making available the author's interpretation of the play for an English-reading public.[87] Right from the initial stages of composition, Rabindranath seems to have been anxious about the reception of this play – both in the Bengali original and the English version – and the transition from *Raktakarabi* to *Red Oleanders* seems to have mattered considerably to him.

Described as "A DRAMA IN ONE ACT", *Red Oleanders* is less of translation and more of transcreation – as has been the case with most of Rabindranath's auto-translated works. In *Red Oleanders*, too, he takes liberties with the original to ensure its easy reception among the target readers/viewers. For instance, the reference to *Pous* in the song becomes *Autumn* in the English rendition; "*Pouser roddur*" is made the "September sun". The Bengali month of *Pous*, however, corresponds to the winter months of December–January. But Rabindranath draws the equivalence on the premise of the harvesting season; so the English version of the song mentions the "basket" of Autumn "heaped with corn" (23).[88] In the original, Nandini wears a "*dhani ranger kapar*" (paddy-coloured sari); in the English, this becomes a "grass-green robe" (90): the colour of the unripe paddy is equated to the greenness of the grass, while the "*kapar*" (sari) becomes a "robe" (in consonance with the Western cultural register). The reference to "*Indra*"[89] with his "*bajra*" becomes the non-committal "God sends his thunderbolts" and "*Indradever agun*" is simply the "fire of the gods" (112). Though Bishu and Chandra good-humouredly keep calling each other "*beyai*" and "*beyan*" (parents of one's son-in-law/daughter-in-law) in the original, perhaps because these forms of address would have been alien to Western ears, the English version shifts to the familiar – and safer – "friend" and "brother" (39 ff.), when they do not call each other by their names. Similarly, "*morol*" is simply the "headman" (53) and "*kotal*" is the "police" (85). "*Ma Lakshmi*" (as a form of address, usually to show either tenderness or derision) becomes the innocuous "good woman" (54), glossing over the sarcasm directed at the addressee in the original. "*Para*" (locality) is made "parish" (53), "*japamala*" becomes "rosary" (111), and "*ajagar*" is rendered as the "boa-constrictor" (131) – each of which would be more readily recognized by a Christian/Western readership. On the other hand, "*pronami*" is both "votive fees" (50) and "offering" (52), while the culturally inflected "*Maranchandir brata*" becomes the relatively neutral "fast day of the War Goddess" (34). In search of musical instruments with which the West is more familiar, "*madal*" is given the form of "drums" (86), "*sarengi*" is replaced by the "guitar" (87) and "*sur-bandha tambura*" becomes the "tuned-up lyre" (91).

If in these instances, Rabindranath shows a preference for appropriating the cultural register of the target language, there are other occasions where he retains much of the cultural nuances embedded in the original, as though to familiarize the Western readers/audiences with these. So, the bird "*Nilkantha*" is mentioned as a "blue-throat" but with an added footnote describing it as "a bird of good omen" (82). "*Rahu*" becomes the "Shadow Demon" (17); "*namabali*" is explained as the "wrap printed with the holy name" (51) and again as the "wrap of the Holy Name" (111); "*Kurma avatar*" is annotated as the "incarnation of the sacred Tortoise of our scripture, that held up the sinking earth on its back" (51). There are even attempts at near-literal translations of Bengali idiomatic expressions, even though they may sound strange in the English language. The Bengali statement "*Chenra kalapatar cheye bhanga bhanrer prati manusher hela*" is reworked as "Man despises the broken pot of his own creation more than the withered leaf fallen from the tree" (44), while the Sardar's (Governor) contemptuous "*Saras esechen baker dalke naach sekhat*" is rephrased as the "heron come to teach paddy birds how to cut capers" (49).

There are also instances where the English version omits/alters/abridges sections available in the original. One who has read/viewed the play in the original will particularly miss the song "*O chand, chokher jale laglo joyar*" (41).[90] In the Bengali version, it runs into eight verse-lines (and sounds even longer when sung to the haunting tune to which it is set), but in the English translation it is given a severely truncated prose rendition as "My boat was tied to the bank; the rope snapped; the wild wind drove it into the trackless unknown" (63). The libretto of "*Tor praner ras to shukiye gelo ore*" (34) is retained in the translation but in an abridged form (40). Bishu's "*Ami Ranjaner opith, je-pihe alo pore na*", reads in the English as "I am the obverse side of Ranjan on which falls the shadow" (71), but the masterstroke in the concluding snippet, "*ami amabashya*", goes missing in the English text. Even sections from the encounter between Bishu and Gokul-Chandra (32) get dropped in the English version (38).

Yet, there are also occasions when the author-translator has felt the need to explicate and add to the original, and so 'new' passages have been worked into the English version. No exact Bengali antecedent can be found for Phagulal's angry retort to Chandra in the English text not to 'worry' him about going home: "A thousand times I have told you that in these parts there are high roads to the market, to the burning ground, to the scaffold, – everywhere except to the homeland" (47). The general idea occurs in other parts of their dialogues but there is no precisely corresponding Bengali passage. Chandra's subsequent pleadings with the Governor to be allowed to go home are available in both versions, but the English adds extra references to "our waving fields of barley-corn" and "the ample shade of our banian tree with its hanging roots" (49). When the King demands to know "what use has Nandini" for Bishu, Bishu's reply in the English text has an additional sentence (missing in the Bengali original): "The use which music has for the hollow of the flute" (72).[91]

This transition from *Raktakarabi* to *Red Oleanders* underscores Rabindranath's usual practice in his translations/transcreations – his shifts from one cultural register to another, from the familiar to the strange, from fidelity to the source culture to adaptability to the target culture. What he ultimately achieves is a distinctive sample of transculturation. The source and target cultures crisscross at several points in his translation/transcreation to achieve a unique blend of the two, engendering "genuine variations and expansions".[92] The English *Red Oleanders* reaches out to the Western readers/viewers, trying to familiarize them with cultural nuances of an Eastern society and yet not rendering it so esoteric as to be beyond their comprehension. As a translated/transcreated/transculturated text, therefore, *Red Oleanders* is *and* is not *Raktakarabi*. Much the same could be said for most of his auto-translated works.

Notes

1 This poem, published by Allen & Unwin (London), and later rendered into the Bengali *Sisutirtha*, was inspired by Tagore's experience of seeing a Passion play in Germany in 1930. He was given the offer of having this made into a film by the German film company, UFA. The Bengali version was composed in the same year but included in the volume *Punascha* (published in 1932).
2 For a comprehensive list, see *The English Writings of Rabindranath Tagore*, ed. Sisir Kumar Das, vol. 2 (New Delhi: Sahitya Akademi, 1996, rpt. 2004) 13–5.
3 For details, see Sisir Kumar Das, "Introduction", in *The English Writings of Rabindranath Tagore*, vol. 2, 28–9.
4 Rothenstein, in a letter to Rabindranath dated 4 August 1914, writes: "Everything which now bears your name is gold to Macmillan"; cited in Mary Lago, *Imperfect Encounter: Letters of William Rothenstein and Rabindranath Tagore 1911–1941* (Cambridge: Harvard University Press, 1972) 171.
5 The original Bengali letter uses the compound-word "*rachana-Lakshmi*"; the goddess Lakshmi, then, with her attributes of benevolence and grace, becomes a metaphor for his literary works.
6 This is a reference to the disrobing of Draupadi in the royal court, a public humiliation she was subjected to when the Pandavas lost the game of dice in the *Mahabharata*.
7 Rabindranath Tagore, *Chithipatra*, vol. 6 (Calcutta: Visva-Bharati Granthan Vibhaga, 1957; rpt. 1993) 18–9.
8 "Dhammapadam", translated by Ananya Datta Gupta, in *Pracin Sahitya. Annotated English Translation and Critical Essays*, ed. Nilanjana Bhattacharya and Sayantan Dasgupta (Calcutta: Visva-Bharati Granthan Bibhag, 2017) 157–72; here quoted from 170–2.
9 Cited in Shyamal Kumar Sarkar, *Collected Papers on Rabindranath Tagore* (Calcutta: Deys, 2013) 158.
10 This English translation of the original Bengali letter was made by Indira Devi herself. It was published under the title "Genesis of English *Gitanjali*", in *Indian Literature*, vol. II, no. 1 (New Delhi: Sahitya Akademi, October 1958–March 1959) 3–4. It has been cited by Sisir Kumar Das in "Introduction", in *The English Writings of Rabindranath Tagore: Poems*, vol. 1, 10–11. Also cited in Shyamal Kumar Sarkar, *Collected Papers on Rabindranath Tagore*, 160.
11 Cited and translated in Shyamal Kumar Sarkar, *Collected Papers on Rabindranath Tagore*, 163–5; emphases added.
12 Rabindranath Tagore, *Chithipatra*, vol. 11 (Calcutta: Visva-Bharati Granthan Vibhaga, 1974) 171–2.
13 Sujit Mukherjee, *Translation as Discovery* (New Delhi: Allied Publishers, 1981) 103.

14 Sujit Mukherjee, *Translation as Discovery*, 112.
15 Sujit Mukherjee, *Translation as Recovery* (Delhi: Pencraft International, 2009) 85.
16 Aditi Ghosh, *Literary Translation and Bengali* (Calcutta: The Asiatic Society, 2008) 23.
17 Sukanta Chaudhuri, *Translation and Understanding* (New Delhi: Oxford University Press, 1999) 46.
18 Sukanta Chaudhuri, *Translation and Understanding*, 43.
19 Shyamal Kumar Sarkar, *Collected Papers on Rabindranath Tagore*, 163.
20 Sisir Kumar Das, "Introduction", *The English Writings of Rabindranath Tagore*, vol. 1, 17.
21 Sisir Kumar Das, *The English Writings of Rabindranath Tagore*, vol. 1, 17.
22 Tagore to Yeats, Urbana, Illinois, 26 January 1913. Yeats Papers, New York Public Library; as cited in Bikash Chakravarty (ed.) *Poets to a Poet* (Calcutta: Visva-Bharati, 1998) 163.
23 Tagore to Ernest Rhys, [London], 31 May 1913. Rabindra Bhavana archives; also cited in Bikash Chakravarty (ed.) *Poets to a Poet*, 112–3.
24 Tagore to Pound, Urbana, Illinois, 5 January 1913; cited in Bikash Chakravarty (ed.) *Poets to a Poet*, 275.
25 *Chithipatra*, vol. 11, 156, 162, 172, 175.
26 Letter to Indira Devi, London, 6 May 1913, trans. Indira Devi; cited in "Introduction", *The English Writings of Rabindranath Tagore*, vol. 1, 10.
27 Letter to Indira Devi, London, 6 May 1913; as cited in "Introduction", *The English Writings of Rabindranath Tagore*, vol. 1, 20; emphases added.
28 Rosanne Dasgupta, "Not Praise, but Love", cited in Bikash Chakravarty (ed.) *Poets to a Poet*, 5.
29 See Bikash Chakravarty (ed.) *Poets to a Poet*, 11.
30 As reported by Rothenstein, Curzon's argument was "there were more distinguished men in India than Tagore"; see *Men and Memories: 1872–1938* (London: Vintage Publishing, 1978; originally 1938) 266.
31 Tagore wrote the Bengali essay "Choto o Boro" ("The Small and the Great") in 1917; it was later included in *Kalantar*, now published in *RR*, vol. 13, 248–64.
32 "The Bengal Renaissance was the outgrowth of the grafting of a foreign culture onto a more-than-willing native culture." Sudipto Chatterjee, "Mise-En-(Colonial)-Scene: The Theatre of the Bengal Renaissance", in *Imperialism and Theatre*, ed. J. Ellen Gainor (London: Routledge, 1995) 19–37; here quoted from 20; also "English literature was not merely a literature of the masters but it was literature, a source of non-denominational spirituality, a harbinger of a secular outlet." Jasodhara Bagchi, "Shakespeare in Loin Cloths: English Literature and the Early Nationalistic Consciousness in Bengal", in *Rethinking English: Essays in Literature Language History*, ed. Svati Joshi (Delhi: Oxford University Press, 1994) 146–59; here quoted from 149–50.
33 *The Call of Truth* (1921); originally published in Bengali in *Prabasi*, and later in English in *The Modern Review*. Reprinted in *The Mahatma and the Poet: Letters and Debates between Gandhi and Tagore 1915–1941*, ed. Sabyasachi Bhattacharya (New Delhi: National Book Trust, 1997; rpt. 1999) 68–87; here quoted from 84.
34 W.B. Yeats, "Introduction", *Gitanjali* [Bilingual version] (Santiniketan: Rabindra Bhavana, Visva-Bharati, 1999) 13.
35 Cited in Bikash Chakravarty (ed.) *Poets to a Poet*, 155.
36 William Rothenstein to George Bernard Shaw (1 July 1912); cited in Mary Lago, *Rabindranath Tagore* (Columbia: University of Missouri Press, 1976) 65–6.
37 Mary Lago, *Rabindranath Tagore*, 66.
38 "The first group of translations (as well as the original writings) was primarily responsible for the creation and perpetuation of the image of Tagore as a mystic, in conformity with the construct of the Orient." Sisir Kumar Das, "Introduction", *The English Writings of Rabindranath Tagore*, vol. 2, 16.

214 *Rabindranath as theatre-practitioner*

39 These reviews have been quoted in Bikash Chakravarty (ed.), *Poets to a Poet*, 39.
40 Cited in Bikash Chakravarty (ed.), *Poets to a Poet*, 39.
41 W.B. Yeats, "Introduction", in Rabindranath Tagore, *Gitanjali* [Bilingual version] (Santiniketan: Rabindra Bhavana, Visva-Bharati, 1999) 12; emphases added.
42 Reported in *The Times*, 13 July 1912; as quoted in Bikash Chakravarty (ed.), *Poets to a Poet*, 40; emphases added. The occasion was a dinner party at Trocadero Restaurant, presided over by Yeats, and attended by H.G. Wells, May Sinclair, Maud Gonne, Cecil Sharp and others. Yeats's presidential address was in line with what he had written in the "Introduction" for Song-Offerings. And a Bengali rendition of Rabindranath's speech was published in *Probasi* (*Bhadra*/Aug–Sep issue). See also Prasantakumar Pal, *Rabi Jibani*, vol. 6, 317–18.
43 Alex Aronson, *Rabindranath through Western Eyes* (Calcutta: Rddhi-India, 1978) 15.
44 This has been discussed in the "Introduction" to Bikash Chakravarty (ed.), *Poets to a Poet*, 43–8.
45 While the Viceroy's office bristled at the "insolence of resigning an honour conferred by the King", the English dailies interpreted his action as a "challenge he has flung at the authorities" (*Indian Daily News*, 3 June 1919), and even tried to scoff at it in derision: "As if it mattered a brass farthing whether Sir Rabindranath Tagore who has probably never been heard of in the wilds of Punjab, and who as a writer is certainly not so popular as Colonel Frank Johnson approved the Government's policy or not! As if it mattered to the reputation, the honour and the security of British rule and justice whether this Bengali poet remained a Knight or a plain Babu!" (*The Englishman*). For details, see Prasantakumar Pal, vol. 7, 419–23.
46 Letter from Robert Bridges to Rabindranath (15 June 1920); as cited in Bikash Chakravarty (ed.), *Poets to a Poet*, 67.
47 Letter from William Rothenstein to Max Beerbohm (5 Aug 1920); as cited in Mary Lago, *Imperfect Encounter*, 269.
48 Rabindranath Tagore, *Letters to a Friend*, ed. C.F. Andrews (London: Allen & Unwin, 1928) 7.
49 *Chithipatra*, vol. 11, 299–301.
50 Mukherjea changed his original title, *The Message of Office*, into *The Post Office*, and introduced changes in the language at Rabindranath's instruction: see Sisir Kumar Das, "Introduction", *The English Writings of Rabindranath Tagore*, vol. 2, 22.
51 The first draft of the translation was given to Rabindranath in 1912, with the title *King*; the longer title was Rabindranath's addition.
52 The same production was repeated in London on 10 July 1913.
53 To cite a few instances of its performance in the West – premiere show in Dublin on 17 May 1913, repeat performance in London on 10 July 1913; on 18 November 1916, at Hollywood Library auditorium at Los Angeles; on 4 June 1921 at Berlin Theatre; on 4 October 1926 at Dresden, and another in 1926 at Prague. For details, see Rudraprasad Chakrabarty, *Rangamancha O Rabindranath* (Calcutta: Ananda, 1995)138–9; also Prasantakumar Pal, *Rabi Jibani*, vol. 7 (Calcutta: Ananda, 1997) 214; vol. 8 (Calcutta: Ananda, 2000) 51–2; Prabhatkumar Mukhopadhyay, *Rabindra Jibani*, vol. 3 (Calcutta: Visva-Bharati, 1952; rev. 1961) 261. Perhaps the most memorable instance of this play's performance was the1940 production by Janusz Korczak at the Warsaw Ghetto, to prepare Jewish orphans for their deaths, before being taken away (in 1942) to the Treblinka extermination camp by the Nazis.
54 The earliest performance of *Chitra* may have been the one in Boston on 8 February 1915, with another in London in February in 1916. On 27 April, *Chitra* was given at St. James Theatre, London. There was also a performance in China at Peking Normal University on 8 May 1924, in which Nandalal Bose, accompanying the Poet in his China tour, helped with the costume and make-up. Two other performances remain unconfirmed – one, at Munich Theatre in 1916, as claimed by the German radio but heavily disputed by English and American news agencies;

the other in the USA for which a contract was signed in November 1916, but the performance itself remained unreported. All these refer to performances during the Poet's lifetime. See details in Prasantakumar Pal, *Rabi Jibani*, vol. 7 (Calcutta: Ananda, 1997) 213–14, 263; vol. 9 (Calcutta: Ananda, 2003) 107–8.

55 "the basic problems with *The Post Office* were its awkward and inconsistent attempts at overcoming regional and cultural differences." Ananda Lal, *Rabindranath Tagore, Three Plays* (Calcutta: MP Birla Foundation, 1987) 90–91.

56 Originally published in *Visva-Bharati Quarterly*, New Series, 38, vol. 3 November 1972–January 1973, 25–40; subsequently reprinted in Shyamal Kumar Sarkar, *Collected Papers on Rabindranath Tagore* (Calcutta: Deys, 2013) 141–54.

57 There are eight manuscripts of the translation in the Rabindra Bhavana archives at Santiniketan.

58 This draft (ms 67) may be considered the final revised text of the translated *King of the Dark Chamber*. This was published in *Rabindra-biksha*, no. 14 (1990): 11–64.

59 Mary Lago has unearthed a letter from Macmillan to Rothenstein: "Macmillans now propose to bring out the plays separately. The Post Office and Chitra are accessible, but have you got the King of the Dark Chamber?" See *Imperfect Encounter*, 173.

60 Cited in Prasantakumar Pal, *Rabi Jibani*, vol. 7, 22; emphases added.

61 Rabindranath's letter to Rothenstein, dated 8 July 1914 in Mary Lago, *Imperfect Encounter*, 170.

62 Ananda Lal, *Rabindranath Tagore, Three Plays*, 100.

63 For details, see Prasantakumar Pal, *Rabi Jibani*, vol. 8, 28.

64 As cited and translated in Shyamal Kumar Sarkar, *Collected Papers on Rabindranath Tagore*, 164.

65 Sukanta Chaudhuri, "Rabindranath Tagore and the Traffic of Texts", in *Towards Tagore*, ed. Sanjukta Dasgupta, Ramkumar Mukhopadhyay and Swati Ganguly (Calcutta: Visva-Bharati, 2014) 309–19; here quoted from 313–5.

66 A letter from Rabindranath to Ramananda Chattopadhyay, dated 9 March 1920, seems to indicate that the English translation of *Karna-Kunti Samvad* was sent to *The Modern Review* for publication; see *Chithipatra*, vol. 12 (Calcutta: Visva-Bharati Granthan Vibhaga, 1986) 70.

67 The translated text has six drafts (comprising manuscripts and typescripts) preserved in the Rabindra Bhavana archives at Santiniketan, identified as 72, 74, 75, 81 (i), 81 (ii) and 81 (iii). Of these, 74 appears to be the corrected typescript of 81 (iii), while 72, 81 (i) and 81 (ii) are interrelated, with the last occurring as the final typescript. No date occurs in any of the drafts. The date mentioned in the archival entry of the drafts is 1917.

68 Only one handwritten manuscript of *Sacrifice* is preserved in the archives, with additions/alterations/deletions marked in it by Rabindranath himself.

69 *Sacrifice*, in Rabindranath Tagore, *Collected Poems and Plays* (Delhi: Macmillan, 2001; 1st Indian reprint, 1991; originally 1936) 679, 689.

70 See, for instance, Edward Thompson, *Rabindranath Tagore: Poet and Dramatist* (Delhi: Oxford University Press, 1948) 93.

71 For these details, see the respective manuscripts in *Bichitra: On-line Tagore Variorum*, School of Cultural Texts and Records, Jadavpur University, bichitra.jdvu.ac.in

72 *Chitra*, in *Collected Poems and Plays of Rabindranath Tagore*, 205–6; emphases added.

73 This is the "Note" by Sturge Moore, appended to *Chitra*, the manuscript of which he was helping to prepare for publication; as included in *Collected Poems and Plays of Rabindranath Tagore*, 207.

74 Sturge Moore talked to Arabindomohan Bose, nephew of Jagadishchandra Bose, and revised the statement.

75 Letter from Sturge Moore to Rabindranath (25 January 1914); as cited in Bikash Chakravarty (ed.), *Poets to a Poet*, 194.

216 *Rabindranath as theatre-practitioner*

76 The text begins, for instance, with the stage direction: "The stage should be divided in two by a raised dias parallel [*sic*] with the footlights and stretching from wing to wing. On it the plane of the Gods./ In front of it the mortal plane. A dark curtain to relieve the figures is the only background desirable, scenery would be out of place./ While the gods are present the mortal plane should be in a shadowy half-light". For details, see Prasantakumar Pal, *Rabi Jibani*, vol. 6, 330.
77 In fact, in the later reprints of *Collected Poems and Plays*, the stage directions have been withdrawn from the text of *Chitra*.
78 Reported in *Manchester Evening News*; as cited in Prasantakumar Pal, *Rabi Jibani*, vol. 7, 156.
79 Moloy Rakshit, *Raktakarabi: Path O Pathantarer Bhabnay* (Calcutta: Dey's Publishing, 2009) 52.
80 In recalling these visits later, he mentioned the "Titanic" wealth of these capitalist nations, and went on to contrast the elegance of Lakshmi with the acquisitiveness of Kubera; see "Sikshar Milan" (Aswin 1328, 1921), *Siksha, RR*, vol. 11, 669.
81 The Bengali original *Muktadhara* (1922) appeared first in *Probasi*, April 1922, and then was published as a book in June 1922. The auto-translated *Waterfall* appeared in between, in *Modern Review*, May 1922.
82 This has been written on two exercise books, identified as ms. 151 (iii) and 151 (iv); the first book has pages 1–59.
83 See also Moloy Rakshit, *Raktakarabi: Path O Pathantarer Bhabnay*, 43, 59–60.
84 For instance, *Visarjan* of 1890 and *Sarodotsav* of 1908 became the auto-translated *Sacrifice* in 1917 and 1919 respectively. *Raja* (1908), translated by Kshitischandra Sen, and *Dakghar* (1912), by Devarata Mukherjea, became *The King of the Dark Chamber* and *The Post Office*, both published in 1914. The translation of *Phalguni* (1915) as *The Cycle of Spring*, in which Rabindranath collaborated with C.F. Andrews and Nishikanta Sen, appeared in 1917.
85 Significantly, this English version, appearing first in *Visva-Bharati Quarterly*, was embellished with the Cubist illustrations that Gaganendranath made for this playtext.
86 For *Muktadhara* (1922) also, the translated version, *The Waterfall*, followed close on the heels of the original. The Bengali original appeared first in *Probasi*, April 1922, and then was published as a book in June 1922. The auto-translated *Waterfall* appeared in *Modern Review*, May 1922.
87 In fact, an explanatory note as "*Natya-parichay*" [Introducing the play] had already found place in the second draft, i.e., ms. 151(v). Yet another note as "*Prastabana*" [Prologue], also explicating his views about the play, was ready before the Bengali playtext was printed in book form in 1926. This published version of 1926 carried both these pieces. When the play was reprinted in 1945, the new edition shifted the second passage to the end as "*Kabir abhibhasan*" [The Poet's address], under "*Grantha-parichay*" [Introducing the text]. For details, see Moloy Rakshit, *Raktakarabi: Path O Pathantarer Bhabnay*, 570–7.
88 Page numbers refer to the Macmillan edition of *Red Oleanders* (Delhi: Macmillan India, 1962; 1st edn. 1925).
89 Like Zeus/Jupiter of the Greco-Roman mythology, Indra was the king of the gods in the Hindu pantheon and wielded the thunder as his primary weapon.
90 These numerals refer to the line numbers in the respective Bengali and English texts of the play.
91 Significantly, when Nandini asked the King what he saw in her, his 'Voice' had replied "The dance rhythm of the All" (30), which appears to fall short of the more suggestive Bengali version, "*Vishwer banshite naacher je chhanda baje sei chhanda*" (18).
92 Sukanta Chaudhuri, "Rabindranath Tagore and the Traffic of Texts", *Towards Tagore*, 315.

12 Conclusion

The present study has been concerned primarily with Rabindranath's contributions – both as a writer and a practitioner – to the Bengali theatre of his times. The earlier chapters have tried to relate his dramatic/theatrical output – in particular his experimentations after his relocation to Santiniketan – to his concerns with nation-building. His theatrical explorations, then, were inscribed with certain ideological underpinnings that informed his notions of a modern Indian theatre that would serve as a viable alternative to the colonial mimicry then available in the contemporary theatre. As has been reiterated at several points in the preceding discussions, if he was imagining a new nation he was also imagining a new theatre for that emergent nation.

This ideological thrust – emerging from his notion of Nation and *samaj* and egging him on to dream of a new theatre – has also determined Rabindranath's role as theatre-practitioner, which the later chapters of this book have attempted to reconstruct. In the combined roles of author-actor-producer-director, who often also supervised matters related to stage décor or costume or make-up, Rabindranath's sharp pragmatic sense of the theatre enabled him to keep in sight the material circumstances of production and reception of his plays. In fact, his astuteness as a theatre-practitioner also rubbed off on his role as a dramatist. The dramaturgical structures of his plays were often conditioned by his awareness of the practical stipulations of performance. Most of this has been dealt with in the preceding chapters of this volume.

It has also been argued in the course of the study that, though Rabindranath did assume certain theoretical positions vis-à-vis his notions of a 'new' theatre (notably in the essay "Rangamancha" and some other works), he did not allow his theorist self to dominate the theatre-practitioner in him. Consequently, he has often shifted ground, to cater to the more immediate requirements of theatrical performance. For an evolving artist like him, ever given to experiments and innovations, rigidity in theoretical formulation was perhaps neither possible nor desirable. This would be even more true when he negotiated with a living theatre, which, by its very ephemeral nature, was subject to the logistics of production/reception. Despite these factors, many of his pronouncements and/or practices do suggest postures that we would today identify as "theoretical". For instance, in the discussion of "Rangamancha", it has been pointed

DOI: 10.4324/9781003110279-13

out that his ideas about the role of the spectator closely resemble what has been later propounded by Western theorists of Performance Studies.

Rabindranath's innovations in the theatre – in fact, in all his attempts to provide alternatives to colonial ventures – would also seem to be in tune with what more recent theorists have argued about reclaiming of one's national history and culture in order to construct a nationalist/decolonized identity. To recall Fanon's formulation:

> A national culture is a whole body of efforts made by a people in the sphere of thought to describe, justify and praise the action through which that people has created itself and keeps itself in existence.[1]

In certain ways, this reminds us of Rabindranath's emphasis on *atmasakti* (self-empowerment), a prerequisite for a nation to gain its own identity – social, economic, political, or cultural. Like Rabindranath, for Fanon, too, cultural nationalism is a prerequisite for national liberation, though the latter's acquiescence of violence as a possible means of resistance[2] would possibly not be approved by the former, who prioritized an awakening of the inner self, hence of *atmasakti*. Interestingly, Fanon's opinion that political governance should be decentralized and the elite classes opposed[3] may have an equivalence in Rabindranath's advocacy of governance emerging out of the rural community (*swadeshi samaj*) rather than a centralized political system.

The study in this book has analysed how Rabindranath, with his theatrical experiments, has invoked the roots of indigenous traditions, and, in turn, tried to build up a cultural nationalism through his theatrical practices (as through similar engagements in other fields of activities). He has conceptualized his theatre as an alternative cultural artefact, moving away from the European model, and has inscribed it with performance idioms available in Eastern traditions. In doing so, his theatre has prioritized the cause of the 'nation as community', which retained collective memories of its historical/mythical past available to all sections of the *samaj*/community, over that of the 'nation as state', encapsulated in the colonially imported concept of a centrally organized political state organ, operating through its executive-bureaucratic-militaristic appendages, chiefly located in the urban metropolis. Yet, it also needs to be mentioned that Rabindranath, despite his declared preference for the folk theatre idiom, did not reject other samples available. As has been argued in earlier chapters, though the *asram* of Santiniketan afforded him with the space to indulge in his experimentations, he took these experiments to proscenium theatres of Calcutta, Bombay, Madras or Colombo. He could not reject the architecture of those playhouses but tried to reinscribe them with Indian cultural motifs through the performance. Moreover, the audiences at these venues comprised chiefly the urban middle classes. So, on the one hand, the theatrical innovations tried out at Santiniketan were placed before these urban spectators for their scrutiny and approval; on the other, through these innovations/experiments an attempt was being made to expand and reorient their expectations of theatre. What has been observed of the '"urban folk' theatre"[4] in the context of post-1947 Indian theatre is also largely true of the drama/theatre engineered by Rabindranath: "The mythic, ritualistic, and primal narratives of folk culture offer a refreshing counterbalance to the textures of urban existence, ...".[5] Rabindranath's theatre may, in fact, be seen as a prototype of this kind of 'urban folk'. This 'urban folk' is ultimately a 'hybrid' theatre that has emerged out of the efforts of dramatists and theatre workers (primarily hailing from urban origins) to rejuvenate their urban theatre by infusing into it elements from folk theatre, albeit for an urban viewership: "urban folk theatre is not a replication of folk performance but an autonomous form with its own aesthetic, cultural, and political objectives in relation to a predominantly urban audience."[6] If the likes of Viyay Tendulkar or Girish Karnad (as playwrights) or Habib Tanvir or Ratan Thiyam (as practitioners) have been trying to create this new idiom of the 'urban folk' theatre, Rabindranath had already been a pioneer in this path much before them. He had borrowed from the folk resources, not to replicate the folk theatre, but to offer an alternative model of the Bengali theatre, which could cater to audiences at Santiniketan as well as in urban centres. Unfortunately, Dharwadker or the other scholars pay scant regard to this path-breaking contribution of Rabindranath, even if the scope of their studies may have limited them to a different time frame.[7]

In fact, through his kind of 'urban folk'/hybrid theatre, Rabindranath often seems to be egging his audiences to straddle two kinds of spaces, less geographical, more imagined – the spaces offered by the real present and the imagined past (imagined through a reclaiming of folk or mythic sources); often the present was reconstituted in terms of that imagined past/alternative space. This happens rather pointedly in plays like *Dakghar* or *Raktakarabi* or *Tasher Desh*. In the first instance, the immediate present of the ailing Amal is variously infused with other spaces/times – recalled through the memories and/or visions of the curd-seller, the watchman, the young boys at play, Sudha culling flowers, and most notably Thakurda/Fakir with his tales of imagined lands; even Amal participates in these back-and-forth movements through time and space as he recounts his visit to the curd-seller's village or has reveries of the postman journeying through distant lands. The temporal and spatial denominators, though circumscribed by the restrictive confines of the patient's room and the repressive presence of the physician or the headman, ultimately move beyond those barriers into the more expansive imagined space offered by, say, Sudha or Thakurda/Fakir.[8] In *Raktakarabi*, the *Ramayana* myth is invoked to define the prevalent situation of *Yakshapuri* (itself an analogy for the modern acquisitive society), and this informs the play with parallel registers of space and time. Moreover, there is an ongoing tussle between the immediate space/time of *Yakshapuri* and a different space/time from which the miners have been uprooted and of which they retain a shared memory (as of the harvesting rituals of "*Nabanna*"); even the harvest-song (invoking *Pous*/Autumn) comes from afar and wafts into *Yakshpuri* intruding upon its spatio-temporal set-up. Armed with this song, Nandini (who is both within and outside of the space/time of *Yakshapuri*) knocks on the door of the King, inviting him to step out. In *Tasher Desh*, the imagined space/time of the Prince's dream is instilled into the reality of the cardland to free it from the regimentation of its sociopolitical system. Many of these analyses – particularly in relation to the two later instances – have been dealt with in the earlier chapters. But what is intriguing is that in his collapsing together of the real and imagined spaces/times, Rabindranath, in certain respects, almost seems to be in tune with the concept of 'heterotopias', postulated by Foucault:

> Places of this kind are outside of all places, even though it may be possible to indicate their location in reality. Because these places are absolutely different from all the sites that they reflect and speak about, I shall call them, by way of contrast to utopias, heterotopias.[9]

Admittedly, Foucault is more immediately concerned with the problematic of modern urban space/place; Rabindranath, differently situated in history, could not have engaged with the issue in the same way. Yet, with his merging together of different templates of space and time – in the plays mentioned, for instance – he almost seems to be using an early sample of Foucault's notion of 'heterotopias', but with obvious differences.

One must also remember that, posited at a historical juncture when ambivalent responses to the culture of the colonizer (theatre included) were symptomatic of the Bengal Renaissance,[10] Rabindranath could not evade his 'in-between' position. After his relocation to Santiniketan he did try to carve out for himself an alternative position both as playwright and theatre-practitioner. This position, in its attempts at a conscious departure from the Western influences, may be viewed as a reaction to the early excessive colonial importations, and, at times, even seemed to offer a distinct anti-colonial/postcolonial corrective – reaching a crescendo perhaps in the political discourse of a play like *Raktakarabi* or the theatrical semiology of a play like *Phalguni*. However, it has also to be conceded that in many respects he was promoting the agenda of acculturation that the Bengali theatre had given itself from the time of Madhusudan, and which, in turn, defined its hybrid character. Not only did he emulate Western traditions in his early experiments with the opera or Shakespearean tragedy, but also, in a later phase, he did not shy away from performing on proscenium stages at metropolitan venues, though, by then, most of his plays usually premiered at his *asram*-school which offered a non-urban ambience more conducive to his experiments and innovations. This movement between the urban and rural cultural registers, between Santiniketan and the cities, could be viewed as a step in the direction of the "urban folk" (as discussed above). Though he was quick to identify the colonial with the urban and the national/*swadeshi* with the folk, he ultimately found use for all the diverse traditions for his theatre. The story of acculturation, which started in the Bengali theatre with Madhusudan Dutt, reached a full circle in Rabindranath – more so, when he attempted to move beyond the binaries of the colonizer–colonized models and explore other available cultural resources. He was increasingly adopting a more syncretic model where the urban and the folk, the oriental and the occidental, the national and the global, could coexist in a harmonious fusion.

What was ultimately on offer was a more eclectic kind of theatre in which non-realistic theatre idioms (like that of the Indian *jatra*) could be deployed to inflect productions even in the West-influenced proscenium theatres in different metropolitan venues. This syncretic quality of his theatre was available, for instance, in the Jorasanko-production of *Dakghar* (1917–18), with the stage décor done by Abanindranath Tagore and Nandalal Bose; what was particularly lauded was the attempt at *"adaptation of western technique to eastern drama*; everything we saw was true to reality. The dress of the actors, their speech, their gestures, the furnishing and appearance of the room, were 'true to life'. *Yet the whole play was Indian through and through.*"[11] The scenographic realism was so inscribed with overt Indian/Bengali rustic signifiers that it could hardly be dismissed as an instance of colonial mimicry but rather exuded a markedly Indian ambience, in which urban and folk, colonial and *swadeshi* were blended together. In fact, the chapter on "Theatricalizing cultures" has been concerned with how, with his growing emphasis on a more inclusive cosmopolitan worldview, Rabindranath's theatre – like his other modes of cultural articulation – grew beyond the mere 'in-between'/hybrid model (with transactions between cultures of colonizer and colonized) towards a fuller intermingling of cultures – Eastern and Western, urban and rural, local and global. Evoking different cultural inventories, therefore, his theatre was able to achieve a synthesis of various cultural codes and, in turn, emerge as a more syncretic model, but firmly sited in the Indian milieu.

Rabindranath was not merely satisfied with imagining a new theatrical model for the new Indian nation that he had envisioned. He was trying to give it shape through his own practices. Intensely disappointed by the conditions of the contemporary public stage, he was dreaming of a new performance space for this 'new' theatre. In that context one may recall his invoking the concept of the 'little'/'parallel' theatre already germinating in the West by then, to conceptualize a similar experimental ludic space for our cultural purposes, veering away from the usual practices of the contemporary commercial theatre. Much of what he envisaged as a parallel/alternative theatre was articulated in *Nachghar*, the theatre journal edited by Hemendrakumar Roy, on 3 June 1927. He thought of a relatively small-sized playhouse, accommodating a select but discerning group of spectators, with performances following a kind of repertory system, so that neither would plays be repeated several times in the same week nor would actors be saddled with the same role for consecutive evenings. This would be an appropriate venue to carry out experiments in the theatre, which the conditions of the contemporary public stage disallowed.[12]

To reiterate an issue already raised at the very outset of this study, Rabindranath's contributions – whether as a playwright with innovative dramaturgy, or as a theatre-practitioner offering not only new performance idioms but even conceptualizing a new site for experimental theatre, or even as one of the founding fathers of our nation imagining new cultural spaces through communicative modes like theatre or music or dance – have, unfortunately, not received due attention. In the academia, Tagore scholarship, when investigating his plays, has been largely concerned with issues like theme, characterization, philosophical message, at most of dramaturgical structure. Only a handful of scholars, small in number but discerningly insightful in their analyses, have seriously engaged with the theatrical potentiality of his dramatic output.

The situation in the theatre, too, has been hardly encouraging. Actors and directors of the Bengali theatre have generally tended to stay away from Rabindranath's plays, betraying misgivings about their stageworthiness. In the pre-Independence commercial Bengali theatre, leading practitioners like Sisirkumar Bhaduri or Ahindra Chowdhury, despite warnings from their friends and fellow-players, had mounted some of Rabindranath's plays, but were persuaded against further experiments in this direction by the unfortunate failure of these plays at the box office. Only after the arrival of a new kind of parallel theatre, spearheaded by the stalwarts of the Indian People's Theatre Association (IPTA) and the Group Theatre movement – Sombhu Mitra, Utpal Dutt, Ritwik Ghatak – did Rabindranath find acceptance on the Bengali stage. The IPTA production of *Visarjan* (1951), starring Ritwik Ghatak, Utpal Dutt, Kali Banerjee, etc. and the Bohurupee productions, were significant ventures. Among the troupes that emerged with the Group Theatre movement, Bohurupee determinedly continued with their productions of Rabindranath's plays, under the stewardship of Sombhu Mitra and Tripti Mitra – *Char Adhyay* (1945), *Raktakarabi* (1954), *Dakghar* (1957), *Muktadhara* (1959), *Visarjan* (1961), *Raja* (1964), *Ghare Baire* (1974)[13] – and subsequently followed by Kumar Roy doing *Malini* (1986) and *Muktadhara* (1996) for the same group. More recently, there have been experiments with different plays of Rabindranath, trying to locate in them contemporary relevance[14]: *Visarjan* (Theatre Workshop: 1984; Natyam: 1989; Theatron: 1991; Gandhar: 1991, Rangakarmee: 2006), *Tapati* (Theatre Centre: 1991), *Raktakarabi* (Pathasena: 1997; Tritya Sutra: 2006; Arghya: 2009), *Phalguni: Suchana* (Chetana: 2003), *Malancha* (Anya Theatre: 1992), *Grihapravesh* (Kalapi: 1998), *Chirakumar Sabha* (Kalapi: 1993; Calcutta Performers: 1996; Durgadas Smriti Sangha: 2007; Chetana: 2009), *Raja* (Sangbarta: 2000; Natyam: 2000; Blind Opera: 2003), *Dakghar* (Sangbarta: 1992; Kalakshetra: 2006; Swapnasandhani: 2007), *Sesh Raksha* (Rangrup: 2005), *Valmiki Pratibha* (Baikali: 2004; West Bengal Correctional Services: 2004), *Veerpurush* (Swapnasandhani: 2011), *Tasher Desh as prose play* (Natyam: 2005; Kaler Jatra: 2019).[15] It has been mentioned earlier that the birth centenary year (1961) had seen a flurry of dance drama performances, which more often than not, tended to collapse into a conventional mould. And the sesquicentennial celebrations (in 2011) occasioned the revival of his plays as recensions with sociopolitical contemporaneity. Yet, one has to wait and see whether all this has been a mere passing trend or is here to stay with us, so that Rabindranath is finally assigned his rightful place in Bengali theatre. One may bring down the curtains with a final caveat: till Rabindranath is given his due recognition for his contribution to the Bengali theatre and accepted as our contemporary whose plays have relevance even today in our theatre, we shall remain the losers, not Rabindranath.

Notes

1 Frantz Fanon, *The Wretched of the Earth* (London: Penguin, 1967) 188.
2 "decolonization is always a violent phenomenon": Frantz Fanon, *The Wretched of the Earth*, 27.
3 "The national government, if it wants to be national, ought to be governed by the people and for the people, for the outcasts and by the outcasts": Frantz Fanon, *The Wretched of the Earth*, 165.
4 See Aparna B. Dharwadker, *Theatres of Independence: Drama, Theory, and Urban Performance in India since 1947* (New Delhi: Oxford University Press, paperback edition, 2008; originally 2005) 320.
5 Aparna B. Dharwadker, *Theatres of Independence*, 317
6 Aparna B. Dharwadker, *Theatres of Independence*, 322.
7 Dharwadker refers to Rabindranath's essay "Rangamancha"/"Theatre", but seems to mistake Rabindranath's use of a term like "poetry" to mean exclusively the genre of poetry and not "literature" at large, and thinks that she dismisses "the idea that performance is an intrinsic aspect of drama" (58). She misses the subtext of Rabindranath's argument when he writes that *drishyakavya* ("poetry performed") is only less independent than *sravyakavya* ("poetry merely heard") in that it has to rely upon the performance (by actors) for its reception among others (audience), and that drama and performance are mutually interdependent for a complete wholeness ("To display its splendour, it [art of acting] must rely on the graces of the play text": "The Theatre", 95). Dharwadker also does not focus upon Rabindranath's interpretation of the role of the spectator whom he empowers with the ability to 'read' the performance text (as though in anticipation of recent theories of reader-response or audience-reception). But the main thrust of the tract is Rabindranath's envisaging an alternative model of theatre (as has been amply discussed in earlier chapters), where also Dharwadker goes off-track when she cites Kathryn Hansen to see Rabindranath (along with others) contributing to "the campaigns against popular culture" (Hansen, 255; cited in Dharwadker, *Theatres of Independence*, 141).
8 This found a visual corroboration in the production of the play by *Bohurupee* in Calcutta (first staged by the group in 1957; revived in 1973). When the royal physician ordered the opening of all doors and windows, the walls of the room seemed to silently move apart, leaving the view of an open expanse, with the cyclorama at the back and moonlight streaming in.
9 Michel Foucault, "Of Other Spaces", trans. Jay Miskowec, *Diacritics*, vol. 16, no. 1 (Spring 1986), 22–7; here quoted from 24.
10 Homi Bhabha, for instance, offers a postcolonial position that would want to revise "those nationalist or 'nativist' pedagogies that set up the relation of Third World and First World in a binary structure of opposition": *The Location of Culture* (London: Routledge, 1994) 173; in doing this Bhabha moves beyond Fanon or Edward Said.
11 C. Jinaraja Das, "The Future Indian Drama", *New India*, 12 January 1918; emphases added.
12 A fuller excerpt from this article has already been cited in the chapter on "Theories of Theatre".
13 In particular, *Char Adhyay* (1951), *Raktakarabi* (1954), *Dakghar* (1957; revived 1973) and *Raja* (1964) have made history in the Bengali theatre.
14 This is just a sample of instances, not an exhaustive list.

15 Of these, special mention may be made of two productions: Blind Opera's *Raja* (2003), directed by Shubhashis Gangopadhyay, and the West Bengal correctional Services production of *Valmiki Pratibha* (2004), directed by Alokananda Roy. In the former, a visually challenged Sudarshana's search for Raja in the Dark Chamber resonated with deeper significances, while the latter was a powerful instance of theatre used as therapy to give a new meaning to the lives of the prisoners, recruited as the cast.

Appendix I
Plates (of photographs/paintings of Rabindranath's performances)

Plate 1 Valmiki Pratibha: Rabindranath Tagore as Valmiki (an early performance, c.1881)

Plate 2 Valmiki Pratibha: Rabindranath as Valmiki, with the robbers (later performance)

Plate 3 Valmiki Pratibha: Rabindranath as Valmiki; Indira Devi Chaudharani as Luxmi

Appendix I 227

Plate 4 Visarjan: Rabindranath as Raghupati, bent over the dead body of Joysingha (Arunendu Tagore) in the last scene (early performances, from 1890 to 1900)

Plate 5 *Visarjan*: Rabindranath as Joysingha; the stage décor by Gagendranath Tagore (later performance in Calcutta in 1923)

Appendix I 229

Plate 6 Phalguni: Rabindranath with the cast of the prologue, added for the later performance in Calcutta (1916).

230 *Appendix I*

Plate 7 Phalguni: Rabindranath as Kavisekhar in the prologue; painting by Abanindranath Tagore (production in Calcutta, 1916).

Appendix I 231

Plate 8 Phalguni: Rabindranath as the blind *baul* in the main play; painting by Abanindranath Tagore (production in Calcutta, 1916).

232 *Appendix I*

Plate 9 Dakghar: Rabindranath as Thakurda (Gaffer), Ashamukul Das as Amal and others; the stage décor was by Nandalal Bose and others, supervised by Abanindranath Tagore (production in Calcutta, 1917)

Plate 10 Dakghar: Rabindranath as Thakurda (Gaffer), Ashamukul Das as Amal and others in the final scene of the play

Appendix I 233

Plate 11 Programme brochures for several productions (*Natir Puja, Sesh Varshan, Navin* and *Shapmochan*)

Plate 12 Programme brochure for *Natir Puja*, first performance in Calcutta (1927)

Plate 13 Programme brochure for *Natir Puja*, first night of later performances in Calcutta (1931)

Plate 14 Natir Puja, a scene from the film made by New Theatres studio (1932); Lalita Sen replaced Gouri Bose as Srimati in the film

Appendix I 237

Plate 15 Natir Puja, a scene from the film; Upali (Rabindranath) pays his homage to the dead Srimati; the film replicates the stage performance.

Plate 16 Natir Puja: Upali and Srimati, at the beginning of the play; painting by Gaganendranath Tagore.

Plate 17 Natir Puja: painting by Abanindranath Tagore.

Plate 18 Natir Puja: the dance of the Nati (dancing girl), made famous by Gouri Bose (who was cast as the first Nati) showing how she discards her ornaments as she dances; painting by Nandalal Bose, who was also in charge of costumes.

Plate 19 Tasher Desh: a poster for the play by Nandalal Bose, who also designed stage-setting and costumes.

242 *Appendix I*

Plate 20 Tasher Desh: Rabindranath with the cast of the play.

Plate 21 Chitrangada (dance drama): performance at New Empire (1936); Rabindranath is seated on stage, left of the dancers; the singers and musicians are seated at the rear of the stage.

Appendix I 243

Plate 22 The Poet and the Dance: woodcut by Ramendranath Chakravarty, suggesting the proximity of Rabindranath to the dancers as he sat (possibly onstage) reciting lines.

Plate 23 Event celebrating the Poet's last birthday (1941), performed on the porch of Udayan, his residence in Santiniketan; he sits on a chair facing the dancers.
Source: all plates have been accessed through public domain.

Appendix II

Rabindranath Tagore: A brief chronology of select events and works, 1881–1941

Since the focus of the present book is Rabindranath Tagore's career in drama/theatre, the scope of the timeline here has been set from 1881 (when his first plays were written) to 1941 (his demise). An attempt has been made to include all dramatic compositions, unless information has not been available, could not be accessed, or even overlooked through inadvertency. Of his fictional (novels and short stories) and non-fictional writings (essays, life stories, travelogues, etc.), select works have been mentioned here. The date is the date of publication, unless otherwise specified. The works which appeared before 1841 have not been included in this chronological table. Major events that affected his life and career have been mentioned sometimes, though selectively, either in the main document or in the endnotes.

The two major sources from which most biographical information has been gathered are Prabhatkumar Mukhopadhyay, *Rabindra Jibani*, 4 vols. (Calcutta: Visva-Bharati Granthalay, 1933–52) and Prasantakumar Pal, *Rabi Jibani*, 9 vols. (Calcutta: Ananda Publishers, 1982–2003). Data has also been collected from Prabhatkumar Mukhopadhyay, *Rabindra-barshapanji* (Calcutta: Dey's Publishing, 2007; originally 1962); Samir Sengupta, *Samakal o Rabindranath: Ghatanapanji* (Calcutta: Pratikshan Publications, 1991); and Gourchandra Saha, *Rabindrajibanprabaha* (Calcutta: Patralekha, 2012). Another valuable source of information about the texts has been *Granthaparichay* of *Rabindra Rachabali*, vol. 16, edited by Rabindrakumar Dasgupta, Sankha Ghosh, Bhabatosh Dutta, et al. (Calcutta: West Bengal Government, 2001). Extensive help has also been drawn through the entire book from Rudraprasad Chakrabarty, *Rangamancha o Rabindranath: Samakalin Pratikriya* (Calcutta: Ananda Publishers, 1995).

Table A.1 Rabindranath Tagore: A brief chronology of select events and works, 1881–1941

Date	Non-dramatic works (select)			Dramatic works	Remarks (related mostly to theatrical performances/ public readings, etc.)
	Poetry[1]	Fiction[2]	Essay, etc.[3]	(including different dramatic forms used)[4]	
1881	Bhagna-hriday [The Broken Heart][5]		Europe Prabasir Patra [Letters from a sojourner in Europe] (collection of letters)	Valmiki Pratibha [The Genius of Valmiki] (musical drama); revised in 1886. Rudrachanda (verse-play)[9]	Valmiki Pratibha is described as "geeti-natya" (in Bengali), in which the performers sing their lines on stage; as such it may be seen to have affinities with the Western opera.[6] 26 Feb: first performance at Jorasanko for Viddyajana Samagam [Assembly of Intelligentsia].[7] Rabindranath enacted the role of Valmiki,[8] while his family members (including female relatives) played the other roles. Performed several times, including the 1891 staging in honour of Lady Lansdowne, wife of the Viceroy.
1882	Sandhyasangeet [Evening Songs]			Kal Mrigaya [The Fatal Hunt] (musical drama)	
1883	Pravat Sangeet [Morning Songs]	Bouthakuranir Haat [The Young Queen's Market]			9 Dec: Rabindranath marries Mrinalini (originally Bhabatarini)

Appendix II 247

Date	Non-dramatic works (select)			Dramatic works (including different dramatic forms used)	Remarks (related mostly to theatrical performances/ public readings, etc.)
	Poetry	Fiction	Essay, etc.		
1884	Chobi o Gaan [Pictures and Songs], Saisab Sangeet [Songs of Childhood], Bhanu Singha Thakurer Padabali [The Songs of Bhanu Singha Thakur]			Prakritir Pratisodh [literally, Nature's Revenge; but later translated as Sanyasi, or The Ascetic] (verse drama)	19 Apr: the suicide of his sister-in-law, Kadambari, left an indelible impression on Rabindranath; he dedicated many of his early works to her.[10] Though Prakritir Pratisodh was not staged by the Poet, he considered it significant enough to merit attention in his life story, Jibansmriti.
1885				Nalini (first prose play composed)[11]	The writing of Nalini probably started out as a collaborative effort, but later it appears Rabindranath took charge to give it the final shape.[12]
1886	Rabichhaya [Shadow of the Sun/Rabi] (songs)			Started writing short comic sketches, collected later in Hasya Kautuk (1907)	18 Jan: his first public lecture on Rammohun Roy given at City College.[13]
	Kori o Komol [Sharps and Flats]			Valmiki Pratibha revised, with inclusion of songs from Kal Mrigaya.[14]	20 Feb: revised Valmiki Pratibha staged at Jorasanko.[15] Also staged at Star Theatre, to raise funds for Adi Brahmasamaj.[16]
1887		Rajarshi [The Royal Sage]			

248 *Appendix II*

Date	Non-dramatic works (select)			Dramatic works (including different dramatic forms used)	Remarks (related mostly to theatrical performances/ public readings, etc.)
	Poetry	Fiction	Essay, etc.		
1888				*Mayar Khela* [The Play of Illusions] (musical drama)	29 Dec: earliest performance of *Mayar Khela*, was at Bethune School, under the aegis of Sakhi Samiti (a women's organization, founded by the Poet's sister, Swarnakumari Devi)
1889				*Raja o Rani* [The King and the Queen] (verse drama; uses the Shakespearean five-act tragic structure and blank verse)[17]	Oct: *Raja o Rani* is said to have been first performed at either the Park Street or the Birjitala residence of Satyendranath and Jnadanandini;[18] it was directed by Satyendranath. The date of performance remains uncertain.
1890	*Manasi* [Images of the Mind]			*Visarjan* [literally, Immersion; translated later as *Sacrifice*] (verse drama; like *Raja o Rani* emulated Shakespearean tragic form)	*Visarjan*, based on the earlier section of the novel *Rajarshi*, was revised many times; but the version in circulation now is based chiefly on the 1903 edition. Opinions differ over the date of the earliest performance, but it is agreed that Rabindranath played Raghupati in these early performances of the play.
1891			*Europe-jatrir diary* [Diary of a traveller to Europe], vol. 1.		

Appendix II   249

Date	Non-dramatic works (select)			Dramatic works (including different dramatic forms used)	Remarks (related mostly to theatrical performances/ public readings, etc.)
	Poetry	Fiction	Essay, etc.		
1892			"Sikshar Her Pher" [Difference in Education] (in *Sadhana*)	*Chitrangada* (verse-play) published in Sep 1892, illustrated by Abanindranath.	17 Dec: *Chitrangada* was staged in the public theatre (Emerald Theatre) in Calcutta.
				Goray Galad [Wrong at the Start] (comedy)	Amateur performance of *Goray Galad* by Sangeet Samaj
1893			*Europe-jatrir diary*, vol. 2	*Bini Poysar Bhoj* [A Free Repast] (farce)	*Bini Poysar Bhoj*, a farce for mono-acting, was performed several times by Akshaykumar Mazumdar.
			"Ingrejer atanka" [The Englishman's Panic], "Ingrej o Bharatbasi" [The English and the Indians] etc.	Continues to write farces (1893–1901), published later in the collection *Vyangakautuk* (1907)	Rabindranath reads "Ingrej o Bharatbasi" at a literary conference in Calcutta, with Bankimchandra presiding.[19]
		Publication of *Choto Galpo*, a compilation of 16 short stories published earlier			
1894	*Sonar Tari* [The Golden Boat]	*Bichitra galpo*, 1 & 2; *Katha Chatushtoy*: three compilations of short stories featuring stories published earlier.[20]	"Raja o Praja" [The King and the Subject], "Sahityer Gourab" [Glory of Literature], "Bideshiya atithi o deshiya athithya" [Foreign visitor and local hospitality][21] (in *Sadhana*)	*Swargiya Prahsan* [A Celestial Farce] (farce)	28 Apr: at the memorial convention of Bankimchandra, held at Star Theatre, Rabindranath was requested for a song by the audience, for which they were duly rebuked by the Chairman, Gurudas Banerjee.[22]
				Viday Abhishap [Farewell Curse] (lyrical playlet), completed in 1893, now published in book form.[23]	*Viday Abhishap* is a retelling of an episode of Mahabharata.

Date	Non-dramatic works (select)			Dramatic works (including different dramatic forms used)	Remarks (related mostly to theatrical performances/ public readings, etc.)
	Poetry	Fiction	Essay, etc.		
1895		*Galpo-dasak* (collection of short stories)	Relinquishes the editorship of *Sadhana*.		28 July: at the commemoration of the 5th death anniversary of Vidyasagar, at Emerald Theatre, Rabindranath reads "Vidyasagarcharit".[24]
1896	*Chitra* [25] [Images], *Nadi* [River]			*Malini* (verse drama)	*Malini* was probably written during his travel from North Bengal to Orissa.[26] The inspiration came from Rajendralal Mitra's *The Sanskrit Buddhist Literature of Nepal* (1882); this was also the source for many of his works related to Buddhist tales.[27]
1897			*Pancha-bhut* [The Five Elements] (collection of essays)	*Baikunther Khata* [Manuscript of Baikuntha] (farce)	*Baikunther Khata* was written at the request of Khamkheyali Sabha; amateur performance of the farce in March, with Rabindranath in the role of Kedar, and Abanindranath as Tinkori.[28]
				Writes the lyrical plays *Gandharir Abedan* [literally, The Appeal of Gandhari; later translated as The Mother's Prayer]; *Narakvas* [literally, Sojourn in Hell; later translated as *Somaka and Ritvik*]; *Sati* [Faithful Wife; later translated as *Ama and Vinayaka*]	Most of these lyrical playlets were probably written during his sojourn in Santiniketan, Nov-Dec; but these were published in *Kahini* (1900)[29]

Appendix II 251

Date	Non-dramatic works (select)			Dramatic works (including different dramatic forms used)	Remarks (related mostly to theatrical performances/ public readings, etc.)
	Poetry	Fiction	Essay, etc.		
1898	"Duhsomoy", "Hatabhagyer gaan", "Madan bhasmer purbe", "Madan bhasmer por", "Devatar Graas" (in *Bharati*)		"Kantharodh" [Stifling], "Bangabhasha" [Bengali Language], "Coat ba chapkan" [Coat or chapkan], "Aitihasik Upanyas" [Historical Novel], (in *Bharati*)[30]		12 Feb: the Poet read *Gandharir Abedan* at a meeting of the Calcutta University Institute at the Institute hall. Some even viewed the playlet as Rabindranath's protest against the Sedition bill;[31] this protest was more directly available in his essay "Kantharodh".[32]
1899	Composed many narrative poems, using varied sources: Buddhist tales ("Pujarini", "Abhisar", "Parisodh", etc.)[33]; Sikh history ("Sesh Siksha", "Bondi Veer")[34], tales from Rajasthan[35] ("Nakal Garh", "Hori Khela", "Ponrakha").[36] *Kanika* [Particles]			*Lakshmir Pariksha* [The Trial of Lakshmi] (a comic verse drama, with all-female cast; also composed *Karna-Kunti Sanvad* [literally, Karna Kunti Episode; also translated as *Karna and Kunti*], a lyrical playlet, based on *Mahabharata*.[37]	*Lakshmir Pariksha* was a comedy in rhymed verse, with all-female cast. As such, it was later often played by girl students at the Santiniketan school. Some of the narrative poems composed in this period, and later anthologized in *Katha* or *Kahini*, also became sources for later dramatic compositions (like *Natir Puja* or *Shyama*).
1900	*Katha* [Stories],[38] *Kahini* [Tales], *Kalpana* [Imagination or Muse], *Kshanika* [The Fleeting One]	*Galpaguccho*, 2 vols. (collection of 32 short stories).			16 & 27 Dec: Sangit Samaj staged *Visarjan*, with Rabindranath playing Raghupati. The first performance on 16 Dec was in honour of the King of Tripura, Radhakishore Manikya.[39]

252 Appendix II

Date	Non-dramatic works (select)			Dramatic works (including different dramatic forms used)	Remarks (related mostly to theatrical performances/ public readings, etc.)
	Poetry	Fiction	Essay, etc.		
1901	Naivedya [Offertory]	"Nastanir" [The Broken Nest], a novella (serialized in Bharati; May- Nov). Chokher Bali [A Speck in the Eye] (serialized in Bangadarshan till Nov 1902).	"Nation ki?" [What is the Nation], "Prachya o Paschatya Sabhyata" [Eastern and Western Civilizations], "Bangla Byakoron" [Bengali Grammar], "Kumarsambhav o Sakuntala (in Bangadarshan)	Bashikaran (farce)	20 Dec: Raja o Rani was performed by the students of Bangabasi College at the Corinthian Theatre.
1902	Poems written in memory of his wife (pub. in Bangadarshan; later included in Smaran [Remembrance], Utsarga [Dedication]).		"Rangamancha" [The Theatre] (in Bangadarshan, 30 Dec 1902). "Bharatbarsher Itihas" [History of India], "Atyukti" [Exaggeration] (in Bangadarshan)		"Rangamancha" [Theatre] is his major treatise on theatre in which Rabindranath enunciates his theories of theatre. Pointing out the shortcomings of Western realistic theatre and arguing for an alternative that recalls indigenous traditions, he is envisaging a model that would be a serious departure from the urban and colonial form then in use. A performance of Visarjan at the Santiniketan school in winter. Harishchandra Haldar, a family friend, came from Calcutta to paint the scenery (in contradiction to Rabindranath's opinions in "Rangamancha"). The stage was erected behind the dining hall.[40]

Appendix II 253

Date	Non-dramatic works (select)			Dramatic works (including different dramatic forms used)	Remarks (related mostly to theatrical performances/ public readings, etc.)
	Poetry	Fiction	Essay, etc.		
1903	An early edition of *Sisku* [The Child][41] published (19 Sep); the poems were being composed from July; more written subsequently.	*Chokher Bali* published in book form (5 Apr). *Noukadubi* (being serialized in *Bangadarshan*).	Writes a preface for Dineshchandra Sen's *Ramayani Katha*; later included in *Prachin Sahitya* [Ancient Literature].		22 Dec (afternoon of 7 Pous): second performance of *Visarjan* at the Santiniketan school.[42]
1904			"Swadeshi Samaj" [The Indigenous Society][43] (in *Bangadarsan*).		22 July: reads "Swadeshi Samaj" at a crowded public meeting, at Minerva Theatre. 31 July: a second reading of the address was arranged at the more spacious Curzon Theatre.[44]
			"Bangabhivag" [Division of Bengal], "University Bill", "Desher Katha" [About the Country] (also in *Bangadarshan*)		26 Nov: the Poet witnesses a performance of *Chokher Bali*, at Classic Theatre (dramatized and performed by Amarendranath Dutt).[45]
			Ingreji Sopan [Steps to English], Part I (a textbook for learners of English)		

254 Appendix II

Date	Non-dramatic works (select)			Dramatic works (including different dramatic forms used)	Remarks (related mostly to theatrical performances/ public readings, etc.)
	Poetry	Fiction	Essay, etc.		
1905	Composed several patriotic songs as part of the agitation against the Partition of Bengal (chiefly after he withdraws to Giridih). Within a month, he composed almost 22–3 songs; most of these were written on the reverse of the manuscript of *Kheya*.[46] For the purpose of Rakhi Bandhan, he composed the "Rakhi sangit".		"Saphalatar sadupay" [Honest means to success], "Chatrader prati sambhashan" [Address to the Students], (in *Bangadarshan*); "Imperialism" (in *Bharati*); "Abastha o byabastha" [Situation and Remedy] (in *Bangadarshan*); "Banga-byabacched" [Partition of Bengal], "Partitioner siksha" [Lessons of Partition], "Bilater Phaans" [England's noose], (in *Bhandar*), *Atmasakti* (collection of essays)		11 Mar: Rabindranath reads his essay "Saphalatar sadupay" [Honest means to success][47] at Minerva Theatre, at a session of Bangiya Sahitya Parisad. 30 Mar: at Classic Theatre, he read "Chatrader prati sambhashan", [An address to the students] organized by Bangiya Sahitya Parisad. 25 Aug: read "Abastha o byabastha" at the Town Hall in Calcutta. Reported to have sung one or more of his patriotic songs (among them perhaps "Amar sonar Bangla").[48] It was reported that on 3 Sep the agitating students marched in procession "singing a national song composed by Babu Rabindra Nath".[49] In an address "Deshiya naam", among other things, he appealed to the theatre proprietors to rename their theatres (Star, Classic, Grand, Unique) with Bengali names.

Date	Non-dramatic works (select)			Dramatic works (including different dramatic forms used)	Remarks (related mostly to theatrical performances/ public readings, etc.)
	Poetry	Fiction	Essay, etc.		
1906	*Kheya* [Ferry], published on 10 Aug. Makes a Bengali translation of Sarojini Naidu's "Palanquin Bearers" as "Palki-beharar gaan" (in *Bangadarshan*)[52]	*Noukadubi* [The Wreck] published as a book by *Basumati*, on 2 Sep.	"Rajbhakti" [Loyalty to the King]; "Deshnayak" [Leader of the Country] (pub. 18 May; subsequently also in *Bhandar* and in *Bangadarshan*),[50] "Siksha-samasya" [Problems in Education] (in *Bhandar*).		23 Jan: reads "Rajbhakti" at Field and Academy Club.[51] 26 Apr: reads "Deshnayak" [Leader of the Country] at the meeting convened at Pashupatinath Bose's house in Bagbazar to protest against the Barisal atrocities.[53] 6 June: read "Siksha-samasya" [Problems in Education] at Overtoun Hall 16 Sep: a public performance of *Lakshmir Pariksha* before all-female audience at a Swadeshi Mela [National fair].
		Gora (serialized in *Probasi* from Sep 1907–Feb 1909).	*Bharatbarsha* (collection of essays) *Ingreji Sopan* [Steps to English], Part II		

Date	Non-dramatic works (select)			Dramatic works (including different dramatic forms used)	Remarks (related mostly to theatrical performances/ public readings, etc.)
	Poetry	Fiction	Essay, etc.		
1907	"Namaskar" expresses the Poet's respects for Sri Aurobindo (pub. in *Bangadarshan*).[54]		*Charitrapuja* [Tribute to Great Lives], *Sahitya* [Literature], *Prachin Sahitya* [Ancient Literature], *Adhunik Sahitya* [Modern Literature], *Lok Sahitya* [Folk Literature], *Gadya granthabali* vols. 1–7 (between Apr-Dec).[55]	*Hasya-kautuk* and *Vyanga-kautuk* (collections of farces, written earlier)	8 & 12 Jan: two consecutive performances of *Kal Mrigaya* to raise funds for a women's body founded by Hiranmoyee Devi.[56]
					19 Jan: for the literary meet at the Exhibition Grounds Rabindranath read "Sahityasammilan"; Surendranath Banerjee presided.[57]
	After losing Samindranath, his youngest child on 24 Nov, he sought solace in the songs that he composed, beginning with "Antara momo bikoshito koro" at Shilaidah (13 Dec). This was also published as a poem, "Prarthana" [Prayer] (in *Bangadarshan*).		"Byadhi o Pratikar" [Disease and Remedy] (in *Probasi*).		17 Feb: "Ritu-utsav" [Celebration of Seasons] was staged in Santiniketan, by the Poet's youngest son, Samindranath and his friends, with costumes and properties. Rabindranath was not present at Santiniketan.
			Rabindranath writes the preface for Dakshinaranjan Mitra Majumder's *Thakurmar Jhuli* [Grandmother's Tales], a collection of Bengali fairy tales (6 Sep)		

Appendix II 257

Date	Non-dramatic works (select)			Dramatic works (including different dramatic forms used)	Remarks (related mostly to theatrical performances/ public readings, etc.)
	Poetry	Fiction	Essay, etc.		
1908	Katha o Kahini (brings together the poems of Katha and Kahini of 1900)	Golpoguccho, 2 vols (of proposed 5 vols)[58]	Gadya granthabali, vols. 8–14.[59] Also volumes that collected his essays and speeches: Raja Praja [King and Subject]; Swadesh [Country]; Samaj [Society]; Siksha [Education]; Samuha [Others]		21 May: at Minerva Theatre, Rabindranath reads "Path o Patheya", for Chaitanya Library.[60] Even though absent from the school, Rabindranath encouraged the presentation of Varsha Utsav [Celebration of Monsoon] at Santiniketan through songs, readings and recitations.[61] This event happened towards the end of the monsoon months, around Aug.[62]
			Individual essays continued to appear in several periodicals: "Path o Patheya" [Way and the Means], "Deshhit" [Welfare of the Country], "Samasya" [The Problem] (in Bangadarshan); "Sadupay" [Honest Means] (in Bharati).[63]	Sarodatsav [Autumn Festival] (prose play) completed on 23 Aug; published on 20 Sep.[64]	24 Sep: before Puja vacation, Sarodatsav was staged in Santiniketan. This play, in writing and performance, marked a turning point in his dramaturgical career.
				Mukut [The Crown] (prose play)	The novella, Mukut, published in Balak, was dramatized for performance by young boys of the school.
1909	Begins composing the poems and songs of Gitanjali [Song Offerings] in English translation.		Santiniketan, vols. 1–8.[65] (collections of essays or addresses)	Prayaschitta [Atonement] (historical drama, in prose)	Prayaschitta is the dramatization of the historical novel Bouthakuranir Haat.
	Chayanika (anthology of his select poems) published in Sep.[66]		Gadya granthabali, vols. 15–16.		In Dec (for Pous Utsav), Visarjan was staged, under Rabindranath's supervision. Boy students enacted female roles.[67]

Date	Non-dramatic works (select)			Dramatic works (including different dramatic forms used)	Remarks (related mostly to theatrical performances] public readings, etc.)
	Poetry	Fiction	Essay, etc.		
1910	*Gitanjali* (published on 5 Sep[68], consisting of 157 poems and songs.	*Gora* (finished in *Probasi*, published as book in Feb)[69]	*Santiniketan*, vols. 9–11.	*Raja* [translated later as *The King of the Dark Chamber*] (prose play); first draft completed by 11 Nov in Shilaidah.[70]	8 Feb: when Rathindranath arrived in Santiniketan with his newly wedded wife, Pratima, the students performed *Malini*. It was performed again on 23 Apr, with Rabindranath in charge. Boys played female roles on both occasions.[71]
	Rabindranath urges Kshitimohan Sen to translate Kabir's poems. Vol. 1 appeared in Sep; the remaining volumes completed by Aug 1911.		"The Problem of India" (in *Modern Review*, Aug).[72]		8 May and 4 Oct: in Santiniketan *Prayaschitta* was performed twice. For the second performance, Rabindranath played Dhananjoy Bairagi.[73]
					In July, girl students acted ~~Lakshmi~~ *Lakshmir Pariksha*. Pratima Devi, his daughter-in-law, played Kshiro. No male member was present among the audience.[74]
					25 Dec: reads "Jishucharit" [Life of Jesus] at the Christotsav celebrations.[75]
1911			His autobiography, *Jibansmriti* [My Reminiscences], serialized in *Probasi* (Aug 1911– July 1912).	*Achalayatan* [Immovable] (prose play) composed in Shilaidah, published in 1912 in book form.	19 March: premiere of *Raja* in Santiniketan. 8 May: second performance, on the occasion of the Poet's 50th birth anniversary.[76]
			"Bhagini Nivedita".[77] *Santiniketan*, vols. 12–13.	*Dakghar* [*The Post Office*] (prose play) composed in Santiniketan possibly by 17 Sep[78]; published in 1912 in book form.	25 Sep: *Sarodotsav* was performed at the school before Puja vacation. Sannyasi was played by Rabindranath.

Appendix II 259

Date	Non-dramatic works (select)			Dramatic works (including different dramatic forms used)	Remarks (related mostly to theatrical performances/public readings, etc.)
	Poetry	Fiction	Essay, etc.		
1912	When his England tour is called off due to illness retires to Shilaidah (March–April); composes songs/poems of *Gitimalya*; also begins to translate poems of *Gitanjali* into English.		*Jibansmriti* (already serialized in *Probasi*) published as a book (on 25 July), with 23 illusrations by Gaganendranath and one by Jyotirindranath.	Publication of *Achalayatan* and *Dakghar*.	25 Jan: for Maghotsav at Adi Brahmasamaj, Rabindranath addresses the assembly; "Jana Gana Mana" is sung as a Brahmo-sangit.
			Chinnapatra (collection of 145 letters, 8 to Srishchandra, the rest to niece Indira)[79]	Translation of *Dakghar* as *The Post Office* done by Devabrata Mukherjea, and of *Raja* as *The King of the Dark Chamber* done by Kshitischandra Sen.	2 Feb: student wing of Bangiya Sahitya Parishad felicitate Rabindranath at the Town Hall; he addresses in response. 3 Feb: the students perform *Baikunther Khata*.
	The Poet arrives in London, in June; gives Rothenstein manuscript of the English *Gitanjali*;[80] Rothenstein circulates copies; Yeats, enthused, reads the poems before other literati.				16 Feb: *Baikunther Khata* performed by his friends at Gaganendranath's residence.

260 *Appendix II*

Date	Non-dramatic works (select)			Dramatic works (including different dramatic forms used)	Remarks (related mostly to theatrical performances/ public readings, etc.)
	Poetry	Fiction	Essay, etc.		
	On 1 Nov, English *Gitanjali* (*Song Offerings*) with an "Introduction" by W.B. Yeats published by India Society in London (750 copies).[82]				16 March: reads "Bharatbarsher Itihaser Dhara" [The Course of Indian History][81] at Overtoun Hall.
					22 March: a performance of *Valmiki Pratibha* at Asutosh Chowdhury's house, attended by the Poet himself. Dinendranath played Valmiki.
					23 April: the *asram* school inmates performed *Raja o Rani*. The Poet plays no role.
					19 June: Sukumar Ray reads a paper on "The Spirit of Rabindranath" at W.W. Pearson's house in Hampstead Heath in London; the Poet was present.[83]
	The first review appears on 7 Nov in *Times Literary Supplement*.[84]				30 July: at Royal Albert Hall, London, performance of Tagore's short story "Dalia" as *The Maharani of Arakan* (translated and dramatized by George Calderon); Sybil Thorndike was part of the cast.[85]

Appendix II   261

Date	Non-dramatic works (select)		Essay, etc.	Dramatic works (including different dramatic forms used)	Remarks (related mostly to theatrical performances/ public readings, etc.)
	Poetry	Fiction			
					The Poet moves to USA with son and daughter-in-law and stays in America for 6 months (Oct 1912–April 1913) and lectures at different institutions. In Urbana, he gives a series of lectures at the local Unity Club.[86]
1913	Urged by Ezra Pound, Harriet Munro, the editor of *Poetry*, (Chicago-based journal), publishes 6 poems of Tagore (9 Dec issue).[87]				
	Gitanjali (*Song Offerings*) popular edition published by Macmillan.		While in the USA, begins to write his first serious prose essays in English, to be given as public addresses.	*Chitra* (English translation of the verse-play *Chitrangada* of 1892, pub. by India Society in Jan)[88]	23 & 26 Jan: lectures at Chicago University
	On Nov 13, news of the Nobel award announced by the Swedish Academy in Stockholm.[89]		*Sadhana: Realisation of Life* (pub. in Nov by Macmillan), collecting together his addresses in English, given chiefly in UK and USA.	Translates *Sarodatsav* as *The Autumn Festival*, partly inspired by some of Yeats's shorter plays.[90]	30 Jan: delivers talk on "Race Conflict" at Rochester. Meets Rudolph Eucken.[91]

262 *Appendix II*

Date	Non-dramatic works (select)			Dramatic works (including different dramatic forms used)	Remarks (related mostly to theatrical performances/ public readings, etc.)
	Poetry	*Fiction*	*Essay, etc.*		
					14 Feb: four lectures at Harvard University, and one at Harvard-Andover Divinity School.[92]
	The Gardener (pub. in Oct by Macmillan)[93]			A playlet in English, *The King and the Rebel*, was written and sent to Ajitkumar Chakravarty before summer vacation of the school, perhaps for performance by students to add to their knowledge of English.[94]	After Rabindranath's return to England (in April), *Post Office* is staged by Irish Abbey Theatre Company on 17 May in Dublin and on 10 July in London.[95]
	The Crescent Moon (pub. in Nov, by Macmillan)[96]				19 & 26 May and 2, 9 & 16 June: Westminster Lectures at Caxton Hall, London (later included in *Sadhana*).
					23 May: talks on "Realisation in Love" at Manchester College, Oxford.
					30 Sep: before Puja vacation, performance of *Valmiki Pratibha* at Santiniketan; this turned into a welcome reception for the Poet who returned from his foreign trip on 29 Sep.[97]
					The King and the Rebel performed by students at Santiniketan.

Appendix II 263

Date	Non-dramatic works (select)			Dramatic works (including different dramatic forms used)	Remarks (related mostly to theatrical performances/ public readings, etc.)
	Poetry	Fiction	Essay, etc.		
1914	29 Jan: Bengal Governor, Lord Carmichael, in Calcutta, hands over to Rabindranath the Nobel award received from Sweden.[98]	*Eyesore*, English translation of *Chokher Bali* being serialized in *Modern Review*.		*The King of the Dark Chamber*, English translation of *Raja*, by Kshitischandra Sen; published by Macmillan (in June), in the name of Rabindranath, despite his distinct reservations, as was trying to revise the translation radically.[99]	24 Jan: on the day of Maghotsav, reads "Choto o Boro" [The Big and the Small] at Adi Brahmo Samaj. 28 Jan: reads "Ekti mantra" at Sadharan Brahmo Samaj.[100]
	Utsarga [Dedication] (published 28 May); *Gitimalya* [Garland of songs] (published 2 July); *Gitali* [Short songs] (published in Oct).	Begins on the novel *Chaturanga* (which appeared in *Sabuj Patra*, Nov 1914–March 1915; yet to be given its final shape.		*The King of the Dark Chamber*, a partially revised draft done when in USA, appeared in the theatre journal *The Drama* (May issue) from Chicago.	Andrews, on his return from South Africa (via UK) was welcomed with a newly composed poem of the Poet, and greeted by the *asram* inmates.[101]
	While at Ramgarh (in May) begins composing poems of *Balaka* and several songs; also, with the help of Andrews, he starts collecting poems for *Fruit Gathering*			*The Post Office*, translation of *Dukghar*, done by Devabrata Mukherjea, but published by Macmillan in the name of Rabindranath.	25 Apr: a welcome was arranged for Nandalal Bose (who joined the school) at the *Amrakunja* [mango-grove], decorated with lotus leave and flowers and *alpona* in the traditional style.[102]

264 *Appendix II*

Date	Non-dramatic works (select)			Dramatic works (including different dramatic forms used)	Remarks (related mostly to theatrical performances/ public readings, etc.)
	Poetry	Fiction	Essay, etc.		
					26 Apr: before start of summer vacation, a performance of *Achalayatan* was staged, with the role of Acharya Adinpunya played by Rabindranath.[103]
	26 Dec: Rabindranath translates the school anthem "Amader Santiniketan" as "She is our own, the darling of our hearts, Santiniketan".		"Ma ma hingshi" [Refrain from violence] published in *Tattwabodhini* (Oct issue)		Aug 5: with the outbreak of World War, Rabindranath reads his "Ma ma hingshi" [Refrain from violence] address at the Santiniketan Mandir.
					8 Dec: Sangit Sangha organized a staging of *Valmiki Pratibha* at Theatre Royal, Calcutta, to raise money for War Relief Fund. Dinendranath played Valmiki. Attended by Lord Carmichael, with wife, the royals of Natore, Burdwan, Coochbehar, Mymensingh, etc.[104]
1915	"Shakespeare", a commissioned poem for the tercentenary celebrations of Shakespeare's death; later included in *Balaka*.[105]	Starts writing *Ghare Baire* after school closes for summer vacation in end-April. The first instalment appears in *Sabuj Patra*, Baisakh issue (Apr).	"Palli Unnati" [Progress of the Village] (in *Probasi*)	*Phalguni* [The Cycle of Spring] (prose play), published in *Sabuj Patra* (in March)	10 March: reads the draft of *Phalguni* (named *Vasantotsav* then) at Jorasanko before a select gathering.

Appendix II 265

Date	Non-dramatic works (select)			Dramatic works (including different dramatic forms used)	Remarks (related mostly to theatrical performances/ public readings, etc.)
	Poetry	Fiction	Essay, etc.		
					6–11 March: Gandhi visits Santiniketan and meets the Poet, though briefly.[106] Prompted by Gandhi, on 10 March, the students and teachers carry out all menial chores themselves.[107]
					20 March: Bengal Governor, Lord Carmichael was welcomed at *Amrakunja*, on a dais decorated with *alpona* in the traditional style.[108]
	Kavyagrantha, vols. 1–6.	Macmillan asks for translations of his short stories. Apart from exiting translations (by Sister Nivedita, etc.) efforts are on to induct new hands (Thompson, Andrews, Surendranath)			25 April evening: *Phalguni* staged at Natyaghar in Santiniketan. The Poet played the blind *baul* [minstrel].
	From East Bengal, Rabindranath collects folk songs (including songs by Lalan Fakir or Gagan Harkara). *Probasi* (Aswin/Oct issue) carries "Lalan Fakirer Gaan" [Songs of Lalan Fakir], with Rabindranath mentioned as the collector.				Possibly on 25 April morning, younger boys performed *King and Rebel*.

266 *Appendix II*

Date	Non-dramatic works (select)			Dramatic works (including different dramatic forms used)	Remarks (related mostly to theatrical performances/public readings, etc.)
	Poetry	Fiction	Essay, etc.		
			"Sikshar Bahan" [Medium of Learning] (in *Sabuj Patra*).		18 June: King George V conferred knighthood upon Rabindranath.[109]
					10 Dec: he reads the essay "Sikshar Bahan" at the hall of Rammohan Library; Brajendranath Seal presided.
					Performances of Rabindranath's plays were being done in the public theatre: *Raja o Rani* (7 May & 21 Jun at Star Theatre); *Abhimanini* (from "Shasti", 13 Jun, at Star); "Akalanka Sashi" (from "Didi", 31 Oct, at Star).[110]
1916	*Kavyagrantha*, vols. 7–10	*Ghare Baire* [the English translation ultimately was titled *Home and the World*]	*Santiniketan*, is published by Indian Publishing House.	To the original *Phalguni*, he added the prologue (as introductory scene), "Bairagya sadhan" [Practice of abstinence]; this would add to the length and also serve to introduce the play.[111]	29 Jan, 9.15 pm: *Phalguni* was performed for the Bankura relief fund at Jorasanko, with the prelude "Bairagya sadhan" in which Rabindranath, Abanindranath, Gaganendranath, Pearson, etc. took part. Rabindranath also played the blind baul in the main play. It was repeated on 31 Jan at 5.30 p.m.
	Balaka [A Flight of Geese]	*Chaturanga* [Four Episodes][112]	*My Reminiscences* (translation of his life story, *Jibansmriti*, by Surendranath) serialized in *Modern Review*, Jan–Dec.		

Appendix II   267

Date	Non-dramatic works (select)			Dramatic works (including different dramatic forms used)	Remarks (related mostly to theatrical performances/ public readings, etc.)
	Poetry	Fiction	Essay, etc.		
	Fruit Gathering by Macmillan	*Galpo saptak* (collection of short stories)			
	Stray Birds (on 15 Nov) by Macmillan[113]	*Hungry Stones and Other Stories* (his short stories translated by various hands), pub. by Macmillan (on 26 Sep, from UK and on 27 Oct, from USA).[114]		*Phalguni*, with the newly added prelude, "Bairagya sadhan", is published by Indian Publishing House.	19 March (the evening of *Vasantatsov*): an open-air performance of *A Midsummer Night's Dream*, under the supervision of CF Andrews.[115]
	While in Japan, writes an original English poem "The Song of the Defeated" (in *Modern Review*, Oct).[116]		In Japan, he was also preparing some of the lectures he intended to deliver in America	On his voyage to Japan, he translates *Visarjan* (as *Sacrifice*), *Raja o Rani* (as *The King and the Queen*) and *Malini*.[117]	During his visit to Japan (29 May to 3 Sep), though Rabindranath appreciated many aspects of Japanese culture (their dance, modern painting, Haiku poetry[118], tea ceremony, flower arrangement) but he was severely critical of Japan's aggressive nationalism.[119] He delivers several lectures at different cities of Japan, warning the Japanese people against imitating the Western model of nationalism.[120]
	In Japan, he translates several poems from *Kanika*, later included in *Stray Birds*			Translates *Prakritir Pratisodh* as *Sanyasi, or the Ascetic*.	

Date	Non-dramatic works (select)			Dramatic works (including different dramatic forms used)	Remarks (related mostly to theatrical performances/ public readings, etc.)
	Poetry	Fiction	Essay, etc.		
	Palataka [The Escapee]				At a reception at Kobe, Japan, he reads the translated *Sanyasi*. At Idzura, he visited the grave of Kakuzo Okakura to pay his respects. He planted a fir tree in the memory of his friend. Reaching America on 18 Sep, the Poet undertakes a hectic lecture schedule. Pond Lyceum manages his itinerary and lecture tours in USA.[121] George Brett, of New York Macmillan, also helped with the arrangements of the tour, and personally met Rabindranath on 19 Nov when the Poet was again in New York.[122] Rabindranath's most widely read paper in USA was "The Cult of Nationalism". He read this at different venues and different cities, as this constituted his cardinal message to America and the West.[123] He also read from other essays, later included in *Personality*.

Appendix II 269

Date	Non-dramatic works (select)			Dramatic works (including different dramatic forms used)	Remarks (related mostly to theatrical performances/ public readings, etc.)
	Poetry	Fiction	Essay, etc.		
					Rabindranath read from his works at different cities. Apart from reading from his poems, he also read from his plays (at Columbia Theatre, San Francisco, 5 Oct), and from *Sanyasi* (in Urbana, 27 Dec).
					Overseas News Agency (of Berlin) claimed a staging of *Chitra* at Munich Theatre "for the first time".[124]
					A proposal from Madam Alla Nazimova to do *Chitra* in USA had apparently been finalized but no evidence of any performance of this play has been found.[125]
					18 Nov: *Post Office* was staged in Hollywood Library auditorium at Los Angeles.[126]
					Though initially planned till April 1917, the hectic nature of the itinerary was too taxing and the Poet decided to cut short his tour.[127]

270 *Appendix II*

Date	Non-dramatic works (select)		Essay, etc.	Dramatic works *(including different dramatic forms used)*	Remarks *(related mostly to theatrical performances/ public readings, etc.)*
	Poetry	Fiction			
1917	"The Sunset of the Century" (*Modern Review*, June)		"Nationalism in the West" [revised version of "Cult of Nationalism" (in *Atlantic Monthly*, March 1917)][128]	*The Cycle of Spring*, pub. by Macmillan, 28 Feb.[129]	The Poet, still in America, continues to read "The Cult of Nationalism" at different venues.
					The people of Lincoln, Nebraska, present Rabindranath with a printing machine for his school on 8 Jan.[130]
			My Reminiscences (trans. Surendranath) pub. by Macmillan, 25 Apr.		Rabindranath returns from his overseas tour, and reaches Santiniketan on 16 March; he is brought to the *asram* along a newly constructed path, Nepal Road.[131]
			Personality: Lectures delivered in America, pub. by Macmillan, 17 May	*Sacrifice and Other Plays*, pub. by Macmillan, 30 Oct.	14 Apr: conducts the morning prayer; in the evening reads "The Cult of Nationalism" and "Woman" at Santiniketan.
			Nationalism (compiles in one volume his "Nationalism" essays in English), pub. by Macmillan, 14 Sep.[132]		15 Apr: reads "The Second Birth" and "Nationalism in India".
					27 Apr: a show of *Chitra* at St James Theatre, London.

Appendix II 271

Date	Non-dramatic works (select)			Dramatic works (including different dramatic forms used)	Remarks (related mostly to theatrical performances/ public readings, etc.)
	Poetry	Fiction	Essay, etc.		
			Plans were made for "Visva-vidya-sam-graha", with writings on world knowledge.[133]		3 May: first performance of *Dakghar* (in Bengali) at Mary Carpenter Hall, with Ashamukul Das as Amal.[134]
					7 May: he read before the guests (at Santiniketan) "The Nation" and *Sanyasi* and *Sacrifice* (English versions of *Prakritir Pratisodh* and *Visarjan*)
					8 May (evening): *Achalayatan* was performed with Rabindranath playing Acharya.
			"Kartar icchay karma" (in Bharati); English translation of this essay as "Thou Shalt Obey", by Surendranath Tagore, in *Modern Review*, September issue.		9 May: read *The King and the Queen* at the Santiniketan house
					4 Aug: reads "Kartar icchay karma" [literally, Work according to the order of the Boss], at Rammohun Library.[135]
					26 Sep: *Baikunther Khata* performed chiefly for female audiences;
					28 Sep: same play, performed for male audiences.
			"The Medium of Education" (translation of "Sikshar Bahan") in *Modern Review*, Oct.		10 Oct: *Dakghar* staged at Vichitra in Jorasanko. Amal was played by Ashamukul Das.[136] Rabindranath played Thakurda, Prahari [Guard] and Baul.[137]

272 *Appendix II*

Date	Non-dramatic works (select)			Dramatic works (including different dramatic forms used)	Remarks (related mostly to theatrical performances/public readings, etc.)
	Poetry	Fiction	Essay, etc.		
			"The Small and the Great" (a translation of "Choto o Boro" by Surendranath Tagore) appeared in *Modern Review*, Dec issue.		14 Nov: reads "Choto o Boro" at Vichitra. 16 Nov: reads the same essay at Rammohun Library.[138] 23 Dec: *Lakshmir Pariksha* acted in Santiniketan. 26 Dec: reads "India's Prayer" at Congress session 31 Dec: *Dakghar* performed at Vichitra, Jorasanko in Calcutta. The special invitees included Besant, Gandhi, Malaviya and other Congress delegates; the Poet acted in it.[139]
1918	"India's Prayer".[140] (*Modern Review*, Jan)	Instalments of *At Home and Outside* (translation of *Ghare Baire* by Surendranath) appear in *Modern Review* from Jan issue.[141]		Reworks *Achalayatan* as *Guru* (prose play)	4 Jan: *Dakghar* performed again at Vichitra, the last in this round of performance of the play; the Poet was also among the cast, playing Thakurda (Gaffer), Prahari (Guard) and Bhikshuk (Beggar).[142]

Appendix II 273

Date	Non-dramatic works (select)			Dramatic works (including different dramatic forms used)	Remarks (related mostly to theatrical performances/ public readings, etc.)
	Poetry	Fiction	Essay, etc.		
	Palataka [The Escapee]	Tota kahini was published in Sabuj Patra, in Jan (Magh)		English translations of lyrical playlets were being done by the Poet: Narakbas (Visit to Hell), Gandharir Abedan [as The Mother's Prayer], Karna-Kunti Samvad (as Karna and Kunti)[143]	14 Apr: after morning prayers at Mandir on Navavarsha, a session of songs and readings was held; the Poet also participated.
	Lover's Gift and Crossing (includes some translated Baul songs and Vaishnav poems) pub. in Apr by Macmillan	"The Parrot's Training" (translation of Tota kahini by himself) in Modern Review, March.[144]			24 Apr: a variety programme at Vichitra, Jorasanko, with songs, music and poetry. The Poet also took part, singing and reading from his poems.
		Mashi and Other Stories (translated 14 short stories by various hands) pub. by Macmillan			16 May: his eldest daughter, Madhurilata, dies of consumption.
					The staging of Sarodotsav before the Puja vacation fell through as Dinendranath was down with fever; instead a Sanskrit play and Autumn Festival (English version of Sarodotsav) were staged.[145]
		Stories from Tagore (translated 10 stories, with Andrews) pub by Macmillan (Oct)			23 Dec (8 Pous): foundation laid for Visva-Bharati.[146] The idea of Visva-Bharati germinates from an urge to build up a centre for humanistic learning.

274 *Appendix II*

Date	Non-dramatic works (select)			Dramatic works (including different dramatic forms used)	Remarks (related mostly to theatrical performances/ public readings, etc.)
	Poetry	Fiction	Essay, etc.		
1919		*The Home and the World* (translation of *Ghare Baire* by Surendranath Tagore) pub. by Macmillan	*Japan-jatri* [Traveller to Japan]	*Swarga-marta* [Heaven and Earth] (comic play)[147]	12 Jan: reads "Message of the Forest" in Bangalore, and "The Centre of Indian Culture" at different venues in South India; reads this again on 21 March in Empire Theatre of Calcutta.[148]
			The Centre of Indian Culture (pub. by Society for Promotion of National Education, Adyar)		15 Apr: students organize 'Anandabazar', selling food items and handicrafts; the profits went for the aid of the indigent. Some students had the brainwave of setting up an 'archaeological display', with exhibits like "Rama's sandals" (Ramananda Chattopadhyay's footwear), "Ashoka's script" (handwriting of a student named Ashok), "Buddha's relics" (from a student Buddhadas).[149]
			Message of the Forest (in *Modern Review*, May)		
			Autumn Festival (in *Modern Review*, Nov)	8 May: on Rabindranath's birth anniversary students perform *Visarjan* and the Sanskrit play *Mahvir-charit* (3rd Act).	

Appendix II 275

Date	Non-dramatic works (select)			Dramatic works (including different dramatic forms used)	Remarks (related mostly to theatrical performances/ public readings, etc.)
	Poetry	Fiction	Essay, etc.		
					31 May: in a protest against the massacre at Jallianwala Bagh (13 Apr) the Poet writes an open letter to Viceroy, Lord Chelmsford, and renounces his knighthood given by the British Empire.[150]
					26 Aug: the Poet accepts Romain Rolland's invitation to join in the Declaration of Independence of the Spirit.[151]
					23 Sep: before the commencement of Puja vacation, *Sarodotsav* was staged in Santiniketan; the Poet played Sanyasi.[152]
					In Nov, when in Sylhet, he is impressed by Manipuri dance and wants to introduce this dance form in the Santiniketan school.[153]

276 *Appendix II*

Date	Non-dramatic works (select)			Dramatic works (including different dramatic forms used)	Remarks (related mostly to theatrical performances/ public readings, etc.)
	Poetry	Fiction	Essay, etc.		
1920				*Arupratan* [Formless Jewel] (prose play), a revised version of *Raja*	19 Apr: a performance of *Chitra* in Baroda on the occasion of the Poet's visit (as part of his tour of Western India).
					On a tour of Europe, reaches England on 5 June; meets friends in London, Oxford and Cambridge.[154]
					But in Aug, he leaves England disappointed with the British Parliament's response to the Jallianwala Bagh massacre.
					In London, Rabindranath goes to see a performance of *Beggar's Opera*, but walks out in disgust.
					11 July: girls of Clifton Boarding School, Bristol, enact *The King of the Dark Chamber* before the Poet.
					He reads to them from *Lakshmir Pariksha* and *The Crescent Moon*.
					28 July: at Wigmore Hall, five of his lyrical playlets were staged. Sarojini Naidu summarized the contents of each before it was enacted. The dumb-show used as a prelude for *Kach and Devjani* was much appreciated.

Appendix II 277

Date	Non-dramatic works (select)			Dramatic works (including different dramatic forms used)	Remarks (related mostly to theatrical performances/ public readings, etc.)
	Poetry	Fiction	Essay, etc.		
					In Paris, he watches a performance of *Faust*.
					3 Nov: enjoyed Twain's *The Prince and the Pauper*, starring Faversham, at Booth Theatre, New York; after his Europe tour, the Poet was in USA from 28 Oct (till March 1921).
					7–10 Dec: four matinees of *Sacrifice* and *The Post Office* at Garrick Theatre, New York, organized by Union of East and West.[155]
					24 & 25 Dec: in Santiniketan, *Baikunther Khata* performed; the Poet was in USA.
1921	*The Fugitive*, pub. by Macmillan	*The Wreck* (translation of *Noukadubi*) pub. by Macmillan	*Glimpses of Bengal* (translation from *Chinnapatra*)	*Rinsodh* [Repayment of Debt] (prose play; revised version of *Sarodotsav*)	13 Feb: in Santiniketan, a moonlit celebration of *Vasantotsav* (Festival of Spring) with singing of songs (mainly from *Phalguni*) and the site decorated with *alpona*.
					In USA, meets Helen Keller[156], Leonard Elmhirst; invites the latter to come to Santiniketan to help with rural reconstruction.

Date	Non-dramatic works (select)			Dramatic works (including different dramatic forms used)	Remarks (related mostly to theatrical performances/ public readings, etc.)
	Poetry	Fiction	Essay, etc.		
			"Sikshar Milan" [Co-ordination of Learning] published from Santiniketan Press as a booklet on 14 Aug.[159] Also published in *Sabuj Patra*, *Bharati* and *Probasi*, Sep-Oct.		2 Apr: an open-air performance of *The Farewell Curse* (translation of *Viday Abhishap*) was given at Hampstead, by the Union of East and West.[157] 27 May: delivers his Nobel acceptance speech at the Swedish Academy, Stockholm.[158] 4 June: his voice is recorded at Berlin, by Prussian Academy.[160] 4 June: saw *Post Office* at Berlin Theatre 6 Aug: (having returned to India on 16 July from his trip abroad), reads "Sikshar Milan" [Co-ordination of Learning] at Santiniketan. 15 Aug: reads the essay again at University Institute Hall, Calcutta.[161] 18 Aug: another lecture on education at Alfred Theatre in Calcutta.[162]

Appendix II 279

Date	Non-dramatic works (select)			Dramatic works (including different dramatic forms used)	Remarks (related mostly to theatrical performances/ public readings, etc.)
	Poetry	Fiction	Essay, etc.		
					29 Aug: reads "Satyer Ahowan" [Call of Truth] at University Institute Hall, Calcutta.[163]
					2–3 Sep: open-air performance of *Varsha-mangal* at Jorasanko, Calcutta.[164]
					Despite Gandhi meeting him in Aug and again on 6 Sep, Rabindranath could not fully agree with several tenets of Gandhi's Non-Cooperation movement.[165]
					2 Oct: *Rinsodh* staged in Santiniketan, with students and teachers performing together; the Poet played Sekharkabi.
					9 Nov: Sylvain Levi and Madame Levi welcomed at *Amrakunja*
					23 Dec: officially Visva-Bharati is declared open and handed over to the people at the first session of Visva-Bharati Parisad, chaired by Brajendranath Seal.[166]
					23 Dec: in the evening, scenes from the Sanskrit play, *Benisamhara*, and Rabindranath's *Visarjan* were performed for the entertainment of the guests.

280 *Appendix II*

Date	Non-dramatic works (select)			Dramatic works (including different dramatic forms used)	Remarks (related mostly to theatrical performances/ public readings, etc.)
	Poetry	Fiction	Essay, etc.		
1922	*Lipika* [Notes or Writings] (prose poems), pub. by Indian Press Ltd, 17 Aug[167]		*Creative Unity*, pub. by Macmillan	*Muktadhara* [literally Free Flow; but translated as *The Waterfall*] (prose play). The Bengali original appeared first in *Probasi*, Apr. and then published as a book in June. The auto-translated *Waterfall* appeared in *Modern Review*, May issue.[168]	7 Feb: *Muktadhara* is read before a select gathering at Jorasanko residence; 21 July: reads it again publicly at Rammohan Library. Reacting to Gandhi's arrest on 10 March, Rabindranath cancelled *Vasantatsov* and the performance of *Muktadhara*.[169]
	Sishu Bholanath [The Carefree Child][170] (poems for/about children)			21 Feb: Elmhirst read "Robbery of the soil", which impressed the Poet so much he wanted to translate it. 28 July: Elmhirst read it again at Rammohan Library, chaired by Rabindranath.[171]	15 Apr: Anandabazar at Shaalbithi of Santiniketan. 16 May: Constitution of Visva-Bharati was registered; published on 22 May.[172] This Constitution mentions the date of establishment of Visva-Bharati as 22 Dec 1921.

Appendix II 281

Date	Non-dramatic works (select)			Dramatic works (including different dramatic forms used)	Remarks (related mostly to theatrical performances/public readings, etc.)
	Poetry	*Fiction*	*Essay, etc.*		
					July: public reading of *Muktadhara* at Rammohan Library to raise funds for Visva-Bharati Sammilani.[173]
					7 Aug: celebration of *Varsha-mangal* at Santiniketan; the Poet also sang and recited his poems.[174]
					16, 17, 19 Aug: *Varsha-mangal* performed at Rammohan Library Hall, Madan Theatre and Alfred Theatre in Calcutta.[175]
					16 Sep: *Rinsodh* performed at Alfred Theatre, Calcutta, with the Poet playing Sanyasi/Vijayaditya.[176]
					18 Sep: a second performance at Madan Theatre.[177]
					4 Oct: Indian Press, Allahabad, makes over to Visva-Bharati the rights of publication and sale of Rabindranath's books in Bengali.
					24 Dec: on the occasion of *Pous Utsav*, performance of *Macbeth*, Act II, and *Mudrarakshasa*, Act III, in the evening.

282 *Appendix II*

Date	Non-dramatic works (select)			Dramatic works (including different dramatic forms used)	Remarks (related mostly to theatrical performances/ public readings, etc.)
	Poetry	Fiction	Essay, etc.		
1923			April: the first issue of *Visva-Bharati Quarterly* was released, edited by Rabindranath and with contributions from Winternitz, James H. Cousins, O. C. Ganguly, Ferdand Benoit and the Poet himself.[178]	*Vasanta* [Spring] (musical drama), pub. by Visva-Bharati.[179]	7 Jan: the Poet presides over Elmhirst's lecture on "Rural Reconstruction" at Rammohan Library.
					22 Jan: on the day of Sri Panchami, celebration of *Vasantotsav* at the asram.
					Gretchen Green shot a film on work being carried out in Surul; even the Poet was shot on location. The title of the film was "Sriniketan".[180] This change in name from Surul to Sriniketan is a significant shift, though the official adoption of the name seems to happen in 1923 when Elmhirst presents his annual report (26 Dec 1923) of Sriniketan Department of Agriculture.

Date	Non-dramatic works (select)			Dramatic works (including different dramatic forms used)	Remarks (related mostly to theatrical performances/ public readings, etc.)
	Poetry	Fiction	Essay, etc.		
				The writing of *Raktakarabi* probably started in Shillong,[182] at least of the first few drafts;[183] the play initially was not named *Raktakarabi*, but *Nandini*, and sometimes even referred to as *Yakshapuri*.	19 Feb: in bidding farewell to Elmhirst (before his departure to China and America), the Poet bestowed on him the title of *Desika* (Guru or Acharya, who is a guide to the way of Truth)[181] 25 & 27 Feb: *Vasanta* staged in Calcutta, at Madan Theatre and University Institute Hall respectively. 23 Apr: farewell of Vincent Lesney at Kala Bhavana He reads the new play at several private gatherings, in Calcutta (2 Oct) as well as in Santiniketan (19 Oct).[184] He definitely had performance in mind; and did not want it published before it was staged.[185] But he was never able to stage *Raktakarabi*, apparently for want of a proper player for Nandini. 26 July: the Poet makes over to Visva-Bharati the copyright of all his Bengali books till 1923.

Date	Non-dramatic works (select)			Dramatic works (including different dramatic forms used)	Remarks (related mostly to theatrical performances/ public readings, etc.)
	Poetry	Fiction	Essay, etc.		
				Rathajatra (a prose play) pub in Probasi, Nov; this was inspired by a play by Pramanath Bishi.[186]	25, 27, 28, 30 Aug & 1 Sep: performances of Visarjan at Empire Theatre, with the 62-year old Poet playing young Joysingha, with Ranu Adhikari as Aparna.[187]
					25 Dec: during the morning service, the Poet pays his respects to Pearson[188] and the other deceased; in the evening, he conducts the prayer of Christotsav.
					25 Dec: at a meeting of Visva-Bharati Samsad, Visva-Bharati was given the management of the Santiniketan Trust.[189]
1924		Gora (trans of Gora by Pearson) pub. by Macmillan		Raktakarabi (prose play) in Probasi (Aswin,1331 BS/ Oct 1924);[190] published as a single playtext in 1926.	9 Feb: celebration of Vasantatsov at Santiniketan with songs on the evening of Sri Panchami; decorations by Nandalal Bose and Suren Kar.[191]
					1–3 March: three lectures at Calcutta University; later published in Bangabani.
				The Car of Time (translation of Rathajatra of 1923) in VBQ, Jan.[192]	13 Apr–29 May: moves through China, addressing gatherings at different places (Shanghai, Nanking, Peking, Taiyuan, Hankow). All through, Tsemon Hsu serves as Rabindranath's interpreter.

Appendix II 285

Date	Non-dramatic works (select)			Dramatic works (including different dramatic forms used)	Remarks (related mostly to theatrical performances/ public readings, etc.)
	Poetry	Fiction	Essay, etc.		
				The Curse at Farewell (translation of Viday Abhishap by Edward Thompson)	8 May: at the Peking Normal University auditorium, for his birth celebrations, *Chitra* is staged.[193]
				Red Oleanders (prose play); English translation of *Raktakarabi*, pub. in *VBQ*, Special Sharadiya (Autumn) Number, in Sep (Aswin 1331 B.S.)[194]	22 May: at Taiyuan, after his lecture, *Sannyasi* is staged.
					Returns to Santiniketan in July; sets up a tea club named Sushimo Chaa-Chakra[195]
					17 Aug: Rabindranath visits Sisirkumar Bhaduri's new theatre, Monomohan Natyamandir (inaugurated on 6 Aug); *Sita* was staged.
					15 Sep: *Arupratan* staged at Alfred Theatre, Calcutta; Ranu Adhikari mimed the role of Sudarshana; Sahana Bose sang songs of Surangama; Dinendranath and others sang in chorus; the dialogues were spoken by the Poet.
					6 Nov–3 Jan 1925: during his forced stay in Argentina (cancelling his Peru trip due to ill health), with Victoria Ocampo attending him, he developed a penchant for doodles while cancelling out lines of his poems; these were the early signs of his moving towards painting.

Appendix II

Date	Non-dramatic works (select)			Dramatic works (including different dramatic forms used)	Remarks (related mostly to theatrical performances/ public readings, etc.)
	Poetry	Fiction	Essay, etc.		
1925	*Purabi* (dedicated to "Vijaya") pub. by Visva-Bharati in Aug.[196]	*Broken Ties and Other Stories*, pub. by Macmillan.	*Talks in China* (lectures given in China) pub. by Visva-Bharati[197]	*Red Oleanders* (prose play); English translation of *Raktakarabi*, pub. in book form by Macmillan	10 March: *Sundar* was to be staged at Santiniketan, to celebrate the advent of spring. But the performance had to be cancelled for storms and heavy rains. It was later given on 13 Apr (*Varsha sesh*) at Konark house. Also at Jorasanko in Jan 1929.[198]
	Prabahani (collection of songs)		*Sankalan*, (a collection of his non-fictional prose writings) pub. by New Artistic Press, in Aug.[199]		14 Apr (*Navavarsha*/Bengali New Year): staging of *Lakshmir Pariksha*, also on the porch next to Konark.[200]
					19 July: *Varsha Mangal* in Santiniketan.
			Prasantachandra Mahalanobis, in charge of Visva-Bharati Publications, considered introducing a 'House Style', and standard spellings.[201]	*Grihapravesh* (prose play: "Sesher Ratri" dramatized) pub. by Visva-Bharati Granthalay in Oct, and also in *Probasi* (Aswin/Oct issue).	25 July: Rabindranath saw a performance of *Chirakumar Sabha* at Star Theatre; the first show had been staged on 18 July. Dinendranath was in charge of songs; the Cubist stage setting was by Gaganendranath.[202]
					4 Aug: arrangements were made to celebrate autumn with songs; but a sudden outburst of showers, saw a spontaneous shift to songs celebrating the rains.

Appendix II 287

Date	Non-dramatic works (select)		Dramatic works (including different dramatic forms used)	Remarks (related mostly to theatrical performances/ public readings, etc.)
	Poetry	Essay, etc.		
		"Red Oleanders: Author's Interpretation" (in *VBQ*, Oct)[203]	*Sesh Varshan* (musical drama) pub. in *Sabujpatra*, Kartik/ Nov issue	11 Sep: *Sesh Varshan* performed at Vichitra, in Calcutta, as a blend of acting, singing, miming and some rhythmic bodily movements.[204] 15 Sep: second performance to raise funds for Pearson Memorial Hospital. 17 Sep: special performance for Belgian royals, Lord and Lady Lytton, etc. 19 Sep: probably yet another show on public demand.
		"Swaraj sadhan" in *Sabujpatra* (Aswin/ Oct issue); "Striving for Swaraj", the English translation (possibly by Surendranath) in *Modern Review*, Dec.[205]	*Sodhbodh* (prose play: "Karmaphal" dramatized) in Annual *Basumati*;[206] pub as book in June 1926	5 Dec: Art Theatre premieres *Grihapravesh* at Star Theatre, with Ahindra Chowdhury, Sushilasundari and Niharbala in the lead roles. Dinendranath and Gaganendranath were in charge of music and stage design, respectively. 19 Dec: the Poet went to see the third performance.[207]

Date	Non-dramatic works (select)			Dramatic works	Remarks (related mostly to theatrical performances/ public readings, etc.)
	Poetry	Fiction	Essay, etc.	(including different dramatic forms used)	
1926	Begins to give shape to the poems of *Lekhan* while convalescing in Hungary.[208]		Essays read during tour of East Bengal (7–28 Feb) appeared in journals; "The Meaning of Art" (*VBQ*, Apr); "The Rule of the Giant" (*VBQ*, July-Sep), "Eker Sadhana" [The Quest for the One] (in *Bharati*).[209]	*Natir Puja* (prose play)[210] *Raktakarabi* (in Bengali) pub. in book form by Visva-Bharati *Shodh bodh* (prose play) pub in book form by Visva-Bharati[212] *Chirakumar Sabha* (prose comedy)[213]	8 May: performance of *Natir Puja* in Santiniketan; initially an all-female cast, the lead role was played by Gouri, the daughter of Nandalal Bose. The introduction of dance to create the dramatic was a major innovation.[211] 4 Oct: witnesses a performance of *Dakghar* (*Post Office*) at Dresden, Germany, played to a packed auditorium. Sees another performance of the play in Prague.[214]
1927	*Lekhan*[215]			*Paritran* (prose play) *Riturangasala/ Riturananga* (medley of seasonal songs)[217]	28, 29, 31 Jan, 1 Feb: *Natir Puja* was performed at Jorasanko, Calcutta, to raise funds for Visva-Bharati.[216] *Paritran* was a revised version of *Prayaschitta*. 18 March: first performance as *Riturangasala* at Santiniketan. 8 Dec: given as *Rituranga* at Jorasanko, Calcutta.[218]

Appendix II 289

Date	Non-dramatic works (select)			Dramatic works (including different dramatic forms used)	Remarks (related mostly to theatrical performances/ public readings, etc.)
	Poetry	Fiction	Essay, etc.		
1928	*Fireflies*, pub. by Macmillan[219]		*Letters to a Friend*[220]	*Sesh Raksha* (comedy) [Salvaged at last]	*Sesh Raksha* was the revised version of *Goray Galad* (of 1892)
				Shiver Bhiksha (dramatic dialogue)	14 July: Rabindranath, on the occasion of *Varsha-mangal*, introduced the ritual of *Vriksha-ropana* (planting of a sapling).
					15 July: *Halakarshana* or *Halachalana* was celebrated at Sriniketan.[221]
1929	*Mahua*	*Jogajog* [Communication]; *Sesher Kabita* [The Final Poem]	*Jatri* [Traveller][222]	*Tapati* (prose play)	*Tapati* was the reworked version of *Raja o Rani* of 1889.
					26, 27, 29 Sep & 1 Oct: *Tapati* performed in Jorasanko, with the 68-year old Poet playing the King.[223]
1930			*Bhanusingher Patrabali* [Letters of Bhanusingha]		Delivered *The Religion of Man* as the Hibbert lectures at Oxford, in May.

290   *Appendix II*

Date	Non-dramatic works (select)			Dramatic works (including different dramatic forms used)	Remarks (related mostly to theatrical performances/public readings, etc.)
	Poetry	Fiction	Essay, etc.		
1931	*The Child*, pub. by Allen & Unwin, London.[224] The Bengali version, *Sishutirtha*, came in August.		*The Religion of Man: Being the Hibbert Lectures for 1930*, pub. by Allen & Unwin, London	*Nabin* (musical drama), completed in Feb 1931; included in *Banabani*.[225]	17, 18, 19 & 22 March: *Navin* performed at New Empire Theatre, Calcutta. This was more a musical drama than a dance drama, with a narration used to string the songs together.[226]
					14, 15, 17 Sep & 1 Oct: *Sishutirtha* performed in dance format, in Calcutta.
	Banabani [Voice of the Forest]		*Russiar Chithi* [Letters from Russia]	*Shapmochan* [The Redemption] (dance drama)	May be considered as the starting of the dance drama form ("nritya natya")
	Gitabitan (compilation of more than 1500 songs)				31 Dec & 1 Jan 1932: *Shapmochan* performed at Jorasanko in Calcutta.
	The Golden Book of Tagore				
1932	*Parisesh* [At the end]			*Kaler Jatra* [The March of Time] (prose play)	A conflation of the earlier *Kabir Diksha* and *Rather Rashi*[227]
	Punascha [Once more] (prose poems)				Sep: Dinendranath directs a production of *Kaler Jatra* in Santiniketan.[228]
					New Theatres releases the filmed version of *Natir Puja*.
	Sanchayita, a collection of his poems, edited by the Poet himself				*Navin* and *Shapmochan* performed in Lucknow, under the supervision of Pratima Devi, with Asitkumar Haldar helping with the design.[229]

Appendix II 291

Date	Non-dramatic works (select)			Dramatic works (including different dramatic forms used)	Remarks (related mostly to theatrical performances/public readings, etc.)
	Poetry	Fiction	Essay, etc.		
1933	*Bichitrita* [Miscellaneous]	*Dui Bon* [Two sisters]	*Manusher Dharma* [The Religion of Man]; "Bharatpathik Rammohan" ["The Indian Pilgrim Rammohan"]	*Bansari* (prose play).	Affinities between this play and novels like *Ghare Baire* or *Char Adhyay*, have prompted this work to be described as a "novel written in the form of drama".[230]
					10 Feb: Madhu Bose staged *Dalia* (dramatized version of the short story) at Empire Theatre.[231]
					29, 30 March: *Shapmochan* at Empire Theatre, Calcutta.[232]
				Tasher Desh [Kingdom of Cards][233] (prose play, significantly revised by 1939)	*Tasher Desh* is a dramatization of the short story, "Ekti Ashare Galpo" (1892); initially written as a prose play, it was subsequently revised to accommodate more songs and dances.[234]
				Chandalika (prose play)	*Chandalika* has its genesis in a Buddhist tale.
					12, 13, 15 Sep: *Tasher Desh* and *Chandalika* (prose play) first performed at Madan Theatre, Calcutta.[235]
					25, 26 Nov: *Shapmochan*, 27, 28 Nov: *Tasher Desh* performed at Excelsior in Bombay.[236]

292 *Appendix II*

Date	Non-dramatic works (select)			Dramatic works (including different dramatic forms used)	Remarks (related mostly to theatrical performances/ public readings, etc.)
	Poetry	Fiction	Essay, etc.		
1934		*Malancha* [Garden]		*Sravan-gatha* [Song of Sravana] (medley of monsoon songs)	11, 12, 14, 16 & 18 May: *Shapmochan* at Regal Theatre, Colombo, Ceylon. Also performed at Galle and Jaffna.[237]
		Char Adhyay [Four Chapters]			First at Horana, and then at Kandi, he witnesses Kandi dance, which would be inducted into the dance practices of Visva-Bharati.
					24, 28, 30, 31 Oct: *Shapmochan* at Museum Theatre, Madras; 4 Nov: *Shapmochan* at Waltair.[238]
1935	*Sesh saptak* [Last Septet] (prose poems)				16 March: Prose-play *Chandalika* performed at Santiniketan.[239]
1936	*Patraput* [Letters] (prose poems)		*Japan- Parasye* [In Japan and Persia]	*Chitrangada* (dance drama)	The 1892 verse-play Chitrangada was reworked and set to tune.[240]
	Shyamali (prose poems)		*Collected Poems and Plays*, pub. by Macmillan		11, 12, 13 March: dance drama *Chitrangada* given at New Empire Theatre, Calcutta.
					16 March: *Chitrangada* in Patna,
				Parisodh (dance drama) an early attempt to recast the narrative poem (of *Katha*) as dance drama[241]	10, 11 Oct: performance of *Parisodh* at Ashutosh College auditorium, Calcutta.[242]

Appendix II 293

Date	Non-dramatic works (select)			Dramatic works (including different dramatic forms used)	Remarks (related mostly to theatrical performances/ public readings, etc.)
	Poetry	Fiction	Essay, etc.		
1937	Khapchara [Without sense] (rhymes)	Shey [He/That person][243]	Kalantar [A Different Time; also, The End of Time]		24, 25, 26, 27 Feb: Chitrangada given at Excelsior Theatre, Bombay; also performed at Nagpur and Ahmedabad (till early March). The Poet did not accompany the group.[244]
	Chorar chobi [Pictures of rhymes]		Visva-parichay [Introducing the World]		27 March: Parisodh performed at Santiniketan.[245]
1938	Prantik [At the Edges]			Chandalika (dance drama)	The 1933 prose play was refashioned as a dance drama.[246]
	Senjuti [Evening Lamp]				March & April: shows of Chitrangada in East Bengal (10, 11 March: in Khulna; 23, 24 March: in Kumilla; 26, 27 March: in Chittagong; 5, 6, 7 April: in Sylhet; 10, 11 April: in Mymensingh).[247]
				Muktir Upay (prose play)[248]	18, 19, 20 March: dance drama Chandalika performed at Chaya Theatre, Calcutta.[249]
				Swarge Chukratebil Baithak (comic play)[250]	3, 4 Sep: Parisodh in Santiniketan, at Sinha Sadana and in front of the library building.[251]

294 Appendix II

Date	Non-dramatic works (select)			Dramatic works (including different dramatic forms used)	Remarks (related mostly to theatrical performances/ public readings, etc.)
	Poetry	Fiction	Essay, etc.		
1939	Prahasini [She whose laughter is sweet] Akash-pradip [Sky-lamp]		Pather sanchay [Gatherings from the road] (collection of essays and letters)	Shyama (dance drama)	Shyama was the reworked version of Parisodh, which itself was fashioned out of a narrative poem of Katha. 7 & 8 Feb: performance of Shyama at Sree Theatre in Calcutta. 9 & 10 Feb: performance of Chandalika also at Sree Theatre in Calcutta.
1940	Nabajatak [New born] Sanai [Shehnai] Rogsajyay [On the Sick-bed]	Tin sangi [Three Companions]	Chelebela (life story); My Boyhood Days (trans. of Chelebela by Marjorie Sykes)		
1941	Arogya [Convalescence]; Janmadiney [On the birthday]	Galpo-salpo	Asramer rup o bikash [The Form and Progress of the Asram] Sabhyatar Sankat [Crisis in Civilization]		Passes away on 7 August (22 Sravana BS 1348) in Calcutta, where he had been brought for medical treatment.

Notes

1 Anthologies have been italicized; individual poems, considered significant enough to deserve separate mention, are in double quotation marks.
2 Short stories are indicated with double quotation marks; novels are in italics.
3 Essays are entered with double quotation marks; italics have been used for autobiographical writings, travel writings, compilations, etc., which have usually been published as books.
4 Rabindranath's dramatic forms have been varied and often difficult to classify precisely. For instance, his early compositions like *Valmiki Pratibha*, *Kal Mrigaya* or *Mayar Khela* have been identified as "geetinatya" or musical drama, but, as the Poet himself pointed out, though they may have some affinities with the Western opera they belong to a different category and are best described as "drama set to music": see *My Reminiscences* (London: Macmillan, 1917) 194. Also, within this category itself, while *Valmiki Pratibha* and *Kal Mrigaya* present songs woven together for a dramatic structure, in *Mayar Khela* the drama is an excuse for a string of songs: "In this the songs were important not the drama ... this was a garland of songs with just a thread of dramatic plot running through" (*My Reminiscences*, 196). Again, he uses both the terms "kavyanatya" and "natyakavya" for his poetic plays; while the former indicates verse drama (*Raja o Rani*, *Visarjan*, *Malini*), the compositions of the latter kind are more lyrical and less dramatic (*Gandharir Abedan*, *Karna Kunti Samvad* or *Viday Abhishap*). Even in his mature prose plays (like *Phalguni*, *Raja*, *Dakghar*), the language is often so interlaced with poeticism that one is hesitant to label them as mere 'prose plays'. Even among the late dance dramas, the seasonal celebrations in *Varsha-mangal*, *Vasanta*, *Nataraj-Riturangasala* hardly qualify as dramatic pieces; even *Shapmochan*, often referred to as a "kathika" or tableau, seems to exude a flavour somewhat different from the full-fledged dance dramas of his final phase (*Chitrangada*, *Chandalika* and *Shyama*).
5 Though given the external shape of drama, Rabindranath himself denied the work that status, and referred to it as poetry (*kavya*). In the preface he wrote: "This poetic piece should not be mistaken for drama." He was also extremely reluctant to have this published. When Indian Publishing House was trying to get it published in 1911, he sent back the proofs to Charuchandra Bandyopadhyay with the note: "Is this a literary work? And you want to publish it! No, this should not be printed." See Charuchandra Bandyopadhyay, *Rabi-Rashmi: Purba bhag*, vol. 1 (Calcutta: University of Calcutta, 1938) 109.
6 Because the text mentioned Dwijendranath as the copyright-holder, Chandranath Basu, the librarian of Bengal Library, remarked: "Valmiki Prativa by Baboo Dwijendra Nath Tagore was an exceedingly good opera published during the year under review" (cited in Prasantakumar Pal, *Rabi Jibani*, vol. 2, 83).
7 Following Prabhatkumar Mukhopadhyay, *Rabindra Jibani*, vol. 1 (Calcutta: Visva-Bharati Granthalaya, 1933) 99.
8 Prior to this, Rabindranath had acted in other family productions, excelling particularly as Aleekbabu in Jyotirindranath's farce, *Emon Kormo ar korbo na*. His impersonation of the role was so remarkable that the play subsequently came to be known as *Aleekbabu*.
9 This was based on an earlier poetic composition, *Prithvirajer Parajay*, written 1873.
10 Among the early works that Rabindranath dedicated to Kadambari Devi were *Prakritir Pratisodh, Saisabsangeet* and *Bhanu Singha Thakurer Padabali*.
11 Prabhatkumar Mukhopadhyay has dismissed this as a "trivial prose play": see *Rabindra Jibani*, vol. 1, 255.
12 For details, see Prasantakumar Pal, *Rabi Jibani*, vol. 2, 198–9.

13 See Gourchandra Saha, *Rabindrajibanprabaha* (Calcutta: Patralekha, 2012) 45.
14 See Prabhatkumar Mukhopadhyay, *Rabindra Jibani*, vol. 1, 209.
15 Prabhatkumar Mukhopadhyay mentions the performance of the revised version at Jorasanko, but not the date of performance: see *Rabindra Jibani*, vol. 1, 316; however, he mentions the date of publication of the revised edition as 24 February 1886 (316, n. 3). But Gourchandra Saha mentions the date of performance as 20 February 1886 (see *Rabindrajibanprabaha*, 47).
16 As mentioned in Prabhatkumar Mukhopadhyay, *Rabindra Jibani*, vol. 1, 316. Though performance at Star Theatre is mentioned in this biography, the date of performance is not given. However, Prabhatkumar Mukhopadhyay in *Rabindra barshapanji* (Calcutta: Dey's Publishing, 2007; originally 1962) 25, mentions a performance of the revised version on 10 March. Was this, then, the date of performance at Star Theatre?
17 *Raja o Rani* was possibly drafted first in April at Solapur.
18 Prabhatkumar Mukhopadhyay mentions the Park Street residence as the site of the performance: see *Rabindra-barshapanji*, 27; Samir Sengupta, *Samakal o Rabindranath: Ghatanapanji*, 60; and Gourchandra Saha (at 53) follow suit. But Prasantakumar Pal is of the opinion that this took place at the Birjitala residence (vol. 3, 125). This is corroborated in Indira Devi Chaudhurani, *Rabindra Smriti* (Calcutta: Visva-Bharati Granthan Vibhaga, 2010; originally 1960) 32–3.
19 Prabhatkumar Mukhopadhyay, *Rabindra barshapanji*, 30; Samir Sengupta, *Samakal o Rabindranath: Ghatanapanji*, 66.
20 With the publication of *Choto Golpo* (1893) and *Bichitra Golpo*, 2 volumes and *Katha-chatushtoy* (all 1894), all short stories (written till then) were anthologized. For details, see Prasantakumar Pal, *Rabi Jibani*, vol. 4, 32.
21 This essay was prompted by the furore raised by the cremation of Hammergren at Nimtala.
22 See Prasantakumar Pal, *Rabi Jibani*, vol. 4, 2–3.
23 See Prasantakumar Pal, *Rabi Jibani*, vol. 4, 16. *Viday Abhishap* was later translated by Edward Thompson as *Curse at Farewell* (1924), though Rabindranath's own translation bearing the title *Kacha and Devyani* was included in *The Fugitive* (1912); another near-identical version appeared in *New Orient* (1924), with the title *Farewell Curse*. See Ananda Lal, *Rabindranath Tagore: Three Plays* (Calcutta: MP Birla Foundation, 1987) 497–8.
24 Prabhatkumar Mukhopadhyay, *Rabindra barshapanji*, 31.
25 This is an anthology of poems, different from the English translation of 1896 verse-play *Chitrangada* as *Chitra*.
26 See Prabhatkumar Mukhopadhyay, *Rabindra barshapanji*, 32
27 See Prasantakumar Pal, *Rabi Jibani*, vol. 4, 117–118.
28 Details are provided in Abanindranath Tagore, *Gharoa* (Calcutta: Visva-Bharati Granthan Vibhaga, 1941; rpt. 1983) 120–1, and cited in Prasantakumar Pal, *Rabi Jibani*, vol. 4,141. Prasantakumar Pal, however, is not certain about the date of performance, which has been mentioned in Prabhatkumar Mukhopadhyay, *Rabindra barshapanji*, 33.
29 These two, along with *Karna Kunti Samvad*, were dramatizations of episodes from the *Mahabharata*.
30 While poems, short stories and essays were being published individually (chiefly in *Bharati*), no book was published this year (1898); no play either.
31 See, for instance, Prabhatkumar Mukhopadhyay, *Rabindra Jibani*, vol. 1, 420; further details are provided in Prasantakumar Pal, *Rabi Jibani*, vol. 4, 160–2.
32 To fix the date of this play reading as 12 February 1898, Prasantakumar Pal cites a prior announcement in *Amritabazar Patrika* (10 February 1898) and a report (after the event) in a periodical *Samsar* (8 *Phalgun* 1304 BS/February 1898): see *Rabi Jibani*, vol. 4, 160; but Prabhatkumar Mukhopadhyay mentions the date of

Appendix II   297

reading the play as *Agrahayan* 1304 BS/December 1897 (*Rabindra Jibani*, vol. 1, 420).
33   The source was Rajendralal Mitra (compiled), *The Sanskrit Buddhist Literature of Nepal* (1882).
34   The source was J.P. Cunningham, *The History of the Sikhs* (1849).
35   The source was James Tod, *The Annals and Antiquities of Rajasthan* (1829).
36   Most of these poems were included either in *Katha* or *Kahini*.
37   Included later in *Kahini* (1900).
38   Publication of *Katha* (on 14 January), and of *Kahini* (on 7 March); these were later published together as *Katha o Kahini*.
39   See Prasantakumar Pal, *Rabi Jibani*, vol. 4, 305–6, 319.
40   Because Rathindranath, who is the source of this information (*Pitrismriti*, Calcutta: Jijnasa, 1966, 132–33), does not provide any specific date, it is difficult to date this performance.
41   This is not to be confused with the poem *The Child* that he wrote first in English, and later rendered it into Bengali as *Sishutirtha*.
42   Information from Satyaranjan Basu, cited by Prasantakumar Pal, *Rabi Jibani*, vol. 5 (Calcutta: Ananda, 1990) 158. Pal also refers to Jagadananda Roy's memoir, which mentions a possible staging of Shakespeare's *A Midsummer Night's Dream* at Santiniketan during summer vacation of 1903 (111–2).
43   "Native Society" was the English title by which the Bengal Library Catalogue referred to the text printed on the occasion of the second reading. See Prasantakumar Pal, *Rabi Jibani*, vol. 5, 196.
44   The second reading, with important additions, was given at Curzon Theatre on 31 July, for those who could not hear him at Minerva. *The Bengalee* (on 29 July) announced from where tickets for admission could be obtained; but the very next day (30 July) hastened to add that no more tickets were available; 1,200 tickets had been exhausted within four hours. The address was also printed, and sold (2,000 copies of thirty pages each) at 2 annas each. For details, see Prasantakumar Pal, *Rabi Jibani*, vol. 5, 194–6.
45   For details, see Prasantakumar Pal, *Rabi Jibani*, vol. 5, 212–3.
46   See Prasantakumar Pal, *Rabi Jibani*, vol. 5, 259–61 for details.
47   This English title was mentioned in *The Bengalee* (cited in Prasantakumar Pal, *Rabi Jibani*, vol. 5, 220).
48   See Prasantakumar Pal, *Rabi Jibani*, vol. 5, 258–9.
49   As reported in *The Bengalee* (4 September); cited in Prasantakumar Pal, *Rabi Jibani*, vol. 5, 258–9.
50   "Deshnayak", which Rabindranath read publicly on 28 April, was printed as a booklet by the Majumdar Library on 18 May. See Prasantakumar Pal, *Rabi Jibani*, vol. 5, 304.
51   The essay "Rajbhakti" was probably prompted by the visit of the Prince of Wales (later George V) and his wife Mary, who reached Calcutta on 29 December, after touring India, and left for Rangoon on 9 Jan. This was seen as a damage-control measure by the British to alleviate Curzon's aggressive policies.
52   Rabindranath relinquishes the editorship of *Bangadarshan* (new series), after carrying out this responsibility for five years. However, he retains his connection with the periodical.
53   Rabindranath had in mind Surendranath Banerjee in mind, when he read "Deshnayak", but he would be soon disillusioned.
54   From the time of his participation in the anti-Partition protests, Rabindranath was being watched by the British administration; now this poem to Aurobindo brought even his school at Santiniketan under the vigilance of the police. See Prasantakumar Pal, *Rabi Jibani*, vol. 6 (Calcutta: Ananda, 1991) 67.

298 *Appendix II*

55 These were compilations of Rabindranath's essays published earlier in different journals.
56 The performance of 8 January was held at Sangeet Samaj, and that of 12 January at the "Theatre Hall, Exhibition Grounds" (*The Bengalee*, 11 Jan); cited in Prasantakumar Pal, *Rabi Jibani*, vol. 5, 330.
57 Rabindranath was supposed to read this essay at the aborted Barisal literary conference in 1906.
58 In 1900, Majumder Library had published 2 volumes of *Golpoguccho*, anthologizing thirty-two short stories. Now Indian Publishing House arranged to publish all his short stories in five volumes of *Golpoguccho*. Of these proposed five volumes, the first volume was published on 28 September and the second volume on 12 October, 1908.
59 Vol.8 contained *Prajapatir Nirbandha*, vol. 9 contained farces, vols. 10–14 featured essays, among which those on nation-building were the majority.
60 The advertisement for the lecture mentioned, "The paper is intended solely for young men." Rabindranath was keen to prevent the youth from choosing the path of mindless violence. This paper irked the extremists. Though their ideologue, Aurobindo Ghosh, was behind bars, his followers opposed Rabindranath's views in their mouthpiece, *Bande Mataram*. For details, see Prasantakumar Pal, *Rabi Jibani*, vol. 6, 7–8.
61 A similar celebration of the spring season had been organized by Samindranath in 1907, nine months before his untimely demise. This celebration of seasons will become a regular feature among the festivals of Santiniketan.
62 According to Kshitimohan Sen, Rabindranath himself had suggested that celebration of seasons may encourage a closer bond with the world of nature and dispel the darkness from our hearts. Unfortunately, during the 1908 celebration of the rains, he had to stay away from Santiniketan due to commitments at Shilaidah and Patisar. For details, see Prasantakumar Pal, *Rabi Jibani*, vol. 6, 23–4.
63 By this time, the same essay of Rabindranath was being published by several periodicals. So, "Path o Patheya" appeared in *Bangadarshan*, and also in *Bharati*. Again, "Sadupay" was published in *Probasi*, *Bharati* and *Bangadarshan*. See Prasantakumar Pal, *Rabi Jibani*, vol. 6, 9, 22.
64 See Prasantakumar Pal, *Rabi Jibani*, vol. 6, 25.
65 These consisted of addresses given to the inmates of the Santiniketan *asram*-school.
66 This volume was probably edited by Charuchandra Banerji and Manilal Ganguly (as mentioned in a review in *The Bengalee*). More significantly, there were seven illustrations by Nandalal Bose, who was commissioned to do this by Rabindranath himself. See Prasantakumar Pal, *Rabi Jibani*, vol. 6, 96–7.
67 Narendanath Khan played Queen Gunabati, and Sudhiranjan Das played Aparna; see Sudhiranjan Das, *Amader Santiniketan* (Calcutta: Visva-Bharati Granthalay, 1959) 81–4.
68 Prabhatkumar Mukhopadhyay, *Rabindra-barshapanji*, 45, mentions August as the month of publication.
69 This was published by Indian Publishing House; while still being serialized in *Probasi*, on 3 April 1909, a first edition of the novel (though incomplete), with forty-four chapters, was published as "An incomplete social story, reprinted from the vernacular magazine Pravasi ... Published by Purna Chandra Das". See Prasantakumar Pal, *Rabi Jibani*, vol. 6, 59–60.
70 There are two manuscripts of *Raja*. The first manuscript (Ms. 143) begins with the Dark Chamber, while Thakurda and his followers appear in the second scene. In the second manuscript (Ms. 148), the order of the scenes has been transposed, so that the Dark Chamber becomes the second scene. The first printed edition, 6 January 1911, follows the second manuscript. However, in the

Appendix II 299

revised second edition (of 12 April 1921) the original scene order is restored, so that in the version now in circulation the play opens with the Dark Chamber. By then, a shorter "more actable" version had been attempted in *Arupratan* of 1920. See Prasantakumar Pal, *Rabi Jibani*, vol. 6, 180–2. Details also discussed earlier, in Chapter 5: "Preparing the playtext".

71 Sudhiranjan Das and Narendranath Khan played Malini and the Queen respectively.
72 This is the first publication of his writing in English; written in response to the letter received from Myron H. Phelps of New York.
73 Following Prabhatkumar Mukhopadhyay, *Rabindra-barshapanji*, 45.
74 As reported in Prabhatkumar Mukhopadhyay, *Rabindra Jibani*, vol. 2 (Calcutta: Visva-Bharati Granthalaya, 1936) 296.
75 Since 1910, celebration of Christotsav on Christmas Day has become an annual ritual at the Santiniketan Mandir.
76 As was the practice then, boys played the female roles. For the first performance in March, Sudhiranjan Das played Queen Sudarshana; in the second performance (in May) the role was played by Ajitkumar Chakravarty, who had returned to Santiniketan by then.
77 Sister Nivedita had passed away on 13 October 1911.
78 Charuchandra Bandyopadhyay has claimed in a letter that *Dakghar* was written at Santiniketan in three days. See Prasantakumar Pal, *Rabi Jibani*, vol. 6, 236.
79 In 1960, the eight letters to Srishchandra Majumder were dropped and a further 107 letters to Indira Devi were added to expand the volume, now renamed as *Chinnapatrabali*. This was later translated as *Glimpses of Bengal* (1921). Interestingly, in 1913, a collection of English translations of Rabindranath's short stories by Rajani Ranjan Sen, titled *Glimpses of Bengal Life*, published from Madras and Chittagong, was also in circulation.
80 Rathindranath, who was carrying the case containing the manuscript, lost it on the tube train, but it was recovered the next day from the Lost Property office. See, Rathindranath Tagore, *Pitrismriti*, 149–50.
81 This was advertised in *The Bengalee* first as "The trend of Indian History" (9 March), and again as "The Course of Education in Indian History" (15 March). Later, Jadunath Sarkar translated this as *My Interpretation of Indian History*. What Rabindranath was, in fact, arguing in the essay is that India does not have so much of a political history as Europe but rather a cultural history. It suggested the need for a new historiographical approach.
82 The "Introduction" of Yeats was printed on pages vii–xvi; this was followed by the 103 poems covering pages 1–59; a selection was made of Bengali poems from several anthologies that had appeared earlier – *Gitanjali* (53), *Gitimalya* (15), *Naivedya* (16), *Kheya* (11), *Sishu* (3), *Chaitali* (1), *Smaran* (1), *Kalpana* (1), *Utsarga* (1), *Achalayatan* (1).
83 See Prasantakumar Pal, *Rabi Jibani*, vol. 6, 311–2.
84 Encouraged by the *TLS* and other reviews, Rothenstein and Arthur Fox Strangways begin corresponding with Macmillan about publication of Rabindranath's works in English. Interestingly, Fox Strangways's proposal to confer an honorary degree on Rabindranath was turned down by the then Chancellor of Oxford University, Lord Curzon.
85 See Prasantakumar Pal, *Rabi Jibani*, vol. 6, 324–5; Pal also points out that the date was erroneously mentioned as 20 July in "A Chronicle of Eighty Years" by Prabhatkumar Mukhopadhyay and Kshitis Ray.
86 Though initially reluctant to give public lectures, Rabindranath relents upon the requests of the local Unitarian priest, A.R. Vail.
87 The American readers become acquainted with Rabindranath's poems for the first time through these translations that appeared in *Poetry*.

Appendix II

88 See Prasantakumar Pal, *Rabi Jibani*, vol. 6, 465.
89 The Swedish Academy announced: "The Nobel Prize for literature for 1913 has been awarded to the Indian Poet Rabindra Nath Tagore"; Reuter's Services, London, broadcast the news worldwide. The official telegraphic communication, sent from London on 14 November, reached his Jorasanko address in Calcutta on 16 November, and was conveyed to him in Santiniketan. See Prasantakumar Pal, *Rabi Jibani*, vol. 6, 440–3.
90 This is what Rabindranath claims in letters written to Ajitkumar Chakravarty, Charuchandra Bandyopadhyay, Dineshchandra Sen. From these letters the date of the translation may be inferred as 4 January 1913. See Prasantakumar Pal, *Rabi Jibani*, vol. 6, 372.
91 Rudolph Christopher Eucken, who was then at Harvard University as a visiting professor, was the professor of philosophy at Jena University of Germany, and had won the Nobel in 1908. Though Rabindranath had initially declined the offer to lecture at Rochester, he changed his mind as he was eager to meet Eucken. See details in Prasantakumar Pal, *Rabi Jibani*, vol. 6, 363–4.
92 Three of his lectures at Harvard University were on "The Problem of Evil", "The Relation of the Universe and the Individual" and "Realisation of Brahma"; information about the fourth lecture is unavailable. See Prasantakumar Pal, *Rabi Jibani*, vol. 6, 367–8.
93 This included translations from *Kshanika* (25), *Kori o Komol* (4), *Mayar Khela* (3), *Manasi* (3), *Sonar Tari* (9), *Chitra* (6), *Chaitali* (7), *Kalpana* (14), *Utsarga* (6), *Kheya* (4), *Gitanjali* (1) and *Gaan* (50). As expressed in a letter to Jagananda Roy (2 October 1912?), Rabindranath was probably trying to give the Western readers a taste of the variety of moods in his poems, and not remain dubbed only a mystic. See details in Prasantakumar Pal, *Rabi Jibani*, vol. 6, 371–2.
94 The playlet was published in *Rabindra-biksha*, no. 3, 1981, 1–16.
95 Following Prasantakumar Pal, *Rabi Jibani*, vol. 6, 329. In fact, these overseas productions of the English *Post Office* preceded the performance of the original Bengali play, *Dakghar*.
96 Translations of poems, chiefly from *Sishu*, with illustrations by Abanindranath Tagore, Nandalal Bose, Asitkumar Haldar, and others.
97 According to Kalipada Roy, this was the first time *Valmiki Pratibha* was staged in Santiniketan. See Prasantakumar Pal, *Rabi Jibani, Rabi Jibani*, vol. 6, 433–4, 488–9.
98 The Nobel award included a gold medallion, a diploma and a prize money of Kronor 143,010=89; the Chartered Bank cheque was for Rs. 1,16,269/-.
99 The translated text (*The King of the Dark Chamber*) did not have Rabindranath's approval, but went into print bearing his name. The revisions he had been trying to make were ignored, and the version (actually done by Kshitischandra Sen) remained unchanged. This has been discussed earlier in Chapter 11: "Translating the Playtext". See also Shyamalkumar Sarkar, "*The King of the Dark Chamber*: Text and Publication", *Collected Papers on Rabindranath Tagore* (Kolkata: Dey's, 2013) 141–54; Ananda Lal, *Rabindranath Tagore: Three Plays*, 99–100; Prasantakumar Pal, *Rabi Jibani*, vol. 7 (Calcutta: Ananda, 1997) 21–3.
100 Both addresses were later included in *Santiniketan*, vol.16; see Prasantakumar Pal, *Rabi Jibani*, vol. 6, 462–3.
101 See Prasantakumar Pal, *Rabi Jibani*, vol. 7, 3.
102 *Alpona* is a traditional decorative design painted on the floor on auspicious occasions. See details in Prasantakumar Pal, *Rabi Jibani*, vol. 7, 5.
103 Sita Devi reports that among the teachers who acted with the boys were Kshitimohan Sen, Santosh Majumder Jagananda Roy and Dinendranath Tagore. Even Pearson was among the cast and danced to his heart's content on the stage: see *Punya Smriti* (Calcutta: Probasi, 1942) 71–2. For other details, see Rudraprasad

Chakrabarty, *Rangamancha o Rabindranath: Samakalin Pratikriya* (Calcutta: Ananda Publishers, 1995) 116–18.

104 The stage décor seems to have "owed a good deal to English influences" (*The Statesman*, 9 December, 1914); as cited in Rudraprasad Chakrabarty, *Rangamancha o Rabindranath: Samakalin Pratikriya*, 34–5.

105 This was written at the request of Israel Gollancz, and an English translation was sent to England; it appeared in *A Book of Homage to Shakespeare*, ed. Israel Gollancz and Gordon McMullan (Oxford: Oxford University Press, 1916) 320–1.

106 Rabindranath received Gandhi when he arrived at Santiniketan on 6 March but had to leave for Calcutta on 7 March due to prior commitments. He returned on 11 March and met Gandhi at the station as the latter was leaving that very day. For details, see Prasantakumar Pal, *Rabi Jibani*, vol. 7, 68–9.

107 10 March is still observed in Visva-Bharati, Santiniketan, as *Gandhi Punyaha* [Gandhi's auspicious day]. See Prasantakumar Pal, *Rabi Jibani*, vol. 7, 69;

108 A dais was erected for this occasion and was, for long, referred to as the 'Carmichael bedi [dais]'. For details, see Prasantakumar Pal, *Rabi Jibani*, vol. 7, 71–2.

109 The Viceroy had already informed the Poet of this in May, and a formal announcement had been made on 3 June See Prasantakumar Pal, *Rabi Jibani*, vol. 7, 101.

110 Most of these performances, particularly the dramatized versions of the short stories, were staged without proper permission of the author, and were subsequently stopped for copyright reasons. See Prasantakumar Pal, *Rabi Jibani*, vol. 7, 79–80.

111 Since this would be a charity show, it was felt that the original *Phalguni* was too short in length for a respectable duration of performance. Initially there were plans of doing the farce *Bashikaran* along with *Phalguni*; but the two were not compatible together. Ultimately, the addition of the introductory scene ("Bairagya sadhan") was a happy solution. In a letter to Gaganendranath, Rabindranath even advised the printing of a programme note, which would include a summary of the play and the quatrains of Dada (as he felt the audience could miss the impact of these on hearing these for the first time). As cited in Prasantakumar Pal, *Rabi Jibani*, vol. 7, 136.

112 The term "Chaturanga" also denotes the four components on of an army (on land): infantry, cavalry, charioteers and elephant-riding soldiers. It also indicates, therefore, the game of chess.

113 *Stray Birds* are chiefly translations of poems of *Kanika*. These were brief epigrammatic poems.

114 Thompson was reportedly unhappy with the way his contribution to the translations seemed to have been given the short shrift. For details, see Prasantakumar Pal, *Rabi Jibani*, vol. 7, 119–22

115 As reported by Kalidas Roy; cited in Prasantakumar Pal, *Rabi Jibani*, vol. 7, 166. Was this *Brahmacharyasram's* homage to Shakespeare on his tercentennial death anniversary?

116 The rejection by the Japanese people of his views of nationalism prompted the writing of this poem, while still in Japan. It was first published in *Modern Review* (October 1916), and later included in *Fruit Gathering* (also 1916).

117 Pearson, who was carrying a typewriter for the journey, types out copies of the translations. The typed copy of *Sacrifice* found at Rabindra Bhavana has revisions by Andrews. Prasantakumar Pal assumes the copy typed by Pearson was later revised by Andrews. Also, though Rabindranath had made an earlier translation of *Malini* (read by Rothenstein and Trevelyan), he was probably dissatisfied and now made a fresh translation See Prasantakumar Pal, *Rabi Jibani*, vol. 7, 175–8. The significant changes made in the translated texts have been discussed earlier, in Chapter 11: "Translating the playtext".

118 Scholars have put forward the possibility that inspired by Haiku, the Poet took to writing short poems of two or four lines, as may be found in the Bengali poems of *Lekhan* or the English poems of *Stray Birds* and *Fireflies*. They may have particularly served him well to sign autographs. But Prabhatkumar Mukhopadhyay would ascribe the origin of the poems of *Kanika*/*Stray Birds* to the epigrammatic, *sloka*-like short verse already available in the Indian tradition. He distinguishes this from the poems of *Lekhan*/*Fireflies* which he believes had a more Chinese/Japanese antecedent. See Prabhatkumar Mukhopadhyay, *Rabindra Jibani*, vol. 3 (Calcutta: Visva-Bharati Granthalaya, 1952; rpt. 1961) 262, n. 3. See also n. 189 below.

119 It was difficult for the Japanese intelligentsia to stomach Rabindranath's pacifist rebuke of their militant nationalism, more so in times of war; after the initial wave of enthusiasm died down, he was seen as one hailing from a nation in bondage, "a man whose country has lost its independence" (in *Japan Weekly Chronicle*, 17 Aug 1916).

120 Revised versions of the addresses "India's Message to Japan" and "The Spirit of Japan" later appeared as "Nationalism in Japan I & II" in *Nationalism* (1917).

121 Dubbing him "Shakespeare of India", Ponds Lyceum promoted Rabindranath's lectures as a means to fund his school in Santiniketan. When Rabindranath decided to truncate the tour, he was not required to compensate Pond Lyceum as he had already given forty lectures (as per his contract with them); but had the tour continued till April 1917, the financial prospects would have been more lucrative, both for him and Mr. Pond.

122 George Brett was in touch with Rabindranath about the tour, had recommended the name of James Pond (of Pond Lyceum) to arrange for the lecture itinerary, and had even promised to send their local agent "in order to aid you in any way in his power at your landing and also in the details attending your journey to the East" (letter dated 8 October 1916). In their correspondences, they also discussed the possible dates of publication of his forthcoming works and the terms of payment of royalty. Ultimately, when Rabindranath was again in New York, Brett met him in person on 19 November. For details, see Prasantakumar Pal, *Rabi Jibani*, vol. 7, 189, 201, 209–10, 228.

123 "The Cult of Nationalism" was later revised as "Nationalism in the West" and included in *Nationalism* (1917). It contained the major thrust of his message for the Western world, America included: "In this war the death-throes of the Nation have commenced. Suddenly, all its mechanism going mad, it has begun the dance of the Furies, shattering its own limbs, scattering them into the dust. It is the fifth act of the tragedy of the unreal."

124 This was reported in New York *Herald* (4 October 1916). Many saw in this a "political motive" (New York *Sun*, 5 October 1916). Others disputed Germany's claim as this being the first performance of *Chitra*: "The play was acted in Boston by some ardent uplifters of the theatre as long as February 8, 1915, and London saw it played in February of this year" (Chicago *Journal*, 7 October 1916). For details, see Prasantakumar Pal, *Rabi Jibani*, vol. 7, 213.

125 It had been reported in *New York City Times*, (2 November 1916): "Final arrangements for the performance, and the acceptance of the author were completed yesterday...", but nothing seems to have come of it. See Prasantakumar Pal, *Rabi Jibani*, vol.7, 213–14.

126 Mentioned in Prasantakumar Pal, *Rabi Jibani*, vol. 7, 214.

127 New York City *Herald* (2 December 1916) reported that Tagore "has decided to shorten his stay, and will leave San Francisco, Cal., on January 20 for his home" (as cited in Prasantakumar Pal, *Rabi Jibani*, vol. 7, 235). In a letter to Rothenstein the Poet wrote before leaving America: "At last I am going home ... Last three months my world of space and time was completely dislocated – my

Appendix II 303

universe was shattered into bits dancing in a whirlpool" (as quoted in Mary Lago, *Imperfect Encounter*, 233–4).
128 Upon the request of Ellery Sedgwick, the editor of *Atlantic Monthly*.
129 The translation was by C.F. Andrews and Nishikanta Sen. The Poet is believed to have provided his inputs to the translation.
130 On the machine it was inscribed, "THE LINCOLN PRESS/PRESENTED TO THE BOYS OF SHANTINIKETAN/BY THE PEOPLE OF/LINCOLN NEBRASKA, U.S.A/JANUARY 8, 1917". Later this press helped to begin the Santiniketan Press at Santiniketan, which was used to publish several titles of Rabindranath and other authors, as well as books for Brahmacharyasram and Visva-Bharati.
131 The name 'Nepal Road' was chosen for this new path as Nepalchandra Roy, a teacher, took the initiative of laying out this new path with the help of the students.
132 Rabindranath initially wanted to dedicate *Nationalism* to President Wilson of USA, whom he had admired for his anti-war stance. When Macmillan sought the President's consent, he regretfully declined, presumably upon the advice of the British administration: "it seems unwise for me to comply with it, not because of any lack of sympathy on my part for the principles which he so eloquently supports in his book, but because *just now I have to take all sorts of international considerations into my thought* and must err at all on the side of tact and prudence" (as cited in Prasantakumar Pal, *Rabi Jibani*, vol. 7, 243–4; emphases added). Interestingly, though the American edition of *Nationalism* is dedicated to CF Andrews, the British edition has no dedication.
133 Jadunath Sarkar was nominated as the General Editor and Rabindranath the Chief Advisor for this series. The editors for siz sections were also selected – (1) Philosophy: Brajendranath Seal, Narendranath Sengupta; (2) Science: Ramendrasundar Trivedi, Prasantachandra Mahalanobis; (3) History, Geography & Economics: Jadunath Sarkar; (4) Literature, Literary History and Language: Pramatha Chowdhury; (5) Arts: Ardhendukumar Ganguly, Surendranath Tagore; (6) Education: Rabindranath Tagore. See Prasantakumar Pal, *Rabi Jibani*, vol. 7, 268–9.
134 Ashamukul Das, who acted the role of Amal in this performance, was recruited later to play the same role when Rabindranath himself produced the play later in the year. The Poet had not witnessed this performance. See Prasantakumar Pal, *Rabi Jibani, Rabi Jibani*, vol. 7, 263.
135 This essay seems to have been read in support of Anne Besant and Tilak's agenda of Home Rule. Such public support in face of the Defence of India Act was a bold step. Not only did it irk the British, but even the Indian intelligentsia betrayed conflicting views. While leaders like Bipinchandra Pal, despite acceptance of Rabindranath's political position, disagreed with his views about the social conditions, others came out in support of the essay. For details, see Prasantakumar Pal, *Rabi Jibani*, vol. 7, 275–7.
136 As noted earlier, Ashamukul Das had played earlier for the 3 May performance at Mary Carpenter Hall. As he was left an orphan after the death of his mother, he was later admitted to the school in Santiniketan; reported in Prasantakumar Pal, *Rabi Jibani*, vol. 7, 290.
137 For details, see Prasantakumar Pal, *Rabi Jibani*, vol. 7, 291.
138 Following Prasantakumar Pal, *Rabi Jibani*, vol. 7, 296.
139 According to Prasantakumar Pal, the date of the performance is mentioned in the diary of Kalidas Nag; see *Rabi Jibani*, vol. 7, 305.
140 "India's Prayer" comprised two poems – one, originally in English ("Thou has given us to live"); the other ("Our voyage is begun, Captain, we bow to Thee") a translation of a song.

141 The translation was renamed as *The Home and the World*.
142 For this performance, Rabindranath played Thakurda, Prahari and Bhikshuk (Beggar), with Dinendranth, Soumendranath and Nagendranath Ganguly as the 'Beggar's Companions' (from the cast list, as cited in Prasantakumar Pal, *Rabi Jibani*, vol.7, 306). With Dinendranath leading the companions of the Beggar, it may be assumed that the songs were sung in chorus.
143 These were later included in *Fugitive* (1921).
144 *Tota kahini* aimed to satirize the educational reforms being attempted by the Government through the Calcutta University Commission. To make this satire available to a wider readership, this short story was translated as *The Parrot's Training* by Rabindranath himself. The translation was published as a book in May by Thacker, Spink & Co of Calcutta. It carried eight drawings by Abanindranath, and the cover design by Nandalal Bose, and was dedicated to Patrick Geddes.
145 Sita Devi, *Punya smriti*, 193.
146 See Prasantakumar Pal, *Rabi Jibani*, vol. 7, 372–3.
147 This was later included in *Lipika*. *Heaven and Earth* was the name given to the translations made by diverse hands – Bhabani Bhattacharya (in 1932); Indu Dutta (in 1969); Aurobindo Bose (in 1978): see Ananda Lal, *Rabindranath Tagore: Three Plays*, 499.
148 Tickets were sold for this lecture to raise funds for Visva-Bharati.
149 Mentioned by Prasantakumar Pal, *Rabi Jibani*, vol. 7, 483. This fun event still continues in Santiniketan, though now it is observed on Mahalya day, seven days before the start of Durga Puja; usually the Puja vacation begins immediately after the "Anandabazar"
150 His gesture seemed to be the lone action of protest at that point of time, when all the other politicians avoided making definite public statements. For this he was both lauded and vilified, in India and abroad. While the Viceroy's office bristled at the "insolence", Bipinchandra Pal took shelter behind "common prudence" and even Gandhi thought Rabindranath's "burning letter" was "premature". For details, see Prasantakumar Pal, *Rabi Jibani*, vol. 7, 419–23.
151 Along with Rolland, those who were in support of this Declaration de l'espirit included Henri Barbusse, Paul Signac, Frederick van Eeden, Stephen Zweig, Bertrand Russell, Upton Sinclair, Benedetto Croce, Hermann Hesse, Albert Einstein and others. Mentioned in Prasantakumar Pal, *Rabi Jibani*, vol. 7, 426.
152 Records of accounts suggest that for this performance Nanadalal Bose hired theatrical costumes from Bolpur. Subsequently, Nandalal would take on the charge of designing costumes for the Santiniketan productions. See Prasantakumar Pal, *Rabi Jibani*, vol. 7, 490.
153 At Rabindranath's request, the King of Tripura sent a few Manipuri artistes to go Santiniketan to teach this dance form; among them was Buddhimanta Singh. Eventually, Manipuri became one of the primary dance forms practised at Santiniketan, and widely used in his dance dramas.
154 Contrasted to the enthusiastic welcome with which Rabindranath was greeted on his last visit, a lukewarm reception awaited him this time – even from old friends like Rothenstein or Yeats. One of the reasons could have been his rejection of the knighthood, an honour conferred by the British Empire, the rejection of which did not go down well with the English.
155 Several local stars were inducted for these performances. But Kedarnath Dasgupta, who had come with the Poet to launch the plays professionally, had no experience of the American professional theatre circuit and so suffered badly from inadequate publicity and financial losses. See Prasantakumar Pal, *Rabi Jibani*, vol. 8 (Calcutta: Ananda, 2000), 51–2.

156 Helen Keller had read *Gitanjali* and *Gardener*. On meeting the Poet, she touched his lips and throat to appreciate his readings of his poems. She gifted him a copy of her *The World I Live In*, writing on the title page some lines from *The Gardener*: "To Rabindranath Tagore/Yes, Master, I Forget,/I ever Forget, that the/ Gates are shut every/where in the house/where I dwell alone!/Helen Keller"; the copy is in possession of the Rabindra-Bhavana holdings.

157 The translated text had not yet been published. The players were Henry Oscar and Hazel Jones. The Poet was presumably present on the occasion.

158 Since at the time of the award of the Nobel prize (1913), Rabindranath could not be present the British official in Stockholm had accepted it on his behalf; later it was handed over to him in Calcutta by Lord Carmichael. Now, on visiting Stockholm, he gets the chance to make his acceptance speech in person. Interestingly, that he was going to give a lecture at the Swedish Academy had given rise to "the rumour in this country that he was going to be awarded the Nobel Peace prize also this year" (reported in New India, 11 August 1921; cited in Prasantakumar Pal, *Rabi Jibani*, vol. 8, 111).

159 The Bengal Library catalogue mentioned this as: "The co-ordination of culture. A plea for devising a system of education co-ordinating all that is good in Eastern and western culture"; cited in Prasantakumar Pal, *Rabi Jibani*, vol. 8, 133. Though the original Bengali title referred to *Siksha* (Learning or Education), Rabindranath's concern was for a confluence of cultures achieved through a meaningful exchange of knowledge. This was also the underlying principle of his university, and he had serious misgivings because of the boycott policies.

160 A speech ("The Message of the Forest") and a song were recorded. The recording was done by Dr. Dogen, director of the recording unit of Prussian Academy, Berlin. See Prasantakumar Pal, *Rabi Jibani*, vol. 8, 116.

161 Saratchandra Chattopadhyay opposed Rabindranath's arguments in his "Sikshar Birodh". This is an instance of how the Poet's discourses were being misunderstood and he was being continuously castigated by his fellow countrymen.

162 *The Indian Daily News* (18 August 1921) announced that the lecture would be on "The Problem of Education" (different from the University Institute lecture); but Sita Devi noted that he did not read any prepared speech but spoke impromptu. Interestingly, the Chairman, Prafullachandra Ray, remarked that India may discard everything European but not the Sciences and Literatures of Europe, for that would damage her own interests. See Prasantakumar Pal, *Rabi Jibani*, vol. 8, 134.

163 In this address Rabindranath was more directly critical of Gandhi's political agenda of non-cooperation. Though slogans were raised from certain quarters in the name of Gandhi during his speech, he continued unfazed and completed his address. See Sita Devi, *Punya Smriti*, 228.

164 The stage was erected in the open space behind Vichitra; Nandalal Bose was in charge of the stage décor. As Prabhatkumar Mukhopadhyay reminds us, this *Varsha-mangal* was a musical recital comprising songs and recitations; dances were yet to be accepted as entertainment fit for the 'refined' tastes of the *bhadralok* (polite) classes (*Rabindra Jibani*, vol. 2, 217). Santidev Ghosh mentions that this was the first programme in which boys and girls participated together (*Rabindrasangeet*, Calcutta: Visva-Bharati Granthalay, rev. edn., 1958, 229). But according to Prabhatkumar Mukhopadhyay, the first event in which boys and girls of Santiniketan performed before the Calcutta audience was the 1922- *Varsha-mangal* at Vichitra (*Rabindra Jibani*, vol. 3, 125–6); see also n. 158 above. But the first performance by students of the school in Calcutta was in the fundraising show (for Bankura famine relief) of *Phalguni* in 1916, in which girls had not played any role; see Prabhatkumar Mukhopadhyay, *Rabindra Jibani*, vol. 2, 534–5.

Appendix II

165 Rabindranath, though supportive of the spiritual strength of Non-Cooperation, disagreed with Gandhi's modes of practical politics – his siding with the narrow-minded Khilafat movement to achieve Hindu-Muslim unity; his boycott policies, including boycott of education by students in the schools; or even his proposition that *swaraj* could be gained by spinning the charkha for six months. "Poems I can spin, Gandhiji, songs and plays I can spin, but of your precious cotton what a mess I would make!" was the Poet's rejoinder to Gandhi's urge to spin the *charkha*. There were wide rifts between supporters and opponents of Gandhi's policies – in India, in Calcutta, even in Santiniketan – and members of each group were trying to enlist Rabindranath's support on their side, much to the Poet's vexation. Even Gandhi met him personally (in Calcutta) in August and September 1921, but Rabindranath remained unconvinced about Gandhi's *modus operandi*. In fact, though their meeting of 6 September was kept away from public gaze, Elmhirst learnt about it later from the Poet himself and noted it down. Krishna Kripalani, in recounting Elmhirst's version, reports: "Tagore said, 'Come and look over the edge of my verandah, Gandhiji. Look down there and see what your non-violent followers are up to. They have stolen cloth from the shops in the Chirpore Road, they've lit that bonfire in my courtyard and are now howling round it like a lot of demented dervishes. Is that non-violence?'" (*Tagore: A Life*. New Delhi: National Book Trust, India, 1986; originally 1961, 169); also see Prasantakumar Pal, *Rabi Jibani*, vol. 8, 135, 143–4.

166 On this occasion, Rabindranath declared: "Today is the first session of the Visva-Bharati Parisad. The work of this institution, Visva-Bharati, has been going on for some time. Today we shall hand her over to the people. The friends of Visva-Bharati, in India and abroad, who share its ideals and will not hesitate to receive her, to them we offer her today... Though Visva-Bharati is a product of India, she will have to emerge as a seat of learning (*tapasya*) for all humanity" (as cited in Prasantakumar Pal, *Rabi Jibani*, vol. 8, 164–5; translated).

167 The compositions of *Lipika* (initially called *Kathika*) date back to at least 1920, and individual poems were also published in different periodicals (*Bharati, Probasi, Sabuj Patra, Bangabani*, etc.). But Bengal Library Catalogue mentions the date of publication by Indian Press Limited as 17 August 1922. See Prasantakumar Pal, *Rabi Jibani*, vol. 8, 32, 156, 180, 209, 224.

168 Following Prabhatkumar Mukhopadhyay, *Rabindra Jibani*, vol. 3, 116, and Prasantakumar Pal, *Rabi Jibani*, vol. 8, 208–9, 214.

169 See Prasantakumar Pal, *Rabi Jibani*, vol. 8, 276. In fact, no records seem to exist to show that this play was ever acted in Santiniketan within the Poet's lifetime.

170 But Bholanath is also an epithet of Siva, a god famous for his carefree ways.

171 Prasantakumar Pal mentions both occasions (see *Rabi Jibani*, vol. 8, 173, 195, 218, 282); Prabhatkumar Mukhopadhyay refers to the second occasion only: see *Rabindra Jibani*, vol. 3, 125. Both state that the second occasion in Calcutta was organized by the Visva-Bharati Sammilani/Society, though Mukhopadhyay does not mention the venue (Rammohan Library Hall).

172 This was printed in a 36-page booklet, titled "VISVA-BHARATI/ (THE SANTI-NIKETAN UNIVERSITY)/ MEMORANDUM OF ASSOCIATION/ STATUTES & REGULATIONS". The solicitor, Hirendranath Dutta, took care of the legal details.

173 Following Gourchandra Saha, *Rabindrajibanprabaha*, 129.

174 Mentioned in Prasantakumar Pal, *Rabi Jibani*, vol. 8, 220. See also Prabhatkumar Mukhopadhyay, *Rabindra Jibani*, vol. 3, 125–6.

175 Following Prasantakumar Pal, *Rabi Jibani*, vol. 8, 221–2. The event consisted of songs and music; dances were yet to be made a part of performances. See also Prabhatkumar Mukhopadhyay, *Rabindra Jibani*, vol. 3, 126.

176 Though Prabhatkumar Mukhopadhyay holds that what was performed in Calcutta was not the reworked *Rinsodh* but the earlier version of *Sarodotsav*, yet Prasantakumar Pal argues that it was the revised *Rinsodh* which was performed on this occasion, though advertised as *Sarodotsav* (in *Anandabazar Patrika*, 9 September 1922). Also Prabhatkumar Mukhopadhyay mentions 17 and 18 September as the dates of performance; but from contemporary accounts and press reports it appears the play was given on 16 and 18 September. For details, see Prabhatkumar Mukhopadhyay, *Rabindra Jibani*, vol. 3, 127–8; Prasantakumar Pal, *Rabi Jibani*, vol. 8, 226–30; and Rudraprasad Chakrabarty, *Rangamancha o Rabindranath: Samakalin Pratikriya*, 89. Also, as happened during the *Varshamangal* performance, objections were again raised about students, especially girls, performing on the public stage. Rabindranth responded to the letters of Lalitmohan Das, a Brahmo leader, and Krishnakumar Moitra, editor of *Sanjeevani*, but decided to go ahead with the performances. See Prasantakumar Pal, *Rabi Jibani*, vol. 8, 226–7. Again, since Dinendranath's father suddenly fell critically ill, he had to drop out of the production, and was replaced by Abanindranath in the role of Thakurda (Gaffer). Pramathanath Bishi, who was given the task of the prompter, mentions how Abanindranath, who had not been able to memorize his lines, depended heavily on the prompter's cue (*Rabindranath O Santiniketan*. Calcutta: Visva-Bharati, 1959; rpt. 1975, 76). The stage décor was by Nandalal Bose and Surendranath Kar.

177 Following Prasantakumar Pal, *Rabi Jibani*, vol. 8, 282, and Rudraprasad Chakrabarty, *Rangamancha o Rabindranath: Samakalin Pratikriya*, 89; but Gourchandra Saha mentions the date as 19 September (*Rabindrajibanprabaha*, 130). See also n. 176 above.

178 The *Visva-Bharati Quarterly* will be referred to as *VBQ* in subsequent entries.

179 *Vasanta*, dedicated to the poet Nazrul Islam, happened to be the first book published by Visva-Bharati, after the contract with Indian Press, Allahabad, was terminated. As in the revised *Phalguni* or *Rinsodh* (the revised *Sarodotsav*), in *Vasanta*, too, he started with a King and his court, more as an excuse to present a string of songs, than to create a well-knit dramatic narrative. Some dance-like movements may have accompanied the songs, but it was not dance proper. See Prabhatkumar Mukhopadhyay, *Rabindra Jibani*, vol. 3, 135–6; Prasantakumar Pal, *Rabi Jibani*, vol. 8, 252–3, 255–7.

180 This was a documentary film of the work being done at Sriniketan; it was shot to help Elmhirst to show actual documentation of the work during his visits to China and America in March 1923. When there was a preview in Calcutta, the Poet was present among the viewers. The title-card read: "The Taj-Mahal Film Company produce 'Sriniketan'/ Under the direction of Gretchen Green/ Photographed by N. Senyal Gupta"; as given in Gretchen Green, *The Whole World and Company* (New York: Reynal and Hitchcock, 1936) 151–6.

181 See Gretchen Green, 156. It may be noted that now the highest honorary degree awarded by Visva-Bharati is *Desikottama*, the Supreme *Desika*.

182 Rabindranath went to Shillong on 26 April, with a large group, including Rathindranath, Pratima, grand-daughter Nandini /Poupee (adopted daughter of Rathindranath and Pratima), another grand-daughter Nandita (daughter of Mira), Ranu Adhikari, and Gretchen Green.

183 This is the assumption of many scholars; see, for instance Prasantakumar Pal, *Rabi Jibani*, vol. 9 (Calcutta: Ananda, 2003) 8.

184 Following Gourchandra Saha, *Rabindrajibanprabaha*, 136.

185 He once wrote to Ramananda Chattopadhyay: "I do not wish to have it published before its performance"; see letter to Ramananda Chattopadhyay, dated 5 September 1923, in *Chithipatra*, no. 12 (Calcutta: Visva-Bharati Granthan Vibhaga, 1986) 86.

308   *Appendix II*

186 Rabindranath acknowledges in the footnotes that he had been inspired to write this play by a composition of Pramanath Bishi, who had, in fact, written a play by the same name and read it before the school inmates on 26 July 1923, when Rabindranath was in Calcutta. The Poet read the work later and was moved to write his own play (also named *Rathajatra*). This is the earliest version of what later emerged as *Kaler Jatra* (1932). For details, see Prasantakumar Pal, *Rabi Jibani*, vol. 9, 33–34; also Pramathanath Bishi, *Purano sei diner katha* (Calcutta: Mitra & Ghosh, 1958) 178–9.

187 Initially announced for 31 July, 1 Aug and 3 Aug, the performance had to be rescheduled as Rabindranath was taken ill with dengue. Even on the later occasion, Ranu was unavailable on the first day (25 August) as she was down with fever, and was replaced by Manjushree Tagore. Sahana Devi had temperature on the second day (27 August) but decided to perform nevertheless. Not only was the quality of acting much applauded, but with the stage décor and costumes designed by Gaganendranah, Abanindranath, Nandalal and Suren Kar, this staging emerged as a very different presentation (from the 1890 or other subsequent productions of the play till then). Details provided in Prasantakumar Pal, *Rabi Jibani*, vol. 9, 17–18.

188 Pearson died in Italy on 25 September 1923, after accidentally falling off a train on 18 September; the news reached Santiniketan on 30 September.

189 The resolution adopted was: "Visva-Bharati undertakes the management of the Santiniketan Trust so far as possible in accordance with the spirit of the original Santiniketan Trust Deed.". The meeting was chaired by Surendranath Tagore. See Prasantakumar Pal, *Rabi Jibani*, vol. 9, 85.

190 Prasantakumar Pal has cited a letter of Rathindranath that indicates there were certain printing errors in the *Probasi* text of *Raktakarabi*, which left Rabindranath unhappy; he wanted those errors rectified in keeping with pages 21 and 22 of the English text of *Red Oleanders*; see Prasantakumar Pal, *Rabi Jibani*, vol. 9, 155.

191 *Vasantotsav* being observed on the day of Sri Panchami, Nandalal Bose and Suren Kar decorated the site with two replicas of the *veena* to suit the occasion, not so much as religious emblem but more as aesthetic motif. Was this an attempt to overlay the religious overtones of Sri Panchami with the more secular celebration of *Vasantotsav*?

192 Though the final version of this play (in Bengali), *Kaler Jatra*, would appear in 1932, that the translation already bears the name *The Car of Time* anticipates the direction in which the play would move.

193 Nandalal Bose helped with the costumes and make-up. The young amateur actors belonged to the Crescent Moon Society and spoke in impeccable English. See Prasantakumar Pal, *Rabi Jibani*, vol. 9, 108.

194 The text of *Red Oleanders* that appeared in *VBQ* had illustrations by Gaganendranath, and it was dedicated to Elmhirst. When this English translation appeared in a book form, published by Macmillan the next year, the dedication was missing.

195 The name was given to honour the poet Hsu Tsemon who was his interpreter throughout the China trip.

196 "Vijaya" was Victoria Ocampo. He wrote most of the poems of *Purabi* during his sojourn at Buenos Aires, where Victoria Ocampo was his hostess. He sent her a copy of the Bengali original with a caveat: "I have dedicated it to you though you will never be able to know what it contains" (Ketaki Kushari Dyson, *In Your Blossoming Flower-Garden: Rabindranath Tagore and Victoria Ocampo*, 373; as cited in Prasantakumar Pal, *Rabi Jibani*, vol. 9, 242). Ketaki Kushari also reports that the copy she found among the Ocampo collections contained the second edition, with the inscription "To/ Vijaya/ with love/ Rabindranath/

July 30/ 1940. Only after Khitishchandra Ray brought out an English translation in 1960 was Ocampo able to read the poems in English. See Prasantakumar Pal, *Rabi Jibani*, vol. 9, 242 for details.

197 An earlier edition was printed in September 1924. But the Poet was unhappy with certain lapses in print; so that early edition was supressed and a revised edition was issued around January 1925. See Prasantakumar Pal, *Rabi Jibani*, vol. 9, 242.

198 See Prasantakumar Pal, *Rabi Jibani*, vol. 9, 193. Santidev Ghosh, however, reminds us that *Sundar* of 1925 and *Sundar* of 1929 were not quite the same text, there were major differences between the two: see Santidev Ghosh, *Rabindrasangeet* (Calcutta: Visva-Bharati Granthalay, rev. edn. 1958; originally 1942) 253.

199 As *Chayanika* had been a collection of his select poems, *Sankalan* was a collection of his select non-fictional prose writings that included thirty essays ("Sikshar Bahan", "Sikshar Milan", etc.) and sections from *Jivansmriti, Chinnapatra, Europe-jatri, Japan-jatri* and *Paschim-jatrir Diary*. In fact, this was the first time that *Paschim-jatrir Diary* appeared in print. *Paschim-jatrir Diary* would again be included in *Jatri* of 1929. See also Prasantakumar Pal, *Rabi Jibani*, vol. 9, 242.

200 Amita Tagore (daughter of Ajitkumar Chakravarty, who married into the Tagore family) played Khiro in *Lakshmir Pariksha*. She mentions the occasion as the Poet's birth celebrations, which Prasantakumar Pal considers an inadvertent error, as the shifting of the Poet's birth celebrations to the *Navavarsha* day (14 April) happened later. See Prasantakumar Pal, *Rabi Jibani, Rabi Jibani*, vol. 9, 311.

201 Nothing happened immediately and it was decided that, for the time being, the original manuscripts of Rabindranath will be followed in print. A body for standardization of spellings will come into effect as late as in 1935–36. See Prasantakumar Pal, *Rabi Jibani*, vol. 9, 243.

202 According to Sisirkumar Bhaduri, Rabindranath had initially given the play to him for staging, but, being busy with other plays, he kept it for future performance. In the meanwhile, the Art Theatre Limited convinced Rabindranath that Sisirkumar was not interested in doing the play, and thereby obtained the rights of production. Opening on 18 July 1925, the play went down well with the audiences in the commercial theatre. See details in Prasantakumar Pal, *Rabi Jibani*, vol. 9, 194–5, 237–8.

203 The Poet had verbally analysed *Raktakarabi/Red Oleanders* for Victoria Ocampo when in Argentina. Elmhirst, who was present as his Secretary and travel companion, made a transcript of this analysis, which now appeared *Visva-Bharati Quarterly*.

204 Santidev Ghosh describes how this musical drama used opera-like blend of simultaneous on-stage singing and acting ("*geetabhinay*"), with mute miming ("*mukabhinay*") and rhythmic movements of the body. See Santidev Ghosh, *Rabindrasangeet*, 238.

205 In these essays, Rabindranath continued articulating his ideological differences with Gandhi, and to ensure a wider circulation made them available in both Bengali and English versions; they might have been prompted by Gandhi's recent visit to Santiniketan (29 May to 2 June 1925), when Gandhi once again failed to make the Poet agree to his views.

206 Rabindranath had initially promised to give the dramatized version of the 1903 short story "Karmaphal" to *Probasi*, and this was announced in the earlier issue of the journal. However, when both *Grihapravesh* (dramatization of "Sesher Ratri) and *Sodhbodh* (dramatization of "Karmaphal") were simultaneously available, *Probasi* chose the former for its Aswin/October issue. Then

310   Appendix II

Rabindranath gave *Sodhbodh* to *Basumati* for its Annual Number. See details in Prasantakumar Pal, *Rabi Jibani*, vol. 9, 254–5.

207 On seeing the performance of *Grihapravesh*, Rabindranath was, on the whole, pleased but thought some revisions were needed. He made the changes in the original, reduced the number of songs and even introduced a couple of new characters (including that of a young girl). He was supposed to go and see the revised text in performance on 9 January 1926, but no records are available to confirm whether he actually went on that day. See Prasantakumar Pal, *Rabi Jibani*, vol. 9, 264.

208 The Preface to *Lekhan* has a Bengali and an English version; in the English preface (dated November 7. 1926) he writes: "The lines in the following pages had their origin in China and Japan where the author was asked for his writings on fans or pieces of silk". The Preface mentions the place as Balatonfured, Hungary.

209 "The Meaning of Art" and "The Rule of the Giant" were both given at the Curzon Hall of Dacca University, on 10 February and 13 February (1926) respectively; the former, was published in the *Dacca University Bulletin XII* and also in *VBQ*; the latter in VBQ. "Eker Sadhana", later published in *Bharati*, was an address at Kumilla Abhayasram, which made an interesting reference to the difference between the European theatre and the indigenous jatra. See Prasantakumar Pal, *Rabi Jibani*, vol. 9, 281–9.

210 When he found that preparations were being made to present his poem "Pujarini" as a dumb show, the Poet decided to recast the poem as a play. It initially had an all-female cast. Due to certain contingent factors related to the later performance in Calcutta, Rabindranath created the only male character, Upali, and played it himself. See discussions in Chapter 6: "Selecting the cast". A translation, *The Dancing Girl's Worship*, appeared in *VBQ*, old series 5 (April 1927); it was subsequently translated as *Natir Puja* by Marjorie Sykes in *VBQ*, new series 10 & 11 (1945); and by Shyamasree Devi as *The Court Dancer* (1961): for details, see Ananda Lal, *Rabindranath Tagore: Three Plays*, 501.

211 Prior to this, though dance-like movements had been employed, dance *per se* had not been directly used in Rabindranath's theatre. Gouri Bose's rendition of Srimati's dance in *Natir Puja* opened up the possibilities of using dance as a language of the theatre. Also see discussions in Chapter 9: "Acting the role".

212 The play had already been published in the Annual Number of *Basumati* in October 1925.

213 Though first serialized in *Bharati* (1901–3) and then published in *Rabindra Granthabali* (September 1903) as a story with the title *Chirakumar Sabha*, when it was published as a single text it was given the form of a novel and was named *Prajapatir Nirbandha* (1908); then it was reworked again as a full-fledged comic drama and the earlier title, *Chirakumar Sabha*, was restored (1925); this was published in 1926.

214 Following Prabhatkumar Mukhopadhyay, *Rabindra Jibani*, vol. 3, 261.

215 Prasantachandra Mahalanobis was excited when he found in Germany a new technique of printing: the manuscript written directly on an aluminium plate, using a special kind of ink, could be directly printed without the intervention of the compositor. This was used for *Lekhan*. See Prabhatkumar Mukhopadhyay, *Rabindra Jibani*, vol. 3, 262.

216 There was some hesitation, even among residents of Santiniketan, to stage *Natir Puja* in Calcutta which would mean Gouri Bose would have to dance on the public stage. To resolve the problem, Rabindranath created the only male character, Upali, and played it himself. Prabhatkumar Mukhopadhyay (*Rabindra Jibani*, vol. 3, 270) inadvertently mentions the year of performance in Calcutta as

Appendix II 311

1926. For more details, see discussions in earlier chapters, especially in Chapter 6: "Selecting the cast" and in Chapter 9: "Acting the role".
217 Published in *Bichitra* (*Ashar* 1334 BS/June 1927), with illustrations by Nandalal Bose; published as *Rituranga* in *Mashik Basumati* (*Pous* 1334/December 1927); the two versions, collated and revised, were published tgether as *Nataraj-Riturangasala* in *Banabani* (in 1931); following Prabhatkumar Mukhopadhyay, *Rabindra Jibani*, vol. 3, 274, n. 1.
218 On this occasion, a booklet of forty-four pages, titled *Rituranga*, was published, possibly for distribution among the audience. See Prabhatkumar Mukhopadhyay, *Rabindra Jibani*, vol. 3, 274, n. 1.
219 *Fireflies*, based on the poems of *Lekhan*, bears this prefatory remark: "*Fireflies* had their origin in China and Japan where thoughts were very often claimed from me, in my handwriting on fans and pieces of silk" (Macmillan, New York publication). This echoes what he wrote in the Preface to the Bengali *Lekhan* in 1926.
220 Letters to CF Andrews; revised and enlarged version of the 1924 *Letters from Abroad*.
221 See Prabhatkumar Mukhopadhyay, *Rabindra Jibani*, vol. 2, 351. These two events are still celebrated yearly in Visva-Bharati, though the first on the death anniversary of the Poet (22 *Sravana*, usually 7 August) and the second on the following day. Though Prabhatkumar mentions the second ritual as *Halachalana*, this is now observed as *Halakarshana*.
222 In 1961, two travelogues emerged out of this one volume – *Paschim jatrir diary* and *Java jatrir patra*
223 Following Prabhatkumar Mukhopadhyay, *Rabindra Jibani*, vol. 3, 359–60.
224 A poem written originally in English, inspired by a Passion play he saw in Germany in 1930; a Bengali translation, *Sishutirtha*, was made later.
225 Following Prabhatkumar Mukhopadhyay, *Rabindra Jibani*, vol. 3, 397, n. 5.
226 See Prabhatkumar Mukhopadhyay, *Rabindra Jibani*, vol. 3, 307, n. 4. *Navin* was a musical drama in two sections, in which the songs were interlinked through a commentary. The first section celebrated the advent of spring, and the second showed the exit of spring.
227 These were revised versions of *Rathajatra* (1923) and *Shiver Bhiksha* (1928).
228 Following Rudraprasad Chakrabarty, *Rangamancha O Rabindranath: Samakalin Pratikriya,* 262.
229 Prabhatkumar Mukhopadhyay claims that this was the first occasion when students of Visva-Bharati performed dance dramas outside Bengal; see *Rabindra Jibani*, vol. 3, 469.
230 See Prabhatkumar Mukhopadhyay, *Rabindra Jibani*, vol. 3, 475.
231 Rabindranath not only dramatized the short story but also added two songs for performance. Madhu Bose also made a film out of this play, which Rabindranath went to see; following Prabhatkumar Mukhopadhyay, *Rabindra Jibani*, vol. 3, 360, n. 2, 468.
232 Rabindranath revised *Shapmochan* before this performance, and this became the accepted version.
233 Krishna Kripalani translated the play as *Kingdom of Cards* in *Visva-Bharati Quarterly*, New Series 4 (February 1939): 264–89.
234 Though written as a prose play, *Tasher Desh* has been traditionally performed as a dance drama.
235 *Chandalika* was labelled as a "Harijan Tragedy", while *Tasher Desh* was mentioned as a "musical Burlesque" in the advertisements in *The Statesman* and *The Liberty*. *Chandalika* was a solo recital by Rabindranath, interspersed with songs; *Tasher Desh* was performed by the full team. For details see Rudraprasad Chakrabarty, *Rangamancha O Rabindranath: Samakalin Pratikriya*, 263–4; also

312   *Appendix II*

      Granthaparichay, RR, vol.16, 773–86. Prabhatkumar Mukhopadhyay, however, mentions the dates of performance as 2 and 4 September (*Rabindra Jibani*, vol. 3, 487).

236 While *Shapmochan,* enacted through songs and dances, was an instant hit, *Tasher Desh* floundered on the very first evening (27 November), probably because the Bengali dialogues were an impediment for those who did not follow the language. Prabhatkumar says that for the next day's performance he added more songs and dances (see Prabhatkumar Mukhopadhyay, *Rabindra Jibani*, vol. 3, 489). Eventually, by the second edition of 1938, the play was majorly revised, with dialogues reduced and more songs (and dances) added.

237 See Prabhatkumar Mukhopadhyay, *Rabindra Jibani*, vol. 3, 498–9, 500; also Dilip Kumar Roy, *Rabindra samakale Rabindranataker abhinoy* (Calcutta; Sramik Press, 1999) 173–4.

238 When certain members of the audience were restless, Rabindranath rebuked them.

239 Daughter Prakriti was played by Gouri Bose and the Mother was Indulekha Devi; see Rudraprasad Chakrabarty, *Rangamancha O Rabindranath: Samakalin Pratikriya*, 265.

240 In January 1936, Pratima Devi was trying to make a dance-cum-mime out of the 1892 verse-play *Chitrangada*; on noticing this, the Poet began with composing new songs and ended with refashioning out of the verse-play a new dance drama. For details, see Santidev Ghosh, *Gurudev Rabindranath o Adhunik Bharatiya Nritya*. (Calcutta: Ananda, 1978; rpt. 1983) 177, 183.

241 *Parisodh* would be further transformed to evolve into the dance drama *Shyama* by 1938.

242 Following Rudraprasad Chakrabarty, *Rangamancha O Rabindranath: Samakalin Pratikriya* (Calcutta: Ananda, 1995) 297.

243 "Shey" denotes another individual in the third person, singular number; the work seems to imply the being is a male.

244 From around this time, the dance dramas were being performed under the supervision of Santidev Ghosh.

245 The performance was "in open air in front of the library building" (Visva-Bharati News), as cited in Rudraprasad Chakrabarty, *Rangamancha O Rabindranath: Samakalin Pratikriya*, 299.

246 When the Poet converted *Chandalika* from a prose play to a dance drama (in 1938), he ensured that the lines of the prose narrative were easily set to tune.

247 These were the last performances of *Chitrangada* during Rabindranath's lifetime.

248 Dramatization of the story by the same name.

249 Subhaschandra Bose was present on the first evening; following Rudraprasad Chakrabarty, *Rangamancha O Rabindranath: Samakalin Pratikriya*, 266–7.

250 Revised version of *Swarga Marta*.

251 Following Rudraprasad Chakrabarty, *Rangamancha O Rabindranath: Samakalin Pratikriya*, 300.

Bibliography

Primary works

Tagore, Rabindranath. *Collected Poems and Plays of Rabindranath Tagore.* Delhi: Macmillan, 2001; 1st Indian reprint 1991.

Tagore, Rabindranath. *The English Writings of Rabindranath Tagore.* Ed. Sisir Kumar Das. 3 vols. New Delhi: Sahitya Akademi, 1994–2004.

Tagore, Rabindranath. *Gitanjali* [Bilingual version], with Introduction by W.B. Yeats. Santiniketan: Rabindra Bhavana, Visva-Bharati, 1999.

Tagore, Rabindranath. *Glimpses of Bengal: The Letters of Rabindranath Tagore, 1885–1895.* London: Macmillan, 1921.

Tagore, Rabindranath. *Letters to a Friend.* Ed. C.F. Andrews. London: Allen & Unwin, 1928; revised and expanded version of *Letters from Abroad*, 1924.

Tagore, Rabindranath. *My Boyhood Days.* Trans. Marjorie Sykes. Calcutta: Visva-Bharati, 1961. Reprinted by Delhi: Rupa 2005.

Tagore, Rabindranath. *My Reminiscences.* Trans. Surendranath Tagore. London: Macmillan, 1917; rpt. 1933.

Tagore, Rabindranath. *Nationalism.* New Delhi: Rupa, 2005; originally 1917.

Tagore, Rabindranath. *The Post Office.* Trans. Devabrata Mukherjea. London: Macmillan, 1914; rpt. 1961.

Tagore, Rabindranath. *Pracin Sahitya [Ancient Literature] Annotated English Translation and Critical Essays.* Ed. Nilanjana Bhattacharya and Sayantan Dasgupta. Calcutta: Visva-Bharati Granthan Bibhag, 2017.

Tagore, Rabindranath. *Rabindranath Tagore: Three Plays.* Trans. Ananda Lal. New Delhi: Oxford University Press, 2001.

Tagore, Rabindranath. *Selected Letters of Rabindranath Tagore.* Eds. Krishna Dutta and Andrew Robinson. Cambridge: Cambridge University Press, 1997.

Tagore, Rabindranath. *Selected Writings on Literature and Language.* Eds. Sukanta Chaudhuri and Sisir Kumar Das. Oxford, New York & New Delhi: Oxford University Press, 2001.

Tagore, Rabindranath. *Three Plays.* Trans. Marjorie Sykes. Bombay: Oxford University Press, 1950.

Thakur, Rabindranath. *Rabindra Rachanabali* [Complete Works of Rabindranath] Birth Centenary edition, 15 vols. Calcutta: West Bengal Government, 1961.

Thakur, Rabindranath. *Rabindra Rachabali* [Complete Works] Popular edition (issued on the occasion of 125th birth anniversary), 15 vols. Calcutta: Visva-Bharati, 1986–1992.

Thakur, Rabindranath. *Chithipatra* [Letters], 19 vols. Calcutta: Visva-Bharati, 1942–2004; rpt. 1993–2015.
Bichitra: On-line Tagore Variorum, *School of Cultural Texts and Records*, Jadavpur University, bichitra.jdvu.ac.in.

Secondary works

Ahsan, Nazmul. *Shakespeare Translations in Nineteenth Century Bengali Theatre*. Dhaka: Bangla Academy, 1995.
Alam, Fakrul and Radha Chakravarty (eds.). *The Essential Tagore*. Cambridge: Harvard University Press, 2011.
Al-din, Salim. *Madhyjuger Bangla Natya* [Medieval Bengali Theatre]. Dhaka: Bangla Akademi, 1996.
Anonymous. "Natyamancha samparke Rabindra-chintan" [Rabindranath's Thoughts on the Stage], *Gandharva*, Rabindranatya sankha, 1368 [Number on Rabindranath's Theatre, 1961], 72–73.
Aronson, Alex. *Rabindranath through Western Eyes*. Calcutta: Rddhi-India, 1978.
Bagchi, Jasodhara. "Shakespeare in Loin Cloths: English Literature and the Early Nationalistic Consciousness in Bengal", in *Rethinking English: Essays in Literature Language History*, ed. Svati Joshi. Delhi: Oxford University Press, 1994, 146–159.
Bagchi, Jatindramohan. *Rabindranath o jug sahitya* [Rabindranath and Contemporary Literature]. Calcutta: Brindaban Dhar & Sons Ltd, 1947.
Bagchi, Mani. "Peshadar Rangamancha O Rabindranather Natak" [The Professional Theatre and Rabindranath's Plays] in *Gandharva*, Rabindranatya sankha, 1368 [Number on Rabindranath's Theatre, 1961], 82–84.
Bagchi, Mani. *Sisirkumar o Bangla Theatre* [Sisirkumar and Bengali Theatre]. Calcutta: Jijnasa, 1960.
Bandyopadhyay, Arundhati. *Banglar loknatya jatra o satti Rabindranatak* [Jatra, the Folk Theatre of Bengal and Seven Rabindra-plays]. Calcutta: Department of Comparative Literature, Jadavpur University, 1987.
Bandyopadhyay, Brajendranath. *Bangiya Natyasalar Itihas, 1795–1876* [*The History of Bengali Theatre, 1795–1876*], 7th edn. Calcutta: Bangia Sahitya Parishad, 1998; originally 1933.
Bandyopadhyay, Charuchandra. *Rabi-Rashmi: Purba bhag* [The Ray of Rabi: Early Phase] (Vol. 1). Calcutta: University of Calcutta, 1938.
Bandyopadhyay, Charuchandra. *Rabi-Rashmi: Paschim bhag* [The Ray of Rabi: Later Phase] (Vol. 2). 3rd edn. Calcutta: A. Mukherjee & Co., 1939.
Bandyopadhyay, Debjit. *Natir Puja: Rabi Parikrama* [Natir Puja: An Appraisal]. Calcutta: Signet Press, 2019.
Bandyopadhyay, Rabindranath. "Kaljoyee natakkar Girishchandra Ghosh" [Immortal Playwright Girishchandra], in *Korok Sahitya Patrika: Bangla Natak o Natyamancha*, ed. Tapas Bhowmik, Autumn issue (2013): 76–88.
Banerjee, Sumanta. *The Parlour and the Street: Elite and Popular Culture in Nineteenth Century Calcutta*. Calcutta: Seagull Books, 1989.
Basu, Bishnu. *Rabindranather Theatre* [The Theatre of Rabindranath]. Calcutta: Pratibhas, 1987.
Basu, Sibaji Pratim. *The Poet and the Mahatma: Engagement with Nationalism and Internationalism*. Calcutta: Progressive Publishers, 2009.
Bhabha, Homi (ed.). *The Location of Culture*. London: Routledge, 1994.

Bhabha, Homi (ed.). *Nation and Narration*. London: Routledge, 1990.

Bhaduri, Pinakesh. "Natyacharya Sisirkumar and Natyasurya Ahindra Chowdhury", in *Korok Sahitya Patrika: Bangla Natak o Natyamancha*, ed. Tapas Bhowmik, Autumn issue (2013): 304–326.

Bhanja, Gouri. "Natir Puja 1333", transcribed by Alpana Roy Chowdhury, *Visva-Bharati News* (April 1978): 176–178.

Bhattacharji, Sukumari. "Sanskrit Drama and Tagore", in *Rabindranath in Perspective: A Bunch of Essays*. Calcutta: Visva-Bharati, 1989, 118–126.

Bhattacharya, Arnab and Mala Renganathan (ed.). *The Politics and Reception of Rabindranath Tagore's Drama: The Bard on the Stage*. Abingdon and New York: Routledge, 2015.

Bhattacharya, Ashutosh. *Bangla Natyasahityer Itihas, 1852–1952* [The History of Bengali Dramatic Literature, 1852–1952]. Calcutta: A. Mukherji & Co Ltd, 1955.

Bhattacharya, Bijanbehari. *Lipibibek* [Scripting Memories]. Calcutta: Bookland, 1962.

Bhattacharya, Charuchandra. *Kabi Smarane* [Remembering the Poet]. Calcutta: Basudhara Prakashani, 1961.

Bhattacharya, Gourisankar. *Bangla Loknatya Samiksha* [An Appraisal of Bengali Folk Theatre]. Calcutta: Rabindra Bharati University, 1974.

Bhattacharya, Ramkrishna (ed.). *Manche Rabindranath: Bharati Parishad Barshiki* [Rabindranath on Stage: Bharati Parishad Annual Number]. Calcutta: Bharati Parishad, 1978.

Bhattacharya, Sabyasachi (ed.). *The Mahatma and the Poet: Letters and Debates between Gandhi and Tagore 1915–1941*. New Delhi: National Book Trust, 1997; rpt. 1999.

Bhowmik, Spandana. "Playwright versus Dramatist: Writing for Performance, Writing Raja", *Sangeet Natak*, vol. XLVI, nos. 1–4, 2012: Special issue on "Rabindranath's East-West Encounters: Performance and Visual Arts", ed. Abhijit Sen and Saurav Dasthakur. New Delhi: Sangeet Natak Akademi, 2013, 109–120.

Bishi, Pramathanath. *Purano sei diner katha* [Remembering Those Fond Old Days]. Calcutta: Mitra & Ghosh, 1958; rpt. 1986.

Bishi, Pramathanath. *Rabindra Natya-prabaha* [*The Drift of Rabindra Plays*], 2 vols. Calcutta: Orient Book Company, 1958.

Bishi, Pramathanath. *Rabindranath O Santiniketan* [*Rabindranath and Santiniketan*]. Calcutta: Visva-Bharati, 1959; rpt. 1975.

Bose, Mandakranta. "Nrityanatya, Rabindranath o Bangasamskritir nutan diganta" [Dance Drama, Rabindranath and a New Horizon in Bengali Culture], *Balaka, Special issue: Natyabyaktitwa Rabindranath*, year 19, no. 29 (November 2010): 56–68.

Chakraborti, Basudeb. *Some Problems of Translation: A Study of Tagore's "Red Oleanders"*. Calcutta: Papyrus, 2005.

Chakrabarty, Rudraprasad. *Rangamancha o Rabindranath: Samakalin Pratikriya* [Theatre and Rabindranath: Contemporary Responses]. Calcutta: Ananda Publishers, 1995.

Chakrabarty, Rudraprasad. "Abhineta o Nirdeshak Rabindranath" [Rabindranath as Director and Actor], in *Korok Sahitya Patrika: Anya Rabindranath*, ed. Tapas Bhowmik, pre-Autumn issue (2010): 181–190.

Chakravarty, Amiya (ed.). *A Tagore Reader*. New Delhi: Rupa, 2003; originally 1961.

Chakravarty, Bikash (ed.). *Poets to a Poet, 1912–1940: Letters from Bridges, Rhys, Yeats, Sturge Moore, Trevelyan and Pound to Rabindranath Tagore*. Calcutta: Visva-Bharati, 1998.

Chakravarty, Radha (ed.). *Shades of Difference: Selected Works of Rabindranath Tagore*. New Delhi: Social Science Press, 2015.

Bibliography

Chakravorty, Swapan (trans.). "The Theatre", in *Rabindranath Tagore, Selected Writings on Literature and Language*, ed. Sukanta Chaudhuri and Sisir Kumar Das. Oxford, New York & New Delhi: Oxford University Press, 2001, 95–99.

Chanda, Rani. *Gurudev*. Calcutta: Visva-Bharati, 1962.

Chatterjee, Partha. *Lineages of Political Society: Studies in Postcolonial Democracy*. New York: Columbia University Press, 2011.

Chatterjee, Sudipto. Mise-En-(Colonial)-Scene: The Theatre of the Bengal Renaissance, in *Imperialism and Theatre*, ed. J. Ellen Gainor. London: Routledge, 1995, 19–37.

Chattopadhyay, Basantakumar. *Jyotirindranather Jibansmriti [Jyotirindranath's Reminiscences]*. Calcutta: Prajnabharati, 1919.

Chattopadhyay, Khagendranath. *Rabindra Katha [About Rabindra]*. Calcutta: Parul Prakasani, 2015; originally 1941.

Chaudhurani, Indira Devi. *Rabindra Smriti [Rabindra Memories]*. Calcutta: Visva-Bharati Granthan Vibhaga, 2010; originally 1960.

Chaudhurani, Sarala Devi. *Jibaner Jharapata [Faded Leaves of Life]*. Calcutta, Allahabad: Rupa, 1975.

Chaudhuri, Sukanta. "Rabindranath Tagore and the Traffic of Texts", in *Towards Tagore*, ed. Sanjukta Dasgupta, Ramkumar Mukhopadhyay and Swati Ganguly. Calcutta: Visva-Bharati, 2014, 309–319.

Chaudhuri, Sukanta. *Translation and Understanding*. New Delhi: Oxford University Press, 1999.

Chowdhury, Darshan. "Rangamancha" prabandha o Rabindranather theatre bhabna [The Essay "Rangamancha" and Rabindranath's Ideas of Theatre], *Uddalak: Special number on Rabindranatak*, ed. Santosh Kumar Mandal, 2nd year, nos., 2 & 3, April–September 2002, 101–115.

Dalmia, Vasudha. *Poetics, Plays and Performances: The Politics of Modern Indian Theatre*. New Delhi: Oxford University Press, 2009; originally 2006.

Das, Sisirkumar (ed.). *The English Writings of Rabindranath Tagore*, vol. 1. New Delhi: Sahitya Akademi, 1994.

Das, Sisirkumar (ed.). *The English Writings of Rabindranath Tagore*, vol. 2. New Delhi: Sahitya Akademi, 1996.

Das, Sudhiranjan. *Amader Santiniketan [Our Santiniketan]*. Calcutta: Visva-Bharati Granthalay, 1959.

Dasi, Binodini. *Amar Katha [My Life-Story]*, ed. Soumitra Chattopadhyay, NirmalyaAcharya, et al. Revised and expanded. Calcutta: Subarnarekha, 1987; originally 1912.

Dasgupta, Sanjukta, Ramkumar Mukhopadhyay and Swati Ganguly (eds.) *Towards Tagore*. Calcutta: Visva-Bharati, 2014.

Das Gupta, Uma. *A Difficult Friendship: Letters of Edward Thompson and Rabindranath Tagore*. New Delhi: Oxford University Press, 2003.

Das Gupta, Uma. *Rabindranath Tagore: A Biography*. New Delhi: Oxford University Press, 2004.

Deb, Chitra. *Thakurbarir Andarmahal [Inner Precincts of Tagore Household]*. Calcutta: Ananda Publishers, 1980.

Devi, Maitreyee. *Mongpu te Rabindranath [Rabindranath in Mongpu]*. Calcutta: Rupa, 1967.

Devi, Maitreyee. *Swarger Kachakachi [Close to Heaven]*. Calcutta: Prima, 1981.

Devi, Pratima. *Nritya [Dance]*. Calcutta: Visva-Bharati, 1948; rpt. 1965.

Devi, Sahana. *Smritir Kheya [Ferrying Memories]*, 5th edn. Calcutta: Prima Publications, 2011; originally 1978.

Devi, Sita. *Punya Smriti* [*Sacred Memories*]. Calcutta: Probasi, 1942.
Devi, Surupa. "Sudhar Smriti" [Sudha's Memories], in *Balaka: Natya-byaktitwo Rabindranath*, ed. Dhananjoy Ghoshal, no. 19 (November 2010): 27–30; originally published in *Rabindra Bharati Patrika*, January–March 1979.
Dharwadker, Aparna Bhagava. *Theatres of Independence: Drama, Theory, and Urban Performance in India since 1947*. New Delhi: Oxford University Press, paperback edition, 2008; originally 2005.
Dutta, Harindranath. "Rangalaye Rabindranath: Smriticharan" [Rabindranath in Theatre: Recapitulations], in *Manche Rabindranath*, ed. Ramkrishna Bhattacharya. Calcutta: Bharati Parishad, 1978, 13–18.
Dutta, Harindranath. *Rabindranath o Sadharan Rangalay* [*Rabindranath and the Public Stage*]. Calcutta: Tagore Research Institute, 1983.
Dutta, Satyendranath. "Sahare Phalguni" [Phalguni in Town], *Bharati*, 39th year, no. 11, Phalgun 1322 (1916): 1098–1110.
Dutt, Utpal. *Ashar chalaney bhuli* [*Led Astray by Hope*]. Calcutta: Paschimbanga Natya Academy, 1993.
Fanon, Frantz. *The Wretched of the Earth*. London: Penguin, 1967.
Foucault, Michel. "Of Other Spaces". Trans. Jay Miskowec, *Diacritics*, vol. 16, no. 1 (Spring 1986), 22–27.
Ghosh, Aditi. *Literary Translations and Bengali*. Calcutta: The Asiatic Society, 2008.
Ghosh, Ajitkumar. *Thakurbarir Abhinay* [*Acting of the Tagore Family*]. Calcutta: Rabindra Bharati Society, 1988.
Ghosh, Girishchandra. "Abhinay o Abhineta" [Acting and the Actor], *Girish Rachanabali*, ed. Debipada Bhattacharya, vol. 3. Calcutta: Sahitya Samsad, 1946, 829–841.
Ghosh, Girishchandra. "Pouranik Natak" [Mythical Drama], *Girish Rachanabali*, ed. Rabindranath Roy and Debipada Bhattacharya. Vol. 1. Calcutta: Sahitya Samsad, 1944, 731–735.
Ghosh, Sankha. *Kaler Matra o Rabindra Natak* [*Rabindra Drama and the Measure of Time*]. 3rd edn. Calcutta: Dey's Publishing, 1985; originally 1969.
Ghosh, Santidev. *Gurudev Rabindranath o Adhunik Bharatiya Nritya* [*Gurudev Rabindranath and Modern Indian Dance*]. Calcutta: Ananda, 1978; rpt. 1983.
Ghosh, Santidev. *Rabindrasangeet* [*Tagore Songs*]. Calcutta: Visva-Bharati Granthalay, rev. edn. 1958; originally 1942.
Ghosh, Subroto. *Rabinataker Natyakatha* [*Dramatic Narrative of Rabi-plays*]. Calcutta: Signet Press, 2017.
Ghoshal, Dhananjoy (ed.). *Balaka: Natya-byaktitwo Rabindranath* [*Balaka: Theatre-Personality Rabindranath*], year 19, no. 19 (November 2010).
Goswami, Parimal. *Smriti chitran* [*Memorial Reconstructions*]. Calcutta: Prajna Prakashani, 1958.
Granthaparichay [Bibliographical Information], *Rabindra Rachabali*, vol. 16, ed. Rabindrakumar Dasgupta, Sankha Ghosh, Bhabatosh Dutta, et al. Calcutta: West Bengal Government, 2001.
Green, Gretchen. *The Whole World and Company*. New York: Reynal and Hitchcock, 1936.
Gupta, Bepinbehari. *Puratan Prasanga* [*Of Yesteryears*], ed. Asitkumar Bandyopadhyay. Calcutta: Pustak Bipani, 1989; originally 1966.
Haldar, Asitkumar. *Rabitirhe* [*Rabi Pilgrimage*]. Calcutta: Anjana Prakashani, 1958.
Kar, Sudhir Chandra. *Kabi Katha* [*About the Poet*]. Calcutta: Suprakasan, 1951.
Kripalani, Krishna. *Tagore: A Life*. New Delhi: National Book Trust, India, 1986; rpt. 2011; originally 1961.

318 Bibliography

Kundu, Pronoykumar. *Rabindranather geeti-natya o nritya-natya* [*Rabindranath's Musical Drama and Dance Drama*]. Calcutta: Orient Book Co., 1965.
Lago, Mary. *Imperfect Encounter: Letters of William Rothenstein and Rabindranath Tagore 1911–1941*. Cambridge: Harvard University Press, 1972.
Lago, Mary. *Rabindranath Tagore*. Columbia: University of Missouri Press, 1976.
Lal, Ananda. *Rabindranath Tagore: Three Plays*. Calcutta: MP Birla Foundation, 1987; later revised version from Oxford University Press, 2001.
Lal, Ananda. "Tagore in Calcutta Theatre: 1986–2010", in *Towards Tagore*, ed. Sanjukta Dasgupta, Ramkumar Mukhopadhyay and Swati Ganguly. Calcutta: Visva-Bharati, 2014, 515–546.
Mitra, Rakhi. "Chitrangada Bitarka O Kabichitter Vibartan" [The Chitrangada Controversy and Its Impact on the Poet's Mind], *Parikatha*, year 14, no. 1 (December 2011): 161–184.
Mukherjee, Sujit. *Translation as Discovery*. New Delhi: Allied Publishers, 1981.
Mukherjee, Sujit. *Translation as Recovery*. Delhi: Pencraft International, 2009.
Mukhopadhyay, Amartya. *Politics, Society and Colonialism: An Alternative Understanding of Tagore's Responses*. New Delhi: Cambridge University Press India Pvt. Ltd., 2010.
Mukhopadhyay, Prabhatkumar. *Rabindra Jibani* [*The Biography of Rabindranath*], 4 vols. Calcutta: Visva-Bharati Granthalay, 1933–1952; rev. edn., 1960–1964.
Mukhopadhyay, Prabhatkumar. *Rabindra-barshapanji* [*Rabindra Chronology*]. Calcutta: Dey's Publishing, 1962; rpt. 2007.
Mukhopadhyay, Sourindramohan. *Rabindra Smriti* [*Rabindra Memories*]. Calcutta: Sisir Publishing House, 1957.
Nandy, Ashis. *The Illegitimacy of Nationalism: Rabindranath Tagore and the Politics of Self*. Delhi: Oxford University Press, 1994.
Nussbaum, Martha. "Patriotism and Cosmopolitanism", *The Boston Review*, XIX (5), October–November 1994, 3–16.
Pal, Prasantakumar. *Rabijibani* [*The Life of Rabi*]. 9 vols. Calcutta: Ananda Publishers, 1982–2003.
Poddar, Arabinda. *Tagore: the Political Personality*. Calcutta: Indiana, 2004.
Quayum, Mohammad A (ed.). *The Poet and His World: Critical Essays on Rabindranath Tagore*. New Delhi: Orient Blackswan, 2011.
Rakshit, Moloy. *Raktakarabi: Path O Pathantarer Bhabnay* [*Raktakarabi: Reflections on Alternative Textual Readings*]. Calcutta: Dey's Publishing, 2009.
Ray, Niharranjan. *Aitihya o Rabindranath* [*Tradition and Rabindranath*]. Calcutta: Dey's Publishing, 1994.
Renganathan, Mala and Arnab Bhattacharya (ed.). *Rabindranath Tagore's Drama in the Perspective of Indian Theatre*. London: Anthem Press, 2020.
Rothenstein, William. *Men and Memories: 1872–1938*. London: Vintage Publishing, 1978; originally 1938.
Roy, Anuradha. "Bangali buddhijibir chokhe British sashan" ["British Governance in the Eyes of the Bengali Intelligentsia"], in *Unish Sataker Bangalijiban o Sanskriti* [Bengali Life and Culture in the 19th century], ed. Swapan Basu and Indrajit Chaudhuri. Calcutta: Pustak Bipani, 2003, 254–272.
Roy, Dilip Kumar. *Rabindra samakale Rabindranataker Abhinoy* [*Acting of Rabindranath's Plays in his Times*]. Calcutta: Sramik Press, 1999.
Roy, Hemendrakumar. *Soukhin Natyakalaye Rabindranath* [*Rabindranath in Amateur Theatre*]. Calcutta: Indian Associated Publishing Co. Pvt. Ltd., 1959.

Roy, Hemendrakumar. *Prabandha Samkalan [Collected Essays]*. Compiled by Deviprasad Ghosh. Calcutta: Agami, 1990.

Roy Chowdhury, Subir and Swapan Majumdar. *Bilati Jatra theke Swadeshi Theatre [From English Jatra to Swadeshi Theatre]*. Calcutta: Dey's Publishing, 1999; originally 1972.

Samaddar, Sekhar. *Visarjan: Rupe, rupantare [Visarjan: In Different Manifestations]*. Calcutta: Papyrus, 1992.

Samaddar, Sekhar. "Rabindranather Natyabhavna" [Rabindranath's Ideas of Theatre], in *Punascha Rabindrakriti*, ed. Sabyasachi Bhattacharya and Bratin Dey. New Delhi: National Book Trust, India, 2012, 215–283.

Sanyal, Abantikumar. *Kabir Abhinay [The Poet's Acting]*. Calcutta: Rabindra Bharati University, 1996.

Sar, Ramenkumar. "Sadharon rangamanche Rabindranath byartho!" [Rabindranath a Failure in Public Theatre!], in *Balaka*, ed. Dhananjoy Ghosal, year 19, no. 19 (Nov 2010): 181–188.

Sarkar, Pabitra. *Natmancha Natyarup [The Stage and the Theatrical Form]*. Calcutta: Proma Publications, 3rd edn. 1999.

Sarkar, Pinakesh (ed.). *Harano Diner Natak [Plays from Forgotten Years]*. Calcutta: Sahitya Samsad, 1999.

Sarkar, Shyamal Kumar. *Collected Papers on Rabindranath Tagore*. Calcutta: Dey's Publishing, 2013.

Sen, Amita. *Ananda Sarba Kaaje [Joy in Every Sphere]*. Calcutta: Tagore Research Institute1983.

Sen, Amita. *Santiniketane Asramkanya [The Daughter of Asram in Santiniketan]*. Calcutta: Tagore Research Institute1977.

Sen, Asok. "Rajnitir pathakrame Rabindranath" [Rabindranath in the Lessons of Politics], *Bangadarshan*, 11 (July–December 2006).

Sen, Kshitimohan. "Vedmantrarasik Rabindranath" [Rabindranath Versed in Vedmantra], *Visva-Bharati Patrika* (Baisakh 1350 B.S., April 1943) 601–603.

Sen, Nilima. "Amar Chelebela" [My Childhood] in *Durer Nilima*, ed. Arundhati Deb, 2nd edn. Calcutta: Thema, 2018: 173–8.

Sen, Pulinbihari and Kshitis Roy (eds.). *Rabindranath Tagore: A Tribute*. New Delhi: Sangeet Natak Akademi, 2006; originally 1961.

Sengupta, Samir. *Samakal o Rabindranath: Ghatanapanji [Rabindranath and His Times: A Chronology]*. Calcutta: Pratikshan Publications, 1991.

Sinha, Biswajit. *Encyclopaedia of Indian Theatre – 5: Rabindranath Tagore*, Part I. Delhi: Raj Publications, 2003.

Tagore, Abanindranath. *Gharoa [Household Reminiscences]*. Calcutta: Visva-Bharati Granthan Vibhaga, 1941; rpt. 1983.

Tagore, Jyotirindranath. *Jyotirindranather Natya Sangraha [Collected Plays of Jyotirindranath]*. Compiled by Sushil Roy. Calcutta: Visva-Bharati Granthan Vibhaga, 1969.

Tagore, Rathindranath. "Looking Back", in *Rabindranath Tagore: A Tribute*, ed. Pulinbihari Sen and Kshitis Roy. New Delhi: Sangeet Natak Akademi, 2006; originally 1961, 45–52.

Tagore, Rathindranath. *Pitrismriti [Memories of Father]*. Calcutta: Jijnasa, 1966.

Thompson, Edward J. *Rabindranath Tagore: Poet and Dramatist*. Delhi: Oxford University Press, 1948.

Index

Achalayatan 2, 65, 70, 71, 80, 98, 100, 101, 103, 112n21, 141, 153, 176, 183n55, 258, 264, 271, 272
Adhikari, Ranu 70, 74n29, 85, 121, 122, 134, 140–1, 154, 173, 177, 284, 285, 307n182
alternative theatre/parallel theatre 29, 31, 47, 48, 77, 86–7, 151–2, 221
Andrews, C.F.152, 199, 204, 263, 265, 267, 273, 301n117, 303n129
Arupratan 2, 68, 84, 85, 100, 103, 105–7, 113n49, 121, 122, 134, 140, 147n72, 173–4, 276, 285
asram-school/*Brahmacharyasram* 2, 42, 47, 48–50, 63–72, 123, 151–2, 191, 220
audience/spectator 28, 29, 36n92, 47, 67–9, 77–9, 83–4, 85, 88, 107, 120, 123, 125, 132, 135, 138, 140, 143–4, 150–1, 154, 157, 163, 165, 166, 169–71, 173, 174, 179, 191–2, 208, 218, 249, 301n111, 312n238
Autumn Festival, The 76, 119, 257, 261, 273, 274

Baikunther Khata 39, 118, 137, 164, 176, 250, 259, 271 277
Bansari 65, 80, 108, 291
Bhaduri, Sisirkumar 1, 21, 26, 29, 30, 35n73,n74,n75 & n78, 36n89, 87, 88, 104, 158, 222, 285, 309n202
Bishi, Pramathanath 80, 96, 110, 138, 146n57, 308n186
Bohurupee 1, 158, 222, 223n8
Bose, Amritalal 4, 6, 9n10, 22, 23, 26, 28, 35n82, 85, 133, 135, 157, 177–8
Bose (Bhanja), Gouri 68–9, 70, 118, 122–4, 127n40, 132, 168, 288, 310n211 & n216, 312n239

Bose, Nandalal 49, 70, 71, 118, 152, 154, 157, 214n54, 221, 263, 284, 288, 298n66, 304n152, 308n191 & n193
Bose, Subhaschandra 56, 108
Bouthakuranir Haat 26, 37, 103, 150, 246, 257
boy-actors in female roles (in Santiniketan) 49, 66–7, 73n15, 119–21, 138, 142, 152–3, 191, 257, 258; female actors in same/similar roles (later productions) 67, 68, 74n29 & n30
Buddhist influences/sources 39, 81, 90n36, 96, 100, 250

cast selection 61n83, 66, 67, 70, 116, 117, 118, 121, 122, 135, 191, 251
celebration of seasons 99–100, 188, 308n191; see also individual seasonal plays and musicals
Chaitanya, 18
Chakravarty, Ajitkumar 66, 67, 70, 73n8, 119, 120–2, 197, 200, 205, 262
Chakravarty, Amiyachandra 124, 192, 198, 199, 203
Chandalika 2, 31, 50, 64, 83–4, 90n29, 100, 103, 108, 116, 135, 136, 155, 158, 168, 188, 189, 191, 205, 291, 292, 293, 294, 311n235, 312n246
Chattopadhyay, Ramananda 112n28, 122, 274
Chattopadhyay, Saratchandra 30–1, 111, 305n161
Chirakumar Sabha 26, 29, 36n89, 65, 98–9, 172, 183n74, 222, 286, 288, 310n213
Chitra 203, 206, 207–9, 214–5n54, 215n73, 216n76, 261, 269, 276, 285, 302n124 & n125, 309n202

Chitrangada 2, 27, 31, 39, 49, 50, 65, 69–70, 82–5, 96, 100–1, 103, 117, 123, 124–5, 136, 155–6, 168, 188 189, 191, 205, 206, 208–9, 249, 261, 292, 293, 312n240 & n247

Chokher Bali 28, 252, 253, 263

Chowdhury, Ahindra 1, 26, 29, 35n73, n76 & n77, 36n89, 87, 88, 158, 222, 287

Chowdhury, Pramatha 117, 150, 303n133

costume and make-up 48, 49, 50, 70, 71, 121, 129, 136–7, 154–5, 158, 170, 171, 173, 175, 176, 183n60, 189, 214n54, 217, 304n152, 308n193

Cycle of Spring, The 48, 99, 149, 151, 204, 264, 270

Dakghar 2, 9n8, 31, 50, 64, 65, 70, 71, 72, 80, 81, 97–8, 101, 117–8, 132–3, 134, 141, 142, 147n77, 153, 154, 157, 158, 165, 173, 175, 176, 177, 179, 180, 188, 203, 219, 221 222, 258, 259, 263, 271, 272, 288, 299n78, 304n142

dance 71, 81, 123–4, 155, 188–9, 310n210; introduction in *Natir Puja* 68, 81, 155, 188, 310n211; dances from different cultures 71, 188–90, 193n9; hostile responses and criticism 68, 123, 167–8; measures to scotch criticism 124–5, 168, 191; positive responses 68–70, 123–4; social respectability gained 124, 191, 192

dance drama/*nrityanatya* 69, 71, 81–4, 90n27, 100–1, 103, 108, 116–7, 118, 25, 36, 155–6, 158, 168, 188–92, 193n20, 222, 242, 292, 293, 295, 295n4, 304n153, 311n229 & n232, 312n240

Das, Sajanikanta 6, 70, 83, 125, 163, 192

Das, Sudiranjan 2, 66–7, 70, 73n15, 120, 121–2

Devi (Bose), Sahana 70, 122, 132, 134, 142–3, 169, 173–4, 175–6, 285, 308n187

Devi (Kripalani), Nandita 121, 122, 133–4, 190

Devi Chaudhurani, Indira 25, 48, 96, 152, 168, 196, 199, 259, 299n79,

Devi Chaudhurani, Sarala 67, 163

Devi, Jnanadanandini 25, 73n14, 116, 125n1, 248

Devi, Mrinalini 25, 34n60, 63, 116–7, 125n1, 246

Devi, Pratima 71, 81, 107, 109, 136, 138, 188, 258, 290

Devi, Sita 5,152–3, 167, 169, 175, 176, 183n55

Devi, Swarnakumari 117, 163, 248

Dutt, Amarendranath 20, 28, 33n40, 253

Dutt, Michael Madhusudan 14, 15–16, 24, 157, 220

Dutt, Utpal 222

Dutta, Satyendranath 6, 48, 60n59, 117, 118–9, 153

eclectic/inclusive/syncretic theatre 71, 85, 86, 156–7, 186, 188–9, 190, 192, 220–1; see also alternative/parallel theatre

Elmhirst, Leonard 57–8n13, 210, 277, 280, 282, 283, 306n165, 307n180, 308n194, 309n203

Gandharir Abedan (*Mother's Prayer, The*) 101, 112n22, 204, 206, 207, 250, 251, 273, 295n4

Gandhi, M. K. 45–6, 57–8n13, 135, 265, 272, 279, 301n106, 305n163, 306n165, 309n205

Ganguly, Nitendranath 180

Ghosh, Girishchandra 20, 21, 22, 28, 29, 34n44, 80–1, 164, 166, 172, 179, 180; his rhythmic pattern ("Gairish chhanda") 164; resentful towards Rabindranath 27–8

Ghosh, Sankha 3, 180, 245

Ghosh, Santidev 67, 70, 71, 118 120–1, 135–6, 305 n164, 309n204

Gitanjali (*Song Offerings*) 104, 195–7, 199–202, 212n10, 257, 259, 258, 260, 261, 299n82

Goray Galad 6, 35n74, 39, 103–4, 104, 130–1, 131–2, 164, 249, 289

Goswami, Parimal 68, 139, 172

Grihapravesh 26, 35n76, 64–5, 80, 88, 222, 286, 287, 309–10n206, 310n207

Haldar, Asitkumar 70, 71, 119, 134, 153, 154, 290

Haldar, Harishchandra 117, 150, 152, 162, 181n12, 252

Hasyakautuk 119

internationalism/universalism 45–6, 81, 85, 186, 200, 304n151

Irving, Henry 130, 159n6, 163, 177

322 Index

Jataka tales see Buddhist influences
Jallianwala Bagh massacre 41, 58 n15, 202, 214n45, 275, 276, 304n150,
jatra 13, 16–7, 18, 24, 34n62 & n64, 47, 63, 76–7, 81, 85, 101, 117, 143, 150–1, 187, 193n7, 221, 310n209

Kaler Jatra/Rather Rashi 31, 50, 60n69, 65, 80, 110–1, 115n86, 172, 290, 308n186 & n192
Kal Mrigaya 2, 26, 84, 90n35, 150, 187, 246, 247, 256, 295n4
Kalidas 14, 78
Kar, Surendranath 70, 71, 154, 307n176
Karna-Kunti Samvad (*Karna and Kunti*) 101, 112n22, 204, 206, 215n66, 251, 273
Katha o Kahini 257, 297n38
King and the Rebel, The 195, 262
King and the Queen, The 104, 206, 248, 267, 271
King of the Dark Chamber, The 203–4, 215n58, 258, 259, 263, 276, 300n99

Lakshmir Pariksha 39, 67, 85, 120, 251, 255, 258, 272, 276, 286, 309n200
Lebedeff, Herasim 13–4

Macmillan 95, 204, 212n4, 215n59, 265, 268, 299n84, 303n132, 308n194
Mahalanobis, Prasantachandra 106, 118, 146n34, 163, 286, 303n133, 310n215,
Mahalanobis, Nirmalkumari (Rani) 122
Majumdar, Akshaykumar 57n3, 117, 129, 249
Malini 39, 66–7, 95–6, 100, 120, 122, 206, 215n67, 222, 250, 258, 267, 301n117
Mayar Khela 26, 67, 84, 150, 187, 248
Mitra, Dinabandhu: 18; see also *Nildarpan*
Mitra, Rajendralal 16, 100, 250
Mitra, Sombhu 3, 7, 88, 222
mixed casting 67–8, 74n27, 116–7, 120–1, 305n164; oppositions 68; problems resolved 69–70, 168
Muktadhara 30, 50, 53, 60n67, 64, 65, 80, 98, 101, 103, 108, 109, 110, 153, 172, 205, 209–10, 222, 280, 281
Mustafi, Ardhendusekhar 20, 26, 80–1, 163, 164

Naidu, Sarojini 2, 53, 107, 204, 276
Narakavasa (*Somaka and Ritvik*) 204, 206, 207

Nataraj-Riturangasala 2, 64, 188, 295n4, 311n217
nation/nationalism 3, 7, 30, 31, 39–46, 48, 50, 51, 53, 56, 57n12, 59n49, 65, 76, 87, 108, 150, 186–7, 200, 217, 218, 221, 267–8, 301n116, 302n119
Nationalism 43, 44, 51, 195, 270, 302n120 & n123, 303n132
National Theatre 18, 19, 20, 21, 22, 23, 26, 28, 87
Natir Puja 2, 4, 30, 49, 67, 68–9, 70, 72, 81, 85, 100, 109–10, 116, 118, 120, 121, 122, 123–4, 125, 127 n50, 131, 132, 153, 155, 167–8, 188, 191, 205, 251, 288, 290, 310n210 & n216
Navin 64, 135, 139, 143–4, 188, 290, 311n226
Nildarpan 18–20
nineteenth-century Bengali theatre 7, 13–23, 27–8, 150; colonial influences 13–4; urban theatre 16–17, 33n19; indigenous forms marginalized 16–18; Reformist Revivalist trends 14, 15, 186; anti-colonial urges 18–20, 21, 22–3; Shakespeare translations 14–15, 20; categories of plays: historical 20–1, mythological/religious 21, romances 22, satires and farces 22–3; relation with Tagore family 23–6, 36n95; charges against Rabindranath 26–8, 35n82; defence of charges against him 29–31

Ocampo, Victoria 222, 309n203
opera/*geetinatya* 26, 81, 84, 150, 187, 246, 295n4

Parisodh 84, 100, 123, 125, 190, 251, 292, 293, 294; see also *Shyama*
Pearson, W.W. 119, 195, 260, 266, 284, 300 n103, 301n117, 308n188
Phalguni 2, 5, 6, 30, 31, 47, 48, 55, 64, 67, 70, 71, 72, 77, 80, 81, 98, 99, 101, 116, 117, 118–9, 136, 137, 149, 151, 152, 153, 165–6, 167, 170, 173, 176, 177, 179, 204, 220, 222, 264, 265, 266, 267, 277, 295n4, 301n111
Post Office, The 9n8, 203, 214n50 & n53, 258, 259, 262, 263, 277, 300n95
post-1947 productions 222, 223n8 & n13, 224n15
Prajapatir Nirbandha 98
Prakritir Pratisodh 64, 79, 80, 99, 101, 247, 267, 271, 295n10

Prayaschitta/Paritran 30, 67, 70, 103, 120, 138, 146n60, 257, 258, 288
proscenium theatre 13, 24, 85, 86, 153, 156–7, 167, 169, 188, 218, 220, 221

Rabindranath and public theatre 26, 29, 35n73, 35n76, 86, 87, 149–50, 221
Rabindranath as actor (and approaches to acting style) 80–1, 130, 132, 138–9, 164–5, 166–7, 168–9, 171, 174–5, 176–7, 177–8, 178–9; in *Dakghar* 173, 175, 304n142; in *Phalguni* 81, 165–6, 167, 173,179; in *Prayaschitta* 258; in *Raja* 166–7, 173, 175; in *Sarodotsav* 165, 167, 175; in *Tapati* 158, 170–1, 174, 179; in *Visarjan* 5, 71, 130, 138, 139, 163–4, 169; vocal acting, 6, 69, 83, 171–4, 181n10
Rabindranath as director 2,3, 6, 66, 85–7, 121–2, 130–2, 133, 134–7, 139, 141, 156–7, 167, 169, 175–6, 188, 217; in *Chandalika* 136; in *Chitrangada* 136; in *Goray Galad* 6, 130, 131–2; in *Natir Puja* 131; in *Phalguni* 136; in *Raja* 106–7, 131, 135; in *Shapmochan* 135; in *Tapati* 136–7; in *Visarjan* 6, 130–1, 169
Rabindranath as translator (and views on translation) 196–8, 202; abridgement of original 206–7; additional details (for target readers) 207; power relations between languages 199, 202; *tarjama* 198, 203, 205; transcreation 198, 203, 205, 210; translations by other hands 195, 200, 204–5
Rabindranath's improvisations/innovations 137–8, 139, 140–1, 218; for accidental errors/events 138–9, 140; for lapse of memory 137–8; for theatrical exigency 131, 132–3, 136, 139, 140–3; in *Achalayatan* 141; in *Dakghar* 141, 142; in *Natir Puja* 123, 168; in *Visarjan* 138–9, 140–1, 142–3; in *Valmiki Pratibha* 138
Raja 2, 5, 31, 50, 53, 55, 64, 65, 66, 67, 68, 70, 71, 72, 80, 81, 84, 85, 98, 100, 101, 103, 104–7, 108, 116, 120, 121–2, 131, 133, 135, 140, 142, 153–4, 157, 166–7, 173, 175, 177, 179, 182n.37, 188, 203, 222, 258, 259, 263, 295n4
Raja o Rani 2, 25, 26, 28, 30, 31, 50, 55, 64, 77, 80, 103, 104, 116–7, 118, 122, 129, 130, 140, 150, 163, 164, 166, 187, 206, 248, 252, 260, 266, 267, 295n4
Rajarshi 55, 95, 103, 104, 247, 248

Raktakarabi 51–3, 56, 57, 61n76, n77 & n78, 64, 65, 80, 90n45, 96, 98, 101–3, 107, 108, 109, 110, 112n28, 113n.32, 114n59 & n61, 122, 127n38, 140, 153, 158, 165, 172, 203, 205, 209, 210, 211, 212, 216n.87, 219, 220, 222, 283, 284, 288, 307n185, 308n190, 309n203
"Rangamancha" 29, 47, 49, 57, 63, 67, 76–7, 78–9, 85, 88 also n2, 108, 117, 119, 143, 144, 150–1, 157, 164–5, 187, 191, 217, 252
Red Oleanders 51, 53, 107, 114n61, 140, 203, 209–12, 285, 286, 287, 308 n190 & n194, 309n203
rehearsals 82, 129, 131, 132, 134–6, 137, 139, 175
revisions and recensions 1, 2, 95, 103–4, 139–40, 141–2, 147n87, 198; *Achalayatan* revised (as *Guru*) 103; *Chandalika* revised 83, 84,103; *Chirakumar Sabha* revised 98–9; *Chitangada* revised 83, 84, 103; *Grihapravesh* revised 35n76, 310n207; *Parisodh* revised (as *Shyama*) 83; *Raja* revised (as *Arupratan/Shapmochan*) 104–7, 140, 142; *Raja o Rani* revised (as *Tapati*) 50, 103, 104, 140, 170; *Raktakarabi* revised 107, 140; *Sarodotsav* revised (as *Rinsodh*) 99, 103; *Tasher Desh* revised 50, 53, 107, 141–2; *Visarjan* revised 95, 104, 139–40
Rinsodh 68, 99, 103, 277, 279, 281, 307 n176
Rituranga 2, 100, 188, 288, 311n218
Rothenstein, William 201, 202, 204, 212n4, 213n30, 215n59, 259, 299n83, 302n127, 304n154
Roy, Dwijendralal 20, 21, 22, 29, 150; farces 22; historical plays 21; reproaching Rabindranath 27, 28, 112n24
Roy, Hemendrakumar 6, 29, 86, 117, 124, 172–3, 221
Roy, Jagadananda 70, 72, 118,119, 121, 297n42

Sarodotsav 2, 5, 39, 47, 48, 55, 63, 64, 66, 70, 71, 76, 79, 80, 81, 98, 101, 119, 121, 136, 137–8, 140, 151, 152, 165, 175, 176, 179, 187, 258, 273, 275, 307 n176
Santiniketan community 46, 48–9, 50, 63, 65–7, 72, 116, 123, 217, 220

324 Index

Sati (Ama and Vinayaka) 204, 206
Sen, Amita 70, 82, 131, 132, 134, 135
Sen, Kshitimohan 70, 96, 99, 107, 118–9, 258
Sesh Raksha 26, 35n74, 57n2, 65, 104, 222, 289
Sesh Varshan 2, 64, 100, 188, 287
Shapmochan 2, 9n9, 36n92, 50, 65, 81–2, 82–3, 84, 90 n36, 100, 103, 107, 124, 135, 140, 144, 155, 168, 188, 189, 190–1, 290. 291, 292, 295n4, 311n232
Shyama 2, 6, 31, 50, 65, 69–70, 83–4, 100, 108, 116, 125, 155, 156, 158, 168, 188, 190, 192, 251, 294, 295n4, 312n241
Sodhbodh 65, 287, 309–10n206
sources for the plays 52, 95, 100, 101–3, 207, 219, 251; for *Achalayatan* 100; for *Chandalika* 100; for *Chitrangada* 96, 100–1; for *Dakghar* 97; for *Malini* 95–6; for *Natir Puja* 100,; for *Raja/Arupratan/Shapmochan* 100; for *Raktakarabi* 52, 96, 102–3; for *Rather Rashi/Kaler Jatra* 110, 115n.82; for *Shyama* 100; for *Tasher Desh* 107; for *Visarjan* 95; for short playlets 101
Sriniketan 46, 48–9, 50, 53, 61n82, 66, 118, 282, 307n180
stage setting/stage décor 64, 70, 71, 149–56, 188, 217; painted scenery (and its rejection) 76–7, 150–1, 152; use of Indian motifs 85, 154, 157, 218; in *Chandalika* 155; in *Chitra* 208–9; in *Chitrangada* 155–6; in *Dakghar* 70, 157, 188, 221; in *Mayar Khela* 150; in *Phalguni* 48, 152–3, 165; in *Raja* 85, 153–4, 157, 188; in *Raktakarabi* 51; in *Rinsodh* 152; in *Sarodotsav* 71, 152; in *Shyama* 156; in *Tapati* 176; in *Visarjan* 85, 130, 150,154, 157, 169, 176; in *Valmiki Pratibha* 150, 163
Sturge Moore, Thomas 196, 199, 208, 215n73
Sundar 2, 14, 64, 155, 156, 188, 193n10, 286, 309n198
"Swadeshi Samaj" 41, 42, 43–4, 46, 47, 55, 56, 57, 58n26, 76, 106, 253

Tagore, Abanindranath 70, 71, 82, 116–9, 121, 129–30, 133, 134, 137–8, 140, 150, 152, 154, 158, 163, 171 188, 221, 249, 250, 266, 300n96, 304n144, 307n176

Tagore, Amita 70, 85, 121, 122, 127n34, 130, 133, 134, 136, 154, 158, 170–1, 174, 309n200
Tagore, Devendranath 63, 100
Tagore, Dinendranath 26, 35n76, 60–1n69, 71, 117, 118, 119, 133, 134, 139, 169, 173, 176, 177, 260, 264, 273, 285, 286, 287, 290, 304n142
Tagore, Dwarakanath 24, 162
Tagore, Gaganendranath 70, 71, 82, 85, 116, 117–8, 119, 121, 133, 136, 154, 163, 169, 176, 216n85, 266, 286, 287, 301n111, 308n194
Tagore, Jyotirindranath 22, 24–6, 116, 117, 129, 162–3, 181n5, 259
Tagore, Nitindranath 116, 150, 163
Tagore, Rathindranath 39, 103, 116–7, 119, 120, 139, 152, 154, 169, 258, 299n80
Tagore, Samindranath 63, 99, 256, 298n61
Tagorc, Satyendranath 24, 25, 116, 125n1, 129, 162, 248
Tapati 2, 5, 26, 30, 47, 50, 68, 77, 85, 103, 104,113n38, 122, 133, 136–7, 140, 151, 155, 157–8, 170–1, 174, 176, 177, 179, 205, 222, 289
Tasher Desh 2, 31, 50–1, 53–5, 56–7, 64–5, 80, 98, 101, 103, 107–9, 141, 153, 205, 219–20, 241, 242, 291, 311n235, 312 n.236; as prose play 108, 311n234, 312n236
teachers and students performing together 49–50, 65, 66, 70, 71, 99, 118, 119, 136, 191, 279, 300n103
theatre as dance 81, 82–3, 135, 155, 187, 188, 191
Thompson, Edward 49, 66, 81, 112n23, 153, 179, 195, 285

Uday Shankar 124
urban-folk 169, 218–9, 220; see also alternative/parallel theatre

Valmiki Pratibha 2, 25, 26, 84, 90n35, 116, 118, 129, 138, 149, 159n3, 163, 164, 187, 222, 224n15, 246, 247, 260, 262, 264, 295n4, 300n97
Varsha-mangal 67–8, 99, 120, 125, 180, 188, 279, 281, 289, 295n4, 305n.164
Vasanta 36n92, 188, 120, 157, 188, 307n.179
Vichitra Hall (Jorasanko) 2, 67, 82, 85, 156, 271, 272, 273, 287, 305n164

Viday Abhishap (*Kacha and Devyani/ Curse at Farewell*) 101, 112n23, 204, 206, 207, 249, 278, 285, 295n4, 296n23

Visarjan 2, 5, 6, 26, 30, 39, 47, 55, 64, 70, 71, 76, 80, 85, 95, 103, 104, 116, 118, 119, 120, 121, 122, 129–30, 131, 133, 134, 138–9, 140, 142–3, 150, 152, 154, 157, 158, 163–4, 166, 169, 171, 173, 175–6, 177–8, 187, 206, 207, 222, 248, 251, 252, 253, 255, 257, 267, 271 274, 279, 284, 295n4, 297n40, 308n187

Visva-Bharati 2, 6, 9n9, 46, 49, 60n61, 65–6, 68, 70, 83, 106, 118, 120, 123, 124, 125, 154, 165, 173, 186, 192, 273, 279, 280, 281, 283, 284, 288, 292, 306n166 & n172, 308n189

Waterfall, The 109, 209–10, 216n81 & n86, 280

Yeats, W.B. 97–8, 199, 201, 203, 214n 42, 259, 260, 299n82, 304n154